W9-CFT-712

And still
they fly!

by
Guido Moosbrugger

Steelmark

Copyright © 2004 by Guido Moosbrugger

All rights reserved. No part of this book may be reproduced in any form or by any electronic or mechanical means including information storage and retrieval systems without permission in writing from the publisher.

Published by
Steelmark LLC
8086 South Yale, Suite 173
Tulsa, OK 74136
(918) 827-6453
www.steelmarkonline.com

And Still They Fly! By Guido Moosbrugger

Second edition, paperback
ISBN 0-9711523-1-4

Second edition, hardback
ISBN 0-9711523-2-2

First edition, paperback, 2001 (out of print)

Printed in the USA

Although the author and the publisher have researched many sources to ensure the accuracy and completeness of the information contained in this book, we assume no responsibility for errors, inaccuracies, omissions or any other inconsistency herein. Any slights against people or organizations are unintentional.

German to English tranlation corrections by Christian Frehner, Marianne Schmeling and Mike Whelan. English proof reading and editing by Mary Jane Shippen, Jason Steele and Mike Whelan. Front and back cover design by Jason Steele. Front cover picture #228 was taken by Billy Meier on March 8, 1976 in Bachtelhörnli, Switerland. The back cover photo insert #84 was taken by Billy Meier on March 18, 1975 at Ober-Sädellegg, Switzerland.

For more information on the Billy Meier case:

Visit: *www.andstilltheyfly.com*
www.steelmarkonline.com
www.billymeier.com
www.figu.org

or write to:

FIGU Society USA
P.O. Box 730
Mounds, OK 74047
or

Semjase Silver Star Center
CH-8495 Schmidrüdi / ZH
Switzerland

See *Official Addresses* page for more information on regional groups.

Table of Contents

CHAPTER 3

CHAPTER 4

CHAPTER 5

CHAPTER 6

Foreword

The author, Guido Moosbrugger, born on February 14, 1925 in Dornbirn (Austria), had already revealed his great desire to work for the well-being of the public by his choice of profession as a teacher and later as the director of the "Volksschule" (German elementary school) in Hirschegg. He has studied ufological and astrophysical questions for many years as well as questions pertaining to the size, structure and origin of the universe. His keen interest in the realm of all natural sciences also persuaded him to take part in an Austrian expedition to Morocco in 1951 lasting nine weeks in total, with the objective of conducting geographic research on several "white spots" high in the Atlas Mountains. He further undertook educational trips to almost all European countries, as well as North Africa (Morocco, Tunisia, Algeria, Egypt, Lebanon and Turkey), Mexico and South America.

Guido Moosbrugger read his first UFO book with great interest as early as 1954 and came to the conviction that the so-called UFOs could very well exist. At that time, he had no one he could talk to about these things. The time for this finally came more than 20 years later: A simple newspaper announcement had drawn his attention to the monthly UFO lectures in Munich. During 1975 and 1976 Guido attended these lectures regularly and purchased a number of ufological publications, which he eagerly plowed through.

Eventually, Guido had his first brief encounter with Billy Meier in April of 1976 when Billy presented a slide lecture in Munich. Billy's slide material was so fascinating that Guido made up his mind to get to the very bottom of the entire case. He immediately wrote a letter to Billy and asked if and when he could visit him. To his great joy, Billy promptly answered and invited him for a visit to Hinwil. Guido was also fortunate enough to accompany Billy at various flight demonstrations by the Pleiadians in the first few months. In addition to this, he was also granted permission to take photographs of two night demonstrations and of various landing tracks. Since May of 1976, Guido has been a member and board member of FIGU[1] and therefore has made great efforts to contribute to Billy's difficult mission.

I learned of Billy at just about the same time as did Guido, since I had met with the ufologist, Lou Zinstag, in Basel, Switzerland on my numerous European trips to visit relatives and acquaintances, and he, at that time, told me immediately about Billy's contacts and showed me his excellent pictures. Lou could not decide whether or not to publish Billy's experiences in a book, as she apologetically admitted the ideas and philosophies of Billy and the Pleiadians would go against her grain as a Swiss patriot. I must not forget to mention Lou in a very commendable way as, despite her opinion, she did a great service by making the truth known on her last trip to America by giving the top American ufologist, Colonel Wendelle C. Stevens (Ret.),[2] a thorough account of Billy and his many pieces of contact evidence. Wendelle Stevens, in turn, traveled several times to Hinterschmidrüti in Switzerland along with other UFO researchers to conduct a thorough investigation of the Meier UFO case. As a direct result of this, several books and video films appeared in the USA about Billy's contacts with the Pleiadians.

The reader can look up a great deal of the well-founded contact evidence on pages 204–207 and pages 234–258 in Gary Kinder's book, *Light Years*. For many months, I also corresponded with the Air Force Colonel who was interested in the

Brazilian contact case in the city of Mirascol in the district of Sao Paulo (investigated by Maria de Lourdes and Ney Matiel Pires). This, in fact, is how we were presented with a copy of Billy Meier's book, *UFO Contact from the Pleiades*, by Wendelle Stevens, as a gift.

With respect to our early impressions of Billy, we could consider ourselves quite fortunate that, despite his poor state of health, he devoted more than two hours to my sister and me during our stay at the Semjase Silver Star Center. Our visit ended with Guido relating the content of *UFO Contact from the Pleiades*, whereupon we agreed to try to translate the book into Portuguese and possibly find a publisher. Guido's main concern here is to represent the entire case of Billy Meier and his contacts with the Pleiadians as objectively and truthfully as possible.

Finally, an attempt could now be made to build a small bridge spanning from this book to those scientists who have curbed their haughtiness and arrogance enough to recognize that in the smallest of atoms, as well as in the most gigantic expanses of the cosmos, a spiritual force is at work—a force which was intended by Creation for all existing life. Should our politicians ever succeed in gaining greater insight, our earthly wars would disappear of their own accord, nature would no longer bestow tellurian misfortunes upon us, and the cosmos would no longer threaten us with the invasion of comets. Thereby, an alternative by the Pleiadians would come into the realm of possibilities. When we see the shambles of our earth before us, we should not hesitate in supporting the peace efforts of FIGU because, in doing so, we can actively contribute to the preservation of global peace.

Brazil, January 1991, Dr. Walter Bühler

Author's Foreword

The challenging title of this book, *And Still They Fly!*, is intended first of all to remind us of the saying, "And still ... it moves!," attributed to the famous Italian naturalist, Galileo Galilei (and his observations of Jupiter's moons). Back then this idea was a substantial influence in sweeping the erroneous ideas of the Middle Ages under the table in order to make room for the new knowledge and to make a triumphant entrance into the era of the New Age possible.

We citizens of the 20th Century are in an amazingly similar situation today; that is, in dealing with the radical revision of out-dated and false teachings. The cardinal question of primary concern is whether planets other than earth are inhabited by human civilizations or whether we enjoy a uniquely superior status. And if extraterrestrials actually exist, the next spontaneous question is whether they are technologically so far advanced that they can conquer the supposedly unconquerable barrier of space and time and visit us with their spacecraft. From a logical point of view, there is only one answer, at least to the first question. As every school child knows today, our earth, viewed from a cosmic standpoint, is no more than a tiny speck of dust. Therefore, in my opinion, it is just short of megalomania to imagine that earth is the only place in the endless expanse of the entire universe where life forms exist that are endowed with reason. Now, happily enough, the opinion seems to prevail that, slowly but surely, earth people are not the only ones who exist and are by no means the crown of Creation, as opposed to what has been arrogantly propagated up to this point. As far as that goes, considerable progress has been made in the realm of this reorientation process, but it looks as if the ultimate and decisive break-through will keep us waiting a while as the majority of earth humanity cannot or simply will not admit that there actually are UFOs, which have been sighted sporadically all around the world for decades, so their existence is just as controversial as it has ever been. And thereby, we have once again come to the sum and substance of the sentence: "And still ... they fly!"

In the first two chapters of this book, you will learn the meaning of these mystery-shrouded UFOs and why their presence has been documented on our globe so frequently in this particular day and age. In *Chapters 9* and *Chapter 14*, two interesting questions are answered, namely, why extraterrestrial spacecraft do not land publicly and what do the extraterrestrials want here, anyway.

In *Chapter 2*, I have roughly described the lifestyle of the Pleiadians from planet Erra as best I could according to the information provided by the contactee, Eduard Albert Meier. These Pleiadians from planet Erra are not ethereal beings, but people of flesh and blood just as we are, yet much more highly evolved. Their home planet Erra is located in the sun system Tayget, which is in the open star cluster of the Pleiades and able to sustain life. The system exists within another dimensional space-time continuum. In comparison to our SOL System and earth, planet Erra is displaced into the future by a fraction of a second and is approximately 500 light years away from earth. These facts are, naturally, not readily understandable from our limited perspective.

The Errans are several nose-lengths ahead of us, meaning 3,500 years in technological regard and about 30 million years further in their spiritual development. Due to their enormously high evolutionary level, they master universal space travel almost perfectly. They maintain a great number of bases throughout the entire universe and serve to a certain extent as keepers of cosmic order and as assistants in spiritual guidance to needy civilizations.

We earth people also have been and are still able to profit from this extraordinarily valuable help. They have an entire armada of spacecraft at their disposal to bridge the astronomical distances of universal space. Their space travel technology is so grandiose in development that they can literally jump from one stellar system to another in the truest sense of the word, which, unfortunately for us, shall long remain a dream of the future. Their spacecraft will be comprehensively dealt with in *Chapter 3.*

After that, the subject matter will be about the Swiss contactee, Eduard Albert Meier — known as UFO Billy — who can claim to have contacts with extraterrestrials since his early childhood in the form of telepathy, as well as personal face-to-face contacts. He works as a contactee and mediator between the extraterrestrials and the people of earth. In this section, I have described a few of the most prominent milestones in his turbulent and eventful life and, of course, his extraordinary knowledge and abilities, as well as his unique task in the fulfillment of his mission. Following that, I shall address Billy's contacts with the extraterrestrials—still ongoing at the present time, although not as frequently as in the past—whereby the manner in which they occur will be explained. In the three subsequent chapters, I talk about diverse demonstrations, as well as day and night sightings, which took place in connection with Billy's contacts. Several witnesses reported very mysterious experiences, which were not coincidental but intentionally arranged for the demonstrations and evidence later on. To substantiate the truthful content of the entire episode, Billy was granted permission by the Pleiadians to make a total of eight short films and a few hundred color slides of the various types of Pleiadian spacecraft, their fantastic flight maneuvers and their landing tracks. These pictures are not only the most extensive but also the best of their kind ever produced by a single person anywhere on earth. Incidentally, very thorough investigations have been conducted on this case. American and Japanese UFO researchers have, for example, inspected the landing sites of the Pleiadian spacecraft and have taken various measurements at those locations. These researchers stayed in the immediate vicinity of Billy's residence for weeks and kept tabs on his every move, day and night, with the intention of uncovering any dishonest intrigues. A psychological stress evaluation was also conducted on Billy and on several witnesses. The statements of the witnesses, which were made fully independent of one another in numerous interviews, persistently delivered concurrent results, and all test examinations indicated positive results throughout. To be absolutely certain, Billy's proof material was meticulously examined and analyzed by almost a dozen renowned American specialists and experts who used modern research equipment and computers to scientifically examine:

1. Several color slides and film segments,

2. Whirring sounds of a Pleiadian ship without a protective shield, and

3. Four small metal samples of the material used to construct a Pleiadian space vehicle.

With the help of these scientific analyses, absolutely no signs of falsification or manipulation of any kind were established. On the contrary, new evidence invariably revealed the fact that Billy's contacts were authentic. Due to these solid pieces of evidence, the Japanese produced a total of three television films about Billy's contacts, and a 14-member crew from Hollywood produced a motion picture as well. Over the past fifteen years, a number of books have appeared on the same topic, mostly in the English language. In *Chapter 11*, the most important results of the scientific analyses and several other pieces of evidence are listed. In-depth views of Billy's pictures and the truthfulness of their content will be presented in Chapter 10. Since a great deal of fraud is conducted, especially in the field of ufology, and due to other reasons, it is not at all unusual for UFO contactees and their sympathizers to meet with hostility from their contemporaries. Unfortunately, this is especially true for Billy. Instead of gratitude for the vital messages, wisdom and teachings that he has given us and for exerting himself to the very limit of his strength without regard for his own health in order to fulfill his task as best as he could, he has been attacked worldwide in words and writing. To prevent the spreading of the truth at all costs, his adversaries have attempted to silence him with the cold-blooded intention of dispatching him to eternity. To obtain this goal, no less than thirteen attempts have been made on his life, which are explained in detail in *Chapter 12*. Then in *Chapter 13*, the attacks of the Giza Intelligences will finally be discussed. Here, we are speaking of a negative extraterrestrial splinter group that had caused a great deal of trouble for Billy and the FIGU before the Pleiadians deported them in 1978.

As for the animosity in general, I am sorry to say that Billy does have quite a bad reputation due to defamations, misunderstandings, fallacies and lack of information. This is especially true among the numerous UFO groups, which number about 20,000 worldwide. His adversaries refer to him as something between Einstein, Till Eulenspiegel and Mickey Mouse and vilify him as a liar and a cheat. But despite these false accusations and malicious lies which have been spread throughout the world — partially from the ranks of former group members — not one iota of what these evil tongues would like to fabricate as truth has been proven thus far. Given the fact that would-be contactees are rapidly multiplying and increasingly spreading their professed "wisdom" on earth, it is no surprise that most people have become totally unsure of themselves, continue to grope ever deeper into darkness and no longer know what to think about these matters. It is now more important than ever to examine all information presented to us in this day and age and to carefully analyze it for truthful content and thoroughly reflect upon it. I cannot urge this strongly enough to all who desire to find the way out of the labyrinth of untruths through honest efforts. Speaking for myself, I can assure you that I, under no circumstances, would have dared to appear in public were I not convinced 100 percent of the reality of Billy Meier's contacts. Based on my own experience and long years of research, I can assert with a calm conscience that we are not dealing with *Grimm's Fairy Tales or A Thousand and One Nights* but, plainly and simply, we are dealing with bare facts.

My motive is not based on a craving for fame, sensationalism or anything else of this nature. On the contrary, my sole desire is to represent the given facts as they exist in reality. If this book were to prompt one reader or another to seriously contemplate this question, then I would be quite satisfied.

Although the Billy Meier story is unique to evaluate — especially with respect to its spiritual background — two fully contrary opinions have crystallized in the course of time. The adversaries flatly condemn the entire matter as the most ingenious swindle of all times, whereas advocates speak of the greatest sensation of the 20th century. Of course, the decision of which standpoint is correct must be left up to the reader.

Hinterschmidrüti, January 1991, Guido Moosbrugger

Thanks and Acknowledgments

At this point, I would like to express my wholehearted thanks to all terrestrial and extraterrestrial helpers who have made any contribution to the appearance of this book.

This primarily applies to the contactee, Eduard Albert Meier, for his valuable teachings, information and proof of every kind, as well as to his extraterrestrial friends and helpers from the Lyra and Vega System and from the Pleiades. Above all, thanks and acknowledgment are due to the extraterrestrials Sfath, Asket and the triad Semjase, Quetzal and JHWH (pronounced, ish-wish) Ptaah from planet Erra. Not to be forgotten are all the others, whom we know by name, as follows: Jsodos, Solar, Pleija, Elektra, Nera, Menara, Rala, Alena, Taljda and Hjlaara. Also deserving recognition are the American scientists and engineers who analyzed Billy Meier's evidence and rendered a great service to the authenticity of the entire case through their willingness to publicly announce their findings without considering their own possible loss of prestige.

Furthermore, I would like to thank the American and Japanese research group, headed by Wendelle Stevens and Jun-Ichi Yaoi, for their work, which has been of great benefit to us. Honorable mention is also made in this connection to the American author, Gary Kinder. A cordial thank-you is extended to all those who have helped me in my work, be it with reporting their experiences or the translation of English texts. These are my wife, Elisabeth, Dr. Walter Bühler, Bernadette Brand, Christian Frehner, Rainer Schenck, Hans Lanzendorfer, Engelbert Wächter, Jacobus Bertschinger, Kalliope (Billy's wife), Gilgamesha Meier, Elisabeth Gruber, Brunhilde and Bernhard Koye, Thomas Keller, Herbert Runkel, Mariann Uehlinger, Christina Gasser, Simone Holler, Marete Matern B. Eng., Piero Petrizzo, Louis Memper and the publisher of the German version, Michael Hesemann. For the generous financial support, I offer my sincerest thanks to Marie-Louise and Christian Frehner, Renate Steur, Louis Memper, Mariann Uehlinger, Dr. Walter Bühler and Ernst Kroeger.

I extend my deepest gratitude to Jurij and Rebecca Walkiw of Munich, Germany for taking on the arduous task of rendering the first German-to-English translation of *And Still They Fly!* as well as to Jason Steele, Marc Juliano and Mike Whelan of the FIGU – Los Angeles Study Group, Mary Jane Shippen and Marianne Schmeling. They all worked very hard to finalize the present English version. In addition, I would like to thank Hampton Hsien-Ting Chiu, Mark Gjomarkaj, Willem Mondria, Joseph Royack, Ernest Schwoegler and Mij Shippen who made significant financial contributions in order to bring this publication to fruition.

Guido Moosbrugger

AND STILL THEY FLY! – *Second Edition*

CHAPTER 1

The Mystery of UFOs

On June 24, 1947, the American pilot Kenneth Arnold reported he had observed a formation of nine glowing disks flying at 1,500 kilometers (930 miles) per hour at an altitude of 3,000 meters (2 miles). According to his report, they were skipping around in the sky like saucers on a water surface. In this way or another, the term "flying saucer" probably was coined, which is still in use today, although mostly with a mocking undertone.

For the most part, they are referred to as UFOs, which stands for unknown or unidentified flying objects. For the majority of our contemporaries, these UFOs were and are still a great mystery that has remained unresolved to this very day. The involuntary question arising in view of this phenomenon is what is at the bottom of these mysterious appearances sighted time and again for decades all around the world?

Is there anyone at all who can give us concrete information about UFOs or do we have to settle for vague notions and hypotheses that have been produced so far? Due to our absolutely reliable source of information at FIGU, I am definitely in a position to clarify the mystery of the so-called UFOs. The well-known expression, "all that glitters is not gold," is certainly true in the world of ufology. In other words, whoever is actively engaged in ufology must acknowledge the fact — like it or not — that the majority of presumed UFO sightings have absolutely nothing to do with flying objects, in the true sense of the word.

The wide range of illusions, errors and deceptions is far greater than any layman could possibly imagine. It is thus of vital importance for us to be able to clearly distinguish between inauthentic UFO sightings and authentic spacecraft.

Inauthentic UFO Sightings

The following examples can be categorized as inauthentic UFO sightings:

All Forms of Optical Illusions

These types of sightings occur as unusual appearances in the sky by day or, more frequently, by night, which are mistakenly categorized and thus interpreted as unknown flying objects, and are based on erroneous observations or a lack of knowledge in this field.

Some of these, for example, are bright twinkling planets (Jupiter, Venus), lenticular clouds during the day or glowing clouds at night, polar lights, mirages similar to Fata Morganas,[3] balls of lightning, glowing fumes from a swamp (roaming lights), very high-flying swarms of insects, or other natural phenomena.

Other possibilities, of course, include earthly objects such as various types of balloons (weather, advertisement and sport balloons), colored fluorescent signals, glaring headlights, fluorescent parachutes, airplanes, airships, kites, parachutists, orbiting earth satellites and crashing parts of earthly spacecraft.

All Types of Fraud

This ranges from simple photomontages and diverse trick photography of presumably sighted spacecraft to fantastic descriptions of contacts or space flights with extraterrestrials, and are basically nothing more than pure figments of the imagination. Those responsible for such intrigues are usually notorious liars and swindlers who talk big to attract attention, compensate for an inferiority complex or craving for sensation, among other motives, in order to obtain wide public recognition and admiration.

Occasionally, adolescents, mentally disturbed persons or practical jokers deliberately spread untrue UFO stories to really "pull one off" on their fellow man and royally amuse themselves if they succeed in doing so.

Unconscious Deception Through Suggestion by an Outer Source

This is evoked through the use of spiritual forces with or without the aid of appropriate implements, and is yet another example of how inauthentic UFO sightings can be initiated. The persons affected are firmly convinced that they have sensed or personally experienced something, which in no way conforms to the actual facts. These unsuspecting people have reported extraterrestrial encounters of the first, second or third kind, trips into outer space, and other similar stories. In reality, they were led to believe this entire hocus-pocus by unknown persons (i.e., by way of teleprojection or real vision)[4] in such a convincing manner that they, unfortunately, were unable to recognize the unreality at the bottom of it all. Of course, it would not be fair to label such people as liars. They are completely unaware that unknown forces are misusing them for some reason or another.

Subconscious Deception Through Subjective Autosuggestion

This may be evoked by all kinds of fantasies in a normal state of consciousness or in a trance. People in this state often tell the craziest stories about encounters with extraterrestrials and about giants in outer space with such persuasion that even recognized ufologists fall prey to the stories and write thick books about them based on the statements of these pseudo-contactees. In principle, we ought not to accuse such pitiable people of dishonesty, since they are unaware that their alleged experiences were by no means genuine. They have merely fallen prey to a subconscious self-deception.

Schizophrenic Trance

For quite some time now, more and more people are capable of placing themselves into a schizophrenic trance and have been appearing in public to presumably let foreign beings, the deceased, or ufonauts speak through them. This type of trance is evoked in either an unconscious form through misguided psychic factors, or in a fully conscious form that would indicate deliberate deception. This procedure is very popular at the present time and is practiced worldwide under the catchword: *channeling.*

An Example of an Inauthentic UFO Sighting: The Lights of Kaikoura

Toward the end of December in 1978, several imposing lights that appeared over the city of Kaikoura on the coast of New Zealand created a spectacular UFO uproar. In reality these lights had absolutely nothing to do with UFOs.

I now quote Billy Meier's word-for-word explanation of this phenomenon, observed for about twelve days over Kaikoura:

> **BILLY:** The phenomenon that occurred was based on a graphic 3-D reflection of various SOL planets. Such a 3-D reflection is similar to a Fata Morgana but is so much more realistic and graphic that the planets projected into such a region seem to suddenly move within reachable distance and appear to fly alongside airplanes. For the most part, the planets projected onto the earth seem to have a greater light intensity than when normally viewed with the naked eye. Their size also appears to change. Many of the inhibitory factors of a visual disorder disappear through the Fata Morgana projection. Consequently, the reflected planets appear to be much larger than normal. Such 3-D reflections may include several planets, which, as a rule, appear to be so magnified that even the clouds on them are visible. This is what happened in Kaikoura, which the video film and other pictures have clearly indicated. As far as I know, the 3-D reflection seen in this particular case was a Fata Morgana projection of planets Venus, Mars, Jupiter, Saturn and Mercury. I have no knowledge of whether all five of these planets were seen by the observers. If this were indeed the case, I would then have to say that it was certainly an extremely rare occurrence. When the same phenomenon appeared in the sky over India in 1964 for a period of about eleven days, only three heavenly bodies were sighted.
>
> The 3-D reflection of the SOL planets on earth are caused by light-deflecting rays in outer space which build curved bands, often billions of kilometers long, and move through space-like winding snakes. If such a light-deflecting ray falls within the realm of a planetary system, one or more planets can be projected onto another planet. This is what happened in the case of the lights of Kaikoura. Depending on the circumstances, one or more planets or even an entire solar system located millions or billions of kilometers away could be projected into the wide expanse of outer space. As a result, planets may suddenly become visible in outer space where none actually exist at all.

Genuine Spacecraft

In view of what we have now learned, the impression may have been given that so-called UFOs do not exist at all or only in the fantasy of ufologists and esoteric practitioners. This is not the case. Consequently, we have finally arrived at the question of main importance and relevance today, which is, what do these unknown spacecraft really and truly represent? To answer this, the following categories are among the genuine spacecraft known at the present time.

Physical Spacecraft of Earthly Origin

Yes, that is right — physical spacecraft of earthly origin! These are nothing more than an advanced development of the German and Canadian flying disks which were designed and partially tested as Hitler's secret wonder weapons during World War II but were not ultimately used at the front. East of Leipzig in the vicinity of Prague, fundamental plans for the development of completely new flying machines were worked out in the BMW factory there and in Breslau, as well as in Vienna and other places. It eventually led to the construction of fireballs as well as flying disks (flying gyros) with a fantastic and unprecedented flight technology. The persons primarily involved in the basic research and further development of these machines were the Austrian natural scientist Viktor Schauberger (a genuine UFO contactee), the German experts and flight captains Miethe, Schriever and Habermohl, the Italian researcher Bellonzo, and many others. The disk-shaped spacecraft operated on conventional beam-powered propulsion systems or possibly, new types of propulsion systems.

At any rate, the prototypes were successfully tested for the first time toward the end of World War II and gave commendable performances for that period of time. For example, in mid-February of 1945 in Prague, a flying disk ascended to a height of 12 kilometers (7.5 miles) within three minutes and almost reached twice the speed of sound in horizontal flight. The flying disk was able to hover like a helicopter and perform other similar maneuvers.[5]

At the end of the war, all existing flying disks, as well as their instrumentation and construction plans, were to be completely destroyed to prevent them from falling into enemy hands. This project was not carried out in its entirety. Some of the plans and instrumentation were intentionally (or unintentionally) overlooked during the elimination and promptly fell into the wrong hands. One possible explanation for this is that the occupying forces may have confiscated these valuable documents. Whether or not this was actually the case is beyond my knowledge. According to the Pleiadians, however, secret Nazi groups escaped to safety toward the end of World War II, acquired the confiscated material and continued to develop these new types of flying disks — naturally under a strict oath of secrecy.

The Pleiadians verified in 1976 that the largest craft was as much as 100 meters (330 ft.) in diameter. By continually improving the propulsion, its performance greatly increased as time went on. Judging from appearance alone, these terrestrial flying disks are very similar to the disk-shaped spacecraft of extraterrestrial origin and can easily be mistaken for them. From the standpoint of performance, they were naturally no match for the exceedingly superior extraterrestrial spacecraft, not even with the most modern systems of propulsion.

Since these terrestrial flying disks do indeed exist and are occasionally sighted, two contrary and equally false opinions have been formed:

- Those who are aware of the existence of the terrestrial flying disks are under the false impression that all such objects are either of earthly origin or can be traced back to deceit and fraud, and that extraterrestrial spacecraft are unreal and nothing more than mere fantasy.

- Others mistakenly view all disk-shaped spacecraft as extraterrestrial. They have absolutely no knowledge of terrestrial flying disks or simply do not want to admit they exist.

Extraterrestrial Spacecraft

Now let us finally turn our attention to the spacecraft of extraterrestrial origin. Unfortunately, the majority of people on earth are not well informed about extraterrestrial spacecraft or are informed merely through reports in daily newspapers and magazines. Consequently, they have very vague notions about this topic. These extraterrestrial craft can be divided into two categories: physical spacecraft and nonphysical spacecraft.

Physical Spacecraft of Extraterrestrial Origin

See ~ Photos #4 & #6 – #26

Physical spacecraft are real, visible and tangible objects of solid matter made of high-grade materials such as metal alloys. As for the detection of such objects, it should be stated that the majority of extraterrestrial spacecraft could be shielded, if desired, against acoustical location, radar detection and optical sighting. They are quite capable of evading any detection by us at all. Apart from technological possibilities, the personal disposition of extraterrestrials is a primary factor in determining whether or not they are inclined to let themselves be detected by earth people. For example, the Pleiadians and several other extraterrestrial races take every possible precaution not to be sighted, while others fly around the area without the slightest concern of being observed by us at all.

Just as remarkable are the diverse light effects that can be observed, mostly during night sightings. Depending upon the velocity of the spacecraft, the entire object or specific parts thereof, and its immediate surroundings, may glow in an array of colors. Interplay through rapidly alternating light intensities in an entire palette of colors often takes place. Extraterrestrial spacecraft are often noticeable by their blinking, gyrating and pulsating lights, or beams of light similar to flood lights, as well as various other rays and strong magnetic fields. With direct landings, they commonly leave various tracks behind such as outlines of landing surfaces, depressions, or burnt tracks, etc.

The external form of the ships can vary tremendously. The most famous of these are probably the disk-shaped craft. A large number resemble balls, hats, bells, dumb-bells, cupolas, cigars, rods, spindles, pyramids, cones, cubes, rings, torpedoes, eggs and other similar shapes. The size can also vary greatly, ranging from unmanned telemetric disks, which are only a few centimeters in length, to manned objects that are several hundred meters in length.

The large spacecraft are gigantic in size. For example, the Pleiadians have one such ship[6] with a phenomenal diameter of 17 kilometers (11 miles)! Of course, these wonders of human technology are equipped with the kinds of advanced apparati that we could only dream of here on earth. As a matter of necessity, they are also armed with effective weapons ranging from relatively harmless stunning devices to weapons of total destruction, the effects of which are more devastating than atomic weapons. The reference here is to the overkill weapons that, in their perfection, are capable of disintegrating any type of solid matter into pure energy within a split second. If worse comes to worse, entire planets may be annihilated without leaving behind as much as a small heap of ashes.

A special feature of the extraterrestrial spacecraft is its ability to perform sensational flight maneuvers. The following are a few examples:

- They have phenomenal accelerating capacity that may be significantly increased or stopped within a matter of seconds without the slightest injury to the crewmembers or the craft itself. The terrific acceleration, up to the speed of light (299,792.5 kilometers/second [186,171 miles/second]) and beyond, is something that still seems completely inconceivable compared to our present standards of earth technology.

- Another example is the sudden emergence of a spacecraft — seemingly out of nowhere — and its lightning fast disappearance without a trace. This effect can stem from three different causes:
  1. Optical shielding, so that light rays are projected around the respective spacecraft and therefore, make the object invisible.
  2. An acceleration so rapid that our eyes are not fast enough to register it.
  3. A sudden change of dimension by means of transmission or teleportation. *(See ~ Chapter 5 for more details about this subject.)*

- They have the ability to fly silently and invisibly when the appropriate protective shield has been activated. This does not mean that their system of propulsion functions silently. As already mentioned, the spacecraft can be shielded so we are unable to detect the slightest noise, although they zoom around at tremendous speed. Also worth mentioning is the absence of the notorious sonic boom when they break through the sound barrier.

- They have the ability to hover at any desirable altitude for a long period of time.

- They demonstrate erratic flight patterns, unusual or impossible for terrestrial aerial craft, such as swinging, zigzag, spiral and flutter motions during flight and other similar maneuvers.

Performance capacity naturally depends upon the respective technological level of a planet's inhabitants, especially upon the quality of their propulsion systems. Certain propulsion systems are only suitable for planetary use. Others make extended space flights through interstellar, intergalactic or universal regions possible. According to my knowledge, the fundamental physical principle for all or almost all of the propulsion systems is exactly the same, regardless of how sophisticated the technical level may be. Indeed, it is based on the universal principle of reaction propulsion, which is used throughout the entire universe for space travel.

The different technological levels of the various space races become most apparent in view of their flight times. Some of us may not like to think it possible, but the fact exists that human beings are quite capable of overcoming the tremendous astronomical distances between star systems in the universe, although this can be accomplished in a variety of ways and with enormously different flight times. The travel time required for space flights fluctuates considerably. Distances that only take several minutes, hours or days for some may take months and years for others. Compared to the technology used for space travel on earth at the present time, the extraterrestrial technology is exceedingly superior in every respect.

Nonphysical Spacecraft of Extraterrestrial Origin
See ~ Photos #27–#30

In contrast to the spacecraft previously discussed, there also exist nonphysical spacecraft made of ethereal matter or, in other words, of a certain type of energy, as unbelievable as it may sound. Among these extraordinary objects are:

- *Bio-organic spacecraft,* which penetrate our space-time continuum from dimensions foreign to earth if they so desire, for one reason or another.

- *Pure energy craft* which have very mysterious appearances by our standards. They have an enchanting transformation ability that enables them to assume any form, depending on the crew's wishes. The manufacture and alteration of such nonphysical flying devices are accomplished with the help of spirit force.

In early 1979, two such pure energy ships stayed in space close to earth for several months to fulfill a very special mission. Billy, the Pleiadian contact person, observed them several times at night as they appeared over his residence in Hinterschmidrüti. He was prepared for the extraterrestrial exhibition because the Pleiadians had telepathically informed him beforehand. He was not told of the exact time, but of all other facts concerning the planned days of visit. He then managed to take an entire series of impressive color photographs. *(See ~ Chapter 4: Billy Meier — Contactee of the Pleiadians)*

These pure energy ships originally appeared in the form of a bathtub-shaped object but then assumed a ball-shaped and a rod-shaped appearance. Their size changed on a grand scale from between five to several hundred meters.

Their light radiation was enormous. For example, a hillside was almost illuminated as bright as day on a pitch-black night. Cars parked in front of the Hinterschmidrüti residence and Center averaged five more liters of gasoline per hundred kilometers than usual after their exposure to the radiation of these spacecraft. According to the owners, the cars could no longer be used if they had been exposed a number of times to the extremely intense energy rays of these ships. When energy ships hovered in the vicinity of Billy's office at the Semjase Silver Star Center, the electric typewriter always went "on the blink." The secretary, Bernadette, who worked with this typewriter, can confirm how embarrassing it gradually became for her when the typewriter had to be taken for repair several times. Of course, there was no malicious intent on the part of the crew because they intended no harm to the members of our group.

As we later learned from the Pleiadians, the crews of these energy ships were members of a highly developed dwarf race, the life forms of which are half spiritual.[7] They are called Nabulanians and come from the Andromeda region, which is more than two million light years away from earth.

Who Commands the Extraterrestrial Spacecraft?

Unmanned spacecraft are operated by remote control from stations or mother ships. Aside from these, other fully automatic spacecraft are also in use. Human beings control manned spacecrafts' primary functions, although robots and androids are used as well. These androids, which are created by human beings, look like normal humans. They are half-organic and half-mechanical in composition. With their organic brain, they can think independently within the framework of their programming. They also act according to their own discretion. Nevertheless, they are still machines and can be manually switched off like robots. A main switch or only one switch at a time can either shut down only one or all functions. If the energy supply to the artificial brain is interrupted, a blackout will occur. For security reasons, an android can even switch itself off if its thought capacity is greatly exceeded or overstrained. Androids supervise and work with different robots. They carry out purely human activities as well.

Interestingly enough, female pilots of many extraterrestrial races enjoy the dominant position of commanders because a spacecraft requires relatively little physical strength and women are, in general, more flexible and sensitive in fields of communication than their male colleagues. Among other races that have not yet reached such a high standard of evolution, the exact opposite is true. In other words, the male pilots are the sole commanders of the spacecraft and are under the false assumption that women are less worthy than men are. Among the Pleiadians, the pilots are primarily female.

Footnotes

3 ▪ Fata Morgana – A mirage seen especially in the Strait of Messina formerly attributed to fairy agency.

4 ▪ Teleprojection or real visions are controllable visions (illusions) that, depending upon the wish of the perpetrator, convey certain impressions or experiences to other persons (unaware of this for the most part). The entire incident appears in the form of illusions that are just as real and just as lasting as they would be in reality. As a rule, the real vision cannot be distinguished from reality.

5 ▪ See Literary Index #8

6 ▪ The giant spacecraft is comprised of several large spheres that are interconnected by equally large corridors.

7 ▪ A half-spiritual life form is the term for an intermediate phase that a human being reaches in the course of his/her spiritual evolution. He or she no longer needs a material body but has not yet worked up to the next highest level, that of a purely spiritual life form. The body of a half-spiritual life form does not have a solid structure but can be described as a transparent veil-like nebulous entity.

CHAPTER 2

The Pleiadians, Our Extraterrestrial Friends and Teachers

The well-known seven-star system of the Pleiades is an open star cluster in the constellation Taurus – 420 light years distant from us – and is composed of relatively young stars, planets etc. The designation "seven-star system" is derived from the fact that at least seven sparkling stars can be seen with the naked eye on a clear and starry night in the northern winter sky. However, the planets of this system are in a developmental phase that is still totally unsuitable for human life forms at the present time. The home stars and planets of the Pleiadians, with whom Billy Meier maintains contacts, are located in the same region of the sky. However, they exist in another space-and-time configuration and are an additional 80 light years beyond the Pleiades. One of the sun systems located there bears the name "Tayget," the central star, which is orbited by ten planets; four of these are inhabited. Those human beings living there we call Pleiadians. Yet they call themselves Plejaren (pronounced pleh-yar-en) according to their system, which bears the name Plejaren. The closest planet resembling the earth is called "Erra," and the home of the Errans is located there; human beings of whom the discussion in this book is mainly about.

In this chapter, I would like to impart to you the Pleiadian or Erran ways of life as far as the facts are known to me. I will frequently quote passages from the contact reports[8] because Semjase, Quetzal and Ptaah have already given excellent explanations on many topics — much better than I could do myself.

Much of this may strike some readers as very strange and exotic. Therefore, it is advisable to put aside your preconceived notions and prejudices and critically examine all unusual statements with neutral objectivity. You, dear readers, may then receive several thought impulses, which may compel you to rethink our traditional ways of life and perhaps lead you to new knowledge.

To start, I would like to mention several physical aspects of planet Erra and compare them with our earth. In doing so, incredible similarities will be established. One year on Erra lasts exactly as long as it does here on earth but is divided into thirteen months[9] instead of twelve, with a compensatory adjustment every twenty-three years. A day has 23 hours and 59.4 minutes and one hour correlates almost exactly to an hour on earth.

	EARTH SPECIFICATIONS	ERRA SPECIFICATIONS
Approx. distance to the central sun	150 million kilometers (93 million miles)	150 million kilometers (93 million miles)
Orbital time around the central sun	365.25 days	365.25 days
Inclination of planet's imaginary axis	23.5 degrees	22.99 degrees
Equatorial diameter	12,756 kilometers (7,909 miles)	12,749 kilometers (7,903 miles)
Density	5.5 grams/cm³	5.5 grams/cm³
Atmospheric composition		12% more oxygen than earth
Gravitation		Almost the same as earth's

Fig. 2-1
Dimensional Comparison Between Earth and Erra

In reference to the symbol of planet Erra, Semjase gave the following explanation to Billy:

SEMJASE: I already explained to you that the symbols of your stars date back to our ancestors and were drawn up according to the vibrating and radiating values of the individual stars. In other words, the signs were drawn up according to the individual evolutionary level of the stars, so that each individual sign indicates the evolutionary stage or evolutionary level of the respective star. This is also true of Erra, my home planet, the sign of which was composed from various traditional symbols of our forefathers. Therefore, the same signs the ancients used for the stars of our SOL System (solar system of earth) are common again on earth at the present time. The horizontal form of the symbol represents the mean between above and below, hence the balance. Compare them with the symbols of the SOL System where there is no effective balance but, rather, the domination of either negative or positive forces.

Fig. 2-2
Symbol of planet Erra

Fig. 2-3
Symbol of planet Terra (earth)

The number of inhabitants on planet Erra is about 500 million. It does not exceed the lawful amount due to a permanent birth control policy, which allows for no more than twelve people per square kilometer of fertile soil. In principle, we must emphasize that extraterrestrial intelligences are neither monsters, nor heavenly spiritual figures nor other fairy tale beings, but are human life forms of flesh and blood — just as you and I. The Errans, in particular, are extremely similar to us in appearance. This is probably best documented in the reproduced sketch of Semjase. *(See ~ Photo #5 of a sketch of Semjase)*

Dressed according to earth standards, they certainly would not be recognized as extraterrestrials if they were to take a walk or go shopping in Paris or go anywhere else. According to Billy, who spent several days on Erra as a guest at the end of the 70's, they are not only good-looking people but also very harmonious in manner and outright friendly. The friendliness and courtesy shown him on that day are not only extended to foreign guests but to native inhabitants as well. They all greet one another whether they are acquainted or not, and no one turns around to rudely gaze at a complete stranger even though he or she wears unusual clothing or has a different skin color, etc. As a greeting or departing gesture, an Erran places his right hand over his heart and slightly nods his head. Compared to the people of earth, they are a few stretches ahead of us in evolutionary development. In fact, they are ahead of us from a technological standpoint by about 3,500 years,[10] and from a spiritual standpoint, by about 30 million years.

As a result of the higher vibrations of their home planet, Errans live in a much higher plane of vibration than we do. At this point, I would like to offer a small excerpt from Quetzal's explanations:

QUETZAL[11]: Our vibrations are highly sensitive, and we also react just as sensitively to the vibrations (of other life forms) which penetrate our field of vibration. The vibrations of earthman are still quite unbalanced and negative. If vibrations of the far less sensitive earth human being were to reach us and were to penetrate our field of vibration, they would cause a very strong jolt to our vibratory structure. That is what it also manifests in truth. Consequently for us, the strong external influence would lead to momentary uncontrolled reactions, thoughts and deeds that would trigger unrestrained feelings of anxiety. In other words, when we encounter the vibrations of an earth human being, who today unfortunately still emits very negative vibrations, our momentary reaction time is impaired in many respects and we start to act uncontrollably. That is what happened to Semjase when she fell in the Center and severely injured her head. *(See ~ A Description of Semjase)*

The levels of vibration between earth human beings and us are so fundamentally different and distinct in their negative and positive, as well as balanced, forms that they can lead to severe consequences if they converge. As a rule, vibrations of an earth human being reach a distance of 90 meters (297 ft.), which is why it is essential that this distance be maintained and earth human beings do not get closer to us than this exact distance.

For security reasons, the Errans use respective shielding devices to protect themselves against the vibrations of earth people. With respect to Billy, Quetzal added that a protective measure is not necessary since his vibrations are so balanced they are of no threat to the Errans. *(See ~ Chapter 5)*

Ptaah, Semjase and Quetzal are the names of the three main contact persons about whom we have the following personal information.

A Description of Ptaah

He is about 770 (earth) years old and has three children — two daughters by the names of Semjase and Pleija and one son by the name of Jucata who is no longer alive. Ptaah is the commander of the Pleiadian spacecraft fleet and is vested with the rank of an JHWH,[12] which is comparable to a king of wisdom. In earlier times, this term was translated as God, not in the sense of creator but as a king of wisdom who has the duty to provide his peoples with help and advice. He also presides over other inhabited planets but may never assume the role of despotic ruler, which happened on earth to some extent in earlier times. At the present time, Ptaah presides over three different planets, two of which are known to us as Erra and Terra (earth).

From original sketch drawn by Ptaah, which was later resketched by FIGU Core member, Christian Krukowski*

A Description of Semjase

She is 344 years old, about 1.7 meters (5.5 ft.) tall and is a slender, young, pretty woman with fair skin, sparkling blue eyes and light-blond hair. Her very long and somewhat forward-placed earlobes form a special distinguishing feature. This is the only anatomical difference compared to our women here on Terra. Due to her exceptional knowledge, which far exceeds the average of her home population, she has assumed the rank of half-Jschrjsch, which means a half-queen of wisdom or a half-goddess, as they were called earlier on earth (and which can be read about, for example, in Greek legends). Having occupied herself with

*Sketch by Christian Krukowski

various matters on our planet years before taking up contact with Billy on January 28, 1975, she is by far the best-oriented extraterrestrial concerning our situation on earth. During the period from February of 1965 until June of 1973, she stayed in the DAL Universe[13] with Asket's people. After her return from the DAL Universe to Erra, she came to earth in July of 1973 and continued to carry out the task she had performed here earlier in a hidden station. The first contact with Billy occurred on January 28, 1975. Of all the earth languages, she only mastered German and learned no others. In November of 1984, Semjase finally had to leave the earth for health reasons. Her field of work was exclusively restricted to the European area. She had no authorization whatsoever to become involved in any matters of, or establish contact with, any Pleiadian work groups on earth outside of Europe (neither in America nor Asia).

Unfortunately, on December 15, 1977, she suffered a life-threatening accident in the Semjase Silver Star Center in Hinterschmidrüti and had to be taken to her home planet of Erra immediately for medical treatment and rehabilitation. In May of 1978, she returned to earth and resumed her contacts with Billy until March 26, 1981. From March of 1981 until the end of January 1984, she was again absent because there were other duties she had to fulfill. On February 3, 1984, the very last contact took place between Semjase and Billy. As an after-effect of her accident on December 15, 1977, she suffered a cerebral collapse in the beginning of November 1984 and was transported again as quickly as possible to the DAL Universe where she was healed by the help of Asket and her friends, the Sonaer. Her father, Ptaah, explained that the complete regeneration of her brain and all psi-powers, abilities and memories lost during her collapse would presumably take about seventy years. During this period, Semjase will spend most of her time in the DAL Universe, and it should be noted here that it is absolutely impossible for Semjase to communicate by mechanical or telepathic means with anyone here in our universe. (The only way one could communicate would be to travel to the DAL Universe oneself.) I am giving this detailed information because more and more people are publicly claiming to have established telepathic or even personal contact with Semjase, although this is absolutely out of the question for the time being. On a personal note, Semjase[14] was married but tragically lost her husband after she had been wed for only seven years. Her spouse had participated in a research expedition in a foreign galaxy. At that time, approximately 200 years ago, they did not know the hyperspace technology yet. Of the two research ships dispatched, only one returned home after eleven years, whereas the other with her husband aboard suffered control damage and crashed into a sun. Her marriage was without children.

A Description of Quetzal

If Quetzal had an identification card, it would probably state the following: 464 years of age, 1.9 meters (6.25 ft.) tall, blue-gray eyes and light brown hair. He is spoiled and catered to by four pretty wives and is the father of six children. His wives are very good friends of Semjase and wish she would be the fifth in their marital union. Quetzal and Semjase, however, are of a different opinion in this matter, so this wish will not be fulfilled. During the 11-year contact period (1975–1986), Quetzal was Commander of all Pleiadian stations in our SOL System. According to Billy, Quetzal possesses enormous abilities, especially in the field of technology. He is also quite a distinguished

*Sketch by Christian Krukowski

inventor who has invented and constructed several very useful devices for Billy and FIGU, which have been of great use in the fulfillment of their mission. Regarding various concerns and problems on our earth, the three contact persons, Semjase, Quetzal and Ptaah, have been extraordinarily willing and active in the fulfillment of their tasks. It is our pleasure to express our sincere thanks to them.

Due to their extraordinarily high evolutionary level, the Pleiadians have an almost perfect command of universal space travel. To bridge the astronomical distances, an entire armada of spacecraft is at their disposal. They function, so to speak, as guardians of the cosmic order as well as advisors for the spiritual development of all peoples who are in dire need of their help.

They have a multitude of stations in the universe. Three of them were located on earth, in America, Asia and Europe. These stations were very well hidden and safeguarded in order to avoid detection by our present survey instruments. The European station was located inside a massive mountain in Switzerland and had been in existence for as long as three hundred years. During the 11-year period of contact (1975-1986), this station was continuously occupied by fifty to three hundred Pleiadians. The number varied according to their needs. Although the contacts were officially stopped on January 28, 1986, the Swiss station was still occupied by a crew of seven members whose activities were restricted to all sorts of regulatory and surveillance duties. With the exception of this remaining Pleiadian crew, all other extraterrestrial assistants, consisting of friendly and allied races of the Errans, had left the earth in 1986 after fulfilling their 11-year tour of duty. However, the personal contacts with Billy were officially resumed on November 17, 1989, but only to a limited extent due to his health problems.

A Description of Pleija

We know relatively little about Semjase's sister Pleija. According to Billy, she is a vibrant, adventurous creature with long, black hair. Pleija was once absolutely determined to drive Billy's moped since no such vehicle or anything similar to it is known on Erra. Semjase was of a different opinion. As she put it, she would never seat herself upon such a dangerous vehicle.

Emotions and Feelings

In view of the Pleiadian or Erran behavioral patterns, it would certainly be of interest to know how they deal with emotions and feelings — whether or not they experience joy, sadness, anger, grief, etc. With regard to their considerably higher evolutionary level compared to us, their emotional composure and psychological attitudes are so advanced that we would find them difficult to imagine.

It would be best to let a competent person like Semjase have the word here, since she knows the details of this complicated theme and can give us her report, as follows:

> **SEMJASE:** We also have emotional feelings such as love, friendship, sympathy and antipathy just like you people of earth. In certain respects they are much finer, with more depth and sensitivity. Over the past millennia, we started to exercise too much control and, in doing so, learned to suppress our feelings. We assumed we had to do this in order to protect ourselves against races of a lower evolutionary level. This attitude stems from the fact that all feelings in a higher sphere become increasingly fine-tuned during the course of evolution and, thus, need to be controlled more intensely. This intensification of feelings progresses simultaneously with the entire physical development and substantiates everything venerable that can be comprehended. Consequently, the desire to love and be with someone of the same evolutionary level is much more intense. This is also true for the lower evolved qualities simply because the desire for love is

constant. These feelings cannot be supplanted by knowledge or the ability to communicate, but are actually caused by them. Only through knowledge and the ability to communicate can these feelings evolve and flourish. Therefore, it is not true that certain duties evoke a change in the intensity of our feelings. Since these feelings are highly developed and controlled, they cannot be considered to be changes, only a further evolution of the person. The situation is different among the people of earth however, because their development is still quite low in these areas. This is why they allow themselves to be influenced by their particular work duties to such an extent that a prison guard, for example, may develop aggressive changes in his feelings.

We made the mistake of controlling our feelings too much, which resulted in the fact that we analyzed things according to pure probability values. This was wrong, which we quickly recognized after making your (Billy's) acquaintance, since you frequently gave reign to your feelings. This showed us it was wrong to isolate our feelings toward less developed intelligences through excessive control, which is why this mistake was corrected in the course of the past year. The blockage of emotions had already started to spread and take its toll among our own ranks. But we were able to find our way back in due time and eliminate the damage in a few months before an evolutionary blockage of feelings could take place — in all probability just as it had among other nations. However, among our peoples and races, these manifestations are non-existent. The people of Erra are the most highly evolved in the alliance and are the most progressive in these matters. A sweeping decision made by the Council averted this disorder. In the future, great care must be taken that less developed peoples and races do not make the same mistake. I am speaking of races and nations unknown to us in the wide expanse of the universe.

To the theme of passions, Semjase had the following to say:

SEMJASE: These matters also change depending upon the level of spiritual evolution because, as a rule, passion, sobriety and poise are based on spiritual development. These traits are characteristic features of a certain developmental stage. There are enormous differences in this respect among our peoples and races, just as there are on earth. In this respect, the Errans are completely different one from another because passion and other similar phenomena do not disappear until the physical body has been shed. They only become more refined, depending upon the degree of development in the spiritual realm, as long as they still exist in the physical realm. Passions no longer exist among us in the form in which they are deeply rooted and uncontrolled among you people of earth. By discussion and explanation of these things, we hope to create a better understanding that we Errans are also people just like you people of earth. We are not beings of perfection as often claimed by pseudo-contactees for religious purposes. Those supposedly perfect beings are deceitful and/or power-hungry creatures who would like to bring the people of earth under their control, which has already happened in a few cases. Sometimes, these beings simply exist as fantasies in the imagination of pseudo-contactees.

According to Semjase's explanations, it is obvious that the only difference here is in the degree of feelings and emotions. In my opinion, it has been expressed very plausibly that such highly developed civilizations are also capable of making mistakes to a greater or lesser extent. This fact should be of some consolation to us.

Life Expectancy and Estimation of Time

The average life expectancy of the Pleiadians is 1,000 years. The JHWH, Ptaah, explained the following:

> **PTAAH:** Each form of life has a life expectancy equal to its spiritual level. In early times when their extraterrestrial ancestors begot human beings on earth, their life span was estimated at an average of 1,007 years. Being schooled and taught by their progenitors, they had an enormous degree of spiritual knowledge and skills. At an unexpectedly fast rate, however, they fell prey to (cult) religions with their erroneous teachings and, thus, forfeited genuine knowledge and truth. Inevitably, they also started to act against all natural laws, abandoned them and broke the commandments and laws. Altogether, this led to a loss of their high average life expectancy rate which sank ever lower over thousands of years and leveled off to a mere 20th of that in former times. Only since the beginning of the New Age was there a turn for the better, so now the average life expectancy is once again slowly on the rise. The main reason for this is found in the recognition of truth and the connected spiritual direction. Therefore, the more the spiritual direction turns towards the truth again, the higher the average life expectancy will develop. In this way, the altered genetic factors, as well as other factors that were severely impaired over the course of thousands of years, will regulate and renew themselves.

The present day Pleiadians are the descendants of our common ancestors. This means that here on earth, Pleiadians (or old Lyrians and Vegans, respectively, from whom the Pleiadians descended, just as we have) lived and produced offspring with the human beings of earth (our biblical progenitors). The Pleiadians have remained loyal to the truth, hence to the laws and commandments of Creation, and that is why they have retained their average 1000-year life expectancy. If someone wanted to know how old Semjase would be here on earth, her 344 years must be calculated in relation to our life expectancy. In accordance with this, 1,000 years for the Pleiadians are roughly estimated to be about 100 earth years. Calculated according to our standards, Semjase is a young woman of about 34 years of age.

At this point, I would also like to mention the two different types of time calculation used by the Pleiadians. The first time calculation started with the year of ultimate peace on the Pleiadian worlds approximately 50,000 years ago (exactly 49,728 years ago as figured from the earth year 1994.)

The second time calculation started about 1,968 years before 1994, when the leadership of the Pleiadian peoples and their allies was taken over by the *High Council*[5] of the Cosmic Confederation. *(See section – The Form of Government in this chapter)*

Accordingly, 47,751 B.C. commemorates the time of ultimate peace, which has never yet been interrupted by any form of war. However, the year 26 AD according to our time calculation, marks the beginning of their years of spiritual alignment.

Up to the time of the spiritual alignment, the Pleiadian planets, which are much younger than our earth, were named with simple, specific number values. The Pleiadians then introduced a renewal on request of the High Council. Since the year 26 AD, according to our time calculation, they gave their home worlds harmoniously sounding names, such as Erra, which is the home planet of Semjase, Quetzal, Ptaah, Pleija, Jsodos and others.

Language and Writing

Over the entire planet of Erra, a single uniform language called Sarat is spoken. Unfortunately, I only know two words, arimo and gerasina. The first word is similar to the word "stop" and the second is "mother-in-law." Several languages are spoken on the planets of the Pleiadian system and their allies, but the Kosan language is the common language known by all. Kosan has an intercosmic character because it has already expanded over the border of our galaxy.

Since Semjase speaks perfect German, Billy wanted to know where and from whom she acquired such a mastery of the language. She then gave him the following explanation:

SEMJASE: Just like the people of earth, we must also learn a language. However, this is easier for us and does not require such great effort. We are in possession of all current earth languages and also of those used in earlier times. This means that we possess exact recordings of them in diverse forms. Language courses were established from them. Language specialists do this work as well as machines similar to those you call computers. Other machines of a similar nature are used to transmit and program the language. When connected to such machines, we receive the transmission of the desired language. This is done in a state similar to hypnosis that is induced by the machine. In this way, the language concepts and meanings are implanted and registered. This procedure lasts for 21 days. After that, we need another 9–10 days to be able to speak the language properly. We have to practice correct speech and pronunciation with the help of equipment and language specialists. To learn a language in this manner, we need 30–31 days. The people of earth are already working along similar lines in this area, especially the language institutes, which also use tape recorders in their language courses. This is the first step in constructing equipment and machines like ours and putting them to use. This work is already done in various places on present-day computers.

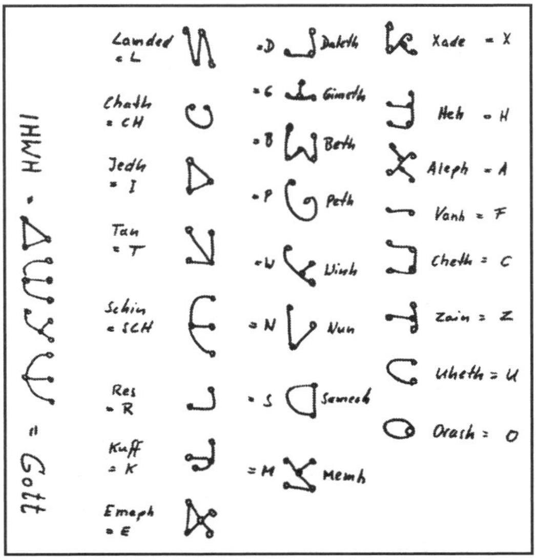

Fig. 2-4-A
The Pleiadian Alphabet as written in Semjase's own hand.

As mentioned in *Chapter 5*, the Pleiadians also have an entirely different method, if they do not master a language, i.e., they use a translator (language converter) that enables them to communicate perfectly. This device can transform any language into another. Besides this, telepathy is used when it is necessary to communicate with someone over great distances. Range of distance itself is never a problem or hindrance when spiritual telepathy is used, of which numerous variations are in use among the different peoples in the universe. (*See ~ Chapter 5: Spiritual Telepathy*)

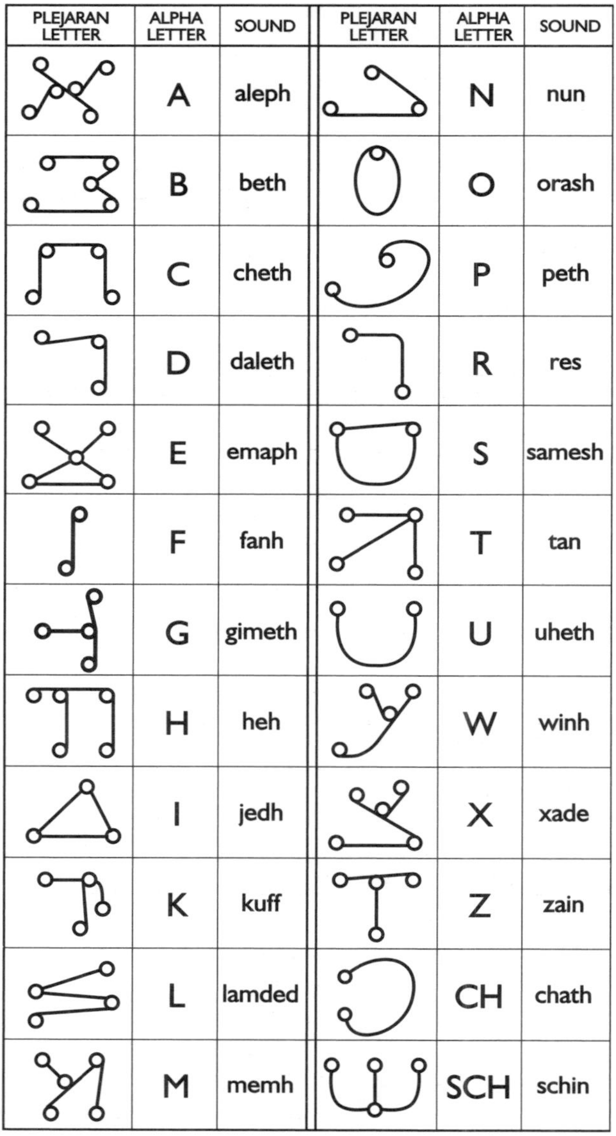

PLEJARAN LETTER	ALPHA LETTER	SOUND	PLEJARAN LETTER	ALPHA LETTER	SOUND
	A	aleph		N	nun
	B	beth		O	orash
	C	cheth		P	peth
	D	daleth		R	res
	E	emaph		S	samesh
	F	fanh		T	tan
	G	gimeth		U	uheth
	H	heh		W	winh
	I	jedh		X	xade
	K	kuff		Z	zain
	L	lamded		CH	chath
	M	memh		SCH	schin

Fig. 2-4-B
The Pleiadian Alphabet reproduced for clarity

As for the alphabetic characters that the Pleiadians use today, Semjase gave the following information:

SEMJASE: The writing we use today is only about 11,000 years old and dates back to those of our ancestors who lived on your earth. Our old written characters are very complicated, whereas the new ones are very simple. Our various scientists who lived on earth back then worked out the characters. They used the constellations visible from earth as a pattern. They connected certain constellations and thus obtained certain forms. If our writing consists of small circles and lines, then these circles depict stars, and the lines were a simple means of connecting them. The people of earth have long forgotten this writing, but it was in use by our ancestors and adopted by the literate earth people for a few thousand years, during which time it was greatly modified. Only a very few scripts used by earth people today date back to our writing, and they have been changed almost beyond recognition.

As a result, it is a fact the earth people did not develop their own writing but adopted it from extraterrestrial ancestors who lived on earth in early times. At the same time, these heavenly sons and daughters were also primarily involved in the development and improvement of earth languages. As for the alphabet of the Pleiadians, it should be said that ch and sch are individual letters whereas i, qu, v and y are not included at all. In place of i, the letter j is used. The vowel combinations ae, oe, ue are also not existing.

**GENERAL OVERVIEW OF THE DEVELOPMENT OF
EARTH LANGUAGES IN RELATION TO THEIR ORIGIN**

Original word	Developed into
WESTAN	all African languages
TRJDJN	all Indian languages such as island languages in the southern and central hemisphere
ARJN	all Germanic, Indo-Germanic, Latin, English and Celtic languages
HEBRJN	Assyrian, Arabic, Hebraic, Babylonian and Aramaic languages
KJDAN	Chinese and Japanese languages
BAMAR	Australian, Near East, Turkish and Osmanian languages
SUMAN	Minoan (from this, the old Greek language was developed), Atlantic, Gobanian, Sumarian and Limurgian languages

Fig. 2-5

The languages listed here are by no means complete but they do give a general overview of the development of earth languages in relation to their origin.

Associated with this, dear reader, I do not want to deprive you of the developmental history of earth languages. The primitive earth Ur-language (ancient and original) called Bro[16] was mixed with seven highly valued old-Lyrian (thus extraterrestrial) languages named Westan, Trjdjn, Arjn, Hebrjn, Kjdan, Bamar and Suman. They developed over time into the ancient fundamental languages of earth and eventually evolved into today's various earth languages.

The above listing is in no way complete, but conveys a valuable rough overview about the origin of the earthly languages.

At this point I would like to mention another matter, which occurred in 1976 when the children of my school classes asked me for Semjase's autograph. At an appropriate moment, I took this request to the contactee, Billy, who further relayed it to Semjase during a personal contact on June 23, 1976. To my joy, Semjase promptly responded during her conversation with Billy, writing four autographs in Latin script with a felt pen that Billy had given her. Because she had little familiarity and practice with this script, she made a small error on her first attempt by writing the word Semjase with a *y* instead of a *j*. Being made aware of this, Semjase then wrote three other samples, this time without a mistake.

Using these original autographs, I made enough copies for all the students in my class. These were not comparable in quality to the originals, but the school children took the copies with joy and wanted to give Semjase a young kitten[17] as a gesture of thanks. Semjase was overjoyed with this gesture but unfortunately, she could not accept the gift for reasons of security.

My own joy soon turned to dismay as I discovered through others that some of the childrens' parents reacted harshly to this action, so that one party already considered filing an official complaint with the school authorities. In my naive and carefree state of mind, I had not expected such a reaction from the parents but I did completely understand the reasoning behind it. As a result, I have decided to be more careful with regard to this sensitive topic.

Living Quarters

If we can visualize the fact that Errans have exactly the same amount of living space on their planet of about 500 million people as do the people of earth with a population of more than 6 billion, we can clearly see that there is ample space on Erra for all forms of life. Literally speaking, the population of our earth should not exceed 529 million people. This number complies with the laws of Creation. We should strive to return to this population count because our extreme overpopulation poses the gravest danger to earth at the present time. *(See ~ Chapter 14 regarding the dangers of overpopulation)*

On Erra there are several cities that have multi-story buildings, but no housing structures are built in the form of high-rise buildings or skyscrapers in which people have to live closely packed together like canned sardines. Extensive park grounds and garden facilities with footpaths are placed between individual residential buildings. There are no streets of any kind — they are not even necessary, for that matter, since Errans do not use any form of surface vehicles at all. All residential areas have their own pedestrian zones. They do not suffer from the noise or environmental pollution we experience from exhaust fumes, sirens, etc.

The majority of inhabitants prefers to live in the country in single-family homes that have semi-spherical or spherical forms and a minimum diameter of 21 meters (69 ft.). Building materials largely consist of a resistant metal alloy or synthetic material, which is extracted from the soil — primarily from sand — and is similar to our silicon. Such homesteads offer sufficient room for a family of five. A woman is permitted to bear as many as three children but this number may not be exceeded. Furthermore, each house is built on its own fertile plot of land, generally at least one hectare (2.5 acres) in size. All families take pleasure in planting and cultivating their own fruit, vegetable and flower gardens. Potatoes and other economically valuable plants naturally flourish here, as well. In general, each available plot of land is used as much as possible and cultivated. Factories and industrial facilities of every kind are built in desolate and uninhabited areas. They are also built underground to ensure environmental protection. On Erra, not a single smokestack pollutes the air with exhaust fumes! Safeguarding nature and the environment has a very high level of priority. Furthermore, the individual residential associations are as self-sufficient as possible, since each home has its own water and energy supply.

Clothing

Unfortunately, we could not learn much about the clothing of the Pleiadians. Semjase said their clothing would appear somewhat strange to us but is much more practical than the garments we wear. However, around the year 2050, our clothing trend will be quite similar to theirs since we will have a change of mind by that time and will prefer practical to "fashionable" clothing. Their footwear is similar to ours. It is no longer made of leather but of synthetic materials. Very close-fitting overalls are specially made for space travel and designed with a ring collar for attaching a protective helmet. The only piece of clothing that a member of our group has ever seen on an extraterrestrial was a lustrous silvery rain cloak that Quetzal was wearing on a walk one night when he was scheduled to contact Billy and stepped in front of the headlights of Engelbert's car. *(See ~ Chapter 8: What is Sneaking Around There at This Late Hour?)*

Nutrition

The Errans nourish themselves according to the laws of Creation, which means that they consume a balanced, measured and nutritious diet of both mineral and vegetable as well as animal foods. Of primary value is nutrition obtained from fruits and vegetables. They categorically reject a purely vegetarian nutrition because negative side effects can result in the form of abnormal mental activities and conscious reaction abilities of an excessively positive nature. Consequently, critical judgment is impaired to the extent that a person can no longer distinguish between what is real and what is unreal. As for the purely physical side-effects, it must be said that adults can tolerate such a one-sided diet over an extended period of time with relatively little harm, but can cause growth disorders and other negative symptoms among children and adolescents. Insufficient vegetarian food or an excessive amount of animal products give rise to the exact opposite effects such as sluggish thoughts and reactions which are also undesirable. Consequently, Errans do not abstain from animal food but never indulge in excessive amounts. They never slaughter domestic animals such as cattle and swine, as we do. Lower animal forms such as rabbits, ducks and chickens are only slaughtered and consumed under extreme circumstances. Nevertheless, people do not have to go without meat specialties, since cutlets, for example, are also on their dietary plan. But how does this relate to the aforementioned? Well, it simply means that the meat used for dietary purposes is artificially cultivated with the help of cell cultures. Therefore, we should not be surprised to find out that on Erra, veal cutlets are produced on an assembly line without having to slaughter a single animal.

According to Quetzal, many earth people unfortunately have very different and erroneous opinions about nutrition that have equally harmful effects on them. The erroneous opinion that a human life form can develop to its full and healthy potential without animal substances is just as false as the assumption that large quantities of animal substances improve the physical constitution. The truth is that great deficiencies appear if either excessive animal substances are consumed or none at all. The entire structure and preservation of human life forms are dependent upon floral and faunal nutrition, at least those pertaining to the physical body. If, for example, faunal nutrition is not available or is abstained from based on erroneous assumptions, then plant substances of equally nutritious value must substitute the lack of animal substances. But this is not yet possible on earth because these nutritious plant substances have remained practically undiscovered. The few that are known are shunned for some unintelligible reasons of disgust.

It would also be interesting to find out what the inhabitants of Erra drink. I do not know enough about this to give a full report, but it is certain that natural juices in all possible variations play a major role. Pure alcoholic beverages are completely unknown. Instead, beverages similar to alcohol are consumed without causing intoxication — not even if a person drinks large quantities.

In my opinion, it would be commendable if our nutritionists would familiarize themselves with the nutritional habits of the Errans in order to give the people of earth appropriate advice on healthy nutrition in the future.

Plants

The ancestors of the present-day Pleiadians who lived on the earth in former times took many types of plants back to their planet and cultivated them. All the plants that we know of today, as well as others we know nothing about, can be found there. Cereals, potatoes, berries, fruits and vegetables are cultivated for daily use among the population, but there is nonetheless a substantial difference between their products and ours. Their fruits and vegetables are so nourishing and thirst-quenching that no other food is necessary to satisfy hunger and thirst for days at a time, even up to the remarkable period of 90 hours! The various types of fruit are much more exquisite in taste and fragrance than those we are accustomed to. Their colors have a greater intensity, as well. The color green, for example, has a rather dull appearance in our natural environment, whereas the unsoiled and lush green on Erra is very pleasing to the eye. One reason for this is the clean air on Erra, which is free from all kinds of harmful toxins. It is due to the robots and androids working there and the exemplary manner in which they properly attend to the plants.

In addition to this, horticulture is practiced on Erra with such captivating results that we on earth would not believe it possible. There are very specific plant cultivations, which grow and flourish in a climate created just for them. Due to their extraordinary size, we have to refer to them as giant plants. Among these are 18-meter (59 ft.) corn stalks with cobs that are 2.2 meters (7 ft.) long and 20–25 centimeters (8–10 in.) thick. Peppermint plants and other similar herbs grow up to 15 meters (50 ft.). However, I have not yet mentioned the largest of these — the apple, pear and cherry trees that soar 120 meters (396 ft.) into the sky. Mammoth apples grow as large as pumpkins and weigh from 20–30 kilograms (44–66 lbs.). Such gigantic fruits are industrially processed and exclusively used for export to other planets where a food shortage prevails. These giant crops are grown for the sole purpose of providing this aid. Although they are the result of excessive cultivation, the fruit tastes just as good and is as nourishing and flavorful as the normal-sized ones.

Flowers

I would now like to comment briefly on the flowers. When Billy visited Erra, he was indeed warmly welcomed, but not with a bouquet of flowers. The Errans, according to Billy's statement, let flowers remain where they grow. No one would ever consider uprooting even a blade of grass to take home and stick in a vase, as is customary here among us. However, the women especially cultivate a flower similar in appearance to our anemone. An exceptional feature characterizes it. After being plucked, the blossoms remain fresh for several hours as if the flower had never been removed. It then starts to dry out similarly to our dried flowers and is used as an embellishment for the women who wear one or more blossoms in their hair. This is the only jewelry they wear since they have no rings, earrings, necklaces, broaches, bracelets, or any other treasures of this kind.

The viewpoint of the entire population basically considers every plant, no matter how small, as an integral part of Creation. They feel bonded in some way to all life forms.

Domestic Animals

In former days when the ancestors of the present-day Pleiadians lived on earth, they returned home with a pair of almost every kind of animal existing on earth and then totally eradicated all animal diseases. Today, as previously mentioned, it is strictly prohibited to import animals from alien planets for security reasons unless they have been 100 percent disinfected so there is absolutely no danger of bringing in a disease.

Despite their love for animal life forms, domestic animals are treated quite differently from the animals here on earth. In view of the fact that many diseases are transferred from domestic animals to human beings, they switched over long ago to keeping all domestic animals on Erra in specially built caged enclosures but never directly in human living quarters. This also holds true for cats, dogs, birds, hamsters, etc. that are often viewed or treated like children or family members here on earth. Out of ignorance and a false understanding of love for animals, this type of treatment can unfortunately lead to very many health problems. It happens that we usually grow most fond of domestic animals. They are often the only form of companionship that prevents elderly and lonely people from feeling so alone and forsaken. However, cats and dogs are also responsible for more than 50 percent of all contagious diseases. According to the Errans, cats and dogs are principle carriers of many deadly diseases and the danger of contagion for human beings is relatively high. The presumed cleanliness of a cat is only an outward appearance since deadly pathogens can be found in its coat only 30 seconds after it has undergone a complete chemical disinfecting. These are facts that hit us earth people especially hard and which we cannot easily digest all at once. In view of the misplaced affection for animals and the incorrect keeping of house pets, our present attitudes on earth will probably not change too quickly. For all those who are fond of house pets, the following should be carefully heeded in one's own interest as well as in the interest of the general public:

- Immediately after petting or simply touching a domestic animal, one's hands should be washed.

- Household pets should not be treated like human beings by kissing them or letting them sleep in the same bed, or similar practices.

Work

When earth people discover the field of esoteric study, they generally would like nothing more than to drop everything else and turn their full attention to spiritual matters. This approach would be a mistake, as we shall establish here. It is far from the truth to assume that the Pleiadians have reached such a high evolutionary level that manual labor is an irrelevant and inferior activity. This assumption is far-fetched and completely untrue.

If people, regardless of the planet they are from, desire to grow in spirit and in knowledge, they can only accomplish this by also performing manual work to the best of their ability. This is not only essential to earn a living but also provides a balance to the study and assimilation of spirit teachings. If people want to live according to the laws and commandments of Creation, they must acknowledge that a certain allotment of physical work is necessary, whether they like it or not, since their efforts would otherwise be in vain. The greater the quantity of learning material and its degree of difficulty, the greater the need for physical activity, since the ability to learn is enhanced by manual activity that has been acquired beforehand.

Provided that the spiritual evolution of a given person is known, then the duration of manual work required of him or her can be calculated. Let's hear what Quetzal has to say about this:

> **QUETZAL:** … The rule exists for earthman that he or she must work in order to promote their spiritual and consciousness-related learning ability and learning activity. Thus, the highest daily average of manual work on earth is eleven hours, whereas it is only two hours per day for the Pleiadians.

All Errans, adults and adolescents alike, perform these two hours of manual work in order to reach a balance between their spirit and consciousness. This daily work quota is performed for the welfare of the general public and is done without payment. In exchange for this, they receive all the necessities of life free of charge. This regulation holds true for the entire planetary region and promotes the feeling of togetherness among the planetary community since other working conditions prevail there as they do here on earth. Errans have such diverse education and skills that they can accomplish practically all the work needed for the general public welfare. Regardless of where a person lives on Erra, they are never restricted to one given place. Whenever and how often it pleases a person, he can change his place of work at any time. Important is only that he carries out his two hours of work for the common good of all, the rest does not matter. For example, he boards his hover craft, flies a few thousand kilometers across the land and touches down where ever he likes. He will then help out in agriculture, another time in an industrial plant. Consequently, they do not have to fulfill their duty year after year at the same place, but can always select new places of employment whenever they please. Should there be a lack of personnel somewhere, provisions have been made for the always-available androids to help out. As a rule, the work in factories is not physically demanding since it largely consists of monitoring the machines and robots. Besides, there are naturally many other jobs, especially creative jobs of a technical and spiritual nature just as we have here.

After completing their two-hour work-duty, every person is free to do whatever they please with the rest of their free time. Naturally they do not laze around, but use their time for meaningful activities. On Erra, it is not unusual for someone to have studied up to thirty different fields of knowledge.

Even the oldest of the elderly do not simply retire but continue to plow their own land or help out with agricultural work on other estates. In so doing, they often encounter people whom they have never met before. In this way, personal contact grows over the entire planet, friendships are made, neighborly love is enhanced, and all things of importance for a harmonious social life are cultivated.

Apart from the agricultural land, fruit cultivation, etc., for public and export purposes, the cultivation of a private garden plays an especially important role in their lives. Although the Errans certainly have adequate mechanical devices to relieve them of the demanding manual work in their own gardens, they make no use of them. We learned from Billy that most of the inhabitants have callused hands, indicating hard physical work. Their private gardens are intentionally worked by hand. This also holds true for Quetzal who has collected such implements as pitch forks, hoes, picks, shovels and all other tools from our planet that are necessary for garden work.

In contrast, the cultivation of soil for general needs and export purposes is done with machines. Here again, we are confronted with such novelties as machines and working robots, which avoid contact with the ground but hover over it instead. They are equipped with short metal arms or long hose-like arms that have a suction funnel at the end. With this suction funnel, the soil is lifted from the ground, conveyed into the machine and spit out the other end, after which the ground is as good as tilled. Similar devices are used to sow seeds, harvest crops or pull weeds. To remove weeds, a special arm is extended that uproots the weeds through suction. They are then processed in the machine and returned to the soil as fresh humus. In general, all the working robots hover over the ground and use the suction principle. This method ensures that the soil is never overburdened by heavy machinery.

Characteristically, the leading powers on planet Erra are the spiritual leaders who have taken the place of politicians. They also perform their two hours of obligatory manual work for the common welfare. Not until after they complete their public work do they pursue their actual work, which consists of functioning as advisors, informers and teachers of the people. Their work simply includes everything that the populace desires and needs to know to align their lives according to the laws and commandments of Creation. These spirit leaders, who number about 2,800 for a population of 500 million, are not bound to any fixed location. Just like the rest, they may also change their residence as they please. Every settlement has a special place where the spirit leaders can fulfill their functions. In larger settlements, relatively more space is available. If another already occupies the place selected, then that occupant packs his bags and moves on, therefore, allowing for continual change. Each inhabitant has the right to select a spirit leader[18] and ask him questions. (Actually, anyone who has ever trusted the insane claims of a pseudo-contactee who has set himself or herself up as a spiritual leader, should blush with shame. According to their claims, extraterrestrial men and women are considered to be supernatural, angelic and ethereal creatures, which by no means is true.)

Since all citizens on Erra receive everything they need and are entitled to, payment by means of money is not necessary. As already mentioned, all able-bodied people work two hours a day without payment for the community as a whole. In exchange for this, they receive all necessities free of charge. Regarding work, I would once again like to stress that the Errans consider every type of work and meaningful activity as a means of promoting their evolutionary process, as no satisfactory coarsely-structured material existence or progressive spiritual evolution would be possible without it.

Transport Vehicles

On Erra there are many vehicles but not a single surface vehicle, so there are no streets as we have here on earth. To cover shorter distances or to take extensive walks, pedestrians only use footpaths between the houses and in the parks. In the open countryside, there are trample paths that invite hiking.

For transportation within a planetary region, the Errans make use of hovering vehicles, which come in two variations, either as: 1. a spherical craft, or 2. a disk-shaped structure somewhat comparable to the spacecraft, which are available in all possible sizes for space flight. A hovering vehicle is designed to accommodate one to five people. Each residence or residential building has at least one means of transportation. The need for a family vehicle is up to the individual. Each adult can request and claim a vehicle for his or her own private use as needed. There are some cases in which two or more people share a common vehicle, but the number of passengers never exceeds five. Therefore, whenever a larger group wishes to travel somewhere together, they do not go by chartered aircraft on Erra. Instead, a corresponding number of hovering vehicles (with five seats each) would suffice. There is probably no need for me to point out that these spacecraft cause absolutely no environmental pollution because they are powered by propulsion systems that do not burn fossil fuel. In addition, they fly almost silently and, if desired, at breakneck speed.

Finally, I would like to call your attention to yet another unique attraction on Erra concerning a "museum of earth vehicles." Every one of the wheeled and tracked vehicles ever built on earth is exhibited here in a huge area of several hectares.

A special experience for the founder of this museum consists of taking an excursion in the wilderness during his free time with nothing other than an earthly Land Rover from his own collection! Space vehicles will be dealt with in detail in the next chapter.

The Problem of Diseases

It would certainly be of great interest for us to know whether the Pleiadians have similar illnesses, such as cancer, and whether they have overcome this scourge of mankind or have never known it at all. Assuming that they have already solved the problem of cancer, could we then profit from their experience and spare ourselves great suffering and sorrow? When asked about this, Semjase responded with the following explanation:

SEMJASE: Our scientists conquered many diseases centuries ago, but afflictions of a pathogenic nature transmitted from other star systems in earlier times still prevail today. However, they no longer exist in a fatal or physically destructive form. They are afflictions of a less harmful nature such as colds, which can develop into pneumonia or other similar afflictions that we ordinarily can constrain very quickly before the pathogens degenerate any further. This also holds true for other afflictions. We, too, are only human life forms like the inhabitants of earth. Consequently, we are also susceptible to certain diseases but are, as a rule, quite capable of controlling and healing them. Moreover, there are certain illnesses unknown on earth that are pathogenic in nature on our planet but which our science has been able to master. As for what you (Billy) refer to as cancer, which is manifested because of a parasite-like, misguided life, we were fortunate enough to eradicate this disease a long time ago. This was not possible until our human race and our scientists started to think and act in new ways and had purged themselves of certain negative attitudes and forms of behavior.

Earthman must acquire the necessary knowledge about these subjects through hard work, because they will then grow from within. Only in this way will they be able to understand many things and, therefore, learn the correct form of behavior. If we were to reveal this knowledge to earthman, we would be handing them a tool, which they, in turn, would use for destruction and annihilation. The knowledge to fight this disease contains too many powerful forces for us to simply reveal and then account for. It is still too early for earthman to possess this knowledge. Only through continual and progressive evolution will they be able to assimilate this much knowledge with its strength and power. At that point they will exercise it moderately and according to the laws and commandments of Creation and will not use it for negative purposes.

With certainty, this explanation will seriously disappoint some of my contemporaries. This does not mean that the Pleiadians are unwilling to help us. They simply may not help us in this particular case — which they exceedingly regret. A premature disclosure of the cure for cancer would load them with great guilt. As an analogy, we would not profit in any form if we were to entrust a juvenile with detailed information on the use of curare, a lethal poison, for purposes of healing. This example should be thoroughly considered by all those who are inclined to accuse the Pleiadians of inhumane behavior and should serve to set their minds at ease, once and for all.

Among other things used by the Pleiadians for purposes of healing are the regeneration machines and other superb equipment that can heal broken bones instantly and do much, much more. Their medication conforms to natural medicine. They always use basic substances that release appropriate activating signals in the body. In contrast, our allopathic drugs function on the theory that chemical residues will bring about healing advantages. Unfortunately, they also produce harmful toxins that burden the body with considerable disadvantages.

We were unable to learn anything about their surgical techniques, but we did receive a comprehensive report from Semjase about organ transplants.

SEMJASE: … This is a developmental type of science, which is still primitive and will continue to have very little success, with few exceptions. Our science, for example, is also working with the transplantation of eyes, but they are only transferred from one living life form to another. This has proven to be a complete success in every respect. However, our scientists only transplant eyes because no form of technology can replace the natural eye. No other bodily organs or limbs are removed from the living or the dead to be transferred to other living life forms. Such transplants involve great dangers in various ways. I would only like to mention two of those that are important. One dangerous factor involves a complete destruction of the body's immune system after undergoing a limb or organ transplant from a foreign body. This means a body that is subjected to transplantation is made fully defenseless by anesthetics and other toxic substances. Its power of resistance is totally destroyed so the transplanted organ or limb will not be rejected. The body therefore becomes dangerously susceptible to all external influences so that even a very small particle of dust is enough to extinguish the body's life and cause the life form to die. The second factor is the existence of the foreign aura inherent in the transplanted part of the donor's body. With all certainty, transmitted auric forces work against the auric forces of the body undergoing the transplant. This gives rise to many dangers and factors that degenerate the body and spirit. We have the capability of a complete regeneration. However, where the possibility of success is in question, the organs are replaced with artificial ones that will probably outlast the life span of the body. This procedure is also used with the loss of limbs. Consequently, this means we do not perform transplants! earth medical science should make endeavors along these lines. The best solution is the production of artificial and purposeful organs that are replaceable.

The possibilities of Pleiadian medicine would thrill the heart of every doctor on earth. All the same, it is comforting to know that we can make great progress in this important sector for the well being of the entire population of earth.

Music, Art and Literature

One day, Billy asked Semjase whether or not the extraterrestrials have musical activities as we do. Semjase answered this question affirmatively and then added:

SEMJASE: Certainly, these things are characteristic of all human life forms in the universe. We also have proper schools for music, but only interested and truly talented people who will later work for the welfare of all can attend them. There are no such things in our world such as musicians appearing in public who produce ear-piercing sounds, as is customary on earth. I often find it dreadful when I listen to earth music, but I am delighted about truly good and harmonious music which has nothing to do with hits that are often bad and discordant.

Billy said that this happens to be barbarous music to which the people of earth are still largely predisposed.

For us earth people, music of the Errans would sound very strange but, on the other hand, it would be so harmonious and enrapturing that we would not be able to withstand it very long. The yearning for this harmonious state would grow to overwhelming proportions within us. For this reason, Billy was not permitted to bring back any music from planet Erra when he stayed there once on a visit. He did explain to us that we have three musical pieces on earth that are somewhat similar in harmony to the Pleiadian music. These pieces are the Bolero by Maurice Ravel, the Valkyrie-ride from The Valkyrie (an opera by Richard Wagner), and the chorus of prisoners from the opera Nabucco by Guiseppe Verdi. Other than that, their composers use completely different instruments from ours. Unfortunately, I do not know any details about their art and literature.

Burial of the Dead

The Pleiadians still have certain practices in common with us despite their very high evolutionary level. This has been established, among other things, by the burial of their dead. Semjase described the facts as follows:

> **SEMJASE:** Burial of the dead in the ground is also known and practiced on our world just as it is on earth. We have special depository facilities that are remote from inhabited areas. From ancient times, we have retained the practice of cremation for very rare cases if desired.
>
> Beside burial in the ground, eliminating the lifeless body is also customary. This matter is left up to the individual so that either form of burial can be used. Burial in the ground is considered to be the natural form and has been practiced in this way since the very beginning. There are no objections to an elimination if no heed is paid to the loss of certain auric forces that linger on for a while within the lifeless body and escape naturally through eliminating or burning. Auric forces can linger on for centuries or, at the longest, until the skeleton has been destroyed.[19]

These auric forces are bound to the physical body and can be a great consolation for those left behind. These forces also linger on objects frequently used by the deceased, such as pieces of clothing, jewelry, etc. Often, a piece of clothing is saved so those left behind have the feeling that the deceased continues to remain among them. These feelings can be traced back to stored auric forces. However, the mistake should never be made of praying to such memorials or idolizing them, as is often done on earth, because people unconsciously deplete their own energy reserves in this way.

The Pleiadians have a distinctly healthful understanding of what death or the dying of a human life form means. Of course, there is sadness and pain over the loss of a loved one, but even so, they are very well informed about what happens after death. They know that only the coarsely-structured body decomposes, whereas the immortal, spiritual form merely crosses over into another dimension in order to thoroughly process the knowledge and impressions accumulated in this life and then to reincarnate into a new body. They also know that a close bond exists between two people who love each other and it does not cease at death but continues far beyond it. Once love has grown, it is lasting and cannot be destroyed.

Due to ignorance and a misunderstanding of these facts, we often mourn intensely, especially when death involves very young people who had to depart this world due to war activities, natural catastrophes, or terror assaults. Exaggerated mourning, which many people succumb to, is for the most part nothing more than self-pity and is zealously nurtured over weeks, months and years. In addition to this, the deceased are sometimes idolized so that all contact with reality is lost. To prevent such unnatural illusions, it is absolutely necessary to carefully examine the question of "life and death" in order to acquire a better understanding, which will also greatly help those affected to better cope with such situations.

Methods of Punishment

It is often assumed that extraterrestrials are superhuman beings who no longer are subject to fault and, hence, no longer need laws and commandments. This assumption is erroneous, for the laws and commandments are only discontinued wherever the order of Creation has become absolutely self-evident. This is only the case, however, in very high dimensions where beings are in a purely spiritual, evolutionary plane in which all that is coarsely mattered belongs to the past. On the other hand, physical life forms of all types and races are still burdened with too many faults to simply ignore the laws and commandments appropriate for their level of evolution.

This implies, no more and no less, that the Pleiadians also err in their deeds and actions now and then. They even burden themselves with guilt and are punished according to the severity of the violation. Semjase once said that she always calls an error by name and stands by it because there is no sense in covering it up, as the people of earth often do. To err is absolutely essential for further development because by making mistakes, we learn how to eradicate the sources of error. Through proper behavior over the course of time, the errors eventually no longer occur. Hence, the Pleiadians are walking along the same path of evolution as all other human life forms in the universe. Naturally, the frequency curve of errors and their severity gradually lessen with increasing maturity. Positive attributes such as carefulness, accuracy, reliability, etc. then take the place of such negative traits as superficiality, forgetfulness, etc. Perhaps it could be said that the road to perfection is paved with many good intentions. It is regrettable that those who neither see their faults nor learn from them must pay more for them, each time.

The legislative process of the Pleiadians corresponds to their spiritual level and is, therefore, more humane. Unfortunately, that cannot be said of our own primitive legislative process. Severe violations in their world are not punished by a death penalty, nor do they inflict other injuries upon the body and mind as "corrections," which are still customarily practiced in a barbarous manner to some extent here on earth.

On all planets inhabited by Pleiadians, a uniform penal system has been introduced which has proved to be excellent. Depending upon the severity of the crime, the guilty are either banished to a very remote island or a specially selected planet — for a lifetime in the case of severe criminal offenses. For well-founded reasons, both sexes may never be banished together. The men are sent to one island and the women to another. The prisoners are left entirely on their own and must literally earn their daily bread by the sweat of their brow. That literally means they may not have machines, nor manufacture any, to help them with their work. To enforce this measure, regular controls are in place to ruthlessly eliminate equipment that has been secretly produced to facilitate their work. Furthermore, care must be taken that the banished are not able to establish or cultivate contact with any other life forms.

According to Semjase's words:

SEMJASE: This form of punishment guarantees the greatest possible security for the maintenance of order. On the other hand, the guilty do not become a burden to the populace. This form of punishment is very humane and useful because the guilty are not inhibited in their development during their life-long banishment.

In primeval times, various criminal life forms from diverse worlds in the universe were banished in this manner to your earth, including some of our own race as well. These early times, though, are also inconceivable to us because we have no accurate data about them.

Some readers may have the impression that this type of prison method is brutal. After careful consideration, I do not feel this way. The realization gradually crystallized within me that banishment was probably the only effective method of fulfilling the punitive measures necessary to guarantee a fundamental commandment of Creation. This commandment plainly states, "every life form has the right to be completely free with respect to its body, its psyche, and its physical and spiritual consciousness." This law is by no means fulfilled through mere imprisonment or through contentious harassment with all kinds of torture or execution. On the contrary, the exact opposite of what mankind really wants is often achieved. After several admonitions, a person guilty of transgressions must be punished until they can see why they have acted falsely and how they can prevent a repetition in the future. There must be punishment, but it must not injure a person's dignity or conflict with the laws of Creation. Punishment is only meaningful when it actually achieves the desired objective. Criminals of all kinds are misguided or mentally sick because they act against the law out of false motives resulting from their illogical thinking. Therefore, they must be offered the possibility of atonement by separating them from society and giving them the opportunity to improve. In this manner they learn to recognize the flaws in their thinking and their actions and begin to act in the right way according to the laws and commandments of Creation. This goal cannot be, and may never be, achieved through any form of torture or the enforcement of a death penalty. Torture is not only a cowardly act of the lowest order but, in my opinion, the most malicious and abhorrent human behavior that anyone could possibly imagine. In comparison, even the death penalty appears rather harmless, although it naturally misses the objective by a long shot. On the one hand, a delinquent is robbed of every possibility of atonement through the death penalty. On the other hand, we are subject to a flagrant fallacy if we believe that we have found an optimal and ultimate solution to the problem by enforcing the death penalty. The opposite is actually the case. The criminal receiving the death penalty is taken out of circulation for a while to the extent that his body decomposes. His immortal spiritual form goes to the next world but cannot stay there very long. It must reincarnate as soon as possible and begin a new life on earth in another body. Since that person did not have a chance to learn the least bit from previous life misdeeds, the reincarnated person continues to think and act as erroneously as before. Any child can figure out what will happen. The same spirit form occupies a new body, and sooner or later the person will commit the same crimes again. There is no improvement, even in imprisonment, because this prison method does not bring about the slightest progress, neither for the criminal receiving the death penalty nor for the general public. Since our terrorists and other criminals do not fear in the slightest the threat of torture or the death penalty, it would have greater meaning to be objective and to use effective measures somewhat similar to the form of correction common among the extraterrestrials.

Forms of Government

The Pleiadians struggled hard to finally win lasting peace in their home worlds about 50,000 years ago. They overthrew the politicians, then the spirit leaders took over their positions and stood by the entire population to advise, teach and help them. This is why there is only a single form of government on Erra and the other three inhabited planets of the Tayget System. Ptaah explained these matters with the following words:

> **PTAAH:** Our worlds are not divided into different countries, as is the case on earth. Every world has its own uniform group of people and a uniform world government, as you would call it in earthly terms. On each world, the government serves as a regulatory and administrative power and they all are subject to the High Council. The High Council constitutes the actual leadership of all of our worlds and is, so to speak, the central government. This central government is not located on our home world (Erra) but on a very special planet.
>
> This is the central governing planet for our races. The High Council, which lives on this planet, consists of half-spiritual and half-physical human life forms. They are the ones who are in a stage of transition and have an absolutely enormous level of knowledge and wisdom. The transition into pure Spirit form means that they leave their material bodies behind and exist as so-called half-spirit forms. They are also the only life forms still called human beings who are able to make contact with the very high pure spirit forms — something absolutely impossible for the physical life forms. Even we Errans are unable to make contact with pure spirit forms, and it is even less possible for the people of earth to do so.
>
> Our people are, therefore, subject to the central government, which is comprised of the half-spirit forms of the High Council. Planetary governments only constitute the administrative agencies and act according to the advice of the High Council. The High Council's form of government is based on the natural laws and commandments of Creation and does not resemble any form of government known to you. For all affairs and order, the creative and natural laws are used according to the manner in which an individual life form must live. Each single life form must comply with every decision of the High Council in their thought pattern, contingent on the fact that each person is approximately on the same evolutionary level in a spiritual sense. Minimal differences are not completely ruled out. Our teachers of spiritual evolution use every means available to continually further the spiritual development of each individual life form. So all of our people live in vibrations of almost the same value.

In addition to this, I would like to say that the High Council — as expressed by its name — is active only in an advisory capacity. In other words, the orders of the central government located in the Andromeda Galaxy may or may not be followed by the people. They are entirely free to accept the recommendations and comply with them or to act at their own discretion.

Cosmic Alliances and Organizations for Order

The Pleiadians are affiliated with a cosmic confederation — a League of Civilizations — consisting of a total number of 127 billion people that extends far into the cosmos and to which many planetary systems belong. They all have an allegiance to the High Council in the Andromeda Galaxy. Of course, other similar types of alliances also exist in the universe, but we have no detailed information on them.

Because other races exist which are in different phases of development from the peace-loving human races, some type of cosmic organization is urgently needed to maintain peace and order.

With this in mind, I would like to quote Semjase's father, Ptaah, once again:

PTAAH: In the entire universe, space travel is practiced by innumerably different life forms ranging from humanoid to non-humanoid races. For the most part, life forms of the same type or like-minded always come together and form alliances with one another. Their values are based on mutual support of every kind and in all matters of evolutionary interest. These combined efforts in all aspects of life are, needless to say, wonderful and even extend into the boundaries of other universes, such as the DAL Universe. The objective of all alliances, whether they be universal, inter-universal, galactic or intergalactic, is peace and progress in all physical aspects of life and spiritual evolution.

The allied partners maintain organizations of order that guard the entire universal realm and beyond. These organizations of order may extend over galaxies separated by extremely vast distances. For such a far-reaching and difficult task, only the so-called giant spacecraft are suitable and are equipped with all imaginable technical possibilities and armed to meet all situations. Fighting cannot be ruled out when non-humanoid life forms attempt to realize their despotic goals by force. Whether we like it or not, they must be confronted since confrontation is an inseparable part of human life.

Basically, the intentions of all highly developed life forms are to peacefully work on their spirit evolution. The universe is inhabited by such diverse life forms that a conflict is often unavoidable. Nevertheless, the Pleiadians attempt to settle all disputes, if possible, through reasonable arbitration before they revert to other measures. Only when no agreement can be reached or the adversaries come up with some type of trick do they resort to the use of force as the last alternative. They then drive away the scoundrels or take them prisoner and ban them to desolate islands or planets. Only in an extreme emergency do they resort to the elimination of persons and material since all species are in need of evolution and, basically, this always takes the same course in their evolutionary phases.

One more word from Ptaah:

PTAAH: Our very early ancestors, who are also actually the forefathers of earthman, were once just as low in their spiritual evolution as earthman is today, as are many other life forms in the innumerable universes.

These cosmic forces of order normally do not intervene in pure planetary affairs unless acts of war threaten the structure of universal space by endangering other planetary systems. In such extreme cases, and if there is simply no other alternative, the forces of order naturally take suitable measures to bring the troublemakers to reason by force.

When inhabitants of a planet are headed on the fastest course to knocking each others' brains out and ultimately destroying one another, as is the case on earth, then the extraterrestrial life forms try to render useful help in the form of teachings and inspirations. Those concerned must decide entirely on their own whether to accept, ignore or reject this help because free will must be upheld at all times and all places. Therefore, it is never within the Pleiadian scope of duty to intervene and force other people to avoid acts of war on their respective planets. The extraterrestrials only intervene if inhabitants of other planets are endangered by the war actions of their neighbors.

Based on a law of Creation, it is not possible that even one single earth person will be evacuated by an extraterrestrial rescue action if we actually would go as far as to transform our earthly globe into a deadly inferno. It is our decision alone to comply with, process and act according to the valuable teachings which the Pleiadians have let us receive and which we must consider with an open mind. Only in doing so will we be able to halt the threatening danger of total destruction and to finally obtain a peaceful existence worth living for.

Marriage

On Erra, they have unmarried people, as we do. Normally, marriage is only practiced in polygamous form. In the entire universe, each human life form is in need of certain regulatory orders and guidelines, which are anchored in laws and commandments. In drawing up the regulatory orders, the extraterrestrials primarily use nature as an exemplary means of orientation. The universal law of love states clearly and concisely that each male life form, as the inseminating part of nature, is able to mate with several female life forms. For the human beings concerned, this explicitly states that every healthy man may enter into the bond of marriage with several women. Only one man can impregnate a woman in the sense of a recipient, which is why she may have only one bond of marriage according to nature.

This law is practiced by the Pleiadians to the fullest extent, so that several women are wed to one husband in each respective marriage. For example, one man is married to four women of his choice and each individual wife has her own house. The husband lives alternately with each individual partner. Of course, this regulation has nothing to do with polygamy, as we know it, a harem or the like. Among the wives concerned, a loving and friendly relationship exists, just as it does with the husband. All forms of jealousy are completely unknown. I would like to stress at this point that the women in a marriage bond are of equal value with their husband in every respect. The laws of incarnation also regulate that men are not favored over women — the sex alternates from time to time in the course of several reincarnations. In this way, a continual balance is achieved and the presumable injustices are herewith eliminated. Admittedly, it will not be easy for some of us to understand or accept these explanations in part, or perhaps, not even at all.

From a spiritual viewpoint of evolution, the full maturity required for marriage on Erra is not reached until approximately 70 years of age. Accordingly, the bond of marriage is not entered into until that time. As a rule, the Errans practice sexual abstinence until that age in order to give undivided attention to their spiritual development.

If two people come together and are of the opinion that they are capable of developing deeper feelings for one another, they have a full three-year period to clarify their feelings and determine if they exist and are genuine. After this period of time, authorized specialists test them to find out if they truly belong together. They are not permitted to unite in a bond of marriage until the test has been successfully passed. This occurs when the necessary requirements such as fundamental feelings, affection and love, are existent. Normally, a marriage bond lasts a lifetime, but it can be dissolved after marriage if the prior clarifications have proven to give a false picture.

The three-year period preceding this test of marriage is divided so that the persons concerned may meet each other once every seven days for several hours. They are free to select how they wish to spend their time, but sexual acts of any kind are not permitted until the intended marriage has undergone a test and is concluded. If the two people are involved in an activity that inevitably brings them together more than once a week, there are no objections. However, a purely personal rendez-vous is not allowed. This rule is intended to give the marriage candidates a period of six days to fully consider everything they have experienced. If they successfully pass the two-year test period, a separation of one year follows. During this time, the two people may not see or meet each other at all. They may even decide to be transferred to foreign planets to fulfill their duties in order to have enough time to ponder everything thoroughly once again. They will not proceed with the test until this has been accomplished. Divorce among the Pleiadians is only permitted in extreme cases where serious violations are made against the laws and commandments of Creation in regard to marriage. Particularly, the breaking of the bond, known to us as adultery, falls in this category. On the high evolutionary level of the Pleiadians, this transgression is very serious and, as a result, the guilty ones are sent into exile for the duration of their lives. *(See ~ Methods of Punishment ~ in this chapter)*

In response to the question of what would happen if a Pleiadian were to fall in love with a person who is from a different planet, Semjase replied:

SEMJASE: If a person from our race were to fall in love with someone from another world inhabited by a spiritually inferior race to the extent that both desired to be joined (in matrimony), the probability of this must first be resolved according to our laws. If the facts show that all necessary requirements have been fulfilled, the bond of marriage may proceed. In this case, it does not matter if the life form from another world exists on a lower spiritual level. This condition can be upwardly advanced in such a case (with the help of special devices) by our scientists to correspond to our spiritual level. Such incidents, though, are quite infrequent.

The topic of jealousy may be of interest, considering how easily sheer jealousy would occur if earth husbands were allowed to have several wives — most of whom would probably get into quarrels regarding such a controversial arrange-ment. I can just hear the clamor when I think about it. If I should be mistaken regarding the Pleiadian practice of multiple marriages for men only (which is contrary to my expectations), I will renounce this statement. But if the roles were reversed, who knows what would happen, regardless of its illicitness, if an earth woman were able to marry several husbands?

What is different for the Pleiadians is that they are no longer plagued with the problems of jealousy within a relationship between a man and woman. In former times, though, they had to endure similar evolutionary stages of learning. In view of this, Semjase said:

SEMJASE: A person who is completely anti-materialistic in his thinking is no longer susceptible to jealousy because his thinking has evolved into universal thinking in which all possessions are respectfully viewed, but not re-vered, and are raised in love and joy as the common property of all. But this only applies if honest affection on both sides exists through the heeding of the laws and commandments.

If two of our people enter into a marriage bond, this does not mean that each partner possesses the other, but simply that they join together in a mutual bond of affection. Rights of possession are not involved — only love, under-standing and the joy of each other's company. Both partners are completely free to choose their own ways of fulfilling the laws and commandments, while the actions and decisions concerning their marriage are jointly discussed until a mutual agreement is reached, thus fulfilling the laws and commandments. In an evolutionary sense and in all respects, mutual clarifications and agreements are required, given through certain rules of order.

For us lowly earthlings, it is somewhat difficult to understand what is actually meant by this, but I would not wish to withhold these comments since they contain some food for thought in order to obtain new realizations. Within the scope of this subject matter, the question of marital quarrels arose. In return, Semjase asked whether we view Pleiadians as super humans. She explained that it is quite natural that differences of opinion will occur between marriage partners, only they may not degenerate into a fight, which is all too common with us.

SEMJASE: As with us and others elsewhere, all life forms are different in their evolution, just as two like poles will never be found together. This would signify a leveling off and nullification of evolution. Therefore, two opposing poles must always meet for an evolution to take place. Both of these opposite poles will inevitably rub against one another and two different opinions will clash. So, for the purpose of evolution, differences in opinions must arise. This is an ir-revocable law of evolution which we and all other life forms of the universe are ordered into.

Footnotes

8 ▪ The contact reports contain the conversations recorded word-for-word between the contactee, Eduard "Billy" Meier, and the extraterrestrials named Semjase, Quetzal, Ptaah, Asket, Menara and Taljda.

9 ▪ A Pleiadian month is called Asar. A Pleiadian day is called Musal. A Pleiadian hour is called Odur.

10 ▪ Since the first publication of the German version of this book in 1991, the Pleiadians are now 8,000 years ahead of earth technology. They have achieved this with the help of a technologically advanced civilization from the DAL Universe.

11 ▪ Quetzal is one of the main contact persons of the Errans.

12 ▪ An JHWH (ish-wish) possesses the highest degree of knowledge and wisdom a person can possibly acquire while still in a physical body. Translated, it means "King of Wisdom."

13 ▪ The DAL Universe is a parallel or twin universe to our DERN Universe. Both came into existence at the same time.

14 ▪ For reasons of posterity, a lock of her hair can be found in the archives of the Semjase Silver Star Center.

15 ▪ Residing in the Andromeda Galaxy, the High Council is the name of the central government of the Pleiadians and their allies within the Cosmic Confederation. Members of the High Council are so spiritually advanced they have reached the stage whereby they exist as half-physical and half-spiritual human state of being.

16 ▪ The original meaning of Bro is "thunder that comes from the mouth."

17 ▪ Due to the danger of transmitting disease bacteria, the Pleiadians are not permitted to bring home any animals from foreign planets.

18 ▪ Spiritual leaders strive to promote the spiritual evolution of the population with all possible means at their disposal.

19 ▪ Contrary to cremation, where the ashes are at least retained in an urn, there are no remains left after an elimination.

CHAPTER 3

Spacecraft of the Pleiadians

The Pleiadians have an entire armada of smaller and larger spacecraft available that can be distinguished by their structure, size and flying range, depending on their use. The following flying objects are included among the Pleiadian spacecraft fleet: Telemeter disks, reconnaissance ships, beamships of various types, giant spacecraft (no information available) and special spacecraft for special missions (no information available).

Telemeter Disks
See ~ Photos #25 and #57, taken at night.
The telemeter disks are exclusively used for surveillance and exploration purposes of all kinds. They can be used for stationary or mobile missions. Their flying range is limited to the planetary region. The telemeter disks of the Pleiadians vary in size from 1 centimeter to 5 meters (.4 in.–17 ft.). They all fly unmanned and are usually operated from fixed stations by remote control. In 1977, a total of 7,000 of these spacecraft orbited around our earth globe. On clear, starry nights from the year 1975–1978, their orbital paths could easily be observed with the naked eye because of their glaring lights with high frequency blinking. This was especially true of those that traveled along relatively low orbital paths. The blinking light was similar to radio signals used exclusively for remote control. As of 1978, the blinking device was replaced by another type of mechanism.

With my third UFO experience in June of 1976, I was able to capture the orbital path of a blinking telemeter disk in a photograph. These telemeter disks are by no means comparable to spacecraft that appear as small points of light orbiting around our globe at an altitude of 20–40 kilometers (12–25 miles) — similar to earth satellites. *(See ~ Photo #57)*

Reconnaissance Ships

See ~ Photos #7, #17 and #18

The reconnaissance ships are primarily used for scouting purposes and sometimes as escort ships. Unlike the telemeter, the reconnaissance ships are manned and have a diameter of 3.5–5 meters (12 ft.–17 ft.). They are not suitable for space flight but are only used within a planetary region. Their flying time is completely unlimited.

Beamships

See ~ Photos #4, #6, #7– #26

The beamships are used for diverse purposes but primarily for transporting people over all possible distances, making personal contacts and conducting all types of research.

The name *beamship* originates from a type of ship used for a period of 400 years and which was equipped with a drive system that emitted rays into the environment. As a result, the entire area beneath the ship was immersed in such a glimmering heat that all objects near and far appeared distorted and blurred while distances seemed to change. To take a picture of one such beamship, a safe distance of at least 90 meters (297 ft.) must be maintained in order to prevent the sensitive film material from being destroyed by the effects of the rays.

In the year 1975, these old ships were put out of commission, returned to their home planet of Erra and scrapped. With the succeeding types, this unpleasant radiating effect no longer occurs, although the name beamship is still in use today.

Billy became familiar with all the various ships used on earth and could photograph and partly film them.

They all have a common disk-shape with a diameter of 7 meters (23 ft.) and occasionally 14 or 21 meters (46 ft. or 69 ft.). A 7-meter ship has enough room for three people but only one pilot is needed for control. The material of the ship's body is made of a copper-nickel-silver alloy and is enriched with gold for special purposes. The walls of the entire ship are fully seamless and without rivets because the entire body is made of one seamless casting. The relatively soft material used has all the characteristics necessary for all kinds of flight maneuvers. This metal alloy is made of pure lead without any added substances and requires a total of seven working processes. Small metal pieces were scientifically examined in the USA. According to the statement of an expert, a cold-welding process is used that is not yet known on earth. *(See ~ Manufacture of the Metal Alloy ~ later in this chapter. Also see ~ Chapter 11: Analyses of Metal Samples)*

The weight of a 7-meter ship is 1.5 tons. The semi-spherical cockpit is found in the upper half of the disk-shaped ship, which is about 2.2 meters (7 ft.) high on the inside. In the newer models, an additional cupola is located on top. The most modern ship that was built by the Pleiadians specifically for use on earth looks similar to a wedding cake. (The function of the many globes around the outside of the ship is to dip into other dimensions.) After having been in service on earth for one year, it had to be taken out of commission. In that short length of time, the craft had been badly damaged by corrosion resulting from the drastic pollution in the earth's atmosphere.

A beamship is capable of undertaking a precise landing at any time of day or night at any desired location. The ship can neither be seen, heard nor picked up by radar when the screening shields are engaged. Upon landing, the ship hovers slightly above the ground so no traces can be found later to indicate what happened there. If the ship does land directly on the ground for demonstration purposes, three landing legs with plate-shaped landing feet serve as helpful supports, leaving three circular areas 2 meters (6.5 ft.) in size of flatly pressed blades of grass. For reasons of security, a landed ship raises two protective shields around it when necessary. (See ~ Chapter 6: Spacecraft Landing Tracks. Also see ~ Chapter 3: Protective Shields of Pleiadian Spacecraft)

Safety Device for Life Forms

If animals or people are within the danger zone of a protective screen during the landing of a Pleiadian spacecraft, a safety device is activated that automatically steers the ship to one side so that no one is injured.

Before this safety device was developed, an unpleasant mishap unfortunately took place on October 4, 1977. It occurred while descending in a small clearing during a landing maneuver. The female pilot of a 7-meter (23 ft.) ship had overlooked a grazing deer hidden among the trees. Unfortunately, it came inside the activated area of a protective shield and was crushed to death instantaneously. The female pilot became very upset when she discovered the fatal accident.

Incidentally, at dusk of the evening on October 4, 1977, Jacobus Bertschinger and Billy's children had briefly observed a luminous flying object that appeared to be landing behind a hill. On the next day, Billy found lightly depressed grass and the dead deer at this landing spot.

This incident gave impetus to the development of the safety device and after its installation in the Pleiadian ships, no such misfortunes have taken place again.

Ship Windows

The orange-colored windows of the ship are actually not windows in the usual sense. Although one can look outside, the specially controlled viewing screens in the cockpit are used for this purpose. The ship's windows have a totally different function, which is the analysis of the atmospheric composition outside the ship. We will learn here why this is useful.

The outside surface of the windows is treated with a special material and assumes various color tones in accordance with the composition of the atmosphere. If the outside atmosphere is tolerable for the ship's crew, this is shown by a very specific color.

The composition of the air on earth is quite suitable for the Pleiadians and, therefore, the ship windows turn orange on the outside and at the same time a yellowish-green light appears on the indirect illuminating system in the cockpit. These colors indicate that the atmosphere is tolerable for Pleiadians and they may leave the ship without a space suit.

However, in the case of toxic compositions, unreasonable atmospheric pressure or dangerous temperatures outside, the outer layer turns yellow, green, blue or red and the illumination system in the cockpit automatically changes. With this system, the crewmembers know precisely, at all times and without further analyses, whether or not the atmosphere outside the ship is tolerable for them.

In the case of unfavorable conditions, they can leave the ship in an appropriate space suit. An automatic safety system allows only those wearing a space suit to disembark into an unsuitable atmosphere, otherwise the exit locks remain closed. The automatic safety is adjusted by touch-buttons that are attached to the space suit.

The entire device functions with such perfection that a failure is totally out of the question. The ship's windows do not actually transform into colorless, transparent panes, as we expect of windows, until the ship enters the vacuum of outer space where there is no atmosphere at all. An additional protective coating on the outside wall prevents any outside radiation from penetrating inside, so all dangers in this regard can be eliminated.

The control-viewing screen enables more accurate viewing and observation, since looking out the ship windows is not especially suitable for taking pictures or filming. The Pleiadians are not familiar with our photo and film equipment. They had to invent special protective devices so that Billy could take fairly useable pictures when he occasionally photographed from the inside of a Pleiadian ship.

Head Antenna

On an older type of Pleiadian ship, a rod antenna was located in the middle of the head plate with a semi-spherical head at the tip. Two functions are connected with it:

- This antenna-type device serves on the one hand as an energy collector, meaning that energy can be drawn in from the surroundings of the flying ship. At any rate, this type of energy collecting is very practical and reasonably priced because it does not cost any money.

- At the same time, the rod serves as an antenna for the videophone via the reception and transmission of the radio communication system with a television-like screen. The people talking on the phone can see each other. This is similar to our modern video telephone devices. However, a special apparatus is necessary so that it works with the transmitter. Otherwise, not a single radio message could penetrate outside because the ship absorbs everything. This videophone can be used on a planet, but only over a short distance in outer space. For gigantic distances in outer space over innumerable light years, the hyper-transmitter is used. (It does not require its own antennas or perhaps the entire ship is an antenna.)

NO. 1: The antigravity shaft with the lock for boarding and disembarking is found on the bottom of the ship. To board the ship, one simply stands beneath the opened access hatch of the antigravity shaft and is lifted inside as if on an elevator by an invisible force. Whoever wants to disembark can be carefully glided to the ground vertically from the cockpit by a transport beam.

NO. 2: There are three oval seating arrangements that can be folded back into a flat reclining sofa on the floor of the cockpit. The elastic synthetic upholstery conforms to everybody so that no pressure points occur. Furthermore, it is possible to turn the folding chair 360 degrees around its own axis and push it in all directions.

NO. 3: The instrument panel in the shape of a horseshoe is equipped with diverse instruments, viewing screens and switches. Numerous drawers and lockers are in the area below. The ship windows, as well as many viewing screens and switches, are on the wall over the main instruments. The most important position is occupied by the navigation console with a control stick for manual steering in case the automatic system is not desired. The ceiling of the cockpit is equipped with an open viewing surface and with a second set of viewing screens so the pilot can also navigate the ship in a reclined position.

Fig. 3-1
Interior Design of a Pleiadian Ship (top view)

Various Viewing Screens

The many viewing screens installed around the navigation console are comparable to our television sets. They can be identified not only by their multiple functions, but also by their profound differences from earthly apparati of this kind.

On several viewing screens, the landscape, people, animals and objects are displayed totally true to reality. On others screens, symbolic forms can be read but must be decoded or analyzed in order to understand the correct meaning (the subconscious of a person, for example). As far as the means of presentation is concerned, it can be said that all pictures and symbols that appear on these screens do so in fantastic colors and in graphic three-dimensional presentations. It is as if everything were really and materially present and not just produced via impulses, as is the case with some of the other viewing sets.

Surface Analyzer

With the surface analyzer, the entire landscape flown over each time can be seen from a bird's-eye view. Individual parts of the panorama can be enlarged as desired to better recognize special details. If one is looking for something special, it is simply programmed and then it automatically appears on a second screen within the main screen. It is, therefore, unnecessary to cast a single glance out of one of the ship's windows, whether to look at the landscape or to make some type of observation.

Thought Analyzer

The thoughts of a person appear on the screen by means of electromagnetic waves in the form of symbols, which have a meaning that must be interpreted.

With the thought analyzer, it is not only possible to accurately read the thoughts from the material consciousness, but to also lure the hidden secrets out of the material subconscious. In this way, the true character of an individual can be recognized because hidden thoughts, among other things, emerge from the subconscious as well, and are brought to light.

In restriction to this, though, I must mention that the Pleiadians only venture into the depths of the material subconscious in special cases. First of all, it is regulated so by law and, secondly, the motto, "the inner secrets are nobody else's business" holds true. In this way, far too many negative facts would be uncovered that would be better off unknown since they cause too much of a burden.

If I am not mistaken, the thought analyzer can be coupled with the surface analyzer and the position indicator.

Position Indicator

The position indicator is an earth globe that always turns in the direction of flight. It gives the position within an exact meter of where the spacecraft is located at any given time. Described in the following contact report is a dialog between Billy and Semjase on how the spherically shaped device locates people known by name, for instance, and displays them on the viewing screen.

> **SEMJASE:** Billy, you can simply hold your hand on this surface. The world sphere then rotates until the desired location appears under this needle attached here. If you place your hand on this plate, you can attract any desired life form on the enlarged map according to your thoughts that are transferred into the apparatus through this receptor. In this manner, you know the exact location of the life form sought at that time. If you press this button, the desired life form appears on this viewing screen.

In conjunction with this, here is an example of reading thoughts:

> **SEMJASE:** If I turn the device on now … So, what do you see now?
> **BILLY:** Man alive! That is Mr. J as he lives and breathes.
> **SEMJASE:** Certainly, you see that he is busy. Now, look here at this scale. Thought vibrations are registered here.

BILLY: That's really quite some wire entanglement…

SEMJASE: … from that we can obtain all values. Look. This figure, for example, represents the subconscious of Mr. J. If I enlarge it … So, what do you recognize now?

BILLY: Girl, those are some real pictures.

SEMJASE: That is right. What do you recognize in them?

BILLY: That … Wait a minute, that, but that is a day. How in the world can I recognize that? I must be going crazy. How can I possibly know that is a day? Man … girl, that is next Wednesday and that … that is a time.

SEMJASE: You are simply fantastic. You know how to read the analyzer without any previous explanations from me. I had to learn it first. You must be well versed in the decoding of pictures. That astounds me since I did not know about it before.

BILLY: Is that really true?

SEMJASE: Certainly.

BILLY: Should I read on?

SEMJASE: Certainly, what else do you see?

BILLY: If I decode it correctly, then the time seen is Wednesday, October 22, 1975, to be more precise, at exactly 11:03 a.m. Is that right?

SEMJASE: (laughing) Certainly, and what else?

BILLY: Mr. J. is reaching for the telephone and is dialing a number. Man, he is telephoning me. He will come by my place around 2 o'clock in the afternoon. However, this time can vary somewhat.

SEMJASE: You decode and recognize the facts very accurately, because your observations are precisely conveyed by the analyzer. Mr. J. is not yet aware of the forthcoming events because he has not yet become conscious of them. His subconscious already knows of the coming events and is now working in this direction. And as you see, we can register these facts with our analyzers and read them. This is how we monitor, control and obtain very accurate information about all things of importance to us. This is also how I discovered that our tasks concerning your influence on certain events are doubted within your own group. I did not look into the future but merely used our analyzers and checked the subconscious minds of various persons in your group concerning these matters.

BILLY: I understand now. But this here, these peculiar forms there. What do they show?

SEMJASE: One moment … So, what do you see in the enlargement?

BILLY: Girl, those are also pictures, but they are constantly changing and in continuous, wild motion. Wait a minute. Aha. I … yes it must be. These pictures can only come from the conscious mind. That must be the conscious mind of Mr. J., or am I mistaken?

SEMJASE: That is correct.

BILLY: Fantastic! With these things, nothing at all remains concealed from you?

SEMJASE: It would actually be so if we were to use it without interrupts (interruptions) But since this is not the case and we still have to learn very, very much, we actually only use these apparati for monitoring and controlling purposes. We acquire all necessities by working in the usual given fashion and that also applies to you, namely, by means of mental work — the normal evolutionary way. Because this way requires that mistakes be made in order to acquire knowledge, we are also subject to wrong decisions, wrong deeds, wrong judgments and misconceptions, just like the people of earth.

BILLY: That is plausible to me. May I now take another look at something else on the analyzer …

Zero-visibility Viewing Screens

A zero-visibility-viewing screen is a special device that receives everything graphically and can optically reproduce what we cannot see with the naked eye or locate with radar equipment. With a zero-visibility viewing screen, spacecraft shielded from vision can, for example, be easily observed.

Billy experienced one such demonstration on the occasion of the Apollo and Soyuz docking maneuver by the Americans and Russians in 1975. He was permitted to follow this exact procedure, namely, from the cockpit of a Pleiadian spacecraft that was in the immediate vicinity at the time of this event. Incidentally, there were also five other spacecraft present as secret observers and they were fully shielded just like the Pleiadian ship.[20]

In addition to this, the Pleiadians have a viewing screen that makes any desired material transparent through the distortion of light rays. An observer can then easily look through all obstacles such as walls and metal walls, discerning all the details behind the scenes as if no walls were there at all. Billy had a few opportunities to admire this technical trick.

One opportunity was during the aforementioned docking maneuver of the Russians and Americans as he looked through the metal wall and saw the cosmonauts and astronauts inside the Apollo and Soyuz ships floating in a state of weightlessness.

Another occasion occurred on September 6, 1977 during a personal contact with Semjase when she hovered with her ship several hundred meters directly over the FIGU Center. During the course of a conversation about various construction projects, it was discovered that Billy had left the necessary construction plans lying on the table of the group room in the shed. Semjase calmly took note of this and finally said that this was no problem for her. This was confirmed immediately because the necessary drawings also appeared on the viewing screen just a moment later. Next, a cellar room was projected on the screen in the same manner and closely examined.

Telepathic Guiding Device

The telepathic guiding apparatus is always used for personal contacts when a designated contact takes place at a location that is not known to the contactee beforehand. In this case, Billy was led along the correct path with the help of this guiding device, which telepathically conveyed necessary instructions from the spacecraft and led him to his destination.

If Billy is completely alone on his way to the contact, the guiding device will direct him to the exact spot where the spacecraft has landed. If someone accompanies him, the guiding device is automatically switched off in the close vicinity of the landing place. This switch-off is something like an alarm signal that prompts the ship's pilot to conduct a personal investigation on the people accompanying him. In doing so, it is determined whether or not their intentions are friendly or hostile or, in other words, whether they are trustworthy or not. This checking deals with a thought analysis that cannot be conducted with the guiding device. If the analysis has a positive result, everything continues according to plan. If not, the designated contact is immediately re-planned or called off and set for a later date.

After activating the control analysis system, the guiding device stores the brain wave patterns of all people who are well disposed towards the event. With the help of this stored information, the guiding device identifies the people concerned at any time, because the brain waves that every person emits are as unique and unmistakable as the papillary lines of a fingertip known as fingerprints.

Healing and Regeneration Devices

Healing and regeneration devices are securely installed in the instrument panel but can also be adapted for use in the cockpit.

Billy was often connected to a regeneration machine when his physical state of health left much to be desired. He felt considerably better each time after such a treatment. *(See sections ~ Healing of Broken Ribs and Healing of Severe Botulism)*

Healing of Broken Ribs

The following are excerpts of the contact conversation between Semjase and Billy on March 28, 1976:

SEMJASE: Do you have pain?

BILLY: A little. I fell from my moped and broke two of my ribs.

SEMJASE: That is not good. Where does it hurt? Let me take a look at it.

BILLY: Oh, it's really nothing serious.

SEMJASE: I wish that you would let me see it. You are much too inclined towards making light of everything.

BILLY: It's really not bad.

SEMJASE: I sense something else, though. Let me see it.

BILLY: Okay, okay. It got me here.

SEMJASE: Take off your over-clothes.

BILLY: That too — good … (I take off my coat, shirt and vest.)

SEMJASE: So, I thought so. How can you still drive your motorcycle? That is irresponsible. Both ribs are broken. You should be resting. Did you know this? I suppose so, yes.

BILLY: Certainly, but one gets used to it. It's the third time that I've wrecked these two ribs. Perhaps I should have it properly repaired sometime with gooey paste or rubber solution.

SEMJASE: As usual, you are unreasonable in these matters. Go home now and lie down to rest.

BILLY: I can't. I have a lot of questions.

Billy went home that day since Semjase did not answer his questions at that time. On Sunday, April 6, 1976, another contact took place. The following are excerpts:

SEMJASE: You are puzzling. Just take off your over-clothes. Here, this device will regenerate your broken ribs. You only have to sit here between these two poles. Your ribs will be fully regenerated after this process. There will be no further indication that they were broken. There, now sit down between them, yes, that is right, that is the way. Now remain in this position several minutes. The entire area is quite inflamed, especially the periosteum.[21] Unfortunately, I cannot relieve the inflammation with this device. It will probably take about two months for it to subside. The next time, I will have it restored to health with a special apparatus.

BILLY: Thanks, that'll be enough, Semjase. If the bones are patched and glued, then the rest is insignificant. It's bearable now.

SEMJASE: Okay, I do not want to pressure you in this matter. I am happy that the ribs are healthy again. So, that is enough. Yes, everything is all right now. Move around a little. There, yes, that is very good.

BILLY: That's super, the worst pain is gone.

SEMJASE: It certainly should be. Now please be more careful in the future.

BILLY: I'll try to. Can I slip back into my clothes now?

SEMJASE: Certainly.

BILLY: So, thanks a lot, dear girl. You're really much more than just a very dear sister.

Healing of Severe Botulism

The following excerpts from the contact conversation between Semjase and Billy on July 16, 1977:

SEMJASE: Your face shows signs of pain and is flushed with fever. What are you suffering from?

BILLY: That's not worth mentioning.

SEMJASE: Sit down over here.

BILLY: What for?

SEMJASE: With this apparatus, I will find out what ailment you are suffering from.

BILLY: That's really not necessary because I know very well what's wrong with me. I've only been poisoned somewhat by a little sausage, which we are all aware of. They've been after me the whole time about it, telling me I should go to the doctor. It's really not so bad, though, because I'm always experimenting a little bit to help myself. I'm halfway all right and can at least creep about.

SEMJASE: I am quite aware of the way you continually minimize the danger. And besides, the symptomatic features of your face reveal something totally different from these explanations of yours. Now sit down over here?

BILLY: If it's absolut…

SEMJASE: You should not disagree, just take a seat over here.

BILLY: All right already, I'll do it. Are you satisfied now?

SEMJASE: Of course, you are sitting just fine. Aha! Just what I thought! You are completely exhausted and, furthermore, it appears that you have not eaten anything for days now.

BILLY: It can't be so bad. How was I supposed to eat, when I was always feeling sicker than a dog?

SEMJASE: Then I am right. Your poisoning is not light in nature but, on the contrary, already quite severe. As the apparatus indicates here, your blood has been poisoned already, while certain cerebral cells have also been affected and that accounts for your sudden pessimism.

BILLY: So what. That's quite normal for meat poisoning.

SEMJASE: It is not as normal as you think, because as I see here, we are not dealing with a usual poisoning, but rather with a far more severe infection caused by meat parasites.

BILLY: You mean there are …

SEMJASE: Certainly, that is why I have to take the necessary action against this. Give me your arm. That is right, that is good.

BILLY: What kind of a thing is this?

SEMJASE: A parasite neutralizer as the people of earth would say, is an apparatus which neutralizes all parasites (that are pathogenic or detrimental toward the physical human life form) as soon as the colorless plate comes in contact with the surface of the skin, just as it is now. The time it takes for neutralization to occur is less than six seconds for the entire human body. The neutralizer automatically adapts to the physical condition and constitution of the human life form concerned within a fraction of a second. As a result, the apparatus neutralizes all the damage caused by parasites, other materials, and substances of a gaseous nature, and that is what has just happened to you and what has taken care of your poisoning.

BILLY: That's terrific! I actually feel well enough to squeal again. But tell me, what do you actually mean with the word parasites in the case of a disease or even a poisoning?

SEMJASE: This includes all kinds of bacilli, viruses, microbes and other pathogenic organisms, the existence of which is still largely unknown to earth scientists. Some of them will be discovered in the course of the next few years.

BILLY: Aha! Then do salmonella and other leeching animalcules also belong to these?

SEMJASE: Certainly.

Helmet-like Memory Machine

The helmet-like memory machine is placed over the head like a hairdryer in order to recall the knowledge and ability stored there from previous incarnations in a very quick and easy fashion. After that, the awakened abilities can never be lost again. However, there is one unchangeable condition involved with this method, meaning that the aforementioned advantage may be used solely for one's own evolution and the fulfillment of the mission.

A safety device located in the brain blocks access to the great wealth of knowledge and ability if the person in question wishes to misuse only a part of it for purely materialistic or demonstrative purposes. Furthermore, the blockade goes immediately into effect should someone risk the attempt to forcefully gain access to this knowledge, by hypnosis, for example, for scientific tests or other such purposes. All such attempts would be doomed to failure from the very beginning.

Comment:
The previous attempts made to hypnotize Billy have shown that his blockade is so effective that anyone daring to forcefully coax something out of him, despite all warnings, would be at risk of losing his life.

Vibration Paralyzer

The vibration paralyzer causes moving land vehicles to come to a stop or puts them temporarily out of operation. With an adequate device, every photo or film camera can be blocked so that not a single picture can be taken.

A device was specially made for Billy to enable him to take a picture, from the inside of a Pleiadian ship and of other things on the outside, without any serious impairment in photo quality, which has always been the case without this device.

Furthermore, a specially constructed mechanism on the inside of a Pleiadian ship was made to meet the requirement for smooth radio communication with our terrestrial transmitters. Otherwise, not a single radio message could escape from the spacecraft because the ship absorbs all radio waves.

Spacecraft Laser Beam Cannon

Of the various weapons on board that every Pleiadian spacecraft carries, Billy was once allowed to use a laser beam cannon to eliminate a dangerous nest of microbes. *(See ~ Chapter 13: Second Strike: A Disastrous Bacterial Infection)*

Contact Conversation Transmitter

By using telepathy, the contact conversation transmitter transmits the exact wording of a contact conversation in symbol form to the contactee, who then translates the received impulses (symbols) into our language and types it on a typewriter. *(See ~ Chapter 5: Mysterious Transmission of the Contact Conversations)*

Manufacture of the Metal Alloy

As mentioned before, the outer encasement of a Pleiadian spacecraft is made of a copper, nickel and silver alloy and is partially enriched with gold for special functions. The outside walls of the ship are completely without joints and without rivets because the entire hull is a single seamless casting. Of course, this relatively soft metal alloy has all of the features required for flight maneuvers of every kind. The material (copper, nickel and silver) is manufactured in seven working cycles from pure lead without any added substances.

In the first working process, the various substances containing lead are first collected from the atmosphere of stars, water or certain plants. These substances are transformed into absolutely pure lead through very complicated processes so that no impurities of any kind remain.

In the second working process, all harmful radiation is withdrawn from the pure lead because every object absorbs all types of vibrations and radiation from the environment, stores them away with greater or lesser intensity and then releases them again into the environment.

The third working process liquefies the lead metal and a transformation takes place through the influence of certain vibrations until a fully new product is developed. Several work processes are necessary for this transformation.

In the fourth and fifth working process, the prospective end product is pressed by intermittent pushes through a cooling spiral by which small metal pieces are formed. The process is repeated several times until the desired features are obtained in optimal form.

In the sixth working process, the complete and final alloy is produced. In the seventh working process, which is also the last one, the manufacture of the metal plates is finally completed and they are ready for use. As already mentioned, the entire metal encasement of a ship's hull is produced from a single seamless piece. The remarkable thing about this manufacturing process is the following:

From chemistry lessons, we know that a metal alloy contains the same fundamental substances that had existed before they had been combined. Brass, for example, is made of 70–80 percent copper and 20–30 percent zinc. The Pleiadians only use pure lead without any additional substances for their copper, nickel and silver alloy and there is no mention of lead in the end product. So, where is the lead?

The Pleiadians use a vibratory technique unknown to us that liquefies metals without heating and can be referred to as a cold welding process.

A direct transformation of materials is also possible in principle, and whoever masters this technique can transform the chemical element of lead directly, without deviation, into the desired alloy. Not even the Pleiadians have discovered the wonder formula for this mysterious process up to this very day. At any rate, it is universally possible to transform the element lead directly into gold, as all alchemists of this world have always attempted time after time. But then again, not even the Pleiadians have found this philosophers' stone up until this very day. *(See ~ Chapter 11 for the results of scientific analyses on extraterrestrial metal samples)*

Aeronautical Capabilities of a Modern Ship

As already mentioned in the foreword, the Pleiadians are almost in perfect command of universal space flight. The latter-known types of spacecraft are not only capable of the flight maneuvers listed in *Chapter 3*, but considerably more because they are capable of performing aeronautical feats that only a few other civilizations in our entire universe can do.

A Pleiadian spacecraft is capable of more than flying absolutely silently and invisibly and landing at any given point of the earth's surface, as are many other extraterrestrial planetarians. What distinguishes the Pleiadians from the others is their ability to jump their spacecraft out of our normal space into a hyperspace. Space and time are paralyzed to null, enabling them to span any imaginable distance in the universe within null-time. Without the command of this super technology, it would be out of the question for the Pleiadians to visit earth at all or so often! Above and beyond this, they are also capable of entering other dimensions (space and time planes) and returning with absolute dependability into normal space. And finally, they are capable of still another mysterious feat: They not only manipulate time by turning back the hands of a clock, but the hours that have already passed can be re-lived from the very beginning. Such manipulation of time may seem like a miracle to us.

What is even more puzzling is the fact that the Pleiadians from planet Erra are capable of traveling in time by jumping either into the past or the future and appearing there along with all of their ships and crewmembers. And I can fully understand that the majority of our natural scientists and engineers are smiling contemptuously about these claims, but it still does not change the actual facts.

Protective Shields of a Pleiadian Spacecraft

- A Pleiadian ship can neither be acoustically nor optically located with the help of radar if the appropriate protective shield is activated around the ship.

- For security reasons, a ship that has landed during daylight is usually enclosed by at least two protective shields. The outer protective shield extends for a distance of 500 meters (1,650 ft.) and causes any uninvited life form to be led astray if it consciously or unconsciously attempts to approach the ship. The invisible and intangible barrier leads the life form in a circle around the protective shield without ever reaching the ship.

  In case someone should succeed in breaking through the outer ring, the second inner protective shield that safeguards the ship within a range of 100 meters (330 ft.) is considerably more effective. The inner shield acts as an invisible and almost impervious wall that can only be penetrated slightly with a tremendous exertion of strength. Bullets of any kind that are fired at it would either be deflected at its periphery, or if they should penetrate slightly, they would be hurled back to a maximum range of 30 meters (100 ft.). It can even successfully ward off atomic or hydrogen bomb attacks with the help of a special shield.

- Every Pleiadian ship has a protective shield that prevents 100 percent against the penetration of negative vibrations, including the relatively low-frequency vibration of earth people. The positive vibrations may pass through unrestrained.

- Another protective shield deflects all obstacles during flight as early as possible so no damage ever occurs. Included among these obstacles are the air resistance within an atmosphere, the interstellar matter in the empty cosmic space (which is never completely empty, besides the diverse energy fields), meteors and comets, cosmic rays and, naturally, all possible space-craft. The protective shield merely causes the aforementioned obstacles to glide away, but does not force them away in the usual manner, producing no kinetic resistance on the ship.

- A Pleiadian ship generates its own gravitational field (becoming like a miniature planet that carries its own gravitational field along with it) and neutralizes all other gravitational fields that do not correspond to its own. Consequently, all manned spacecraft are safeguarded against all kinds of collisions. Protective sensors (either automatically navigated by a half-or-ganic brain or through pilot control) make sure the ship is brought out of a danger zone in time. Should this not function as anticipated, any space-craft will, in every case, be hurled back from the edge of the protective shield if it comes too close. A mistake in the manual control system can be corrected in a flash with the help of an automatic switch if the proper button is pushed.

Furthermore, the modern Pleiadian ships are 100 percent crash-proof. A device is used for this purpose that detects all disturbances and material defects in advance so the anticipated defect can be repaired before it causes any damage.

Footnotes

20 ▪ Four of the five ships belonged to four extraterrestrial races that are friends of the Pleiadians.

21 ▪ Periosteum is the normal portion of bone, made up of a dense outer fibrous tissue layer and a more delicate inner layer. It is the layer of bone regeneration.

CHAPTER 4

Billy Meier ~
Contactee of the Pleiadians

Who is Billy?
He is the man with one arm.
His glance velvet-soft and warm,
As clear as a spring fountain
At its source can only be.
Through love eternal he eases
Man's pain and agony.
Self's greatest hardships he ne'er eschews
To the end of his hidden destiny.
And as springtime each year renews,
Unfolding in blossom splendor abundantly,
He pours forth his knowledge and wisdom
Born of thought and spirit force,
For us men he is an eternal companion.
So be it, until once he is carried forth
And only the memory among us resides
Of a man, with only love as his guide.

By Elisabeth Moosbrugger

I have not exhausted the subject matter of this chapter, but I am offering extensive and fundamental information to convey the clearest picture possible of Billy's personality. To do this has been an important personal desire of mine. It was becoming ever more apparent to me that Billy was often misunderstood, wrongly evaluated and consequently underestimated because of his peculiarity and modesty which, in part, were fully out of place in this day and age. Many people who have known him for years actually know very little or almost nothing at all about his true nature. I would like to make clear that he cannot be studied by normal standards. In this connection, Semjase stated that all of our methods of judging a man would be totally inadequate with reference to Billy, except for an astrological character portrayal. At the present time, there are relatively few experts who are capable of drawing up a highly accurate character analysis.

Billy's civilian name is Eduard Albert Meier. "Eduard" means Guardian of the Treasure, which is a special characteristic of his. He did not adopt the name "Billy," himself. He obtained this name from an American by the name of Judy Reed in Teheran, and with good reason. He always dressed in black and ran around the area like a real cowboy during his stay there. According to a recommendation by the Pleiadians, we should have stopped calling him "Billy" long ago, but the use of this name has become so widespread that a change can hardly be expected now. Incidentally, an old prophecy states the prophet of the New Age would be called "Billy."

He was born on February 3, 1937 at 11:20 am C.E.T., as the son of earthly parents in Bülach in the Zurich Lowlands. And since the times were not particularly rosy for his family, from his earliest childhood he had to help his siblings tackle the daily chores. He often only got around to take care of his schoolwork at night.

Through his contacts with extraterrestrials that occurred for the first time when he was five, Billy did indeed learn a great deal. Consequently, he separated himself more and more from his contemporaries. In this manner, he became an outsider and a troublemaker in both his village and school community, as well as in his own family. This is the only way to explain why he was always held responsible for everything bad that ever happened. But instead of defending himself, he was as silent as a tomb when accusations were unjustly made against him. As a consequence of this, Billy was also declared a problem child and was sent to various reform schools. But, of course, no one wanted to keep such an odd fellow for very long, so he was shoved about from one place to the next. When the constant shuffling back and forth became too much for him, he simply ran away. Billy wandered through the woods, utterly forlorn, and subsisted on anything edible he could find. In the end, he was always seized and brought to a new place where the same game was repeated — this continued for about five years.

One fine day, Billy was finally locked up in a psychiatric clinic where they examined his mental state, among other things. After they had treated him most evilly there, he decided to flee from the country, which he actually succeeded in doing, but under extremely difficult and life-threatening circumstances. In any case, he battled his way over the border to France where he enlisted in the Foreign Legion. Billy was only 15 years old. Although he realized very soon that this step was a mistake, fleeing from the Legion seemed to be impossible. Nonetheless, he managed to accomplish this feat and was able to retreat to the other bank of the Rhine. Once he was back in Switzerland, he reported himself to the authorities. Incomprehensibly, he still kept silent despite all imaginable condemnations. Even after psychologists and psychiatrists at the Rheinau Cantonal Clinic recognized his above-average intelligence, Billy was brought to trial and sentenced to 4-1/2 years of imprisonment. Although he was actually in prison for years as an innocent man, he simply was unable to pull himself together to defend himself. But somehow, even the negative has a positive purpose, and that quite obviously seems to have been the case. This extremely hard lesson served mainly as an excellent preparation for the difficult tasks ahead that he yet had to master. From today's perspective, Billy views this in the following way: "I have to admit that the period of imprisonment and institutionalization was not simply useless, because I learned much more about spiritual matters during this time than I could ever have possibly learned as a free man. A very important learning factor for me was the realization that a man must be modest and selfless to really be a human being."

After he had served his time, there was nothing else to hold him in Switzerland, so he set out on his journey through forty-two countries in Europe, Africa and Asia. Up until his return to Switzerland in 1969, he covered a total of about 3,500,000 kilometers (2,200,000 miles) within twelve years. About 1/10 of this distance was on foot, while the rest was accomplished by bicycle, car, truck, bus, ship, small airplane, helicopter and railway. Of course, the horse and camel were also among his means of transportation, as well as the donkey and oxcart. While in India, Billy used the elephant, naturally. In this way, he was able to become acquainted with a country and its people and gather valuable experience. With absolutely no financial means, he took advantage of every job available in order to earn his daily bread. Forced by necessity, Billy learned and performed, altogether, no less than three hundred and fifty-two different jobs, on a temporary basis. There was often little time left for him to learn a completely new trade so, occasionally, he was granted a somewhat longer learning period. But there was never enough time for an apprenticeship of several years, as is common practice. Sometimes he practiced tasks in which he could put to use his extensive knowledge of theology, theosophy, psychology and psychiatry; namely as priest and pastor, medicine man, village doctor and veterinarian. Other times, he worked as a mason, glass blower and joiner, carpenter, marble cutter, painter and plumber. In addition, he was further experienced in forestry, agriculture, road construction, landscape architecture, and so on and so forth. As far as his typing skills are concerned, he could take on any clerical shorthand typist position. *(See ~ Chapter 5)* In West Pakistan, he started working as a smuggler, which is considered as reputable employment there. Billy also earned a living as a German teacher, blaster, watchman, and special commissioner against criminality and as a private detective. In the latter capacity, he eventually lost his left arm. The practical experience of such jobs was naturally of great benefit to him later on during the construction of the Center in Hinterschmidrüti.

Above and beyond this, Billy devoted himself to the study of all world religions and attained a general idea of all major world views. In order to increase his knowledge, he joined various sects and secret societies for a short while. For the purpose of being taught, he even remained among the wise men in India, whose existence is hardly known to the world because they live in solitude like hermits and almost never appear in public.

A severe blow of fate struck him on August 3, 1965 in Iskenderun, Turkey. As mentioned before, he lost his left arm there in a bus accident. Rescuers left him lying by a ditch for three hours in an unconscious state under the assumption that he was dead. Not until later did they realize their mistake. It was too late by then to save his arm. Regrettably, the necessary amputation was carried out under catastrophic conditions and was anything but professional. Billy will have to endure more or less intense phantom pain in his arm stump for the rest of his life.

On December 25 of the same year, he met his wife, Kalliope, in Greece and became engaged to her on January 25, 1966. In response to internal family problems, he "kidnapped" his bride on February 25, 1966 and married her after diverse complications on March 25, 1966 in Corinth. Three children sprang forth from this marriage. Their names are Gilgamesha, Atlantis and Methusalem. Unfortunately, the problems and conflicts did not stop outside his front door. Consequently, Billy had no easy time of it with his family life. But as incomprehensible as it may sound, dealing with such a myriad of problems actually benefited him by helping him develop two sturdy legs to become strong enough to handle the energy-demanding mission.

Whoever has only met Billy casually or only knows him by hearsay may have discovered or heard to their disappointment that neither his lineage nor his habits indicate anything special. He possesses no material wealth, no esteemed social or governmental status and has no fine-sounding professional title. He does not even have a higher education, let alone a doctorate degree. The only thing he can present along these lines is his honorary title of Sheik Muhammed Abdulla, granted to him by the Ahmdiyya Mosque in Karachi, West Pakistan. (Kalliope received the honorary title of Sheika Aischa Abdulla). In addition to this, in August of 1988 he was also granted the master title of a fifth Dan honoris causa in the name of all Japanese karate clubs. But otherwise, it apparently only concerns an inconspicuous man who may merely want to make himself important. From a superficial viewpoint, he is no more or less than any other man, and has faults as well as attributes to prove so. He also makes mistakes that turn out to be absolutely necessary for his further development. Worst of all is the disappointment of such people who think Billy must certainly wear a halo around his head, which is just not the case. As the old saying goes, outer appearances are deceptive and this definitely holds true for Billy. Actually, only very few people have recognized his true greatness because his talents are concealed to a large extent, and because he does not try to profile himself visibly for the general public. This is one of the main reasons why Billy has given no interviews for years (with few exceptions) — in order to prevent giving the impression that he merely wants to be in the center of the limelight as a world famous contactee. Only those who really know Billy actually realize what he can do and the depth of his integrity. Without exaggeration, I cannot help saying that he is indeed an extraordinary man in many respects. His knowledge and abilities, and especially his versatility, are by all means admirable. His greatest strength is in a totally different realm. Material knowledge of every kind, which he also possesses abundantly, is not what I mean here, but rather, spiritual knowledge that involves totally different facts than usually assumed. Spiritual knowledge and ability can only be acquired by intense study of the spirit teachings. This is mainly a question of studying the universally binding natural laws and commandments of Creation, as well as the use and functional purpose of spirit forces.

To acquire such knowledge and abilities, Billy was dependent on extraterrestrial help. It is thus understandable that he has been in contact with extraterrestrial intelligence since his earliest youth. The contacts are partially in the form of telepathy but are, for the most part, through personal face-to-face contact. Billy has also had contacts through inspirations that he occasionally receives from very high non-physical spirit forms. In the next chapter, I shall go into more detail on this. *(See ~ Chapter 5: Billy's Contacts With Extraterrestrial Intelligences)*

In and of itself, it is not unusual when UFO contactees encounter animosity. Unfortunately, this is especially true for Billy. To prevent the spreading of the truth at all costs, certain circles have tried to silence him by simply intending to dispatch him to the beyond. In 1975–76 alone, three malicious attempts were made on his life. You will learn more about this in *Chapter 12* and *Chapter 13*.

His enemies referred to him as a cross between Einstein and Till Eulenspiegel, or called him a charlatan and swindler, which still occasionally happens today. But despite all the intrigue and slander, (even occasionally from his own ranks), not one iota of what all the wicked tongues would like to conjure up is the truth, nor can these accusations be proven to this day.

A completely new segment of Billy's life began on January 28, 1975 when the 11-year period of contact with the female Pleiadian, Semjase, started. This point can be considered as the actual beginning of the mission work he was to fulfill as prophet of the unadulterated truth and preparer of the way for a better future. Since then, he has no longer practiced a normal profession but has worked in untiring service for the fulfillment of his difficult task.

However, it would be far too much to recount the many commitments and activities that were in store for Billy and all the adverse conditions that had to be mastered. In the spring of 1977, he moved from his original place of residence in Hinwil to Schmidrüti in the Tösstal (Töss Valley) of the Zurich Highlands, where his domicile is found today. It bears the melodious name of *Semjase Silver Star Center* in honor of his extraterrestrial friend Semjase, who did her utmost in all matters in the initial stage of construction. Billy founded the original and central headquarters of the FIGU in August of 1975, but the actual founding assembly did not take place until June 17, 1978 in Hinterschmidrüti. FIGU is the abbreviation for Free Community of Interests for the Fringe and Spiritual Sciences and Ufological Studies. FIGU is a non-profit organization and community of searchers for, and researchers of, universal truth. A few hectares of land used for farming, a farmhouse and several smaller buildings are a part of the overall area of the center. When the farmstead, a miserable ramshackle of a building surrounded by morass, was taken over, and a squalid shed, the land all around was hopelessly overgrown. It took many years of effort and the hardest work of all members to establish its present state, which may be described as paradise-like in comparison to its former state.

The New Age Prophet

A very unpleasant manifestation today is the Babylonian confusion of a concept that is spreading like weeds and blossoming in various fields. Among this field of flowers is the term "prophet." But what does this have to do with Billy? Is it true that he originally claimed he is the New Age Prophet? Now, we have finally reached the core of the matter. It was not Billy who chose this title for himself, but the Pleiadians, who broke this news to him gently. In all honesty, many others as well as I first had to become accustomed to the idea that Billy was a contactee of extraterrestrials, but a prophet? This news just seemed a bit too much of a good thing to me! As can be seen from the contact reports, it was not any easier for him either. When he received the first inspirations from the high spirit plane of Arahat Athersata and was referred to at that time as the New Age Prophet, he vehemently refused to accept it. *(See ~ Chapter 5: Inspirations – Fig. 5-1)*

In a personal conversation with Ptaah, Billy mentioned the following:

> **BILLY:** … He (The Arahat Athersata) pronounced me to be a great prophet, as if my mouth had been shoveled full of wisdom. I found that a bit too pretentious and inappropriate. I find such speeches arrogant because they are out of place. They repulse me and do not fall into my scope. I am truly no prophet. These spirited orations by Arahat Athersata in particular infuriated me and that is why I have set myself against contact with them for the time being. I have suppressed his voice and have not written a single line since then. I have to first consider whether I will continue this work. It is unsuitable and strange for me to stand there as the great prophet because I can never be that … my fellowmen would inevitably accuse me of fraud and megalomania and accuse me of being a liar.

Ptaah had to teach Billy that the people of earth had completely erroneous notions about this, since a real prophet is a life form just like everyone else and is not a powerful being whose head is raised high above all of mankind. Ptaah further advised Billy to retain his former practice of modesty, but to acknowledge his superior knowledge and the wisdom that comes with it. For this reason, no one may accuse him of megalomania. Despite this advice, Billy was only able to gradually become accustomed to his appointed role.

Nowadays, there are many "wise" men around our earth globe who bear the title of "prophet" and make it difficult for truth-seeking people to distinguish between truth and fallacy. The large esoteric market is like a jungle in which one can go astray very quickly if caught off guard. For the comfort of all those who have honestly put forth great effort, it can be said with absolute certainty that every person seeking the truth will sooner or later find the philosopher's stone if they really take pains to do so. The most arduous and strenuous path through the thorny brush must be undertaken and cannot be bypassed or avoided. This arduous journey is considerably easier if one can follow a light that shows a powerful and reliable direction to take. A prophet is entitled to give just that.

According to a law of Creation, each inhabited planet brings forth one or more extraordinarily highly developed human life forms from time to time, with which considerably higher intelligences can make contact in order to guarantee evolution. On earth, these people are called prophets and, unfortunately, they have always been subject to hostility and persecution. That has not changed to this very day. As always, they have been accused of being charlatans, liars and fantasizers by the citizens of earth who do not understand or want to accept the voice of truth and are unable to break away from their false ideas of realism and materialism.

A prophet is schooled and taught by extraterrestrial life forms and only one lives on a planet at any given time. Therefore, his knowledge and wisdom exceeds the normal degree, by far. He receives and propagates trail-blazing and trend-setting messages from very high spirit planes. His proclamations are of a prophetic nature, on which the name prophet is based. A prophet imparts spirit teachings and the laws and commandments of Creation to mankind so they can find their way back to the truth that was abandoned. Prophets of the present day, though, must use completely different work methods than those used in ancient times when they mostly lived in rugged and impassable regions as hermits. They only appeared among the people now and then with powerful words. Teachings of every sort were exclusively conveyed by word of mouth because people were unable to read or write at that time. But this was long ago. The possibility of spreading the truth has undergone tremendous change and improvement, thanks to modern technical means of communication. Whether mankind calls them prophets or truth bringers, their forthcoming mission is determined at conception. Unfortunately, more and more self-appointed prophets or alleged enlightened masters (enlightenment does not take place until the juvenile state or adult age) appear on the world stage to boastfully proclaim earth-shaking events. A true prophet is placed under the control of a higher life form before birth. In Billy's case, this task was taken over by Semjase's grandfather, Sfath, who was responsible for protecting, guiding and teaching him.

All of the earlier prophets who have ever walked on the earth were adequately trained for their mission long before their birth and in earlier lives as well. This corresponds to a law of Creation that no one can ignore. On one hand, higher, responsible spirit forms of higher evolutionary levels predestined them (at the Petale[22] or Arahat Athersata[23] levels, for example). On the other hand, the prophets appointed themselves before birth for the fulfillment of the prophetic mission out of a sense of duty and of their own accord.

The lives of such men develop into prophethood directly after birth. Moreover, an extraordinarily hard existence full of privation awaits them, in which a great deal has to be learned. Despite generous help from extraterrestrial schoolmasters, this in no way means wisdom simply falls into their laps. Furthermore, the prophets have to acquire all the knowledge through their own efforts. A prophet may never lead a carefree, pleasant life. So when alleged conveyers of truth, whose lives were not strewn with the severest of hardships, emerge by their own grace, it can be assumed with certainty that they are not genuine prophets. They proclaim teachings of falsehood that must be continuously revised, whereas true prophets attest to teachings that last eternally and are in no need of change because they possess everlasting validity. To the regret of modern mankind, a prophet pronounces all grievances with aggressive words and spares no one and nothing in doing so. For those who feel personally addressed, this is naturally not very flattering and does not suit them the least bit. But with the current deplorable state of affairs on earth, the necessary clarity cannot be accomplished any other way than with harsh language. Everyone who is bothered by this must bear in mind that aggressive language is necessary to loosen the compacted soil so that fresh seeds can sprout up! In this context, a sentence from *OM: Canon 23, Verse 10* is most appropriate, which states, "It is only the words of the false prophets and frauds and liars who speak and solicit so, and who with flattering words and promises smear stolen honey around your mouth."

Really genuine prophets can be recognized by their clear, unmistakable language that points out and uncovers whatever corresponds to falsehood. With the help of extraterrestrials, Billy began to learn at the early age of five and, thus, acquired enormous abilities in every respect in the course of many years. He learned to find the truth without any outside help, but instead, through an extremely difficult life. A normal earth person would under no circumstances be in the position to undergo and endure such hard lessons. He would perish physically and psychically.

On the other hand, Billy received help that is not given to a normal citizen. He was thus able to undertake time trips into the past with Asket, the kind of experience that normal mortals will probably be denied for many thousands of years to come. At this opportunity, he was able to determine for himself on the spot the truthfulness of historical events that unfortunately are often handed down to us in a falsified form.

The prophethood, which is incumbent upon Billy, corresponds to a destiny that had its beginning on earth more than 10,000 years ago and will find its completion with the Prophet of the New Age. Although this was his predestination, he nevertheless had to renew his decision to continue this difficult task. Just as it pertains to every person, Billy had the freedom to choose whether or not to act in accordance with his predetermination. We are certainly happy that he decided in favor of this.

The Hard Language of Truth

With the regular repetition of a striking clock, the harsh and rough-hewn language in Billy's writings is rejected. A large number of readers are bothered by this fact and prefer to turn to other books, the contents of which do not attack their psyches so fiercely but instead, soothe it like oil and balsam. Their thoughts can continue along the same old track without having to seek new ways through toilsome efforts. Above all, it is much easier to hang on to traditional ideas than be faced with completely new facts that can also be very painful now and then. It must be clear that the truth always sounds hard to a person who finds it annoying and even offensive, so that they feel personally attacked. It also sounds hard because the mirror of their own faults and shortcomings is often held before their very noses, although they assess themselves as being almost faultless. Furthermore, the teachings of the spirit require a completely different interpretation. This happens to be the way it is found in the nature of the matter. There is no further development if a person thinks the same way in spiritual matters as in physical matters. The language of diplomacy, as commonly used among us on earth, serves primarily as a means of gaining some type of advantage at the cost of others. The realities are usually improperly and falsely rendered with this form of language and they degenerate into deadly misunderstandings. The truth can never be spread in diplomatic form. Truth must call the facts by name, as they really are, straightforward, without belittlement or misappropriation. According to the words of Semjase, paraphrasing and sweet-talking give false impressions, with the result that everything is misinterpreted and inappropriately spread and which can lead to renewed false teachings. The language of truth has always been very hard and wherever the attempt was made to paraphrase it, it has been distorted beyond recognition and the real meaning was lost. In the proclaiming of the truth, a falsification cannot occur under any circumstance as it is a question of the laws and commandments of Creation, which are unchangeable and forever valid for all eternity and are in no need of change.

We should thus bear in mind that truth may not be set forth with fine tongues and soft words. People who are far enough in their spiritual development to understand and can bear the hard language do not take offense at Billy's writing style. Naturally, the same fact can be depicted for the reader in various ways, made palatable so that his or her appetite is not spoiled. But Billy makes use of his hard style with full intent because most of our contemporaries are roused to their own thinking only in this manner.

According to the Pleiadians, it will not be easy to make this clear to the people of earth in their present stage of development. They are already too softened and have strayed from the recognition of truth to the point that they energetically resist everything that sounds like the hard truth.

Hence, know thyself. He who bears the hard, undiplomatic language of truth and recognizes its value will find himself on the right path of true evolution. Otherwise, for the time being, this path will remain blocked to him through hindrances that he must first clear away.

Who Finances Billy?

Sometimes, it is absolutely hair-raising to hear or read the mean claims made in regard to Billy's financial situation and which are absolutely unfounded.

Among other things, the erroneous opinion was claimed in a newspaper article that Billy is merely a sectarian leader, just like any other, around whom a number of blind followers have gathered so he can thus lead a free and easy life at their expense. And his organization, economically speaking, is claimed to be remarkably efficient in making hard cash of Billy's works, urging people to work free of charge and relieving them of their money in numerous and varied ways. Word for word it further states, "Billy would not be Billy, had he not let himself be inspired to create a work vacation. He allows his members and those willing to work for him several days or weeks. Of course, this is without pay and these rather misused vacationers have to come up with room and board themselves. Furthermore, it would be meaningful to bring along gifts, some flower seeds, border plants of every kind."

Under item 10 of FIGU's house regulations, it states in writing, "Should the fortunate case arise that you would like to work in the Center for several days or even weeks, the residents of the Center would consider themselves quite lucky. We cannot offer you a night's lodging, board or cash, as stated under points 2, 3 and 4. For board and lodging, we recommend the Freihof Restaurant in Schmidrüti where you can eat well and lay down your weary head for a reasonable price."

First of all, I would like to clearly stress that the Free Community of Interests is not a sect, although it may appear to be in some respects if viewed superficially. Secondly, I emphatically reject the untrue allegations that have been taken out of context with the intent to degrade and defile Billy as an exploiter.

As for point 10 of the house regulations, it can be said that the text, as such, has not been falsely repeated but yields a completely false picture because points 2, 3 and 4 do not appear as in the text. Under point 2, it says, "When you work with or for us, you do this of your own free decision and without any claim to any kind of compensation." In point 4, it explicitly states, "According to the official laws, we are not an inn and, consequently, are prohibited according to law to entertain/ board any persons for work or payment if these persons are not direct family members, relatives or close friends of the Center residents." In point 3, it further states, "Because of the continually increasing prices and because of the law, we are unfortunately not in the position to compensate your work with cash, natural produce, food and board, etc."

Therefore, we not only would make ourselves liable to punishment but would not even be in the financial position to recompense the work of strangers since we are not even able to do so for our own group members. For example, our core group member, Silvano, has worked for years on the farmstead as a farmer and, in a manner of speaking, as all-round-man on a totally voluntary basis. This means he "earns" room and board for his work and a couple hundred francs pocket money given to him as a gift each month from members who are able to pay. We are simply not able to do more . We are happy and satisfied if we financially make ends meet each month without having to take out new mortgages. That is why any outside help is naturally welcome, but on a voluntary basis. And if there are such people who take advantage of this opportunity, it is their business because they know precisely why they are doing it — namely for a good cause. All of us, that is, all core group members of FIGU, as well as all other helpers near and far, are ultimately working for a single, common goal — the fulfillment of the mission. To clarify this, the only remaining question is, "Who finances Billy and what does he and his family live on?" Actually, this would be a matter of Billy's own private concern, but as totally wrong ideas prevail with regard to this, I would like to take a closer look at this question.

Billy receives a modest disability pension and acquires a certain share of the publications sold. And this is, no doubt, his well-earned right since he is the one who telepathically or inspirationally receives the content of the writings, or composes non-transmitted texts himself and puts them to paper. Furthermore, he has the right to reside in the Center with his family for life, just as the other Center members have. Billy and his family do not own any private property whatsoever, neither in the Center nor anywhere else. In other words, the entire area of the Semjase Silver Star Center and everything connected with it is the property of the entire group. Of course, these assets are absolutely bound to the existence of the Center. After long years of construction work, the current, most urgent task of all group members is to keep the center of administration working as efficiently as possible. In this way, it will continue to serve as a place of meeting and instruction and a source for spreading the teachings of truth. As for Billy's financial situation, it has fortunately stabilized in the course of time but he still cannot do any splurging, even today. This was not always the case. In the initial years of construction (since the beginning of this mission work in 1975), he invested his entire savings into this cause as much as was possible for him. If worse comes to worse, Billy would still continue to finance FIGU. Now, it would be the time for him to think of himself and his family for once, because everyone should have a savings account for unforeseen expenses or times of need! As already mentioned, there is no time for him to pursue a regular job while practicing his duties as prophet of the New Age. Because of his anti-materialistic point of view, his inner conflict about money has caused him a lot of trouble. He needed a certain amount of money to support his family and there was not enough to make ends meet, while at the same time he was indoctrinated time and again by his extraterrestrial teacher Sfath that spiritual knowledge may not be sold for money. It took quite a while before Billy finally realized that one could not exist in this materially oriented world without money. Meanwhile, Billy works untiringly, exerting all his energies without compensation for all concerns of FIGU and without taking into account that he has forfeited a considerable portion of his health in doing so. We are greatly obliged to him. With regard to claims of his financial exploitation and profit making at the expense of others and such — no, that is absolutely not the case! All naysayers who use these accusations for their own commercial benefit should once and for all get that into their heads.

Billy's Demonstrations of Spiritual Powers

In earlier times, prophets traveled the length and breadth of the land, spreading their messages through preaching. They displayed their skills in the mastery of spiritual powers by diverse demonstrations. Due to pure lack of understanding, these demonstrations were referred to as miracles, so they went down in history as such. The prophet of the New Age should no longer perform all of these works of wonder because the era is dawning in which every man must use his own reason and find solutions and answers for himself. Therefore, Billy has to keep up with the times and only exercise and use his spiritual powers when no idle spectators are present. Nevertheless, a few group members and a couple of other people have had the pleasure of being convinced of Billy's abilities. The following short reports throughout deal with experiences that I have put to paper, according to the accounts of those concerned.

Guiding Impulse – *A reported experience by Bernadette Brand*

Bernadette lives in Hinterschmidrüti but drives to work in Zurich. On January 11, 1979, she left her job as usual around 4 p.m. and set out on her way home as fast as possible. Following some unknown impulse, she did not take her usual route this time but decided to take a small detour. Due to her poor sense of orientation, she missed the turnoff and drove on in the exact opposite direction and did not find her way again until she reached the "cat's tail." She planned to turn left there and proceeded to pull her car into the driving lane she intended.

But a sudden uneasiness welled up within her, causing her to doubt her intentions. For no apparent reason to her at first, her thoughts at this point circled incessantly around Billy. But then she remembered that the day before, Billy said there were two appliances for sale in Dübendorf that he would like to buy. So she obeyed an impulse once again, made an about-turn and drove straight towards Dübendorf. Acting upon a further impulse, she paid very careful attention to the right side of the road, and whom did she discover at the roadside to the right but Billy, along with his small son. Bernadette immediately stopped, greeted them both and expressed her amazement having so unexpectedly come across them there.

It happened that Billy was waiting for Jacobus, with whom he was going to drive to Zurich for an appointment. Since Jacobus apparently could not arrive on time, Billy would have arrived too late for his appointment in Zurich. Naturally, it was Bernadette's honor to drive Billy immediately there. An appropriate message was left behind for Jacobus.

In Zurich, where Billy was expected, he arrived almost a quarter hour early. And when Jacobus finally did arrive, the business arranged by Billy had already been settled for some time. When Bernadette asked Billy the next day what he had done to arrange this seemingly coincidental encounter with her, he unveiled this small secret and explained:

> **BILLY:** I had somehow a hunch that Jacobus would be unable to arrive on time and I also thought that you would be on your way home about this time. Consequently, I concentrated on you, Bernadette, and lured you to me with a guiding impulse. Such a directing is none other than the transmission of an impulse that triggers certain thoughts and actions in the receiver.

According to Bernadette, Billy's impulses were so overpowering and strong that she could do absolutely nothing else but follow them. Consequently, a coincidence is absolutely out of the question.

Billy's Telephone

When Billy was still in full possession of his spiritual powers before his tragic accident in 1982, he called people to him once in a while by means of telepathy if he urgently needed them for some reason. As an example, I would like to tell you of a short episode that happened in May of 1979 with a young woman who was residing in Munich.

Billy informed her telepathically that she could show up in Hinterschmidrüti on the weekend to settle a certain matter if her time would allow. After transmitting this thought, Billy picked up a small book entitled The Prophet that lay on the living room table. While leafing through it, he did not have the faintest idea to whom the book belonged or who had laid it there or had simply forgotten to take it along. In any case, as Billy leafed through it, he incidentally thought, "this would very well be suitable reading for our group member, Elsi Moser." The young woman from Munich did arrive on the weekend and gave to Elsi Moser (who knew nothing at all of this) a tied package with the comment that she had borrowed the book from a public library in Munich and had brought it for her to read, as requested.

What had happened? The young woman, sensitive to Billy's thoughts, had received his telepathic call that was not at all addressed to her, regarding the book. This led to confusion because the good woman was of the opinion that Elsi had asked her to procure the book. Be that as it may, the actual purpose of the telepathic "telephone" call was at least fulfilled.

Apart from this relatively simple form of communication, Billy also masters spiritual telepathy. The communication in thought between Billy and the extraterrestrials has always taken place in this form. *(See ~ Chapter 5: Spirit Telepathy)*

Tremendous Powers –

According to a report by an extraterrestrial person
who wishes to remain anonymous – abridged.

To outsiders, the following story may seem incredible and fantastic, but many witnesses can vouch for the fact that it corresponds to the truth, word for word. It deals with one of the daring feats that Billy performed on New Year's Eve of 1977. Although he generally is rather reserved with regard to demonstrations, this time he was almost too much of a good thing. At any rate, one of the guests in the course of New Year's Eve came up with the idea that Billy could once again demonstrate spoon bending, as he had done many times before on other occasions.

In the next moment, Elsi Moser gave him a teaspoon she had brought along, which he then actually took between his thumb and forefinger and slowly but surely bent it in front of the entire gathering and finally let it fall, artistically curved, on to the table. Unfortunately, this presentation was obviously not enough because voices arose among about twenty serious observers that Billy should perform other feats. He persistently refused until the constant insistence became just too much. Somehow, it seemed to pain him that his loyal friends demanded evidence of his spirit powers. Deeply saddened, he thus accepted a 10-rappen coin that someone handed him. "What should I do with it?" he asked grievously. It was shouted from somewhere that he should press the papillary lines of his finger onto the coin. "Fine," he replied, with a very grievous tone. Feverishly, he then pressed the coin between his thumb and forefinger and then abruptly smashed his fist onto the tabletop with such dreadful violence that all the guests jumped with fright since they probably assumed Billy had now gone insane. The coin slipped from Billy's fingers, somewhat deformed. His papillary lines were impressed into the hard metal clearly and distinctly.

But this demonstration was still not enough for some and the call for more became increasingly louder. Billy then took a 2-piece franc and a 1-piece franc out of his change pocket, laid them in front of him on the table and asked what he should do with them. After he received no answer in response, he let the 1-franc coin glide into his right hand, clenched his hand into a fist and pressed it closed with visible strain. As he opened his hand again, the coin appeared markedly warped. He did the same with the 2-franc coin. After that, Billy showed visible signs of exhaustion.

The unreasonableness of several witnesses still demanded more. From somewhere, another 2-franc coin was handed to him. With a bitter grimace, he took the coin, let it glide onto his palm and closed his hand again into a fist. Fatigued and exhausted, he said that this was definitely the last demonstration of the night. After that, he raised his arm high and stretched his fist towards Harald Proch, all the while grinning painfully and forlornly in the world. Deep within him, a hell seemed to blaze, probably because they challenged everything out of him and provoked him to the very last. His face looked contorted and strange. But suddenly, his facial features appeared to contort even more. His skin became almost transparent and tears suddenly rolled from his eyes. His physiognomy began to tremble, together with his fist that hovered over the tabletop. His glance was lost somewhere in the eternal distance. All of a sudden, a heavy silence prevailed in the room and no one dared to even utter a sound. It lasted nearly 10 or 15 seconds, then Billy fell in a heap like a puppet. His countenance was snow-white and he struggled for air. He opened his hand spasmodically and let the fully deformed and glowing 2-franc coin fall onto the table as he frantically clutched unto Elsi's arm, helpless and obviously totally exhausted.

Long minutes dragged by before Billy recovered again and was able to speak sensibly. His lips had turned a bluish-white and a burning mark was plainly seen in the palm of his hand. Why? We inspected the 2-franc coin, which was then passed from hand to hand. It was deformed, aglow and burnt. Billy had developed no less than 1,500 degrees heat in his hand — through the purest power of spirit.

The burn on his palm was caused by a sudden decline in concentration through complete exhaustion and extreme fatigue. Because of this, the heat could no longer be controlled and the image of the 2-franc coin was partially burned into his palm where it remained as a burn mark for several weeks.

Afterward, one of the witnesses said, "It must be very clear that none of us will ever make such insane demands of Billy again. We saw everything with our own eyes and personally experienced it ourselves… we have had enough, even more than enough." What can be said about this? Billy is a man just as you and I, but still completely different from us all. How great must this man truly be… he does not use his gigantic powers for his own material advantage, and even in dire need does not resort to them, even in thought!

The Stove – *A report by Bernadette Brand*
On April 30, 1977, Billy and his wife, Kalliope, accompanied by Engelbert Wächter, Hans Schutzbach, Dölf Berroth, Jacobus Bertschinger and Bernadette, sat around the kitchen table late in the evening after a full day of work and chatted with one another enjoying the leisure time. But mixed into this good humor was a drop of bitterness. Something lay like an indigestible lump in their stomachs. It was the thought of moving, as ordered, the heavy cast-iron stove with a mass of 500 kilograms (1,102 lbs.) that was setting on the road. It needed to be picked up in front of the shed and pushed at least one meter to the side.

There was no response to Billy's request for volunteers, but in view of the prevailing fatigue, it could hardly be expected that anyone would as much as lift a finger in this matter on that evening. Instead, those present wallowed in imaginative ideas of how splendid it would be if someone could manage to move the said stove out of the way with the help of telekinesis. No one thought that this wishful thinking could be fulfilled in no time at all — except for Billy. He was suddenly very quiet and fixed his gaze on a certain point of the tabletop, seemingly absent-minded. Very abruptly, he interrupted the laughter round the table and announced quite modestly, "Er isch däne" (it is over there). The weary heads gazed at Billy somewhat skeptically and, perplexed, at once asked, "Öppe de Ofe?" (Do you mean the stove?) Billy confirmed this assumption and explained that he had simply tipped the stove telekinetically onto its side two times on the ground. Due to his tiredness, he simply lacked the strength necessary to lift and transport it.

Since it was already dark outside, those present got a flashlight and went out to the place where the stove was located to see if this was correct and to inspect Billy's work. Naturally, they were fully inspired by his success. In so doing, Billy proved what feats a man is capable of with the help of spirit power, even if he was dead tired.

The Small Difference – *A report by Hans Schutzbach*
On Saturday, November 5, 1977, Billy gave a small demonstration with the use of a plain kitchen chair weighing about 7 kp (70 Newton). Stimulated by a discussion on the use of spirit power, Billy felt compelled to demonstrate two examples which would very clearly point out the difference between the use and non-use of spirit power.

He first demonstrated a bad example, namely, the waste of power if a person only uses his physical power for work without using spiritual powers as well. He then hooked a finger of his right hand under the back of the chair and raised the chair off the ground in a flash by summoning all of his manual strength. In doing so, the jugular veins swelled in Billy's neck, his fingers became white and bloodless — until, after a while, he finally let the heavy kitchen chair glide back to the floor while breathing heavily.

Afterwards, he demonstrated the same practice once more. But contrary to the first example, this time he made use of the power of the spirit. He concentrated, using the same finger movement as before and ripped the chair high up off the ground with unparalleled ease. He then held it in the air for a longer period of time without any apparent strain, as if it were as light as a feather pillow, and finally placed it gently back on the ground.

This minor demonstration was to show how beneficial it can be if a strenuous manual activity is sensibly supported by the use of spirit power.

"At first, I thought I was dreaming ..." – A report by Freddy Kropf

The period of construction in Hinterschmidrüti was strenuous and hard for everyone. The people had to go to work to earn money for a living, but also had to do all sorts of jobs at the Semjase Silver Star Center after work. Consequently, everyone was doubly burdened at that time. In view of this, Billy was known to sometimes use his spirit powers to either relieve himself of physical stress or to occasionally show his hardworking helpers a stunt to keep them in good spirits. He would reward them in this way for their hard work, since there was no other means of compensation in Hinterschmidrüti.

Read now what Freddy, Silvano and Thomas experienced in the Spring of 1983 on their way from Hinterschmidrüti to Pfäffikon while riding a tractor. Billy drove the vehicle on a winding stretch from the Semjase Silver Star Center to Wila and then they continued on southward from there. The three young men were sitting back in the trailer and talking with one another. Suddenly, Freddy stopped talking and leaned forward, hardly believing his eyes. He saw Billy sitting comfortably in the driver's cabin, resting his left arm stump on the upper end of the door frame, with his head snuggled into his upper arm singing a lilting song, as fresh as a daisy. Billy's right hand was not on the steering wheel at all — in fact, the tractor was driving along without any manual help, and the gearshift, brakes, clutch and gas pedal also seemed to be functioning on their own. Who has ever experienced the likes of that! The three passengers felt as if they were in some type of automatic or remote controlled dream car. The small group of men reached the town of Pfäffikon in this manner, purchased the necessary provisions there and, before long, were on their way back to Hinterschmidrüti — in the same manner as they had come. Having arrived home after a long drive of about 40 kilometers (25 miles), Billy stepped out of the tractor cabin and grinned at the young people as if this had been the most normal excursion in the world.

Freddy honestly admitted that he had felt uneasy at first. But after he could see that the trip was safe, brisk and without any complications, he enjoyed the spectacle with obvious pleasure. In any case, he and his friends had seen for themselves what spirit power could do.

"You just have to know how to do it." –

Experiences by Eva Bieri, Bernadette Brand and Guido Moosbrugger

If we want to know something specific, we consult a dictionary and select the proper definition of a term. If a false answer is found, which is quite possible, our search there is in vain, and now we are really in a fix. Actually, something like a universal memory exists in which everything stored there can be found and which also never forgets anything. People well versed in esoteric study already know of what I am speaking. It is the cosmic memory bank — also called the storage block or storage bank. Apart from this cosmic memory bank, every inhabited planet possesses its own planetary memory bank, known in esoteric circles as the Akashic Records. This cosmic memory bank is not coarsely structured, which is tangible or visible, but consists of an energy pool that is responsible for the entire universe. This means that there is only one such memory bank for the entire universe. All logical thought impulses of each and every human life form in that entire universe are received and preserved there forever. All important data and events of the past, present and future are indelibly stored therein and can never be lost. From this memory bank data can be retrieved, which means that if a person is able to tap the reservoir, he receives appropriate answers to his questions in an absolute and truthful manner, namely, about all matters known in that universe. This requires of the person asking the questions the skill of absolutely logical thinking. Unfortunately, the majority of earth human beings is not able to do this yet. Logical thinking means thinking in accordance with Creation and living and acting according to its laws and commandments. Without this ability, it is impossible to consciously call up anything. If this is carried out by the subconscious, that is another matter, since the subconscious, after all, possesses the necessary ability. However, the cosmic memory bank refuses every answer, which the questioner is not yet allowed to know, either because he or she is unable to handle it or because they would jump too far ahead on their natural evolutionary path with the knowledge. In any case, a person can make use of this phenomenal provision if he were consciously or subconsciously capable of doing so. As far as Billy is concerned, we are aware of the fact that he can consciously tap the cosmic storage bank, though he only rarely makes use of it. As a rule, he only resorts to this means when he needs important facts for an article and, further, finds himself pressed for time. That is just how Eva was able to convince herself of this ability of Billy's on October 6, 1983 (just as Bernadette and I had done in mid-August of 1978.)

Let us first hear what Eva tells about this. Billy called her into his office while he sat at his desk holding a ballpoint pen, which was resting on a piece of paper ready for use. Eva was then ordered by him to close the doors and curtains, to sit down and to be silent. He asked her to extinguish the lamp and it became dark in the room. The stillness of the darkened room was suddenly interrupted as Billy started to scribble a few notes on the paper. This did not take very long, though, and before long she could light the lamp again. Billy had tapped the cosmic storage bank and had written the answer to a question on the paper. It is that simple — if one can do it.

It did not happen quite so mysteriously when Bernadette and I were allowed to watch in normal room lighting how Billy does it when he makes an exception, for once, and draws on the cosmic memory bank. The direct reason was that Billy was writing an article for *Voice of the Aquarian Age, Issue #4* of *Facts Worth Knowing* entitled Brain Quotients of the earth People. (*See ~ Appendix B – Clarification of the Concept: Brain Quotient*)

The Door – *A report by Bernadette Brand – abridged*

Sometime in the fall of 1978, I entered the kitchen one evening with the intention of passing through and going in the direction of the threshing floor. The kitchen had four doors at that time. The first and second doors were situated diagonally oppo-site each other. The door for entering the house was 1 meter (3.3 ft.) to the right, in the corner, and just around the corner from it was the door to the threshing floor. Billy also happened to be in the kitchen and we spoke briefly to one another.

With the intention of opening the door to the threshing floor, I started along, while Billy, standing in the other corner, asked whether he should hold the door open for me. I answered no, since it would have taken too long for me to wait be-fore he would have been able to make it over to the door of the threshing floor. As I was passing through, I briefly glanced back over my shoulder and saw how the op-posite door that leads to the toilet corridor slammed shut behind Billy. In the same instant, as I wanted to reach out for the door handle, the door opened as though by a ghostly hand. I took half a step and stood there as if thunderstruck with one leg still in the air. Then, in the crack of the door that was opening outward, Billy looked at me with his grinning and shining face!

I was so rattled and flabbergasted at first that I even forgot to breath. As I gasped for breath, still trembling with amazement and incomprehension, Billy's voice echoed in my ear as if from a very far distance, "So chum äntlich!" (Swiss dialect: "Will you come out, already!")

As if in trance, I descended the two steps to the threshing floor and walked past him, while he stepped into the kitchen. In my head all lights turned red, and I won-dered how in the world he had come around the whole house in less than a tiny fraction of a second. I considered all possibilities and impossibilities until I finally came up with the right idea: He had simply teleported himself from the bathroom corridor to the threshing floor by means of spirit power and had opened the door for me before going back into the kitchen.

The fact that Billy had left the kitchen on one side just to enter it again after a fraction of a second through the opposite door several meters away, was actually the second occurrence. For me, this second occurrence certainly made for a remark-able evening.

The very first time Billy did this was on August 21, 1977 on Maria Wächter's birthday before a gathering of birthday guests. Among the witnesses present, besides Kalliope Meier, were Maria, Engelbert, Conny and Rolf Wächter, Herbert Runkel, his girlfriend Ingrid, Amata Stetter, Margareth Flammer, Olgi Walder, Hans and Koni Schutzbach, as well as Elsi Moser among others.

The distance that Billy would have to cover if he were to blaze around the house in the record sprint of the century was exactly 63.4 meters (209 ft.). Our fast-est sprinter, Silvano, needed exactly 22.1 seconds for the 63.4 meters while Freddy clocked the time. Even the best trained and fastest of runners would've needed at least 10 –15 seconds for this steeplechase around all corners of the house.

But in order to open the kitchen door from the threshing floor outside, Billy had only two possibilities or two ways to choose from. He could either run around the house as described, or he could quite simply teleport himself from one door to the other. In view of the circumstances and lack of necessary time, the latter way is the only remaining possibility.

For all the others and me, such events serve as a source of contemplation on the possibilities of spirit power, if taught and properly used. Not lastly, such examples serve as proof that Billy is neither a charlatan nor a swindler but one who has abilities.

An Episode in the Semjase Silver Star Center –
As told by Christina Gasser

It was the evening of April 28, 1990. Atlant Bieri, (a 10-year-old boy at the time) had just received a telescope as a gift. Naturally, he wanted to try it out and asked me to help him carry the telescope to the yard and set it up. Whoever is familiar with Atlant knows that this venture could not be undertaken without a great to-do.

When the telescope was finally standing, Atlant eagerly began to scan the sky. It was a starlit night and only three days after a full moon. Atlant wanted to take a closer look at the moon that was still almost full. But it was no easy matter to properly adjust the telescope, as he soon would be sure to notice. I would have gladly helped him because I, too, was burning to finally see something. But Atlant was in no way at all willing to yield his place.

In the meantime, Edith Beldi, lured by the commotion, had also joined us. She would also have liked to take one look through the telescope and cast a glance at the most beautiful moon that emerged before us so bright and fascinating. But she had just as little success with her appeal to Atlant as I did, and we had no other choice than to exercise patience.

Christian Krukowski and Adrian Fischer, who had worked at the Center on that Saturday and were ready to set out for home, remained standing with us. We all looked up into the endless expanses of space and exchanged a few words.

Atlant startled us out of our contemplative mood when he suddenly cried out that he had discovered a new moon and danced wildly around the tripod. Billy, who had also come to the front of the house, inspected this "new discovery" and explained to Atlant that this was only a reflection within the lenses. Finally, the telescope was correctly adjusted, and with many "ahs and ohs," we took turns looking at the moon and its craters.

We also searched the heavens for known constellations and suddenly discovered a UFO as large as a star that slowly took its course over the Center. We were closely following its flight when Billy suddenly asked Atlant whether or not he should make the UFO light up. Atlant enthusiastically responded to Billy's question.

We all gazed at the heavens, full of expectation, and had hardly breathed in and out when the flying object grew three times larger and sparkled brightly. While the rest of us fell silent, Atlant absolutely insisted on knowing how that worked and how to do it. Billy told him that it was an unmanned telemeter disk and that he only had to concentrate on it in a proper way whenever he wanted to have such an object light up. On that night, we discovered even more telemeter disks, and it was as if each one of them twinkled a short greeting to us.

The telescope stood abandoned off to one side; we had forgotten our jesting scuffle for the supposedly best place at the eyepiece. Our horizon had been broadened in the true sense of the word. Each of us then went our own way again, but I am certain that this experience lingered a long time in each of our minds.

Billy's Accident and Its Consequences

After the illogical and querulous actions of individual group members, as well as other negative facts, had almost driven Billy into sheer insanity, he understandably wanted to throw in the towel a few times and give up everything. The fact that he stuck to his guns in spite of all adversity is undoubtedly due to an explanation that Semjase had given him one day.

SEMJASE: The fulfillment of your task lies within your own discretion. Therefore, if you want to back out, it would be of great detriment to your mankind. On the other hand, we have no command or constraint over you, so you are free to make your own decision. But please consider that it is solely up to you whether the people of earth attain a very important advantage and are able to take a better path.

I know very well that you think every person must risk their own skin, but that does not suffice. Bear in mind that only very, very few human beings of earth possess abilities similar to yours. Moreover, most of them are unable to muster enough courage to openly reveal the facts. As a human being, it is your duty to spread your knowledge and to help your fellowman in doing so. You knew from the very beginning that everything would be very difficult and that no one would be of much help to you. Therefore, I find that your consideration to put an end to our matters is somewhat hasty.

I see that you are angry because the prospects for help cannot be expected to be great and you will be approached with many things of illogical nature. There is no cause for anger since you must understand that your fellowmen are tremendously far behind you in their spiritual form and first have to learn. Human anger is only called for when knowledge of the laws and commandments and other things clearly exists and is, nevertheless, disregarded. Ignorance ought not to stir up any anger within you since this would violate the laws.

For your benefit, I would like to explain that you should very carefully think everything over once again in peace and quiet before you decide to call it all off. Remember that mankind is in need of your help and that you are capable of giving more than any other person has ever been capable of, with the exception of certain prophets who were disregarded and whose knowledge fell prey to falsification. Remember that no other earth human being has been selected for a contact with a very high spirit form, as in your case, for around 2,000 years. Hence, remember how highly valued you are by us and the beings of the high spirit planes, the Arahat Athersata. This is not without good reason.

You are the first prophet of the New Age and thus the most important person in your world, for you are the fundamental preparer of the way for the new era. You have to fulfill the very difficult preparatory work for the prophets of truth who will come after you. Please think about all this very carefully before you subject yourself to a decision that is only based on anger. We know very well the seething anger within earth human beings, since we have had similar problems with them throughout all ages. Many prophets seethed in great anger due to the lack of understanding and the unreasonableness of their fellowmen. And they were often in need of this anger in order to fulfill their mission. But be fair, for your anger need not exist because your fellowmen are lacking knowledge.

As stated, Billy stuck to his guns, although it was sometimes unspeakably difficult for him. But how could things go well in the long run? He was more or less always under stress. He suffered from overwork and a perpetual lack of sleep. He demanded far more from his body than it was capable of giving. Sooner or later the time was bound to come when he could no longer sustain the long years of overexertion. He repeatedly exhausted himself with heavy manual labor in the construction and renovation of the Center in Hinterschmidrüti, then made himself weary with spiritual work in the fulfillment of his mission (writing of manuscripts, receiving messages, receipt of and writing down of the contact reports, and verbal teachings). Furthermore, irrational and querulous people gnawed at his nerves and continually bombarded him with illogical concerns, which often robbed him of the sleep he always had far too little of anyway. There is no question that certain repercussions from this abuse were largely responsible for Billy's accident and all of its unpleasant consequences.

The calamity finally happened on November 4, 1982 when Billy collapsed into unconsciousness in the bathroom and injured his head so badly in the fall that certain parts of his brain were totally destroyed. Quetzal explained what had caused the accident, as follows:

QUETZAL: As a logical thinker, you are unable to probe the basis of the unbelievably illogical thinking of the earth humans because this is also truthfully impossible. And since you are confronted daily with this illogical reasoning, you have no possibility for a rest in which you could recuperate. In this manner, the electric brain currents increase more and more, amass into a balled energy form, and lead to a consciousness blackout when overstrained, or, in other words, to a short-circuit. Once this overstrain occurs, you lapse into a momentary unconscious state, which holds you captive for awhile. Besides this fact, you can also smash your skull to such an extent upon collapsing into this unconscious state that your life extinguishes.

A while before this accident, the Errans fed Billy's data into an android in order to see what would happen under such adverse circumstances and how they could provide him with help. The result of this test experiment was shocking, the android ultimately found no other way out but to eliminate itself.

The damage caused by this unfortunate collapse will presumably burden Billy more or less for the rest of his life. Apart from a severe cerebral concussion, certain parts of the brain were destroyed so that his memory was severely impaired and lowered to a capacity of 27.2 percent. Dizzy spells, sporadically occurring headaches and frequently reoccurring states of anxiety always reminded Billy from that point on of the misfortune he had suffered and also provided many a sleepless night. In addition, even more deplorable conditions arose. Billy was no longer capable of performing strenuous manual tasks because his head would immediately rebel and start to "spin." And since his brain reacted severely to all sudden jolts, he could no longer afford to take lengthy trips by car or rail. The spirit-telepathic communication with his extraterrestrial friends also had to be restricted more and more because the concentration necessary for this was too strenuous.

Billy had to bear these painful and unpleasant burdens for almost seven years. But whoever is acquainted with Billy knows that he always tries to make the best even of a hopeless situation. He succeeded in recovering a large part of his lost abilities in the course of the passing years. He did so with only the very greatest of will power and the mobilization of all available reserves. What even seems incomprehensible to the extraterrestrials is the fact that his memory is once again functioning excellently. In fact, his memory is so perfect that one would think it had never been damaged or decimated at all. But in spite of all the successes and improvements, sporadic and completely unexpected relapses or entirely new types of physical problems appear from out of the blue time and again. Their causes leave the doctors shaking their heads in bewilderment. Like it or not, Billy must live with this hardship and with the fact that his state of health will improve at times and then worsen again. He has to consider the fact that he will possibly be dependent upon medication for his entire life in order to keep functioning.

The fact that he nevertheless succeeded in completing the work *OM* (the *Book of Books* or the *Book of Truth*, which is about 450 pages long) after his severe physical breakdown by summoning all of his reserves of strength, is what I would certainly call an outstanding achievement. He is absolutely assured of the gratitude of all those who will someday lay their hands on this exceedingly precious book and partake of its valuable content.

I would like to close this chapter with Billy's own words:

BILLY: I call myself a creature of Creation, a creation of Creation, which is what every other life form represents as well. I also recognize myself as a wanderer through space and time, and I mean this in the literal sense of the words. I am, in fact, a wanderer, a traveler through worlds. That I know with absolute certainty. I know that this is what I am and that I am only a stranger everywhere — a traveler who moves on after fulfilling his task and who will fulfill his task at the next place. Neither space nor time nor the particular world and its respective life play a role in this, since I travel through them as a missionary. And only to fulfill this mission is of any significance or importance to me, as well as for the respective life forms of the respective worlds.

As far as I am at all justified to offer a concluding statement, my intention is not to sound too overbearing but also not too modest when expressing the following view. Altogether, Billy is nothing more than a human being like you and I. But he is nevertheless a very special one due to his unique enormous knowledge and his gigantic and extensive abilities, which he does not boast of or peddle to the public. According to the saying, "The best has always been nailed to the cross since time immemorial," Billy, too, is unfortunately not much better off than all the other prophets of this world. Instead of continuing to be hostile toward him in worldwide manner, the perpetual naggers, skeptics and antagonists should finally wake up and acknowledge the true facts. In my opinion, it is high time that we see Billy Meier for who and what he really is.

Footnotes

22 ▪ The highest stage of pure spirit forms or pure spiritual energy beings before becoming one with the Creation

23 ▪ A pure spiritual We-form whose name means "The precious one who contemplates the times"

CHAPTER 5

Billy's Contacts With Extraterrestrial Intelligences

Billy's career as a contactee began in 1942, when he was still only a little boy the age of five. Back then, his first extraterrestrial contact person and teacher was none other than Semjase's grandfather — an Erran by birth named Sfath. He was a venerable and wise man who, like every other mortal, eventually had to depart from this life.

After Sfath's death,[24] an amiable woman known as Asket, who came from the twin universe called the DAL, continued the contacts without interruption. This parallel universe to our DERN Universe originated at the same time as ours. But what does Asket have to do with the Pleiadians? The Pleiadians and Asket's people arose from the same lineage. They were originally at home in the Lyra and Vega Systems ages and ages ago. The old Lyrians and Vegans spread throughout the entire universe and even beyond into the neighboring DAL Universe in the course of millions of years. (Incidentally, many human beings from the Lyra System live on today. They landed here thousands of years ago and their descendants have been settled here since then.)

Asket contacted Billy for the first time on February 3, 1953.[25] Her association with Billy lasted for eleven years and ended in 1964. Those contacts were mostly for Billy's personal benefit.

In order to gain a wealth of experience and new knowledge, Billy's early years were a time of very difficult lessons. Besides learning trade skills of every kind and acquiring material knowledge, the mastery of spirit telepathy and spirit teachings were of utmost importance. The years of instruction and enormous sacrifice and efforts served the sole purpose of preparing Billy for the difficult task that he is now accomplishing as the prophet of unadulterated truth and preparer of the way to a better future for the human race on earth.

After an 11-year interlude, a new contact phase began on January 28, 1975, when the girl from the stars, Semjase, appeared on the scene. This new contact can be considered the actual beginning of Billy's mission. In this contact period which would last yet another eleven years, Pleiadians from the planet Erra were generally the ones who maintained these purely personal contacts. They were Semjase, Quetzal and Ptaah, as well as Pleija, Elektra, Hjlaara, Solar and Jsodos. On occasion, members of other races had contact with Billy, such as the dark-skinned Menara, or the yellow-skinned Taljda, Menara's girlfriend Alena, Rala and others. You readers have already acquired more detailed information about the trio Semjase, Quetzal and Ptaah, in *Chapter 2: The Pleiadians, Our Extraterrestrial Friends and Teachers.* This period of person-to-person contact ended according to plan on January 28, 1986.

At this point, contacts were supposed to continue in a purely telepathic manner by Asket and her helpers, but this was not possible for reasons of Billy's health. In a very restricted form, personal contacts still took place occasionally on a purely private basis. These contacts were primarily for Billy's personal edification and not for the general public.

Contrary to expectations, his health finally stabilized to the point where he could once again shoulder the burden of telepathic communication and prepare the contact reports. The Pleiadians then decided to continue the contacts in their official manner instead of the planned telepathic contacts with Asket. Since that time, this is how they have been taking place.

As for the types of contact, we basically have to distinguish between three of them:

1. Personal face-to-face contacts

2. Telepathic contacts by spirit telepathy. *(See ~ Explanation of the Concept: Spirit Telepathy ~ later in this chapter)*

3. Inspired transmission from very high spirit beings. *(See ~ Inspirations – Fig. 5-1 ~ later in this chapter)*

Billy's Physical Contacts

In principle, every contact is announced through a personal telepathic call. However, Billy is also permitted to request a contact with the Pleiadians at any time on his own behalf, if he wishes to do so for personal reasons or if he considers it necessary in the interest of mission work. To carry out personal contacts, there are several possibilities that may be used depending upon the circumstances:

First Possibility:

Billy receives precise information from the extraterrestrials on the place and time of the planned encounter by way of telepathy. If the stretch of road from Billy's residence to the place of contact is not too far away, he will set out by foot to the appointed meeting place. Otherwise, Billy will either use his own vehicle (moped, private car, tractor) or be driven by a good acquaintance or friend to the vicinity of the contact meeting place. In the latter case, the Pleiadians direct him to go alone the rest of the way to the landing place on foot and have his driver and any companions wait for his return.

Second Possibility:

If for some reason the meeting place is not known or cannot be appointed in advance, a specialized navigation system may be used. It is a guiding device capable of telepathy and is one of the fixtures, so to speak, aboard a Pleiadian ship. The device guides Billy to the meeting place by continuously transmitting which direction to take. In this way, Billy finally arrives at the desired destination.

These were the two possibilities most frequently practiced in the first two years of the contact period, especially when Billy was still living in Hinwil. As landing sites, the extraterrestrials chose either hidden glades or places difficult to approach where people did not normally spend time and where a hiker only seldom strays. These usually were located in the immediate vicinity of Billy's residence. The longest stretch that Billy once had to cover with his moped was about 70 kilometers (43 miles).

Whenever a Pleiadian spaceship lands, it does not touch the ground with its landing legs but hovers about 2–3 meters (7–10 feet) above the chosen place.[26] Boarding and departing take place effortlessly in a comfortable fashion. Whoever is to go aboard simply stands below the opened hatch on the underside of the ship and is then raised vertically into the spacecraft, as if inside an invisible elevator. The hatch then automatically closes again. When departing, the visitor glides very gently and quietly on a transport beam through the opened hatch of the anti-gravity shaft to the ground.

A contact conversation very seldom takes place in open country while sitting on a bench or taking a walk but, rather, inside a spacecraft that usually remains hovering close to the ground or sometimes at a higher position.

Third Possibility:

A completely different method quite frequently used by the Pleiadians and their allies is a controlled transmission with the help of a transmitter machine. This method is often called teleportation, *(See Basic Concepts: Transmission and Teleportation)* and is almost exclusively conducted in this manner at the present time. It has two variations:

- They transmit Billy directly into the interior of a spaceship or even out of the spaceship onto a meadow, street, into his office or anywhere else; in fact, from any place desired.

- The second variation is when the Pleiadians exchange places. They leave their space vehicle in a shielded state hovering in the earth's atmosphere like an invisible balloon and transport themselves from there, by using the teletransmitter, into Billy's office or wherever they want to go. The return into the ship takes place in the same manner. This is undoubtedly the most pleasant method for Billy, since he need not do anything more than welcome them at an undisturbed location.

You will learn of several examples in *Chapter 6: Daytime Demonstrations by the Extraterrestrials.*

The time and duration of the personal contacts can only be labeled as "indefinite and variable." (At any rate, there was and is no appointment book available.) Sometimes not a single contact occurs for several weeks or more. On occasion, several contacts take place one after the other in short consecutive intervals, depending upon whether it is timely for the extraterrestrial visitors or if they consider it necessary for good reasons. As opposed to our common social practice, the extraterrestrial visitors feel free to appear at any time of day or night, as their work permits, or if the respective situation calls for it. The duration of the physical contacts is also subject to great fluctuations. Brief meetings last no longer than a quarter hour and normal encounters for approximately 1–2 hours. On special occasions, this standard measure is more or less overrun so that conversations extend over several hours or expand to even longer marathon sessions. Besides these contacts, Billy also had the honor of taking part in three flight-journeys in universal space, one of which lasted for five full days.

What Happens if Billy Meier is Accompanied by Other Persons?

If Billy is accompanied by persons who are along for the first time, the following happens: The telepathic guiding device registers the presence of the accompanying persons but cannot tell whether they are people with friendly or hostile intentions. When the specialized navigation system is in use, the telepathic guiding device automatically switches off in the general vicinity of the contact meeting place. This alerts the pilot of the spacecraft to conduct a more intense thought analysis of the accompanying persons — even if only superficially — to determine whether they are trustworthy or not. If this thought analysis turns out to be positive, the pilot then continues to guide Billy telepathically to the landing site of the ship so the contact can take place as planned. The persons accompanying Billy must wait at a certain distance for his return. At this time, the telepathic guiding device stores the brain-wave patterns of every single person who has come along. The brain-wave patterns are just as unique for every human being as the papillary lines of their fingertips, which are fool-proof marks of recognition. On the basis of such storage, the guiding device knows immediately which person is accompanying him. If this person ever reappears, a second analysis is unnecessary.

Should the case arise that unknown persons secretly follow Billy when he is underway to the contact place, or if the persons accompanying him prove not to be trustworthy, the extraterrestrials react immediately. They either make new arrangements or shift the contact to another location or call it off on the spot and make up for it at a later date. If Billy has friendly persons along who have accompanied him at least once before and were evaluated as positive, their brain-wave patterns had previously been stored in the telepathic guiding device and so everything takes its normal, intended course.

What are the Accompanying Persons Permitted to Hear and See?

Although the Pleiadians prefer to conceal their presence, it has occasionally come to pass that the whirring sounds of a Pleiadian ship landing or starting could be heard, but only if the appropriate protective shield has been temporarily opened.

It is even more difficult with optical sighting, since another protective shield, developed from a light- and beam-refracting technology prevents any optical or radar detection. In the very best conditions, one could catch sight of a Pleiadian ship landing or taking off in a non-protected state with the closest distance never being less than 500 meters (1,650 feet).

Hardly anyone is capable of seeing landed ships by night, even if they are not shielded, because the splendidly camouflaged natural hiding places in the wooded glades make it impossible.

Security Measures During the Contacts

It is known that prevention is better than a cure, and this is a saying that the Pleiadians take very seriously in every respect. For security reasons, they entirely enclose a landed ship with two protective shields. As explained before, the outer protective shield is located at a distance of 500 meters (1,650 feet) and causes an uninvited life form who, consciously or unconsciously, attempts to come close to be led away. As a consequence of this invisible and intangible barrier, they are led in a circle around the protective shield without ever reaching the ship. If someone or anything manages to break through the outer ring for some reason or another, a secondary inner protective shield with a 100-meter (330 ft.) distance is substantially more efficient in safeguarding the ship. It has the effect of an almost impenetrable wall and can only be slightly broken through with the greatest of force. Even missiles of any kind fired at it would either be deflected at the outermost rim or hurled back after a maximum penetrating range of 30 meters (100 ft.). With the help of a special shield, even an attack with atom or hydrogen bombs could be successfully repelled. As is generally known, Pleiadian spacecraft are capable of flying without sound and can safeguard themselves against detection if the appropriate protective shields are operating.

In Which Language are the Contact Conversations Held?

The contact conversations between Billy and his extraterrestrial friends are held, without exception, in the German language and are, in fact, completely independent of whether the person conversing masters the German language or not. No problems arise with regard to this, for if a Pleiadian does not master our German mother tongue, they immediately make use of a translator. This translating device enables faultless communication in the German language or any other language, provided the appropriate terms are stored in the device and are available for use. Such a language translator is about the size of a pack of cigarettes and is worn on the user's belt. In any case, the device functions so well that every user can communicate perfectly, even if he does not have the vaguest notion about the German language.

Mysterious Transmission of the Contact Conversations

A great part of the personal and telepathic contact conversations that Billy has had with various Pleiadians and a few other intelligences (from January 28, 1975 until today) are recorded word for word in the "contact reports." (Exceptionally few reports have dealt with purely private or internal group matters and were not meant for the general public.) The contact reports have been in print since 1978 and can be obtained by anyone.

The way in which these contact reports come about is quite remarkable and unparalleled on earth. Actually, one would assume that a verbal exchange of thoughts would be recorded on the spot with a type of tape recorder, or possibly even in written form. But nothing of the sort occurs. To guarantee an absolutely true account, to which the Pleiadians attach very special importance, they first make use of a "symbol transmitter." It extracts the exact content of a contact conversation from the subconscious mind (in which absolutely everything is stored) of the extraterrestrial who conversed with Billy. This "symbol transmitter" then transmits to Billy telepathically. This apparatus could relay the telepathic impulses to Billy only if the extraterrestrials had time to make themselves available to Billy. The disadvantage of this was the fact that Billy always had to conform to their time schedule.

At a later time, Quetzal developed a much better transmitting device that made it possible to relay the contact conversations fully independent of the party with whom Billy had spoken. This innovation was clearly an immense advantage for Billy, since he was now able to recall the record stored there, as from a computer, any time he desired, regardless of whether or not the extraterrestrial had time at that moment.

Billy first receives the telepathically conveyed impulses in a picture-like language of symbols, translates it instantly into our language (German), and types everything down with a typewriter.

In the beginning, Billy used a simple mechanical typewriter. When an electronic typewriter was later placed at his disposal, Quetzal not only improved the transmitter again but also the typewriter. From then on, the speed of the telepathic transmission could be increased or decreased as desired. Billy also achieved a 100 percent increase in performance from one day to the next. In my opinion, it would be appropriate to record his highest typewriting speed in the Guinness Book of World Records, since Billy typed a maximum of about 1,200 strokes per minute (20 strokes per second) with only one hand and without the 10-key system! Of course, this again may sound like bragging to the third power, but all the same, this statement expresses the purest truth. This enormous tempo is only possible when Billy's electric typewriter is equipped with Quetzal's magical attachment. We could not type the way Billy does on that typewriter because our electric typewriters do not function in this manner, and because there is another method at the bottom of it. The fact is, Billy predominantly uses his subconscious mind when working, which, by nature, reacts much faster than the conscious mind. When typing, his material subconscious primarily controls the movement of his fingers. Unfortunately, this hyper-fast transmitting and typing process also has disadvantages that are most significant. According to Quetzal, one single minute of telepathic transmitting and typing of this kind is no less demanding than 23 minutes of strenuous manual work. Therefore, one hour is equivalent to 23 hours of hard manual labor and can only be termed as severe labor to the highest degree. The fact that a human being is capable of withstanding this stress is solely based on Billy possessing the rare ability to regenerate his depleted energy reserves relatively fast and effectively.

> **QUETZAL:** This heavy labor not only gnaws away at one's nerves but also one's physical and psychic energy, so that Billy's efforts take a visible toll on him each time. Debilitation, fatigue and world-weariness become evident, as well as visible changes of his complexion, which sometimes cause his skin to become so pallid and translucent that his face appears to be fully crumpled. When transmitting and typing lengthier pieces of work, for example, two or more hours, Billy often endures very severe states of exhaustion.

Quite a few witnesses can attest to this, primarily members of Billy's family.

Taking Billy's faltering health into account, the transmission of the contact conversations had to be discontinued on October 31, 1984 after Quetzal had ascertained that Billy was physically far too overtaxed by the energy-demanding activity, which could no longer be justified. Consequently, he did not write the contact reports again until November 17, 1989. His health had improved enough by then to the point where the transmission of a contact could once again be expected. Unlike the normal 11-year period, which ended on January 28, 1986, the contacts officially resumed on November 17, 1989 in their usual manner.

Much to our pleasure, Billy has been permitted to transcribe the contact reports again since November 1989, but with one restriction: the typewriter is now without the supplementary attachment. Billy can no longer type at the speed of an express train but rather, at a normal typing speed, in order to protect his health as much as possible.

Why are Billy's Speaking Habits Often Clearly Recognized in the Telepathically Transmitted Texts?

The best thing here is to let Quetzal answer this frequently asked question himself:

QUETZAL: The contact conversations that are transmitted and written down by Billy are translated by him from a graphic-symbol language into the German language, so that the exact wording of a sentence is not precisely quoted. Here, the rule is that Billy transforms a sentence or a conversation transmitted through graphic symbols into his own linguistic usage; therefore, it is inevitable that various words used in the sentences or conversations are not the original word or sentence used.

For example, if an extraterrestrial person says, "it was this an occurrence that a long time ago took place," then the wording of this sentence would be transformed by Billy with the later transmission of graphic symbols into such a linguistic form that the transmitted (symbols) would then read as follows: "This was an occurrence that took place long ago." Since the graphic symbols in the transmissions have to be transformed through Billy into his linguistic form and then again into an understandable German language, it should be understandable that the original spoken sentence cannot be repeated verbatim, but undergoes a change of order into its correct form. It is done without falsifying the meaning of the sentence, which, unfortunately, is a common error with translations on earth (from one language into another). Each person has a different sense of understanding and always explains and translates a sentence in accordance with his own understanding. The correct translations are never produced, not even by the very best of interpreters. It is different with Billy, who has always been proven accurate with translations into other languages. Translating a word or sentence from one language into another means that a logical transformation must take place, so that there is an absolutely analogous conversion/translation/conversion. Such a process can only be conducted if an absolutely logical mind is present, one that only recognizes and acknowledges truthful facts. In this way only, is the true sense of a translation guaranteed. Consequently, the transformations and translations of the graphically transmitted symbols through Billy have always been absolutely correct and analogous, since he lives in this logic. Each and every word and sentence has always, unerringly, rendered the original value and meaning in its entirety — without as much as a breath of a change. Billy understands a range of spiritual symbols encompassing 50.2 million units. *(See ~ Chapter 5: Explanation of the Concept: Spirit Telepathy)*

Destruction Mechanisms

In case the Pleiadians take any devices or objects with them to planets, the inhabitants of which are on a substantially lower evolutionary level, it must be strictly heeded that all objects are equipped with a destruction mechanism.

Should any devices or objects of the extraterrestrials be lost or fall into undesirable hands during their stay on earth, they are either burned to ashes or fully eliminated with the help of built-in destruction mechanisms. Practically nothing is left of them. The remote-controlled ignition operates with far-reaching impulse carriers that activate the destruction mechanism built into each device. The reason for this security measure is easy to understand. Planetary civilizations of a lower level should not gain possession of extraterrestrial technology because it could possibly have dire consequences. On one hand, the development of a human race should not progress too quickly, since important phases of learning would be left out that are necessary for the entire evolution.[27]

On the other hand, special caution is advised regarding us earth people for as long as we use and abuse every new invention for military purposes. Viewed from this aspect, we can perhaps better understand why the Pleiadians, as a matter of principle, are not bringing any objects along to give to us on earth. Most objects equipped with a destruction mechanism are made of synthetic material, including the selective warning device.

The Selective Warning Device

Excerpt from the *Contact Report #62* conversation between Billy and Semjase:

> **BILLY:** What is that white thing there?
>
> **SEMJASE:** It is a selective warning device.
>
> **BILLY:** That makes me a lot more knowledgeable, as I have no idea what that could be.
>
> **SEMJASE:** It is an alarm device that produces a sensitive signal tone if someone were to approach us now whose brain-wave pattern[28] is not recorded in the device, by which I mean, registered.
>
> **BILLY:** Aha, and if you lose that device, you would really be in a fix under certain circumstances, wouldn't you?
>
> **SEMJASE:** Not at all, since we always carry a second device with us. Do you see this one here on my belt?
>
> **BILLY:** Okay, you win. But can you perhaps demonstrate once for me how you destroy such a thing?
>
> **SEMJASE:** To further your education, certainly. Look here, I simply throw it on the floor. Now step to the side. Now look at this device on my belt. If you press these two buttons here, the alarm device sets itself ablaze and is reduced to a sticky and brownish-black mass of synthetic material. So there! Observe the device lying there and operate the two buttons.
>
> **BILLY:** (I allow myself to operate it). Fabulous, the thing is literally belching smoke. Does it actually burn to ashes?
>
> **SEMJASE:** Of course, if you let it burn long enough.
>
> **BILLY:** Can I have the remains? You know, I would like to have it analyzed.

SEMJASE: Certainly, but first you ought to extinguish the burning mass, as nothing will be left of it otherwise. Do not touch it, though, until 1 1/2 hours have passed, since certain radiation released through the blaze will leak out until then.

BILLY: Good, don't you think, though, that our scientists will be able to analyze important things from that stuff?

SEMJASE: The possibility is very low as the original composition of this type of synthetic material, which is now beyond recognition, must also be common in a similar form on earth. We should now part ways. I have just heard human voices ahead on the road.

BILLY: It seemed that way to me, too. So long, dear girl, and come again real soon.

SEMJASE: I shall be eager to do so. Farewell, dear friend, and extend my kind greetings to all.

Telepathic Contacts

Besides the personal contacts, the contact conversations between Billy and his extraterrestrial friends take place now and then on a telepathic basis. This is not done with the aid of simple, primary telepathy, but rather in an incomparably more difficult form called spirit telepathy. Very few human beings, who are completely unknown to the public master this on earth today. It is then no wonder that Billy had to be schooled by extraterrestrial teachers for an entire decade or longer in order to learn this complicated form of communication and to renew the knowledge from his earlier incarnations.

Of course utmost concentration is required for the practice of spirit telepathy. That is why Billy always retires to his office where he can work telepathically with as little disturbance as possible. Oddly enough, radio music does not hinder his strenuous work in the least, even if it is quite loud. Things that we regard as rather harmless bother him, such as vibrations emitted from human beings. When Billy pursues telepathic communication in his office, he hangs a warning sign on his office door with the words "Please Do Not Disturb," or he simply locks it so no one can enter unexpectedly. Sounds with normal noise levels do not hinder him in his telepathic work. But when the decibel volume exceeds its usual level, he finds it so annoying that he must interrupt or even put an end to his work. Such a situation can arise, for example, when a child knocks on the office door with a hard object. Besides the obvious interruption, it also has another unpleasant consequence because Billy is extremely vulnerable at these times. In fact, I can well remember how Billy stormed out of his office one day and complained that a very loud knock on the door had struck him like a thunderbolt. As a result of this disturbance, he had to immediately discontinue the spiritual form of telepathic communication. Besides this, the mishap also gave him a headache that lasted two to three days because the extremely loud knocking was like a hammer blow to Billy's head.

As already mentioned at the beginning, the initiative to conduct the contacts almost always comes from the extraterrestrials, but no rule is without exception. In special cases, an exception is made and the impulse comes from Billy's side. To best illustrate this, I will briefly give a concrete example:

schaubare Taten und Wunder ist in der Vergangenheit
dahingegangen und dem Wesen der Vergangenheit an-
heimgefallen. Die neue Zeit fordert nur noch allein
Verstand und Vernunft von dir, um die Wahrheit zu
finden und sie zu erkennen. Suche daher nicht nach
Wunderstätigkeiten der Propheten, denn es wird dir jede Vor-
führung dieser Form im Grossen vorenthalten. Du bist ein
Mensch der zum Neuen gewandelten Zeit, die Wahrheit und
Erkennung fordert. Diese aber erlangst du allein durch das
Suchen und Forschen und durch die stete Arbeit deines
Verstandes und deiner Vernunft, wenn du sie in geistiger
Form nutzbar zur Anwendung bringst. Wundere dich deshalb
nicht, wenn der neue Prophet nicht vor dich tritt und auch
nicht vor die Massen, um sich zu proklamieren. Es sind dies
in der neuen Zeit ~~f~~ falsche Propheten, die das tun. Der echte
Prophet aber hält sich in der neuen Zeit im Stillen und ge-
langt nur in kleine Kreise, um die Wahrheit zu verkünden.
Dem Sinn der Geistesarbeit der neuen Zeit gemäss, kündet
er die Wahrheit in nur kleinen Kreisen und im Haupt-
werk nur durch Schriften, um so ungestört seiner
Mission zu obliegen und um zu verhindern, dass
er zum Idol ernannt und als Heiliger be-
zeichnet werde. Gewiss ist er kraftvoll im Geiste,
um dich von Krankheit und Übel zu heilen, doch
dies im Grossen zu tun ist der neuen Zeit
und der Evolution widerläufig, denn solches
Tun gehört der Vergangenheit an. Nur irrege-
leitete sind diesem Tun noch verfallen und

Fig. 5-1
Inspirations

After Billy and I had pondered over the true structure of the universe and had come up with very dubious results in doing so, I wanted to find out once and for all what it is in reality. Therefore, I kept bothering Billy, again and again, until he finally lost his patience. Since he was also fervently interested in the answer, he finally attempted to telepathically contact his extraterrestrial friend, Semjase, on Saturday afternoon, March 21, 1981, to arrange a personal contact with her. Luckily enough, it went off well at the first attempt, since his wish was fulfilled on that very evening. After returning from almost one hour of communication with Semjase, Billy was so kind as to call on me at once in my camper trailer. He conveyed the most important results to me, with the help of a sketch he had made. My perpetual insistence had paid off after all, since we, thus, were finally able to learn everything we had wanted to know for so long. I would like to add that our expectations were exceeded to a great degree. The marvelous and novel information we learned from Semjase's rich store of knowledge put us in a true state of amazement about the everlasting omnipotence of Creation. It still fills me with joy and gratitude even today when I think that I, an unknowing earthworm, was able to receive a refreshing drink from the cup of universal truth. *(See ~ Explanation of the Concept: Spirit Telepathy ~ in this chapter)*

Inspirations

Besides the personal and telepathic contacts, the inspirations that Billy received from highly evolved spirit beings of the Arahat Athersata and Petale planes must also be mentioned. This form of communication is only one-sided, a one-way street, so-to-speak. This means that Billy can receive messages but is not able to send them. Consequently, he can neither establish thought contact nor ask any questions. Not even the Pleiadians are in the position to do such a thing. For assistance, they too, must turn to the High Council.[29] Only from the lofty spiritual observation point of the High Council is it possible to establish two-way communication with pure spirit beings.

The method of transmission takes place by way of spirit telepathy. Billy receives and writes down the inspired messages. His hand is guided in a mysterious way so correctly that no mistakes in content can slip in, apart from orthographic mistakes. An accurate word-for-word account is guaranteed in all cases. Whoever examines the hand-written draft will be able to notice the following curiosity: On some of the copies, three or four different writing styles emerge, as if several individuals had helped in writing them, even though everything was written by Billy alone. Apart from several peculiarities in the shape of the letters, Billy's own unique handwriting is only faintly detectable, if at all. *(See Fig. 5-1)*

According to Ptaah, inspirations are so extraordinarily energy-demanding that an ordinary earth person, who is unable to quickly replenish his depleted strength, must take a break for several weeks or even months before he is able to have a new contact. A normal earth person would never have been able to handle the mighty achievements demanded of Billy and, inevitably, would have perished from complete exhaustion.

Even for Billy, longer intervals between transmissions had to be maintained, although he possesses the ability to replenish himself relatively fast. Furthermore, only human beings specially schooled for this can receive transmission from this high level. This process is naturally more valuable because it reveals important absolute truths for the human race of earth.

Why, of all People, is Eduard Albert Meier, and No One Else, Permitted to Cultivate Personal Contacts with the Pleiadians?

Interested parties ask this question whenever the opportunity presents itself, and I feel that it is a fully justified question. This very privilege has been an awful thorn in the side of many people among our acquaintances and co-workers who would like to have been in the first position themselves. Unfortunately, some of these people, along with other antagonistic persons, challenged this arrangement, which cannot be changed, and switched over to the enemy camp in order to oppose Billy and his group.

In addition to those named, there are also enough other people who believe they have acquired a legitimate right to have contacts with extraterrestrials because they have intensively studied ufological matters and those of the spirit sciences for decades. Based on their education, knowledge and abilities, they feel that they are more predestined for this than others and, therefore, find it inconceivable that they have not been given the chance despite their alleged superiority. Their extreme ego is offended and out of pure jealousy or other motives, they sooner or later turn to dishonest means to give Billy's contacts an air of incredulity and fraud, primarily because they themselves cannot be what they would like to be. Competitive jealousy also plays a major role in this field.

Former group members also could not accept that they, too, had no chance; that is, unless they were to make great strides in their spiritual evolution within a short period of time. This is absolutely impossible for the people of earth in our present life, even with the greatest imaginable efforts. The Pleiadians have expressed in no uncertain terms on several occasions that physical contact with them is absolutely out of the question for the next few centuries. I would like to explicitly point out, though, that this statement is only valid for the Pleiadians. What other extraterrestrial races practice in relation to contacts with earth people is their concern alone and not up for debate here!

But the saying "no rule without an exception" is also valid in this context. There are very few exceptions. Among these are a few men of particularly high spiritual standing who earlier had acted as Billy's teachers and with whom the Pleiadians had cultivated personal contacts earlier. This is not the case at the present time. As far as I know, there are a few genuine wise men in the region of India who spend their lives as hermits, totally apart from human settlements, and appear in public seldom or not at all. They also never display their spiritual abilities in public and are, therefore, practically unknown among the masses.

Besides the aforementioned exceptions, Billy is the only human being on earth at the present time who has been and still is able to maintain personal contacts with the Pleiadians, regardless of whether we like it or not. All of the conceited or deliberately false claims that have been made public on a grandiose scale around the world for years can do nothing at all to change this fact.

I would like to name here the most important reasons why only Billy is permitted to cultivate personal contacts besides the few exceptions that I have already mentioned. The reasons for this have been stated several times by Semjase. I have merely compiled and partially completed them according to several viewpoints.

- When the Pleiadians establish contact with earth people, they only do so based on the advice of the High Council, which unequivocally states that they may only establish physical contact with Billy for the time being. Although they would be justified not to heed this directive, in accordance with their own free will, as a rule, they choose to follow it. When they realized and understood the necessity of heeding this advice, they tried to fulfill it as much as possible. With regard to the contacts with Billy, there has apparently been no cause to change their mode of behavior in this respect.

- Experience has shown that it is of no advantage whatsoever, if too many people intermingle in the first position because the results are oftentimes more damaging than beneficial, for reasons of rivalry. The well-known proverb, "too many cooks spoil the broth," is undoubtedly appropriate here and hits the nail right on the head.

- The Pleiadians, along with their Lyrian forefathers, have been the teachers of earth people since time immemorial and have always adhered to the decree to only maintain personal contact with the person fulfilling the mission at the time. And at all times, only those people were selected who, in their judgment, were best suited for such. Therefore, it was not purely coincidental that Billy received this privilege because, to be specific, his spirit form had incarnated as several different earth persons who had already fulfilled about the same function thousands of years ago on earth, as he is doing today. As in earlier times, Billy kindly availed himself, again of his own free-will but not until he was requested to do so and not because he had a longing to do so. *He is not doing this for his own pleasure or publicity, fame, honor or similar motives, but solely in the obligatory fulfillment of this mission, which he had decided to take upon himself in the past.*

In view of the relatively high evolutionary level of the Pleiadians, it is quite understandable that they only seriously consider physical encounters with persons who meet all the requirements, which happen to be absolutely essential for their work. Billy was in a position to rise to such a high level of spiritual evolution only because of his similar work in earlier incarnations and also because of his studies during other human lives on earth — not to mention present life teachings by the extraterrestrials. Intensive training is absolutely necessary for a meaningful basis of working and communicating with the Pleiadians. In spite of all degrading remarks that deem Billy to be a simple farmer from Hintertupfing with little formal education, he has, nevertheless, reached the highest level of spiritual evolution on earth. Of course, this achievement must not be confused with the material knowledge acquired in our schools by reading books, but the accumulation of this extraordinary knowledge, by itself, would be far from sufficient for the fulfillment of his task.

Billy also possesses other important attributes that a contactee must always have at his disposal. Among these requirements are, primarily, the mastering of spirit telepathy and the ability to keep his own thoughts under control and, if possible, not to radiate any negative thoughts, feelings and vibrations into his environment. He, further, has the ability to secure the truth independently through his own efforts without the help of literature or his fellowman and is, moreover, absolutely trustworthy and discreet. For example, under no circumstance, whatsoever, may Billy talk about very special information that must remain secret for a given period of time or forever, even if someone tried to force him to do so. For this reason, another skill of great importance is the ability to resist all hostilities and successfully ward off possible attempts to lure or violently force secret knowledge out of him — secrets that people of earth may not be ready to learn for the time being. And finally, there are even more qualities demanded of him that not just anyone possesses.

One last and also important argument is rooted in the aura of the Pleiadians. which has two peculiar effects:

- On one hand, the auric vibrations of the Pleiadians are so intense that they have an irresistible influence on a human being in search of the truth. This happens in such a way that the persons in question would become dependent, so to speak, and would only devote themselves to the study of the truth without any consideration of survival, so they simply would no longer be capable of surviving in our materialistic world. This would be considered a positive degeneration, since the preservation of one's own life must remain guaranteed under all circumstances that may arise.

- On the other hand, if unprotected, the Pleiadians are enormously susceptible to the vibratory realm of an average earth citizen. The unavoidable consequence of this is hopeless confusion combined with feelings of anxiety. This reaction of panic represents a grave danger since it causes the Pleiadians to act and react completely illogically and uncontrollably. I can remember one such accident in this context, which Semjase had on December 15, 1977 in the FIGU Semjase Silver Star Center. *(See ~ Chapter 2 - A Description of Semjase)*

This is why the Pleiadians have to shield themselves against the vibrations of earth people, both in their hidden earth stations and in their spacecraft. Of course, the same is especially true if Pleiadians are in the immediate vicinity of earth people, meaning — if earth people are less than 90 meters (297 feet) from them. For reasons of security, adequate safeguarding mechanisms are used to keep the vibrations away from their bodies so they will not be injured. Unfortunately, the smallest safeguarding mechanism has a very short duration. It protects for approximately 12 minutes at a distance of one-half meter (2 feet). The longest duration of protection is three hours, but a heavy portable mechanism is needed for this.

A question may naturally arise as to why the Pleiadians are able to withstand Billy's vibrations without being injured at all and without a safeguarding mechanism. The answer is actually quite simple. It has to do with his higher evolutionary level and, therefore, his vibrations pose no danger to them. On the other hand, he can adjust equally well to, and is unharmed by, the stronger vibrations of the Pleiadians as well as to the substantially weaker ones of earth people.

Explanation of the Concepts:
Primary Telepathy

The simplest telepathy is transmission of thought, which is finding ever more use among us earth people. Contrary to spirit telepathy, the entire process takes place in the material realm of consciousness and is substantially less complicated.

The thought transmitter sends the thought currents to the receiving person in the form of sentences or words. As incredible as this may sound, these thought currents vibrate as intermittent impulses to the receiver, who receives them with his antenna, that is to say, with both auricles (ears).[30]

The ultra-high vibrations of thought currents are of such high frequency that they cannot yet be detected by our contemporary technology. Man, however, is receptive to and can transform the messages received into intelligible interpretations if they have developed the necessary spiritual abilities. Being ignorant of this fact, it is often assumed that transmitted thoughts resound as an inner voice somewhere in the conscious or subconscious mind. However, this does not correspond to the facts. It is, rather, so that the receiver hears the voice of the person sending the thought inside his head. Nevertheless, human receivers are unable to analyze precisely the area where this voice is located in their head.

Although thought currents are inaudible to the untrained and underdeveloped human ear and recording centers, the vibrations are absolutely real and are received in precisely the same way as acoustical tones are transformed and made audible. The difference to acoustical hearing is that the telepathic voice, when perceived, is a mere whisper in the material consciousness.

Spirit Telepathy

As the name suggests, spirit telepathy is of purely spiritual nature and consequently has unlimited range. It can be referred to as a universal language that enables communication among human life forms throughout the endless expanse of the universe. The process can simply be depicted, as follows:

To start with, every call by means of spirit telepathy commences with a personal code sent to the person designated for conversation. If that person is willing to participate, then the sender transmits his thoughts from his material conscious mind into his material subconscious, which transforms them into symbol pictures. The pictures are radiated out with the help of spirit power as electromagnetic impulses to the receiver at a rate of umpteen-times the speed of light.

In the subconscious of the receiver, the electromagnetic impulses are transformed back into symbol pictures and passed on to the material consciousness, which then translates them into normal language.

Another way electromagnetic impulses are manifested is as soft whispering in the cerebral cortex that penetrate the material consciousness as inaudible thoughts. The spirit telepathy practiced by the Pleiadians functions with the incredible number of 50.2 million symbolic signs. Whoever masters this universal language can make himself understood in the entire universe. That is possible, of course, only for those who are in command of this spirit telepathy. All in all, it is a very complicated process.

There is only one hindrance for this type of communication, and that is the spiritual blockade a person can build around himself by completely shielding himself externally so that no one is capable of establishing telepathic contact with him.

Basic Concepts:
Transmission and Teleportation

If persons or objects disappear from the scene without a trace and reappear "out of nowhere," so to speak, at a different location, this is known as "transmission" or "teleportation."

The transmission (teleportation) is visually illustrated by trick photography in the well-known science-fiction film "Spaceship Enterprise" and is described by the term "beaming." There is a distinction of meaning between controlled and uncontrolled transmissions:

- **Controlled Transmission** – Is a super-fast transport of a body (living being, spacecraft, etc.) from one location to another through dematerialization and rematerialization by the use of a teletransmitter machine, using natural or artificial energies — knowingly and consciously set into action. *(See end of teleportation chapter)*

    ### Examples of a Controlled Transmission:
    This is a contact procedure of the extraterrestrials in which persons of earthly or extraterrestrial origin are "beamed" from any location directly into a spacecraft or, conversely, from a ship to somewhere else.

Of course, all objects can also be transported in this manner. For example, Quetzal (a Pleiadian base commander) "beamed" a sack full of Pleiadian potatoes into Billy's office.

An earthly example is the "Philadelphia Experiment," (provided that it actually took place, which does not seem to be certain.) Supposedly in 1943, an American naval ship suddenly disappeared from the Philadelphia harbor in front of numerous observers. This was due to an alleged experiment that "beamed" a vessel about 640 kilometers (397 miles) to a different location. This incident was repeated back and forth several times. When the experiment was finally stopped, a large part of the ship's crew was missing and the few remaining survivors became mentally deranged or perished.

- **Uncontrolled Transmission** – This type of transmission is super-fast and transports a body from one place to another through dematerialization and rematerialization with the help of natural or artificial energies and is not knowingly generated by human life forms.

- This can also be brought about through: The explosion of a supernova, electromagnetic storms in universal space (relatively frequent), or solar eruptions.

- The formation of dimension portals, as was the case with the Bermuda Triangle up until July of 1977, also in Madagascar and in Japan's Devil's Sea.

Teleportation

A distinction is made here between material as well as spiritual teleportation.

- **Physical Teleportation** – This form also transports a body super-fast (living being, spaceship, etc.) from one location to another through dematerialization and rematerialization with the help of forces of the material conscious mind, thus, without technical means, as follows:

  - triggered consciously by the material conscious mind, or

  - triggered unconsciously by the material subconscious mind.
    (See ~ An Explanation of Dematerialization and Rematerialization)

Examples of An Unconsciously Triggered Physical Teleportation:

- A tribesman was once threatened by a lion. He was seized by mortal fear and wished he could be standing before the hut of his village at home. As a result of his extraordinarily strong feelings of anxiety, his wish actually was fulfilled and he was suddenly teleported into his home village no less than 3,000 kilometers (1,860 miles) away. A disagreeable side effect was that the hair on his head turned snow-white overnight.

- Kalliope, Billy's wife, was going to school in Greece. She had taken an excursion one fine day with her school class into the catacombs. Having arrived at the grave of a saint while sightseeing in the underground vaults the girls of the class stood in line and waited until everyone could pass the grave. As it happened, every schoolgirl was to kiss the glass lid of the coffin while walking by. When it was Kalliope's turn for her kiss, she suddenly found herself standing in the garden before the church doors. What had happened? Based on a strong repugnance against kissing the glass lid, such powerful forces mobilized from within her material subconscious that she teleported herself outside.

Spiritual Teleportation

Such teleportation is super fast and transports a body from one place to another through dematerialization and rematerialization — with the help of spiritual forces of consciousness (without technical aid). In fact, it is set off quite consciously.

If a person is able to teleport such objects as themselves, a spaceship or any other bodies substantially larger over great distances, they must be on an enormously high rung of spiritual evolution. Immense spirit forces are necessary for this. Quite often, a number of spirit forms join together to form a spiritual block in order to reach the desired goal through combined efforts.

An Explanation of Dematerialization and Rematerialization

This mysterious process is used in every transmission and teleportation for superfast transportation of a body from one place to another.

The following three steps take place:

1. In a dematerialization, a body of coarse matter[31] in normal space separates or dematerializes into its component parts in a flash. This means it is transformed into energy (super-fine matter).

2. The energy of the dematerialized body builds an energy packet, which is instantly transported from one place to another. This occurs continuously in a superordinated (Cartisian coordinates) space, which is instantly transported from normal space to hyperspace. In this manner, the energy packet is preserved as an independent and compact unit without mixing with other energies in space.

3. In a rematerialization, the energy packet transforms itself back into a coarse or physical material, which means that the body recomposes itself in a flash at the destination point in normal space.

The entire process is so unimaginably fast that practically no loss of time occurs. One meter-thick (3 feet) concrete walls, steel walls, etc. are of no more hindrance than tremendous distances.

Dematerialization and rematerialization are used, as follows:

- Controlled transmission (also known as "beaming" or "teleportation")
- Uncontrolled transmission
- Material (physical) teleportation
- Spiritual teleportation
- Universal space travel with the use of the hyperspace jump
- Time journeys

Once the process is underway, everything automatically functions as quickly as lightning, so nothing can be corrected any more. Therefore, programming must be absolutely precise in every respect since catastrophic and irreparable mishaps can otherwise occur.

For each body, something similar to a "composition blueprint" is needed in order that, after the dematerialization of the body, the energy packet will rematerialize precisely down to the last detail and the original state of the body will actually be reproduced. Dematerialization and reassembling must be absolutely synchronized. Otherwise, unpleasant surprises would occur, even if only minute subsections of the body were reproduced too early or too late. Serious mistakes in locality can cause time-travelers to be lost forever in space and time. A little carelessness can have very grave consequences, even with "beaming" over a short distance. It is possible that a person could rematerialize in a deep ravine or on a rugged ledge instead of at home. It certainly would not end as fortunately as the time when Billy was "beamed back" to the earth's surface from a Pleiadian spacecraft with the help of a teletransmitter machine and landed on the top of a fir tree.

We must be clear that this is by no means a merely physical process. That is why we have been given just a hint of an explanation about these basic physical concepts for our perusal, just as there is for other phenomena.

One should, therefore, by no means imagine the dematerialization of a body of coarse (physical) matter as a conventional type of explosion. With an explosion, the body would literally be ripped into thousands of pieces and be completely destroyed. The original body could no longer be reassembled from these fragments into its natural form.

This is neither an explosion nor an implosion, and no vacuum is caused, either. Unfortunately, we lack the conceptual tools that are vitally necessary to precisely describe or explain the actual process.

Footnotes

24 ▪ At the time of his death, Sfath was the ripe old age of approximately 900 years old!

25 ▪ See *Chapter 15* for clarification of two photographs of Asket.

26 ▪ The photographic evidence that shows landing track marks were deliberately made by Pleiadian spacecraft for demonstration purposes only. Their crafts rarely have a need to physically land.

27 ▪ By comparison, an apprentice cannot simply leave out or skip over a half-year of apprenticeship without jeopardizing the success of their entire training.

28 ▪ The brain-wave patterns of friendly persons can be stored in the selective warning device just as in the specialized navigation system. After storage, the persons in question can be immediately identified at any time and recognized as friends.

29 ▪ Half-spirit forms, half-spirit beings

30 ▪ The process is similar to a technical radio transmission.

31 ▪ "Coarse matter" can also be considered "physical matter."

Daytime Demonstrations
by the Extraterrestrials

Spacecraft Landing Tracks

For quite some time now, it has not been a secret that extraterrestrial space vehicles land on earth. From time to time, they leave some type of tracks behind, such as expansive landing surfaces or impressions on the ground: footprints, bent branches, depressed shrubbery, diverse radiation and similar things.

If we are fortunate enough to discover such traces, we have an opportunity to conduct a thorough investigation on the spot. And as is customary in our materially oriented society, anything that can be perceived by our senses (especially if it can be measured) has the best chance of being acknowledged as a reality. Therefore, measurable landing tracks serve as excellent means of proof that cannot simply be brushed aside.

In view of this fact and on the basis of his suggestion, Billy's extraterrestrial friends declared themselves willing on occasion to offer that kind of evidence. In general, it is not customary for the Pleiadians to touch the ground when landing, not even when a pilot wants to leave the vehicle. Instead, the spacecraft simply hovers close to the earth without creating any Erran ship landing tracks. However, they did leave about one dozen landing tracks that we were able to inspect at various locations in the Zurich Highlands. None of these were made by accident or carelessness, but were made with full intention to serve as a means of proof.

The appearance and nature of the landing tracks in question would depend on the propulsion system of the space vehicle. As for the landing tracks in the Zurich Highlands, it is a matter of two completely different kinds of track, which will be referred to as *Landing Tracks #1* and *Landing Tracks #2*.

Landing Tracks #1

See ~ Photos #31–#36

Landing Tracks #1 were made by Menara's[32] ship. They show a circular landing surface 3.5 meters (12 ft.) in diameter and appear to be geometrically precise, as if drawn with a compass.

In the summer of 1976, we had the pleasure of having a look at two such circular landing areas at one time, which were next to each other in a meadow near Hinwil (Ambitzgi).[33] Billy showed us the very same type of landing tracks that were in front of a small woodshed in Blitterswil (Oberi Ebni, Juckern) right after he had returned from one of his personal contacts in the late afternoon of October 2, 1976. Although the grass was discolored and badly scorched all around this very recent track, our noses could detect almost no burnt smell during inspection and examination. A physicist who had hoped to detect radioactivity with his Geiger counter had to give up his plans without result. A further peculiarity was discovered on the following day during further inspection — the landing surface must have had a magical attraction for ants. How else could one explain the great number of these industrious insects actively crawling around within the landing surface, whereas no trace of them was found outside of it?

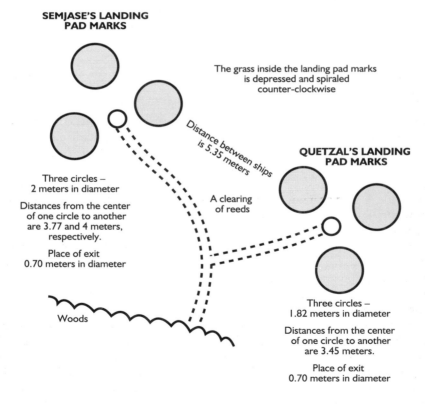

Fig. 6-1
Landing Tracks were left behind in the grass by two Pleiadian beamships
Monday, June 26th, 1976 at 5:30 P.M.

On each of the winter days of November 23, 1977 and February 21, 1978, one such track was laid directly in front of Billy's residence in Hinterschmidrüti. In this cold time of the year, the entire place was covered by a 10–12 centimeters (4–5 in.) thick layer of ice. But as a result of the very hot gas flow that radiated from Menara's ship, the ice had melted almost completely down to the ground at the landing site. In this connection, there is something else worthy of mention. The track of November 23, 1977 was made during a lightning-fast visit of Menara. In fact, the visit took place within 10 minutes, the exact time it took for Billy's wife, Kalliope, to take one of her children to the nearby school and return home. A skeptic would have to figure out how it would be possible for Billy, a one-armed man, to melt such a large area of ice within 10 minutes in broad daylight without being seen by anyone.

Landing Tracks #2
See ~ Photos #37–#44
In various meadows throughout the Hinwil area (Betzholz, Bäretswil, Wetzikon, Adelsriet, Ettenhausen, as well as in Hinterschmidrüti), Semjase, Quetzal and Menara left *Landing Tracks #2* of a 7-meter (23 ft.) Pleiadian ship for observers to admire.

Such landing tracks are made when a Pleiadian ship extended three landing legs from its underside and touched down with its plate-shaped feet directly on the ground. These legs are arranged in triangular form, and each plate produced a circular imprint of about 2 meters (7 ft.) in diameter. Especially impressive were the areas that resembled gigantic circular footprints in the high grass of a meadow. The individual blades were pressed flat against the ground and formed a spiral-shaped counter-clockwise pattern.[34]

We know that grass blades pressed to the ground by a stormy wind (or any other cause) usually rise after awhile and continue to grow. Normally, only dead grass becomes discolored, dries out and remains flat on the ground.

It is baffling to note that the grass blades flattened by the Pleiadian landing gear were neither broken nor otherwise damaged. Furthermore, they retained their original color. But this grass never straightened and continued growing horizontally along the ground as if nothing had happened. New growth quite simply pushed its way through the flattened grass and grew vertically in height, although not as high or as thick as the untouched grass around it.

Our findings showed that the flat blades of grass remained on the ground for weeks, provided, of course, that the meadow was not cut before then. With such a landing track on one's own property in Hinterschmidrüti, it was possible to observe the area for an entire quarter year before the fresh grass completely covered the flattened blades.

The landing tracks that particularly pleased me were the ones left behind in June of 1976 by both Semjase's and Quetzal's spacecraft in a narrow clearing of the Pilgerholz woods overgrown with knee-high reeds. At both landing areas (consisting of three plate imprints each), there were also imprints of slender footprints leading to the southern edge of the wooded clearing. According to Billy's information, the extraterrestrial visitors disembarked there. An exact measurement of the footprints of Quetzal and Semjase's sister, Pleija, showed shoe sizes of 30 centimeters (12 in.) and 26 centimeters (10 in.).

Billy also told us that Pleija definitely wanted to take a ride on his moped, so after he showed her the necessary hand motions, she could no longer be stopped and away she went. At any rate, she had a lot of fun on that short practice drive.

For better understanding, I have included a sketch made by Hans Schutzbach.

And now, back to the landing track on Billy's property. On June 15, 1980, located several hundred meters beyond his residence in Hinterschmidrüti and situated directly at the edge of the woods, we found a track unlike any other landing track we had seen before. It looked as if a whirlwind had swept over it. We promptly received an appropriate explanation from Billy. As he told us, Semjase had landed her space vehicle on this spot during heavy rain showers and a stormy wind. And because weather conditions worsened after her landing, she covered her entire ship all the way around with a security bubble of energy. By doing this, she had "killed three flies with one strike." Firstly, no outsider was able to see the landed vehicle. Secondly, the energy security bubble functioned like a gigantic umbrella, which deflected the torrential downpour to the side. And thirdly, the crew felt as if they were in a Faraday cage — absolutely safe and secure while the tempest raged on outside, accompanied by flashing bolts of lightning and rumbling thunderclaps.

Semjase gave yet another demonstration for Billy that also made a powerful impression. She asked him, jokingly, if he wanted to step outside. Somewhat astonished, Billy drew her attention to the fact that he was not really wearing the most appropriate clothing for stepping out onto the soaking wet turf.[35]

SEMJASE: That is no problem, my friend. Wait a moment.

Semjase presented him with a pleasant surprise. Within a few seconds, she made the flooded turf as dry as if the sun had been shining for many hours. She then let Billy step outside so he could experience the transformation. Billy's reaction to this speaks for itself.

BILLY: Ah, fantastic! Everything is really dry … Uuh, up there, it's raging violently, and the lightning! Man, oh man! It's like a blazing inferno!

Semjase finally added:

SEMJASE: Here, under this protective shield, you can see everything much more sharply and clearly than is possible outside of it.

As a general comment, it can be added that all of the landing tracks were seen and partially photographed by several witnesses, including me.

As for the puzzling nature of the flattened blades of grass, which never returned to a normal vertical position, it was explained in a contact conversation that this effect can be traced to the influence of the anti-gravity propulsion. The Pleiadian ships are equipped with and use such propulsion systems when operating within a planetary region.

A Reported Experience – *By Herbert Runkel*
See ~ Photos #43–#44

On the night of Saturday, June 15, 1980, Billy Meier and I were sitting in the kitchen discussing many topics over a few cups of coffee and a small snack. Shortly before midnight, Billy interrupted the conversation. A familiar smile flitted across his face.

"Is it something special?" I asked.

"No, no," answered Billy, "I shall have company this evening."

"In this lousy weather," I replied, "that can be a pretty mess."

He briefly shrugged his shoulders and then we continued our conversation as if nothing had happened. After we had brewed fresh coffee, Billy looked at his watch and said he had to go.

"Wear something sensible," I said, "or else you'll get soaking wet in this thunderstorm."

"That's all right. So long!" Billy left the kitchen.

A few minutes later, I went outside under the canopy of the farmhouse. The night sky was ablaze with unending bolts of lightning flashing through the low-hanging clouds as torrents of rain pelted down. I lit a cigarette and observed this rare spectacle of nature. After a while, I went back into the kitchen and eagerly awaited Billy's return.

One hour and several minutes had passed when the kitchen door swung open and Billy came in, looking exactly the way he had left, wearing dry light summer trousers, a shirt and sandals. (That is impossible, I thought to myself. How did he arrive at the place of contact without getting wet?) Billy greeted me and asked for a cup of coffee.

"I'm supposed to extend kind regards, and tomorrow we'll have something to photograph," he said and seated himself at the kitchen table.

"What will there be to photograph?" I asked.

"Semjase landed her ship, and I hope a few good tracks remain."

"In this rain, that's certainly impossible," I answered, "but in any case, I'll go down right after sunrise to take a look."

"We can do that," Billy said and drank his coffee. Then he told me a few things that were discussed with Semjase during the contact. As for myself, sleep was now the last thing on my mind. We continued our lively conversation into the wee hours of the morning. The thunderstorm had ceased raging and the cloud cover scattered. Soon the sun was shining over the horizon and we trudged along in our rubber boots to the location where the landing tracks were supposed to be.

The ground was wet and slippery. The grass was lying zigzag, forced to the ground by the heavy rain. But what was that over there? Indeed, there ahead, were three circles, each with a diameter of about 2 meters (7 ft.). The grass had been leveled in spiral formation from the inside to the outside in a counter-clockwise direction. Chaos prevailed everywhere else, but the grass here was lying in a "clean" spiral-shaped order on the ground.

I started photographing immediately, although the daylight was still somewhat inadequate.

"How long was the ship standing here?" I asked Billy, who was also taking photographs with his camera.

"Oh, just about half an hour, I think," Billy replied. "It looks good."

"You can sure say that again," I answered. The sun slowly rose high and the light conditions improved appreciably. The first roll of film was full, and I put a second 36-frame roll of film into my camera in order to take more photos of the landing tracks. It was simply fantastic, although it was not my first time witnessing such an incident.

The photographs that I took at that time still exist today, and whoever wants to see them can do so.[36]

Uninterrupted Beaming

As already discussed in *Chapter 3*, the extraterrestrials quite frequently use methods of controlled transmission, transporting Billy or themselves in a flash from one place to another with the help of the teletransmitter machine. Much to our joy, the Pleiadians conducted such transmissions a number of times, especially for demonstration purposes, and these were seen and admired by several witnesses. Here are a couple of examples:

Disappeared Without a Trace –
An experience filed in the archives by Engelbert Wächter - abridged
The following incident took place at the onset of constructing the Semjase Silver Star Center in Hinterschmidrüti:

The year of 1978, as well as the year before when we "took possession" of Hinterschmidrüti, was a very difficult period of intense hard work for us all. The surroundings and dwellings still were quite deteriorated. Improvements and renovations had to be made everywhere, including the shed. To start with, the previous owner had sorely neglected the roof. It had to be dealt with quickly. The rain leaked through all over and many parts of the beams had to be replaced. Billy formed a work group that included me. One day, I was ordered to the roof to replace a piece of the roof ridge and the outer roof rafter. My work was progressing well and had already reached the point where I began fitting the beams, which had been cut precisely to length and various angles, into the existing girders. I was standing high up on the ridge in order to make the last corrections before the final mounting of a heavy beam, when Billy called to me, "Carpenter, stand outside of the outer edge of the roof. You can hammer in the nails much better from there." As tempting as this advice may have been, I nonetheless "threw it to the winds." I did not have such good command of my spirit forces that I could simply stand way up next to the roof, simply standing in the air. A few minutes later, something completely unexpected took place.

I was standing upright on a narrow board as Billy brushed past my back, as lithe as a cat. As I looked around for him, he had disappeared without a trace! I first thought that he might have fallen from the roof but immediately rejected that notion, since I heard no impact. My colleagues working below me made no indication that someone had fallen or climbed down. It seemed as if Billy had very suddenly vanished into thin air. An immediate search operation within and beyond the shed remained unsuccessful despite an extensive search and loud calling.

About a half hour must have passed. We had resumed our work, when Billy suddenly came walking across the parking lot and very casually returned to his workplace as if nothing at all had happened. He met our curious questions of where in the world he had been with a meaningful smile and explained that Ptaah had beamed him into the ship via teletransmitter, as usual.

At this point, I would like to describe another incident that took place around the same time. Billy had wanted to tell me or show me something important, so he led me to his office. He opened the office door and stepped into the room while I followed close behind. At that moment, Billy walked past his desk. Then it happened again! Billy was suddenly no longer in the room! After inspecting every nook and cranny of the entire room and finding no trace of him, I left the office, undecided and with mixed feelings. I then remembered the incident on the roof and went back to my work.

As later revealed, Semjase had taken Billy, before my eyes, to a contact in her spacecraft with the help of a teletransmitter machine.

If Billy were trying to demonstrate to me a second time how rapidly a man could disappear with the help of very highly developed technology, it escaped my attention. I never asked about it, either.

Locked Out – *A brief report by Guido Moosbrugger*
On another occasion, Billy was beamed from his office onto a Pleiadian spacecraft after a brief advance telepathic call. At that time, both office doors were locked and the keys were sticking in the keyholes from the inside.

After the contact conversation, Billy was not transported back into his office but was set down in the hallway of his residence. You can imagine the rest of the story without much trouble. Since both entrances to the office, as already mentioned, were locked from the inside and no reserve keys were available, a skeleton key had to be specially made in order to get back into the office.

Footprints in the Snow – *A brief report by Guido Moosbrugger*
See ~ Photos #45 and #46
During the night of January 5, 1977, Billy had one of his numerous personal contacts with Semjase. After the contact, he asked her to do him a favor. Curious, she asked what he had in mind. Well, Billy actually wanted nothing more than to be dropped off in the middle of a snowy meadow just for the fun of it. Semjase was happy to fulfill his wish and thus beamed him via teletransmitter into the open country of a snow-covered meadow in Winkelriet, near Hinwil. From that place, he plodded through the snow to the next street. The one-way tracks of his footprints showed quite clearly the way he had taken.

As if by Magic – *Report by Jacobus Bertschinger ~ Part 2 - abridged*
On February 7, 1977, I drove Billy to a pre-announced contact with the beamship pilot, Semjase. Tired of waiting for him to return and the silence of the radio transmitter, I tried after a while to establish radio contact with my friend, Billy, who was in Semjase's spacecraft. But unfortunately, my effort was in vain.

I was startled when, as if by magic, a human form appeared in front of my car. It seemed to have just sprung out of the ground. This form first appeared like a ghost to me in my confusion, but my initial bewilderment soon subsided as I heard Billy's voice coming from the radio transmitter. He cheered me up with his jubilant words, "I'm back already, comrade!" Standing in front of my car was none other than my friend, Billy. He took a seat in the car, grinning from ear to ear, and said, "That surprised you, did it not?" Indeed, I could not deny this, since amazement was written all over my face for quite a while. Billy said that, while inside Semjase's ship and just before he was about to step into the exit shaft, he heard me calling him on the radio. From a height of about 8 meters (26 ft.) above the ground, the transport beam had set him down directly in front of my car simply because he had asked Semjase to do so just to see my flabbergasted face when he suddenly appeared before me as if by magic. His plan, unfortunately, came to naught because he could not see my face in the prevailing darkness.

Semjase gave a night demonstration during and after the return drive. Jacobus Bertschinger tells about it:

Coming from far in the west, an object as large as a soccer ball and shining brightly approached straight toward Hinwil. Billy did not allow me to enjoy the spectacle but asked me to drive him at once to his residence (still in Hinwil at that time) so we could watch Semjase's ship better from there. Well, he should have known better, since two minutes later we reached his residence. His family members, whom he had notified via radio, were all standing outside and watching, completely fascinated by the spacecraft that was shining like a small full moon as it approached. Several groups of people were standing in the streets of their neighborhoods, staring at the passing ship that flew by without a sound. About 3 minutes later, it turned toward a northeasterly direction and disappeared behind a wooded hillside.

I can vouch at any time for the correctness and truthfulness of my statements, even though I run the risk of being called a "crackpot." The truth remains the truth, and that is an unalterable fact.

Night Duty In the Schönberg Region (ZH) during Rain and Mud –
An experience reported by Engelbert Wächter from February 20, 1977 - abridged
Late one evening on February 20, 1977, I, (Engelbert Wächter), Jacobus Bertschinger, Bernadette Brand and Billy were driving in two cars through the pouring rain in the direction of Horgen/Hirzel to bring Billy to an arranged contact site.

After a swampy and hellish drive over a stretch of about 80 meters (264 ft.), we finally reached our destination. After one last check of the radio transmitter, Billy groped his way from tree trunk to tree trunk through the pitch-dark woods, then vanished from our sight.

No sooner had Billy disappeared, when we began to frantically scurry about. To start with, both cars had to be turned around in the swamp-like mire, which was truly no minor undertaking considering the torrential downpour of rain and the soaked, slippery ground. (Our driver, Jacobus, can rest assured that he will always have our sincere gratitude for his feat on that night.)

After swinging the cars around, we had to mount the snow chains in order to be able to leave the swampy terrain. We then stood at the edge of the woods under the protective treetops and waited for Billy's return. The flooding rain splashed down in a harmony of sound. Beating in time, the heavy drops from the dripping trees ran down the backs of our necks and gradually turned our clothes into wet sacks. Every now and then, the wind trifled with the treetops, releasing a true cascade of water. This rain certainly did not contribute to the improvement of our roadway as a small lake was slowly forming around our cars.

While Jacobus was still trying to tighten the chains in the fading light of a pocket lamp, the excited screech of a tawny owl penetrated the dusky woods and two other animals joined in. Seconds later, a peculiar rushing sound filled the air that soon changed into an unfamiliar singing or whirring noise.

We realized what it was — the spacecraft of our mutual friend and mediator of age-old truths, Semjase, with our friend Billy on board. It slowly moved past our heads at a low altitude. No sooner had the whirring faded away over the tops of the fir trees when Billy, to our complete surprise, suddenly appeared in our midst. He was beaming with happiness and wearing absolutely dry clothes despite the rain that was still pelting down. His dry leather coat now gradually became wet and started to shine in the brightness of our cars' headlights. But how could it have been any other way? In Semjase's beamship he was naturally protected from the rain because, as we had learned, no one gets wet in the course of being transmitted by a teletransmitter.

After Billy's return, both vehicles were joined in great haste by a towing rope to tow the smaller car without chains out of the deep mud. Around 1 o'clock in the morning, we heartily took leave of one another in Wädenswil and all drove home in raised spirits despite the mud bath and showery adventure.

Is it a wonder, dear reader, that our mutual friend, Semjase, granted a "small earthworm" like me the gift of a grandiose aerobatic interlude on her beamship in a dream that I had later on.

Incomprehensible for Strangers –
Reported by Engelbert Wächter - abridged

I had hardly reached the roof of our new hen house on Monday, September 21, 1981. I was carrying a chisel and saw to make a few beams fit when I caught sight of Billy as he went off in a vigorous march over the Schmidrüti/Sitzberg Field to a new contact in the direction of "Whirring Meadow.[37]"

I quickly called a friendly greeting to him, which he returned with laughter and a raised hand as he entered the woods. Only a few minutes later, at about 7:20 p.m., I heard the unmistakable whirring of a beamship over the forest of fir trees. It was Quetzal who had called Billy to the contact.

The singing energies resonated for almost an entire minute throughout our high valley before suddenly quieting down and fading away.

After finishing my work on the roof, I seated myself comfortably and observed the Whirring Meadow at the edge of the woods opposite me. My glance darted high up along the giant firs before skimming back across the aforementioned meadow. One minute before 8 p.m. I heard Quetzal's beamship whirring again, and then another unexpected incident took place. Billy suddenly appeared from out of nowhere into the middle of the meadow and set out at a swift pace for the short walk home.

For strangers, this incident would be incomprehensible, but for us, it was almost a daily occurrence. Where there was nothing more than an empty meadow a moment before, there stood a living, benevolent man a moment later. Although we are accustomed to such demonstrations, we are nonetheless deeply impressed anew each time by the technological level of our extraterrestrial friends making such things possible.

To further enrich this documentation from a somewhat higher level, I would like to add a short extract here from the contact conversation between Quetzal and Billy:

QUETZAL: That is understandable, but you should go now, since I still have something to do, and I am bound by time.

BILLY: Naturally. Ah, do you see Engelbert down there? How would it be if you were to let me jump down there — into the middle of a beam he's working on, right in front of his very nose?

QUETZAL: That is too dangerous, my friend. Remember what happened in Winkelriet as you materialized on the top of a giant fir.

BILLY: That was really comical and an emergency landing, so to speak.

QUETZAL: For your sense of adventure, surely, but not for ours. I shall set you down in the middle of the Whirring Meadow and see to it that Engelbert catches sight of you immediately after the materialization, if you would like to surprise him that much.

BILLY: Okay, then forget it. Let me get out now.

QUETZAL: You know your own method of getting out very well, simply by free-falling into space, probably just for the thrill of it.

BILLY: How right you are. I'm just waiting for the moment when the dematerialization machine malfunctions once and I whiz like a rock to the ground as swift as an arrow. I'd like to see how quickly you'd react then and how you'd manage to keep me from being smashed into the ground.

QUETZAL: Your humor is often difficult to understand and not lastly because you superbly understand how to interweave humor and reality, just like now. You joke around and at the same time actually wish that such a situation would occur. Fortunately, I must explain that in this regard it would be impossible for you to jump into the dematerialization hatch if there would be danger of a malfunction, which will never be the case. An energy field would hold you back from the opening.

BILLY: Aha, but if that too were to malfunction?

QUETZAL: You are unrelenting, but it is absolutely impossible.

BILLY: Really absolutely?

QUETZAL: Absolutely.

Extraterrestrial Dwarves (Gnomes)

Among the one dozen or so extraterrestrial races who work together with the Pleiadians and were stationed here on earth, dwarves 115-centimeters (46 in.) tall who reside on a neighboring planet near Erra, were also mentioned.

Their task was to study radiation phenomena and to sound out subterranean displacements that materialize in the earth's interior as a result of various factors and which will influence those regions in the future. In our Center in Hinterschmidrüti, they were specifically busy with totally neutralizing the negative radiation that had accumulated over the years within the residential area. Four of these helpful "brownies" conducted a large-scale housecleaning on February 13, 1977 in the Hinterschmidrüti residence — a job that took several hours to complete. As announced by Semjase beforehand, there was supposed to be a small surprise for us on this occasion, about which Bernadette wrote in a report about her experience.

Semjase's announcement was word-for-word, as follows:

SEMJASE: Out of gratitude, we are always working for you. In less than fourteen days, we will provide photographic evidence to you.

A Strange Little Experience – *Report by Bernadette Brand*
See ~ Photos #47 and #48

Early in the afternoon on Sunday, February 13, 1977, I drove along with Billy, Jacobus Bertschinger, Engelbert Wächter and his wife Maria to Hinterschmidrüti to take a look at the new domicile for Billy, his family and the group members.

Billy and Jacobus had already been to Hinterschmidrüti early that same morning in order to pump out the dirty water from the basement that was almost up to the ceiling. A while after we arrived, the basement was finally emptied, except for a few remaining puddles, and Billy went down to check out the condition of the basement walls. In the meantime, we all stood chatting in front of the basement steps and waited for him, keeping an eye on the basement door.

Then, after a very short while, he emerged with an impish grin and told us that he had found a single small footprint in the north corner of the basement when he was inspecting it a second time. One could tell from his explanation that he had not seen the footprint in question just a few seconds before, during his first check, but it had been left there in the short interval between his two inspections. According to his description, there were not two footprints but only a single one, and it was merely the size of a child's foot, which he explicitly stressed several times. It was really quite strange, since tracks of two shoes should have been left behind in the soft clay of the basement floor if someone had been there. A child could not have gone into the basement, at least not while Billy was there, and would definitely have been seen by us.

Although it was obvious something very peculiar had really happened to Billy and although I reacted as if I were astonished and filled with enthusiasm, I was still secretly suspicious and doubted his description. I searched for a way to convince myself with my own eyes, and since I usually have my loaded photo camera in my car, such a way was indeed open to me. However, misfortune decreed that, of all times, I had forgotten to replace the film. Even worse, I neither had an extra film or a flash unit with me. In a subdued manner, I confessed my stupidity to Billy and he was generous enough to lend me his own camera with a built-in flash so I could go ahead and take the photographs.

Together, we went down into the cellar. The other three persons remained outside and continued to discuss what Billy had reported. Billy and I were all alone in the dim cellar that was now very faintly illuminated by light coming through the open cellar door and a tiny window opening. Occasionally, a bright beam of light from Billy's portable lamp illuminated the cellar and was directed slowly over the ground, along the walls and into every corner, even to the furthermost northern corner where the footprint had been found. Indeed, there was only this one, small, strangely shaped shoe impression in the entire cellar. After carefully inspecting it in the light of Billy's lamp, I proceeded to take photos from all sides of the footprint with Billy's camera. The last of four photographs was taken from a distance of about 1.5 meters (5 ft.), measured from the footprint to where I was standing. Indeed, for a moment, I distinctly had a very strong inclination to turn around and take another photograph from where I was standing straight across the cellar towards the door, but then rejected this notion because I was secretly afraid of making myself ridiculous in front of Billy. How could I have explained to him my impulse to simply shoot a picture into the void, since I was of the opinion that there was nothing more to be found in the cellar.[38]

After I had taken the photos, Billy and I left the cellar to join the others. Presuming to have done my best, I was only superficially interested in these photographs and one or two days later no longer thought about the incident. But the photos regained importance the evening of February 19, 1977 when Billy interrupted my work and asked me to take a look at the recently developed pictures. He also asked Mrs. von Jacobi, a visiting friend, to come along. When I asked whether the photos had turned out at all, he told me that, in addition to the footprint, a helmet and part of a dwarf's shoulder also appeared in the last photo.

I was quite skeptical, since I could not remember seeing anything other than the footprint while taking the photographs. When I saw the photo projected on the AV screen, I was baffled and scarcely able to understand what I had actually photographed. Somewhat to the left and above the center of the photo was the footprint in the cellar clay, and in the right lower corner was a somewhat blurred contour of a helmet, a type of antenna on top of the helmet, and a shoulder. Everything appeared to be entwined with light-gray, gleaming metal strips. The flash of the camera reflecting off the ribbon-like metal threads of the uniform must have blurred the photo at the moment it was taken. The figure that had unexpectedly crept into my photo must have been standing slightly to the right in front of me as I positioned the camera to see the footprint through the lens. To put it mildly, I was more than astonished. I was bewildered for a moment, not comprehending what I was seeing and without realizing that I, myself, actually had the honor of taking this picture. The truth gradually dawned on me, followed by one question after another. Billy patiently explained that the ribbon-like glimmer of the suit in the picture came from mirror-like strips in the dwarf's suit, which served the purpose of making him invisible. Billy also explained that the figure was a dwarf of about 112–115 centimeters (45–46 in.) in size and that this dwarf race worked together with Semjase and her people. What was most astonishing and occupied my thoughts was the fact that I had neither seen anything or anyone else while taking the photos. The following are concluding remarks by Billy:

> **BILLY:** Of the four dwarves present but made invisible, only one of them, unfortunately, could be captured on film. That particular dwarf had made himself visible only during the exposure time needed to take the picture. For this reason, Bernadette was also unable to catch sight of the dwarf with her snapshot.

Not an Everyday Radio Call
As if by Magic –
Report by Jacobus Bertschinger – Part#1 - somewhat abridged
It was the 7th of February 1977 around 6 p.m., and I was driving towards Ottikon with Edi (my nickname for Eduard Meier) to a pre-arranged contact with the beamship pilot, Semjase. I parked my car on a wooded trail. Then Edi got out and walked

in a southeasterly direction to the contact location. I stayed behind in the car and waited. About 15 minutes later, my friend unexpectedly spoke to me through the radio transmitter. That is to say, I felt myself spoken to. Edi was obviously trying to establish contact with the home station, but he did not succeed since the station was not occupied at that moment.[39]

Furthermore, his voice could scarcely be heard over the radio transmitter, which is why I asked permission to speak and pointed out to my friend that the connection left much to be desired. Edi replied that he was in Semjase's spacecraft and would ask her to establish a better connection. Several seconds later, the connection was perfect. Billy's voice was then clear and easy to hear, but in a deeper pitch than usual. Billy said he had detected me on the viewing screen and would direct me to a new location via radio transmitter.

Consequently, I started my car and drove in accordance with Edi's instructions to a rise at the edge of the woods, from which I had an excellent panoramic view. Deep in thought, I sat behind the steering wheel and stared into the clear night. Suddenly, Edi's deep voice rang out again from the transmitter, asking whether I could see the ship located at that point directly over the Kloten Airport. Unfortunately, it was only barely visible as an oval-shaped light disk, which is why I objected to its unsatisfactory appearance. Edi only laughed and replied that Semjase would turn on more light right away. In only 2–3 seconds, the distant spacecraft suddenly started to glow radiantly. I then caught sight of it and observed the glowing object slowly flying away in the direction of Zurich until it disappeared from my field of vision.

My Experience of January 4, 1978 – *Report by Guido Moosbrugger*

As was often the case, I visited the Semjase Silver Star Center in Hinterschmidrüti for a few days at the beginning of the year. On the evening of January 4, 1978, I sat in the warm living room while a snowstorm raged outside and an ice-cold wind swept around the house. Not one of us in the house would've had the notion, even in a dream, to abandon this haven without a compelling reason. But we in FIGU have never been without surprises, so on that very evening events turned out differently from what had been expected. All of a sudden, the "Pleiadian telephone" rang at 9:30 p.m., which means Billy received a person-to-person telepathic call from Quetzal to arrange a contact.

Afterward, Billy called on Jacobus and me to "get everything ready for the contact!" In view of the miserable weather, this request struck like a bolt from out of the blue, but nonetheless, we quickly rose to our feet and set about making the necessary preparations. We put on our weatherproof clothing and thought about which vehicle we wanted to use. After brief consideration, we decided the Volkswagen was best able to meet the demands of the winter weather conditions. We installed our transmitter and eagerly scraped the unwelcome crusts of ice from the windshield. A quarter hour later, the vehicle was in front of the house and ready to go.

Jacobus seated himself at the wheel with Billy next to him on the passenger side and I took a seat in back. We started our drive to an unknown "destination X." On the way, Billy received continuous telepathic directions from the piloting device in Quetzal's spacecraft and gave our driver instructions in which direction he should drive. Although our way was hindered by a heavy blizzard and especially by partially iced-up roads covered with slush, our high spirits could not be dampened.

After a half-hour drive, we reached our destination. We stopped in front of a small bridge at the exit of a wooded area and parked by a narrow wooded trail. From previous experience, Jacobus and I knew exactly what to do. At that point, we were near the contact site and would have to wait for the return of the contactee. Billy got out of the car, hung his radio transmitter over his shoulder and took his leave. With some difficulty, he plodded over a meadow covered with newly fallen snow and straightway headed for a path located higher up. But then what happened? Billy suddenly disappeared from the scene without a trace. Well, Jacobus and I thought instantaneously… "just another one of those lightning-fast actions, as usual!" And indeed, Billy had been transported with lightning speed into the cockpit of Quetzal's spacecraft, which was hovering in the air invisibly and noiselessly. This was nothing special for Billy, since he had often experienced such transmissions.

All at once, Billy's voice called out from our radio transmitter but with a deeper and somewhat darker sound than usual. His radio message was coming from inside of the Pleiadian ship. (Jacobus had already experienced this change of tone on earlier occasions.) Billy's radio message directed us to drive to the nearest homes. He would come down to us at once. As we arrived, Billy suddenly landed with a mighty leap from the slope of the road right in the middle of the street and immediately climbed into our car. Quetzal had dropped him off with the teletransmitter device on the slope of the roadside near our car. We had since ceased to be amazed at the very few snowflakes that could be detected on his leather coat or his Texan hat, although it was snowing heavily. But how could it have been otherwise, since it is commonly known that no snow falls inside a spacecraft?

In retrospect, I still wonder why Billy would leave his residence in that nasty weather to endure such a difficult and troublesome detour, only to be finally beamed into the spacecraft anyway. Quetzal could just as well have transmitted him from his dwelling rather than from the snowfield. It would have been much easier for all concerned.

Well, besides the fact that Jacobus and I would have had one less demonstration to record, the measures taken were somehow related to Billy's failing health. Due to permanent over-taxation through work and business of every kind, his free time was always short and he took far too little notice of his own well being. Therefore, he always lacked the necessary sleep, and especially adequate exercise and fresh air. Repeated reminders from the Pleiadians to pay more attention to his health and to at least take walks as often as possible were almost never heeded, since the fulfillment of his mission left very little time for such things, to his own detriment. His state of health continued to deteriorate from year to year and was finally so ruined that a complete physical breakdown was actually only a question of time. In late fall of 1982, that point was finally reached and led to a tragic accident in the bathtub. Billy sustained a serious cerebral injury, the consequences of which he still suffers to some extent even today.

Unfortunately, the Pleiadians could not prevent this misfortune, although they did not only caution Billy but also forced him, so to speak, to exercise more in fresh air whenever possible, or to free himself now and then from the routine and monotony of daily life. That is why the Pleiadians often sent him to the contact site in all kinds of weather and oftentimes through impassable terrain. When Billy used his moped as a means of transportation to the place of contact, because of the impassable terrain, he often had to carry it over the last stretch to the spacecraft-landing site. Incidentally, the farthest distance from the place of contact was no less than 70 kilometers (43 miles). Occasionally, Billy was intentionally dropped off far away from the starting point so he would have to go back home by foot. Each and every one of these measures served the purpose of improving Billy's health. A brief excursion to Canada served exactly the same purpose. Billy trudged around in the snow with Quetzal for about two hours to "tank up" on fresh air and enjoy the scenic beauty. Unfortunately, the Pleiadians were also overtaxed with work; otherwise they certainly would have offered him such nice surprises more often.

Instructions by Radio Transmission from Semjase's Spacecraft –
Report by Guido Moosbrugger

On Saturday, May 20, 1978, Semjase finally appeared for a personal meeting with Billy after long weeks of absence. Her sister, Pleija, accompanied her. Around 2:15 p.m., Billy received a telepathic request from Semjase to stand by for contact. Half an hour later, he rattled off on his moped with the transmitter slung over his shoulder, as usual. Communication via transmitter proved to be successful in practice, since Billy could now establish contact at any time with the permanent base in the Center or the mobile transmitter installed in Jacobus' Volkswagen. The transmitter's long antenna rod gleamed in the sunshine on top of the VW parked in front of the residential dwelling in Hinterschmidrüti. As a result of the friendly spring weather, most of the group members present either worked in the garden, the meadow or somewhere else outdoors.

In the meantime, Billy was in Semjase's spacecraft located in close proximity to the Center. In the course of the contact conversation, he posed the following questions to Semjase and Pleija:

> **BILLY:** Well, say now, girls, couldn't we fly over to the Center and take a little peek at what's going on over there?
> **PLEIJA:** Certainly. Look, we are already there!
> **BILLY:** Can I use my radio to chat a little with them below?
> **SEMJASE:** Definitely, just connect your device. But please, I would not like to transmit this particular conversation later on.
> **BILLY:** You do not need to, girl. It's enough for me if I can chat a bit with them below. They'll be mighty surprised. Hello, Miranos 5.[40]

According to Billy, Semjase's space vehicle hovered at an altitude of about 700–1000 meters (2,300–3,300 ft.) directly above the Center. From that height, the entire Center could be splendidly seen and the activities of the group members observed in full detail. In the end, we owed our thanks for this situation to a small incident that I now would like to narrate.

Since the Pleiadian ship was shielded against optical detection, it indeed remained concealed from our searching eyes. Then Billy's voice abruptly sounded from the loud speaker of the VW transmitter. Billy's wife, Popi, who happened to be standing nearby, naturally took advantage of the opportunity and excitedly called back:

POPI: Miranos 1, Miranos 1, what's the matter?

Guido Moosbrugger continues: After initial communication difficulties resulting from radio static, Billy's voice suddenly sounded clear and pure but in a deeper tone. Billy then told his wife via transmitter to go into our garden behind the shed and plant strawberries in a very special place. In response to her question as to why, of all things, the seedlings should be planted at the very location where she had intended to plant something else, she received the answer that according to Semjase's explanation, the strawberries would grow and flourish there the best.

Engelbert and I were next to hear instructions from Billy. We were busy erecting a picket fence at the edge of the parking lot. One of us firmly held a sharpened wooden post upright so the other could ram it into the ground with the sledgehammer. Billy, who was watching us from the spacecraft, could not resist giving us exact instructions on where and how to erect the posts so they would be nicely vertical. Incidentally, Engelbert and I intentionally held the ramming posts at wrong angles a few times simply because it was so much fun to be corrected by an invisible teacher.

Not even the chickens that had gone under the parked cars in their diligent search for feed escaped Billy's eagle eyes. When Billy pointed them out to us, this fact was confirmed when we took a look.

Several of the group members soon had stiff necks from constantly gazing into the sky in the hope of catching a glimpse of Semjase's spacecraft. Pleija reacted to this futile undertaking with the words:

PLEIJA: Billy, your friends are all looking up at us.
BILLY: Yes, can they see us?
SEMJASE: No, their efforts are in vain, since the ship is shielded.

Unfortunately, it remained invisible. A skeptical spectator, to whom the entire story seemed rather peculiar, decided to climb up and look around "the pulpit," [41] because he presumed that Billy was hiding somewhere up there instead of actually being in the spacecraft. He thought he could catch Billy in the outrageous act of concealing himself up in the pulpit. Our good man simply had no luck, though. There is no location from which Billy could view all working places, let alone direct his instructions to us via transmitter, without being discovered.

The same is true for any observer who posts himself at an arbitrary point along the mountain road from Sitzberg towards Wila, since observation is also impossible from that perspective. Such a feat could only have been achieved from an observation point in a hovering spacecraft. As there was neither a balloon nor a helicopter in the area, the only other possibility was the Pleiadian ship, a fact the "thoroughly doubting Thomas" simply did not want to acknowledge.

An Extraordinary Speech – *Report by Guido Moosbrugger*

A number of times over the years, several group members had expressed the desire that Semjase might record a few sentences on tape so we could hear the sound of her voice at least once. One fine day, Billy presented this request to Semjase, but unfortunately, with no success. As far as I know, he tried one or two times to secretly record Semjase's voice with a pocket tape recorder hidden in a piece of clothing. To our regret, he did not succeed in this attempt, either, because Semjase discovered his intention early on. So it was astonishing to learn that in early 1983, Quetzal had planned to address our group via Billy's radio transmitter. Apparently, Quetzal wanted to make very confidential information known to us. I could not imagine any other reason for the Pleiadians' change of mind. As it later turned out, my expectation was fully confirmed, as I will now explain.

Since Quetzal was entrusted with diverse tasks and largely overburdened with work, several dates set for the radio transmission were postponed. At last it was agreed to set the final date for March 5,1983, the first Saturday of the month, when we would hold our monthly meeting in the group assembly hall. To say the least, our expectations grew from day to day and excitement continued to mount.

According to Quetzal's suggestion, we were supposed to use our radio transmitters, which had previously functioned very well, but due to special circumstances, problems arose for which we were not prepared.

Before this happened, I personally experienced a pleasant surprise when Billy had knocked at my trailer door shortly before 5:30 p.m. and invited me to accompany him. When asked what was the matter, he answered that a radio message from Quetzal was expected at 6:30 p.m. to test the quality of the radio connection. Of course, I gladly accepted this tempting invitation. We did not have to wait long for the promised event. We were only about 15 meters (50 ft.) away from the trailer, heading in an easterly direction, when it happened. Almost precisely to the second, a voice sounded from Billy's radio transmitter, but it was a female voice rather than a male voice. Instead of Quetzal, who had once again been delayed, it was Taljda[42] who called and talked a short while with Billy in flawless German with almost no accent as far as I could tell.

Afterwards, a man by the name of Solar[43] took over the conversation. Solar used a foreign language that I was unable to understand. Not surprisingly, Billy obviously had no problem communicating with Solar.

Much to our regret, this general rehearsal, if I may call it so, did not have the success hoped for. The transmitter sound level proved to be far too weak for our purpose. It would probably have been adequate for only a few listeners, but not for an entire group. We did not know what to do. We had to find a solution by 8:00 p.m. when our group members would arrive. After some thought, Billy suggested we use a loud speaker to solve the problem. In great haste, we laid a cable from the office over to the assembly hall in the shed. Then a new mishap occurred. Because of the unusual cold for that time of year, the cable froze in a drain that had been carefully scraped out for this purpose, but the stuck cable could not be pulled away from the spot. So this attempt also failed miserably.

A further postponement would've been inevitable if Billy had not come up with another idea at the last moment. No sooner said than done: he had Taljda transmit her message via radio into his office (from the Pleiadian earth station where she was located) and recorded the whole thing there on his recording tape. This simple procedure finally worked out as we had hoped. To the satisfaction of all who were present, the long-awaited event finally took place that same evening. As Billy played the tape recording, we were allowed for the first time since the beginning of the contacts to hear the speech of an extraterrestrial woman. Taljda, by the way, impressed all of the listeners to such an extent that they played the cassette two times in succession. Regarding Taljda, another small but revealing incident has occurred to me. I would not like to keep it from you because it supplies proof that higher-evolved extraterrestrials clearly display thoroughly human habits and are not so "supernatural," as they are often depicted on earth.

As stated by Billy, Taljda visited him several times in his office. Indeed, her presence could be easily detected after each visit — the office would be filled with a pleasant lemon fragrance for several days until it gradually evaporated. As said before, Taljda comes from planet Njssan, the atmosphere of which, according to her statement, has an intense fragrance very similar to our lemons. When Taljda sometimes stays here on earth in the course of fulfilling her mission, she likes to use a perfume with a lemon fragrance because she is pleasantly reminded of her home in this way. And why not?

Demonstration of Laser Beam Pistols

See ~ Photos #49–#52

During the course of the daytime demonstrations, Billy had the opportunity to examine the two different types of laser-beam pistols he had received on loan from Menara to test their functional capabilities.

The first test took place on September 29, 1976 in the area of Hinwil (Ambitzgi/Wetzikon). On that occasion, Billy shot a few twigs of shrubbery in half and then briefly fired at the trunks of two fir trees. They immediately caught fire, causing the resin to flow from their trunks.

For the second test, Billy became acquainted with a substantially older model during a personal contact with Menara and her fair-skinned girlfriend, Alena, on July 6, 1977 in Hinterschmidrüti. Menara parked her space vehicle in a state of suspension above the Semjase Silver Star Center in the broad afternoon daylight and was shielded against optical detection. Menara and Alena were then transported by teletransmitter from their space vehicle directly onto the parking lot in front of the Center's residential building.

Earlier the same morning, Menara had telepathically informed Billy to see to it that no person other than himself would be present in the Center's residential building or its immediate vicinity for the duration of the personal contact, which would last about one hour. Those personally acquainted with Billy know that this presented no problem for him. He simply sent everyone away from the Center to carry out orders or run errands of some kind. He hoped that these people would not return until the extraterrestrial visit was over. But due to an unpredictable circumstance, the visit did not work out as he had planned, though no damage worth mentioning was done to the event. As a security measure against unwelcome surprises, Menara used a special technology to construct a protective energy bell around the entire residential area. Consequently, no outsider was able to observe what was going on inside of the energy bell. Moreover, sensitive warning systems safeguarded the vicinity and indicated the approach of any persons or vehicles. It finally had to be considered that passers-bys, lumberjacks, etc. could come into close vicinity of the residential building, and there would be no alternative than to quickly remove the protective bell and call off the endeavor.

Despite all of these precautions, the participants in the deed took pains to stage the program as quickly as possible. A series of color photographs to be taken with a camera had been planned and at the same time a laser-pistol had been brought along for testing.

This project was almost completely carried out when it was prematurely interrupted. After a good half-hour, the warning system alarm sounded, detecting a vehicle drawing close to the Hinterschmidrüti residence. The two extraterrestrial women were suddenly very pressed for time. At any rate, before Billy could finish his sentence, Menara and Alena had quickly beamed themselves back into their space vehicle and quickly removed the protective energy bell. Consequently, everything returned to normal and no outsider knew what had just happened in Hinterschmidrüti.

Soon after the hurried departure of the two female visitors, the noisy sound of a motor resounded from the road and steadily increased as it approached the residence. Well, it was none other than Jacobus Bertschinger who came rattling along in his tractor and trailer, but without the cement he was supposed to procure from the neighboring village of Wila — the reason for his early return. He had not been able to acquire the desired sacks of cement.

Nevertheless, we were quite content with the outcome of the extraterrestrial visit. As far as the color slides were concerned, they turned out very well. However, the photos showed two distinct abnormalities. In one of them, the vertical corner wall of the residence, as well as the pole with the dog warning sign appeared unusually slanted, although both are perfectly in order and in a correct vertical position. In another photo, part of a tractor is seen in the background, although this vehicle was not at all located in Hinterschmidrüti when the picture was taken but was several kilometers away from the Center at the time. It is the same vehicle, which Jacobus B. was using to pick up the cement sacks in Wila.

At a later time, Billy let Menara explain these peculiarities to him, as follows:

MENARA: The appearance of the tractor resulted from a method of making all matter visible through infra-red radiation, a procedure yet unknown to you. Earth scientists are certainly advanced enough to be familiar with infra-red light and its great potential, such as its possible use to photographically record matter after its removal from the location hours or days before. Up to this point, earth technology has only been capable of capturing shadowy contours on film, whereas our technology is so advanced that an object can be reproduced in complete detail and true to nature long after having been removed from the scene.

The slant of the buildings came about through the simple fact that everything outside the range of radiation of the protective energy bell, appears blurry and distorted, whereas the tractor was within the immediate range of radiation.

Menara's explanations on the laser-pistols are very interesting and that is why I would like to add them here.

MENARA: Take a look at this gun, here. It is similar to the one you once used to irradiate young trees and fir trees (on September 29, 1976 in Ambitzgi/ Wetzikon). This other one is a much older model than that one. Here, this scooping device shows you the target very precisely through the magnifying optics. You can hit a single needle of that fir tree several kilometers away on the hill over there. The tube-shaped optical finder brings the target as close as if it were directly in front of the gun. In contrast, this other one has a very outdated operating apparatus similar to your explosion guns. To emit radiation, you have to pull the index finger back just like you did with my other gun.

These two transparent chambers here on top contain two different elements that are fundamentally necessary to generate the required type of beam emission. When combined, they emit a strong vibration of a type still unknown to you that decomposes or destroys only a few synthetic forms of matter, such as your film material, for example. That is why the gun should not be operated while you are taking photographs. Pressing this button combines the elements of the front and back containers. An incinerating ray develops which disintegrates everything up to a distance of 37.2 kilometers (23 miles) within a split second. Only a few charred bits around the target remain. If only the front container is activated through pressure on this point, the target will merely be stunned. This procedure is only used for purposes of self-defense, whereas the incinerating ray is normally only used for work and clean-up purposes. If necessary, it can be used in extreme cases to damage a hostile vehicle or spacecraft in order to render it non-maneuverable and, therefore, ineffective. The same holds true for other weapons, and so on.

This kind of weapon has not been in use for a long time — about 600 years. Since then, our technology has developed much better ones. The newest weapon of this kind has been reduced to a third of this size. Its function, that is, the operation of releasing the rays, has been fundamentally changed. The operation of the newest weapons has been individually tuned to the carrier so that only their owners can use the gun. The operation of the release is carried out purely on the basis of thought. That is why the brain-wave pattern of the owner must be programmed into the storage unit of the gun's release mechanism. Should the gun pass into the hands of another owner for some reason, a new programming must take place.

BILLY: That is extremely interesting, but I don't understand very much about these things, as you know. That doesn't matter and is of no importance. I'm only somewhat surprised that you speak of an owner of such guns. Can you explain that a little more for me?

MENARA: I refer to the carrier of such guns as owners because this meaning is understood on earth, and because the gun is individually tuned to the person carrying it.

The fact that Billy was given special permission to photograph Menara's girl-friend Alena may indeed be considered a special attraction, with one restriction, though. Under no circumstance was her face to appear in any publication and, therefore, had to be covered. What a pity! But the extraterrestrials are subject to strict regulations with regard to identity, and as far as Billy is concerned, he had no other choice but to strictly comply with these instructions, which he naturally did as a matter of fact.

At the dignified conclusion of the entire event, Billy was permitted to put the laser-pistol into action. Unaided, he fired a shot from a distance of about 20 meters (66 ft.) at the Semjase Tree.[44]

Like lightning, the laser-beam pierced the 24-centimeter (10 in.) thick tree trunk and left a hole as straight as an arrow and as thick as a finger. Since then, the Semjase Tree has become something of a landmark in Hinterschmidrüti. All visitors who know of it want to see it.

Eerie Whirring Sounds

In *Chapter 3*, I pointed out that a Pleiadian spacecraft can shield itself against optical or acoustical detection either completely or in sections by forming a type of energy bell around the entire ship, like a protective cloak. As soon as the acoustical protective shield is partially opened or totally shut off, a peculiar whirring sound can be heard, brought about by the rotation of ring-shaped disks belonging to the propulsion system. In a manner similar to the way the pitch of a spinning top rises with increasing speed, the pitch level and intensity of the whirring sounds are also changed, depending on the number of revolutions of the rotation disks. As already mentioned, the Pleiadians, in contrast to a number of other extraterrestrials, take great care not to be sighted by earth people, so they shield themselves well in order not to be seen or heard. There are exceptions, i.e., when sounds occur at approach for landing, while taking off or shortly thereafter and when the protective shield is momentarily opened. In such cases, the whirring can be heard very clearly, as several witnesses have reported.

A totally different situation occurred when Semjase gave Billy three opportunities to record the whirring sounds, meaning twice in the vicinity of Hinwil early in the year of 1976, and once in Sädelegg/Schmidrüti on July 18, 1980. In the second demonstration of this kind (on Good Friday of 1976), Semjase's spacecraft hovered about 50 meters (165 ft.) above a meadow where Billy had installed his recorder in an area overgrown with reeds. The energy bell was opened in sections with a narrow channel down toward the ground. On one hand, the ship was protected all the way around against optical and acoustical detection. On the other hand, the whirring sounds were channeled unhindered to the recording station and into the surrounding area. Several meters away from where Billy was standing, it was quite easy for the witnesses to establish that the whirring did not come from the speakers of his tape recorder but, rather, from an invisible sender that must have been positioned at an unknown altitude in the atmosphere.

Two days later, the witnesses returned to the scene of the event to conduct a test. They set the recorder in position and let the tape play at full volume. A clear distinction was noted between the original experience and the subsequent playback test. The difference this time was the source of sound (the recorder on the ground). Besides, the volume left much to be desired. The witnesses had to come twice as close to the recorder to hear nearly the same volume of sound as on Good Friday. As mentioned, it was easy to recognize that the original sound triggered hearing sensations different from those produced by the playback of the tape. Be that as it may, these whirring sounds are very peculiar and sometimes seem a little eerie, sounding similar to the whistling of a turbojet engine but with continually changing and merging tone sequences. The only thing that bothered Billy and the witnesses during the demonstration on that Friday were the unwelcome spectators who appeared here, there, and everywhere. It was very understandable, though, that the uninvited but curious onlookers also wanted to be near enough to personally witness such a Pleiadian "spacecraft symphony" in its natural state without having to depend upon the hearsay of others. However, the Pleiadians are known for avoiding uninvited observers and the unwelcome guests came at a very inconvenient time. Their presence led to the sudden interruption of the demonstration, which had only begun 10 minutes earlier. Despite this misfortune, the actual goal was nevertheless achieved: We had new physical evidence, which was now available for scientific investigation. (A copy of this recording can be downloaded for free from *www.steelmarkonline.com*).

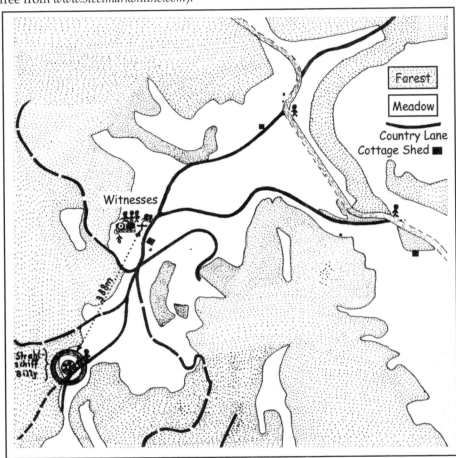

Fig. 6-2
Location map of Billy and his witnesses in Sädelegg (Freddy Kropf)

Beamship Symphony – *Report by Engelbert Wächter - abridged*

The third and last demonstration of whirring sounds was staged in the summer of 1980 at Sädelegg near Schmidrüti. Semjase had given Billy the preparatory instructions in advance. An abrupt interruption, as in the spring of 1976, would be annoying to everyone and was to be avoided. So due to the bad experience caused by the curiosity or intrusiveness of previously unwelcome onlookers, precautions had to be taken. A simple and reasonable solution was offered: All roads approaching the recording location, where Billy was waiting with his tape recorder, had to be temporarily closed to all pedestrians and vehicles for the duration of the demonstration. The only ones who could make this barricade a reality were several members of our group and Billy's family.

Before Billy set out with tractor and trailer laden with recording equipment to the recording location in the middle of a meadow in Sädelegg, he instructed the people at the barricade control points on what they had to do. To be quite certain that no technical malfunction would occur, Billy set up his recording devices at several spots other than just where he was standing.

After the preparations had been made, the event was expected to work out to the satisfaction of the participants, which indeed is what happened.

In addition to my introductory explanation, I am adding this abridged account by Engelbert Wächter:

We (Maria Wächter, Kalliope Meier, Methusalem Meier, Atlantis Meier, Jacobus Bertschinger, Eva Bieri and I) would never have dreamed, in the early morning of July 18, 1980, that we would hear such magnificent sounds in the evening of the very same day.

Billy needed an additional street guard who could prevent even a mouse from slipping through to the recording location, so it became our task to seal off all approaching side roads and throughways.

Somewhat late, we reached Billy, who had already set up and aligned the highly sensitive equipment about 300–400 meters (990–1,320 ft.) from the actual recording location, and was waiting for us. After he had given us the final rules of conduct, he then energetically climbed into his car to drive to the actual recording and contact site. And so we posted ourselves at all of the strategically important points and waited for the events to come.

We then observed Billy arriving at the actual recording location, getting out of his tractor and beginning to hastily fiddle about with the trailer. Shortly thereafter, the tarp flew back and he fastened it in the rod-linkage of the trailer in such a way that a small canopy was formed for protection against the rain that had started to softly fall.

Only a few minutes passed when suddenly a hurricane of air-piercing sound tore through the hills and valleys. A torrent of sound mercilessly beat down on our ears and hammered in our auditory canals. It also caused the inner workings of several sound recording devices to literally melt and become non-functional. We were virtually intoxicated by the engulfing sound waves, an intensity never heard and never experienced before nor since. Not only I, but all of us, stood spellbound at our watch posts and surrendered to this unique backdrop of sound that definitely drifted along and was heard over several kilometers. This fact was not only proven by the elderly married couple who had hurriedly come from a location about 3 kilometers (2 miles) away and were absolutely determined not to be stopped nor sent away — until somewhat harsher words finally produced the desired effect. Then other people drove by "at a snail's pace" with their car windows rolled down, listening to the strange cascades of sound. Several members of a farming family with whom we were acquainted could not keep from swinging themselves onto their tractor and manure tank about 800 meters (2,640 ft.) away to see what was actually going on in the background.

In contrast to Semjase's habit of silencing her ship with an energy shield whenever strangers approached, this time she gave free rein to the sometimes loud and wailing volume of sound. All too often in the past, we have had to work with repeated interruptions and now, even Semjase was at the end of her patience. Not only we, but all the others who were curious and courageous enough to expose themselves to the sounds of a highly advanced technology were granted a rare and deeply impressive experience that lasted nearly 30 minutes.

Highly satisfied about the permission granted to experience a Pleiadian beam-ship in action, and with a feeling of deep gratitude to Billy and Semjase, we set out for home at about 8 p.m. in the rain that was becoming even more intense.

Mysterious Elimination of Fir Trees

In the beginning phase of the contact period when the objective was to take the most convincing photos possible, Semjase was especially fond of using free-standing fir trees in the country as a backdrop. They were splendidly suited as objects of comparison to establish proportions.

Semjase did not choose average trees but selected the giant firs that are found throughout the Zurich Highlands. One of her favorite flight maneuvers was to curve around a giant fir several times with her ship and sometimes touch the outer tips of its branches. In doing so, it was inevitable that the tree in question would receive and absorb radiation emitted by the beam propulsion of the Pleiadian ship.

Semjase explained that the residual radiation lasting several months was not harmful to the trees. But under no circumstances were the Pleiadians allowed to run the risk of giving earth scientists an opportunity to analyze the radiation and, in doing so, gain important knowledge that presently was not allowed to be made known to earthman, the results of which would eventually bring about great disaster for earth. In no way could the Pleiadians take such a risk. Therefore, elimination of the radiation presented a serious problem. The Pleiadians were incapable of either neutralizing the residual radiation or completely extracting it from the tree through technical means. They had no alternative but to make use of a law intended for such cases. This law allows elimination of life forms in exceptional cases when deemed necessary for compelling reasons. Therefore, a total of five giant firs were eliminated in the course of the demonstrations, along with all memories of these trees — altogether, a tremendous job! It is no wonder that a farmer today can no longer remember the presence of one such tree, although he had sawed off its branches for years to burn as firewood. Only Billy was spared this memory deletion at his explicit request and was allowed to keep the photos and films relating to this matter. To make this fairy-tale story somewhat more plausible, on October 17, 1976, Semjase presented us with a smaller, limited demonstration of such an elimination.

My October 17, 1976 Experience – *Report by Guido Moosbrugger*
See ~ Photos #53 and #54

The event started for me, as often before, with a telephone call. Billy's wife, Kalliope called to say that Semjase had announced a demonstration for Sunday, October 17 and that I was invited to take part if I had the time and desire. Naturally, this was fine with me! After arriving in Hinwil, I asked the Meier family about the announced plan and they referred me to Billy, but Billy was extremely reserved on the subject. He could not be persuaded to reveal the details although he had precise information. (The reason for his stony silence was revealed after the event was over.) His only commentary at that time was as follows:

CHAPTER 6 — Daytime Demonstrations by the Extraterrestrials

BILLY: We'll put together a hot air balloon and let it fly tomorrow afternoon with aluminum foil attached to it, to test how the neighboring radar stations will react. In the immediate vicinity of the balloon's starting place where the actual demonstration will take place, I suggest that you observe everything in your surroundings very closely.

Consequently, there was nothing to do but wait patiently and let the event unfold and take us by surprise.

The balloon first had to be fabricated out of thin paper strips. Billy and Herbert Runkel worked diligently for several hours on its construction. And because time was gradually running out, I helped them paste the individual pieces together. With a little effort, we managed to complete the entire balloon hull by Sunday afternoon at 4 o'clock. In the meantime, about a dozen curious spectators had gathered at Billy's residence and impatiently waited for departure to the starting place. Soon thereafter, our small convoy moved through the streets of Hinwil and into the open countryside. Upon reaching our destination, we immediately began the necessary preparations. The photographers assumed their posts and impatiently waited for the first snapshots.

The balloon finally got off to a start around 5 p.m. and functioned as perfectly as in a storybook. Amid the jubilant spectators, the small monstrosity, filled with more than 60 m^3 of hot air, rose into the sky. Broad aluminum strips had been pasted onto the four sidewalls of the rectangle-shaped balloon so it could be better detected on radar. With absolute certainty, we knew this balloon could not escape the radar screens. As a result of clear weather, it was possible to clearly observe the balloon ascending into a cloudless sky. Lo and behold, only a few minutes after the launching, an airplane arrived in the vicinity of our balloon as it floated stalwartly upwards. Was this a pure coincidence or did the airplane happen to have something to do with reconnaissance? (Incidentally, we can attest to the fact that the neighboring radar station, which alleged that nothing of the kind had been detected, subsequently denied the existence of our balloon launching.) So after launching the balloon, we anxiously awaited the actual main attraction. I personally hoped we would finally catch a daytime glimpse of Semjase's spacecraft, but nothing of the kind happened. In the meantime, the balloon had drifted in a northeasterly direction. Billy abruptly mounted his moped and rattled off in the direction of the balloon. We were supposed to meet later at an appointed location but that plan failed because of a misunderstanding. Our disappointment was totally understandable. We finally met again in Billy's apartment where he had been waiting quite some time for us. In great haste, he then led us back to the site where the balloon had been released to point out Semjase's activity on the scene during our absence. He showed us the spot where a 3–5 meter (10–17 ft.) tall fir tree had been growing just a short while before, but in the meanwhile had disappeared in the true sense of the phrase, "without a trace." Semjase had eliminated it in a very mysterious way. An immediate and thorough examination of the grassy earth did not give the slightest indication that a young tree had ever stood there or had ever been removed. Only the one-sided growth of the beech shrub at the same spot made it possible to conclude that the young tree must have actually grown there. The shrub would hardly have grown lop-sided without this hindrance.

We, of course, wondered why Billy had not drawn our attention to the tree before it was eliminated. Billy explained that Semjase had strictly instructed him to maintain absolute silence for security reasons until the elimination was complete. The event would have undoubtedly received a substantially higher interest value if it had not happened so secretly. In this special case, it could not be otherwise.

Footnotes

32 ▪ Menara is a dark-skinned woman from the Lyra System. She belongs to one of the races befriended by the Pleiadians who were stationed on earth for eleven years (1975-86). She often acted as contact person in place of Semjase and Quetzal.

33 ▪ One of the two landing tracks was from Menara's ship and the other from the ship belonging to her friend, Rala.

34 ▪ The diameter of a landing plate on Semjase's spacecraft is 2 meters (6.6 ft.), but only 1.82 meters (6 ft.) on Quetzal's craft.

35 ▪ Billy had been beamed by teletransmitter from his living room directly into Semjase's spacecraft and was thus only wearing light summer clothes and slippers.

36 ▪ The landing tracks described here have absolutely nothing to do with the landing surfaces in the wheatfields of England. For more information, refer to the Contact Report #235 of February 3, 1990 in the *Voice of the Aquarian Age #76*, printed September 1990 and available by FIGU in German and English.

37 ▪ Whirring Meadow was named after whirring sounds of Pleiadian ships that were often heard in an area northeast of the residence in Hinterschmidrüti.

38 ▪ The fact that I did not trust my instinct then, and chose not to run the risk of exposing myself to ridicule, is something that I will no doubt regret for the rest of my life.

39 ▪ The radio station was in the residence of FIGU.

40 ▪ Miranos 5 and Miranos 1 were FIGU code words for the radio traffic.

41 ▪ "The pulpit" is the highest point of the grassy hill, which rises in an easterly direction next to the parking lot at the Semjase Silver Star Center.

42 ▪ Taljda is a yellow-skinned woman from planet Njssan [nis-san] in the Lyra-Vega-System. She had previously been Billy's contact person a few times.

43 ▪ Solar is an extraterrestrial man belonging to the races stationed on earth. He worked many years as an ally of the Pleiadians.

44 ▪ The Semjase Tree, the crown of which was damaged after being pressed flat by Semjase's spacecraft, stands on the side of a small hill in Hinterschmidrüti.

CHAPTER 7

Nighttime Demonstrations by the Extraterrestrials

In the spring and summer of 1976, several impressive night demonstrations by the Pleiadians took place in Hinwil and the surrounding area. I personally had three opportunities to take part in them. Luck played a part in this in two respects:

- My first UFO experience, which occurred the very first time I visited at Billy's place.

- My second and third experiences occurred when the Pleiadians had started to grant permission for outside persons to photograph or film them. Since no other night demonstrations of this kind took place at a later date, these photos are the only ones available and were taken during the night of June 12, 13, and 26, 1976.

My First UFO Experience on May 16 and 17, 1976 –
Report by Guido Moosbrugger

On a weekend in mid-May of 1976, I drove to Hinwil in the Zurich Highlands for the first time. I intended to test the credibility of the Swiss contactee Eduard Meier (in short, known as UFO Billy) and perhaps be given intimate details of his mysterious activity.

In response to a written request, Billy had invited me to visit him at his place and after staying one-and-a-half days in Hinwil, I expected to return home again on Sunday evening. But things worked out differently than planned. Billy suggested in the course of the afternoon that I stay another night because he had a feeling that something special would happen in the night to come. This offer was enticing and seemed promising, so I decided not to start my trip home until the next day — a truly wise decision. Billy was completely right in his guess and I am grateful to him for the suggestion. Because of his help, I finally experienced what I had always longed for — a real UFO experience!

As I sat in the Meier family living room on Sunday evening, May 16, expectantly awaiting the things to come, Billy made a brief comment shortly after 10 p.m.: "Between 12:30 a.m. and 1 o'clock!" When I questioned him, he answered by casually whisking his right-hand through the air several times in wave formations, and at the same time continued to watch the television program as if nothing at all had happened. What in the world did this gesture mean? After all, I was not familiar with the generally accepted circumstances there. Later, in response to my question, I learned that his extraterrestrial friend, Semjase, had telepathically told him to stand by for a personal contact with her at the time mentioned.

At 11:30 p.m., exactly one hour earlier than announced, Billy received another telepathic message from Semjase indicating that she was flying over Billy's place of residence at that very moment. Billy shot up from his seat as if something had bitten him and raced from the living room out into the open. His wife Kalliope, Mr. Schutzbach who was visiting, and I followed right behind. Outside in front of the house, Mrs. Meier threw her arm upward and pointed to the sky. I could hardly believe my eyes at first, but the appearance was really genuine and no dream. A fiery-red luminous object flew silently in a straight line precisely over the Meier residence. Billy's wife was kind enough to lend me her binoculars with which I could clearly see a blinking light on the tail end of the flying object. Full of excitement, we watched it disappear behind a wooded knoll on the northern horizon. Semjase had sent us a greeting in her manner, which made us, of course, exceedingly happy. Mrs. Meier and I trudged up a nearby rise and assumed a better observation point, hoping that the object would show itself again. Instead, Mr. Schutzbach came up to us with the request that we immediately return. We reached the house again in a trot and as we stepped inside, Billy was about to change his clothes. The reason for this, he told us, was that the sign for us to leave had been conveyed several minutes earlier. Therefore, Billy, Mr. Schutzbach and I pulled on warm over-clothes in preparation for the night's excursion, as it was severely cold for that time of year. After that, Billy immediately rattled off on his moped to what remained an unknown meeting place. Since he did not yet know the contact location or the way to get there, as opposed to other contacts, a guiding instrument capable of telepathy located inside Semjase's spacecraft was instructing him. It conveyed the necessary directional data during the entire drive and guided Billy to his destination. Mr. Schutzbach and I followed Billy in my car and stayed close on his heels. We dared not lose track of him, as we had no idea where we were going. To start with, we zigzagged through Hinwil to shake off any pursuers. We then had to stop at two forks in the road and drive a small stretch backwards instead of forwards — and then turn to the right, because either Billy had not understood the telepathic instructions of the guiding instrument or he had accidentally taken a wrong turn. But when we finally arrived at Dürstelen, our leader suddenly stopped in the middle of a country lane. We were now undoubtedly in the vicinity of the contact location. Had Billy been alone, the guiding instrument would have led him directly to the spacecraft, but since he had companions with him, the guiding instrument switched off automatically. This interruption is like an alarm signal and alerts the pilot of the ship to undertake a thought-analysis check of the accompanying persons in order to determine whether they are of friendly or hostile nature and, hence, trustworthy or not. This analysis is a precaution the guiding instrument cannot carry out. If the thought analysis has a positive outcome, the contact will continue according to plan. If not, the contact will be immediately re-planned or called off and taken up later. When the investigation is completed, the guiding instrument stores the brain-wave patterns of all persons of good intent. In this manner, the stored information enables the guiding instrument to identify at any time the individuals concerned, as brain-waves emitted by every human being are just as unique and unmistakable as a fingerprint.

We waited a good quarter-hour on the field path until the action continued. We learned afterward the reason for this pause was that Semjase had received an urgent order to go immediately to the North Sea region (of all times) and had to stop the activity of the guiding instrument at this point. Semjase later had to conduct a thought analysis of us both because our brain-wave patterns had not yet been stored in the guiding instrument.

During this pause, we anxiously searched the heavens for any kind of appearances and suddenly discovered a pin-point sized flying object moving along the horizon that was relatively close to us. During the flight, it continued to blink in short intervals. At first, I thought it was an airplane, although absolutely no engine sounds could be heard. Mr. Schutzbach, a private pilot by profession, doubted my opinion because the frequency of the blinking light appeared very unusual to him. Billy finally said he could determine, just for the fun of it, whether it was an earthly flying object or not. And no sooner said than done — a few seconds later, the blinking light was suddenly extinguished and no trace of the flying object could be seen. Billy explained the procedure with the following words: "I simply commanded the spacecraft to stop blinking — this experiment would not have been successful with an earthly airplane."

(According to Semjase, the "flying object" was an unmanned Pleiadian telemeter disk that is used for reconnaissance purposes. The radio-like impulses, which appear as a blinking light, serve as a means of accurate navigation. If this navigation mechanism breaks down, the telemeter disk becomes uncontrollable and must be returned to the nearest earth station of the Pleiadians.)

After this amusing episode, Billy finally received another telepathic connection from Semjase. He requested that we stay where we were and wait for his return. He would ask Semjase to conduct a small night demonstration but could not promise whether she would agree. In any case, we should continue our observation of the sky and, above all else, keep the northerly direction in clear view.

At this point, he seated himself on his vehicle to cover the last stretch of his journey to the secluded glade where Semjase was waiting for him in her ship only several minutes from where we were standing.

As Billy drove away, I silently wondered what would happen if I were to follow him. Apparently, Semjase must have received my thoughts; otherwise, she would not have said to Billy directly after greeting him:

SEMJASE: You have brought two persons along who are unknown to me. I examined their honesty. Their interest is of an honest nature. Only Mr. Moosbrugger harbored the momentary thought of what would possibly happen if he were to follow you. That is of no further consequence, as it was only his curiosity and his honest interest.

Mr. Schutzbach and I trudged back and forth in the open air and waited for Billy's return. Excellent visibility prevailed and the moon was full in the starlit night. As a result of the unusual cold, we gradually became too uncomfortable and decided to continue our observation of the sky inside the car. We had hardly taken a seat inside when a fiery-red circular disk as large as a headlight appeared in the northern sky above the forest from, as if by magic, out of nowhere. First, it calmly hovered in the air, then swung back and forth like a pendulum and disappeared again. The distance was about 3 kilometers (2 miles), as we were able to establish at a later visit during the day. Shortly thereafter, a snow-white sphere emerged which moved in a circle along a horizontal plane. During this maneuver, the sphere suddenly appeared to triple itself, as another sphere appeared below the left half and one below the right half. We then saw yet a fourth somewhat smaller one that was released like a drop from the central figure but did not descend all the way to the ground. After another pause, a dazzling, silver disk seemed to fly toward us, sparkling and growing ever larger and larger. After a while, it contracted back to its original size and disappeared without a trace. So the short but impressive spectacle, "lumière dans la nuit," (lights in the night) finally came to an end. For this magnificent exhibition we owed our thanks to Semjase as well as to Billy, who had requested this presentation in the course of the contact conversation. Billy himself saw nothing of the occurrence because, during the entire demonstration, he was on his moped traveling back to where we were waiting. It was not long before he joined us again.

After a short break, we managed the drive home without detour, which I enjoyed tremendously because of Billy's unique one-armed-man driving technique. So about half-past three in the morning, we arrived in Hinwil again and immediately retired to the living room to warm our stiff limbs by the warm stove. All in all, for me, it was an absolutely beautiful experience that I certainly will never forget.

As far as the credibility of the entire story is concerned, I would like to make the following comments:

- The witness Mr. Schutzbach confirmed with his signature that I wrote my account truthfully and in absolute accordance with the facts.

- To a possible assumption that the contactee had perhaps staged everything himself, the following can be said: Given the conditions of weather and countryside, it would have been impossible for Billy to join us, even if using his vehicle, within that short time-span after the demonstration. Try as I may, I simply cannot imagine how he could've staged the entire magic. Those brilliant and radiant manifestations can by no means be compared with traditional fireworks or anything similar.

According to the Pleiadians, the phenomena we observed at the time of such night demonstrations was an electrical energy burning, meaning a spacecraft sucks in electrical energy from the surrounding atmosphere, compresses it into a high-density form and then eliminates it through a burning process. The procedure causes the radiant manifestations displayed during the activities I have seen and described here.

In conclusion, I am adding the correlating contact report, as follows: *Contact Report #52, Monday, May 17, 1976 – 12:47 a.m.:*

BILLY: It's much more comfortable here inside. Outside, it is quite cold.

SEMJASE: Sure. You have two persons along who are unknown to me. I had to personally take charge of the guiding again, as I was over the North Sea where I had something to take care of.

BILLY: Aha, were you busy with something special again? That's fine, too. Yes, I have brought along Mr. Schutzbach and Mr. Moosbrugger. Mr. Konrad Schutzbach lives near Hegnau, and Mr. Moosbrugger lives in Walsertal in Austria...

SEMJASE: I checked their honesty and their interest is of an honest nature. Only Mr. Moosbrugger harbored the momentary thought of what would happen if he were to follow you. That is of no importance, as it was only his curiosity and his genuine interest.

BILLY: I'm to greet you from both of them, also from Mr. R. Sch. from Biel. By the way, he also gave me this document to bring along. He wants to ask you whether he can trust it or not. What do you think about it?

SEMJASE: It is a joy for me to be able to be receive these greetings. Extend to them all my joy and my thanks for this. They should also receive my best greetings. But what is the meaning of that in your hand? Do you want to tell me more about it?

BILLY: No, I would like to have an impartial answer from you about it.

SEMJASE: Good, then let me see. — Ah, I am familiar with this document. It is supposed to be a message from extraterrestrial intelligences. But this is not the case; it is a primitive forgery.

BILLY: Then your statement confirms our speculations. Thanks.

SEMJASE: It is my pleasure. But look at this other book belonging to Mr. S. in Lindau. You can now give it back to him. From a theosophical viewpoint, it is an extraordinarily valuable work with astonishing findings in accordance with the truth. The entire work is quite praiseworthy. Please tell Mr. S. that despite the excellent quality of the work, it should nevertheless be emphasized that to be meaningful, the entire work should be changed in its arrangement. The order should be drawn up differently, as everything is somewhat intermixed. All subjects should be properly arranged in the correct sequence. And although the work is astonishingly good and in accordance with the truth, it should not be made accessible to the broad human masses as they are still unable to grasp and understand all of the interpretations and explanations. The work is only suitable for human beings who have already gained a higher spiritual level of knowledge and understanding. If it were distributed among the broad and still ignorant masses, it would cause a confusion that would be quite unsuitable for the whole enlightenment. The work won't actually be understood for another 150–200 years, according to a calculation of probability.

BILLY: Thanks, dear girl, I'll give Mr. S. your assessment. I now have a very specific question. On May 10, I received a world prophecy from the Petale Plane, which I am to cloak in poetic form and interpret. In it, something came up that I am completely unaware of. It has to do with Indians of gigantic stature who live somewhere in Peru and according to the prophecy must have already raided a village about ten days ago. They are supposed to be old enemies of the Incas and supposedly keep themselves hidden in huts covered with leaves and have an underground tunnel somewhere in the jungle. Do you know anything about these giant Indians? If you could give some information about them, I would be very happy, and it would certainly be of interest to other people.

Wednesday, May 19, 1976 — "Blick"

Giant Indians Kidnapped White Women
The savage giants have been missing for over 400 years.

LIMA (Peru) – Savage giants, clothed only in animal skins invaded the Peruvian jungle settlement "La Pampa del Sacrament." With primitive ironwood axes, they struck the village men down. Nine were severely injured. They then picked out the three prettiest white women from La Pampa and kidnapped them.

That was two weeks ago. A few days later, 2.15 meters-tall (7 ft.) men with flaming red hair raided a group of hunters in their forest camp.

"They came with spears and clubs," said a witness of the Peruvian newspaper "Ultima Hora."

Here, again, the savages left injured hunters behind.

The country population now lives in fear and terror. Scientists and historians are puzzled. Who are these great reds? The descriptions of the frightful giants match the traditional description of Indians from the Chanka tribe. The red skins have been missing or extinct for more than 400 years. Back then, the Chankas fought bitterly against the Incas. Later the giant Indians fled from the Spanish plunderers. They successfully resisted every attempt to be civilized. Then they disappeared without a trace. Until now …

SEMJASE: Yes, the existence of these life forms is known to us. They are the distant descendants of an extraterrestrial race and have an average body size of about 210 centimeters (7 ft.). Their skin is as reddish-brown in color as the other Indian races. Their hair growth is red, but partially dyed. About 500 years ago, these giants retreated deep into the jungle where they built a subterranean village and have lived ever since. They also live above ground in huts covered with leaves. However, they have all become wild, clothe themselves in animal skins and live on plants and from hunting.

Recently, they have had problems concerning their women with offspring and have therefore set out over the past several decades to kidnap women from civilized areas, especially white women. Their lineage traces back to the Incas, of whom they are distant descendants. In earlier times, feuds broke out between different Inca tribes so they fought one another to the bloody end. This is what happened between the giants and another Indian tribe of Incan descent who were called Chanaks or Chanka. They fought hard against each other because the Chanaks (or Chanka) fought against the more purely preserved Inca tribes. The giants sided with the more pureblooded Incas and entered the battle against the Chanka (or Chanaks) and caused them severe affliction. Then about 500 years ago, up to which time the giants had been preserved, they suddenly disappeared from the society of all other tribes and retreated deep into the jungle where they have led very hard lives full of privation. They have been considered extinct ever since. Because they are descendants of the Incas, they can only be referred to as Inca enemies insofar as they had feelings of hostility towards the degenerated Incas such as the Chanaks (or Chanka.)

BILLY: That is very interesting. You say Chanka (or Chanaks). Don't you know exactly what they are called?

SEMJASE: These are two terms that have been customary since ancient times. They were known under both names. There is a third name that I cannot give you any information about as I am not accurately informed about it.

BILLY: That doesn't matter. You have already told me more than I expected. I have another question, or rather two of them. They are from Mr. Moosbrugger in Walsertal. Is there an explanation for the astronomical data of the Giza Pyramid, etc., and is there such a thing as the Curse of the Pharaohs?

SEMJASE: I would like to answer the second question first. There is no Pharaohs' curse. This is only a fantasy, like a fable, typical of earth people who believe in various kinds of secrets and see mysteries in all things, as they are still very much confused by their religious fantasies. There have always been fatalities whenever the Pharaohs' graves were plundered, even among your scientists, because they also engaged in the plundering of graves. On the one hand, this can partially be traced back to cases of provoked accidents, and on the other hand, to the protective measures of the old pharaohs and priests who were well aware of the plundering to come. For this reason they developed means of protection. They had slaves gather the hair spinules of the Figidindus cacti and coated them with a poisonous brew. These spinules, which were impregnated with a deadly poison lasting thousands of years, were applied to the bandages of the dead and embalmed pharaohs, and the hair-fine spinules inevitably penetrated the skin and killed whoever came in contact with them at a later time.

BILLY: Fantastic, but by the hair spinules of the Figidindus, do you mean the hair-fine spinules which are on the surface of a cactus fruit?

SEMJASE: Yes, but now for your second question: As the pyramids were constructed, the astronomers of that time had already calculated the future destiny of earth. The measured values of the pyramids were worked out in accordance with the data obtained from these calculations. Their calculations showed that many thousands of years in the future, a catastrophe would again threaten earth from outer space, as it did at the time the pyramids were built. To draw the attention of subsequent earth inhabitants thousands of years later to the threatening catastrophe, the obtained data of astronomical form was, therefore, worked into the pyramids and would be applicable to events that would occur in the distant future. This means that the pyramids were constructed precisely according to the astronomical data and measurements that will coincide with the astronomical data precisely at a time when the catastrophe from space starts to threaten again. The astronomers at that time were very capable and thus calculated the data with extreme accuracy. In their calculations, they even took several world shifts (polar shifts) into account and were thus capable of forecasting the data with the most accurate precision. Just as pre-calculated, earth then toppled over, giving credence to the long past science of that time. Now the time is arriving when the astronomical measurements, which were instrumental and decisive in the construction of the pyramids, as I explained, will gradually align with the astronomical values of the present age and, therefore, announce the events prophesied more than 70,000 years ago. This event will come to pass exactly at the time when the sunlight of a very distant star (a central star — the central sun of the Milky Way as well as of the SOL system) falls in through the pipe-like opening of revelation that extends from outside the Giza Pyramid all the way inside to its center in a straight, unbroken line and illumines a certain point. I am not permitted to say any more about it.

BILLY: It may be important to know this though.

SEMJASE: Certainly, but I may not speak of it. If you want, I can explain it to you alone.

BILLY: Gladly, I'll be as mute as a fish.

SEMJASE: Good, but I will not do it today yet. I will call you alone in thought for this purpose after I have conveyed this report to you.

BILLY: That's fine, but what about certain mysteries that are supposedly entwined around the pyramids, and how were they built, perhaps with machines?

SEMJASE: There are no actual mysteries, except for:

- the existence of the Giza Intelligences *(See ~ Chapter 13 for a more thorough explanation)*

- the concerns about the astronomical measurements in connection with the threatening danger and the significance of the starlight that will fall through the opening of revelation at a certain time. The pyramids were built by the use of telekinetic spirit forces, as you already know, so I have nothing more to say about this.

BILLY: That's quite enough, thanks. I'm still wondering, why, in fact, you were flying around in droves over Hinwil last weekend or shortly before. Did you perhaps lose a golden trifle, which you were looking for? It was quite a grand-scale demonstration. We counted nine ships, although you and Quetzal were there twice, if I received your thoughts correctly.

SEMJASE: Certainly, you are correct with this. No, I did not lose anything, not even such an odd thing as you just mentioned.

BILLY: You make me smile, girl, you really fell for it. You see, a golden trifle also means nothing.

SEMJASE: I will get even with you for that. Anyway, we discovered during surveillance that an army organization looked for our various landing sites with their primitive equipment and dangerous helicopter machines and scanned the area for radiation. I am speaking of the landing sites where I had landed. Since there is always the possibility of radiation deposits, we took the trouble to check it out and scanned and analyzed everything. However, there was no radiation found at any of the sites. You were probably able to observe these primitive helicopter machines yourself, as they made everything unsafe several days ago around the ninth evening hour. Among other things, they also flew around your house.

BILLY: I know, we observed the military scoundrels doing so, but we don't bother with them much as they aren't exactly the most clever of people. You certainly offered us a spectacle, which we enjoyed immensely. Who of you floated northeastward with the floodlight?

SEMJASE: Quetzal. He wanted to make all of you happy.

BILLY: He certainly did that with his spectacular interlude. It was simply grand. Please extend to him our greatest thanks and our greetings.

SEMJASE: Surely he will be very pleased.

BILLY: I also wanted to say, as I was recording the whirring of your ship on tape, many people suddenly appeared out of nowhere. The canton police were also there. Now they're poking their noses also into these matters.

SEMJASE: I observed that, too, but it is not very important as they have no solid clues to go by. How did the photos actually turn out which you had the opportunity to take shortly before Easter?

BILLY: Do you mean the ones where they kept you on the run with their silly jet fighter? I would have liked to have seen the face of that pilot. The pictures are quite good, at least I think so. *(See ~ Photo #16)*

SEMJASE: The pilot had a film or photo camera in his plane, but he was unable to take any pictures with it because I had jammed it. His face was really very funny to see — unbelievable amazement! I have never seen such a dumbfounded face before.

BILLY: I can vividly imagine that. The earthworm often really looks criminally stupid in his amazement. But tell me, didn't you notice anything at 12:20 a.m.? There was some kind of object high above us that blinked in a very unusual rhythm as it flew by. In order to see if it could possibly be a plane, the blinking rhythm of which might have been broken, I tried to give the object a command to put out its light, which it then did after a short while, perhaps 5 or 10 seconds later. Therefore, it must have been a telemeter disk or something similar because, as I told my companions, I am unable to influence a plane. Do you know anything about it? And by the way, Mr. Schutzbach also saw something about 10 minutes later, a red light in the Constellation of the Great Bear, which then was abruptly extinguished.

SEMJASE: I did not detect the second object. It was probably during the moment I was already down here (with the ship in a secluded wooded clearing). The first one, in which you switched the light off, that was one of our telemeter disks. The station notified me that it had been influenced by undetectable forces and had drifted off course. You should be more careful with these things.

BILLY: Is it really so bad if I take the light from such a flitty thing?

SEMJASE: Yes, as the light of a telemeter ship corresponds to a special value, it is used to set the ship's course. As you have already noticed, it exhibits a beam of light at certain intervals and is quite glaring. It is similar to the transmitting impulses that serve as a means of steering. If you extinguish this light through the power of your thoughts, the telemetric ship loses control and moves uncontrollably off course and it must be brought under control again by a station on earth.

BILLY: Then I'll leave this alone in the future. I really had no bad intention.

SEMJASE: Sure, you could not have known about it.

BILLY: Now another question. Is it perhaps possible for you to give my two companions a small demonstration? You know they are interested in everything and, above all, in our task. A small display from you would certainly be extremely valuable to them.

SEMJASE: I understand your wish very well, but you know how difficult everything has become lately as your authorities have been hounding us so much. This is also why I told you to be ready between 12:30 and 1 a.m. and then ordered you here at 11:30 p.m. I want to think about it and consider whether I can give a small demonstration. This is not intended to be a promise, however.

BILLY: Good, that's enough for me. Thanks. Would it be possible for you to give me perhaps two or three types of your food? You know, I'm thinking of little tablets or whatever else it might be. But I don't want to put you in a predicament where you may starve to death.

SEMJASE: Yes, I can comply with your wish, but I have nothing of the sort here. I will have to bring it along for you the next time. The best thing would be something earth-like, something that can also be produced here.

BILLY: Thanks, if you think so. Perhaps it is better that way because if it is something unknown to the planet, it could possibly cause difficulties. You know how the people are here.

AND STILL THEY FLY! – *Second Edition*

SEMJASE: It is about time for me to go, as I have to get back to the North Sea.

BILLY: Then go on, you nightingale… I almost said night owl, but that doesn't fit you. You are more like a nightingale — also in song, by which I mean your voice.

SEMJASE: Your compliments are of rare value and very honest.

BILLY: Thanks, then take all the flowers of the world as proof of my admiration and let their fragrance bring you well-being in joy and love.

SEMJASE: You are very kind, I feel very peculiar inside.

BILLY: You are also very kind — I wish so very much for you, dear girl…that the charming fragrance of the flower world may accompany you in love. So long and see you again soon.

SEMJASE: … I shall be seeing you. My thoughts are with you. For me, it is often very…

BILLY: (I could only hear Semjase's last words very faintly and nothing more of the rest of the sentence, as I glided down through the anti-gravity shaft. I quickly walked away, got on my moped and drove off. I felt that life could sometimes be pretty damn odd and twisted. Anita from Vienna would probably say: Life is sh…)

My Second UFO Experience on June 12–13, 1976 –
Report by Guido Moosbrugger
See ~ Photos #55, #56, #58–#60

This experience was quite different from the one a month before in that everything was announced early and planned in advance. Three days earlier, I had a telephone conversation with Billy and learned that a night demonstration by the Pleiadians was planned for that coming weekend. I was allowed to attend and I could take photos. This piece of good news was of special importance because permission to photograph or film had not been granted to anyone until then, except to Billy.

In view of this promising announcement and my insufficient knowledge of photography, I sought advice from my colleague, Hubert Riese, an occasional photographer, I had never before worked with a telephoto lens in the daytime, let alone at night. According to Hubert Riese's recommendation, I purchased a light-sensitive slide film, which Hubert was kind enough to send to Stuttgart to be developed after my return. He then personally picked it up, checked it over, and then handed it back to me along with the developed slides. On the night of June 12, the announced event was to be launched. After my arrival at the home of the Meier family in Hinwil, I learned from Billy that the action was to start between midnight and one o'clock. To simplify the venture, only persons who had been analyzed by the Pleiadians earlier, as mentioned in my first report, were permitted to take part. Consequently, a total of six persons (the Schutzbach brothers, Mrs. Stetter, Mrs. Flammer, Mrs. Walder and I) were granted permission to take part as spectators.

After a short discussion of the situation, we finally set out one hour after midnight. While Billy drove alone on his moped to the landing site in a secluded glade in Winkelriet/Hinwil, we proceeded in two separate groups to the prearranged observation place in the meadow between Hinwil and Wetzikon, not more than a stone's throw from the sports hall. On a narrow field path, we immediately set up our tripods and adjusted our equipment — two photo cameras and a movie camera aimed in a northeasterly direction toward the edge of the woods near Winkelriet 2 kilometers (1 mile) away. The weather was also in our favor and the visibility was excellent for taking pictures. After one hour of waiting, the spectacle for which we waited with great curiosity and excitement started at 2:15 a.m. As presumed, the first luminous figure appeared in the northeast in front of a wooded rise on the foothills of the local mountain of Bachtel in Hinwil. Oddly enough, I did not have to adjust my camera toward the luminous object, as it was simply and straightway in the correct line of vision. At first, we were able to admire a fiery-red disk as large as a headlight, which disappeared without a trace a few seconds after it appeared on the scene. A while later, an exceedingly beautiful silver disk, shining radiantly, moved toward us. According to the statements of the ladies present, it was said to be in three colors, which I personally did not see as I was busy setting my camera higher. After that, a third disk appeared in a higher position.

Again, after a short pause, a silver disk appeared high above the edge of woods and let something like a fine glittering rain fall diagonally downward. At the end of this short but impressive presentation, we could still see the spacecraft in the form of a red luminous ball for quite some time as it flew away. It first climbed straight up into the sky, gradually swung into a horizontal path and moved further and further away. The luminous ball shrank to a tiny point until it finally disappeared from view. All of this lasted no more than 10 minutes.

Soon thereafter, we heard the distant sound of a vehicle approaching on the narrow path from the direction of Winkelriet. Who could that be? Naturally, it was none other than Billy returning from his contact with Semjase. He enthusiastically said that he had watched the entire night demonstration from the landing site and had also taken photos.

Billy told us that Semjase had flown over to Austria and would land again for a further contact conversation upon her return — but at a different place.

Based on this information, we immediately headed toward Hinwil. We had to stop at a railroad crossing and to wait — as usual.

After a while, Billy set out anew for the contact, but the meeting place or landing site this time was to be in a nearby wooded area. Semjase's approach and landing took place without a sound and was invisible to us as a result of the shielding, just like the first time in Winkelriet. However, the behavior of a few animals became quite peculiar. In the beginning, a deep nocturnal peace prevailed all around. But suddenly, the silence was interrupted by a loud neighing of horses, which resounded from the wooded area where Semjase had landed. At about the same time, we also heard a strange barking, which presumably came from a frightened fox. And finally, a bird the size of a raven fluttered away over our heads. It is well known to us that animals become quite uneasy in the presence of extraterrestrial spacecraft because these craft emit a radiation that sensitive animals can perceive immediately.

When Billy finally returned from his second contact around 4 o'clock in the morning, we all drove back together to our starting place.

I can report the following curiosities about the photos taken during that night:

- The film taken by Mr. Schutzbach shows disk-shaped luminous objects throughout.

- In his black-and-white photos, only worm-like figures appear recognizable as the flight-maneuver patterns of a Pleiadian ship. No disk-shaped craft were visible.

- In my color slides — taken with a telephoto lens — a disk form can only be seen in a single picture which, unfortunately, was overexposed, even though I had exposed it for only 2–3 seconds (without a flash). In one photo, traces of burning in the form of smoke can be seen especially well. I also captured the rain of light mentioned earlier quite well, but here again, no disk was visible although all observers had seen one. The spacecraft flying away, however, was seen as a luminous red point.

- On the other hand, the color slides of Billy's snapshots, which were taken at the landing site and without a telephoto lens, showed quite different luminous objects. One picture, for example, completely surprised us. It revealed a distinct numeral "1." Also remarkable are the intense colors, which are observable only if the projected pictures (slides) are viewed from very close up (and enlarged).

Whoever has once seen these luminous figures has to admit that a firework specialist certainly could not have created them. Skeptics, of course, will undoubtedly offer what they consider to be a sensible explanation for this phenomenon.

My Third UFO Experience on June 26 and 27, 1976 –
Report from Guido Moosbrugger

Fourteen days after my second UFO experience, the Pleiadians, Semjase and Quetzal, wanted to repeat the same spectacle at the same location. Due to unforeseen circumstances, the demonstration arranged for the purpose of filming and photography unfortunately had to be canceled. During the contact conversation with Billy, Quetzal stated the following reason for the cancellation:

> **QUETZAL:** As I have found out, many people in the area are enroute to local events where they are observing the sky very intently for various fireworks in connection with the events. I have further discovered that at the road crossing before Hinwil is an automobile in which two persons of the police authority (two policemen) are keeping a watchful eye on the surroundings.

Quetzal's cancellation of the contact is understandable if we realize that the Pleiadians avoid having uninvited and unwelcome guests at their demonstrations. On this evening, a large dance was held in Hinwil, causing busy auto traffic. Many people were out and about in the open air until late in the night.

The presentation "fell flat" to our great regret, but our efforts were not completely in vain. Although our patience had been sorely tried as we waited out our time in full expectation of the promised event, we were nevertheless rewarded in the end.

First of all, Mr. Hans and Mr. Konrad Schutzbach, Mrs. Flammer, Mrs. Stetter, Mrs. Walder and I had the pleasure of watching several telemeter disks at a relatively low altitude as they majestically passed overhead in the starlit night sky. I took this opportunity to capture the flight path of a blinking telemeter disk on my slide film. At the exact moment I was about to take a picture of Venus with permanent exposure, a telemeter disk appeared and literally flashed into the center of my picture, much to my great joy. *(See ~ Photo #57)*

Secondly, we could follow and photograph the Pleiadian spacecraft as it flew away, looking like a fiery-red luminous ball high up against the firmament, just as once before. But this time the ship sped away at a much faster rate, so I presume that is why a specific photo did not turn out at all, when the ship's path was intersected by another blinking disk.

Night Demonstration on March 14, 1976 –
Report by Jacobus Bertschinger

Jacobus Bertschinger reports of his experience, which took place in the early morning of March 14, 1976 near Bettswil in the vicinity of the Sunnemätteli Children's Home:

At 12:40 a.m., I suddenly caught sight of a dark-yellow light in the northern sky over the top of the fir trees. The light was stationary and had emerged out of nowhere. My first thought was that it could be a house in which the light had simply been switched on. It did seem rather odd to me, though, since no house could actually be situated higher than the crowns of the fir trees and, moreover, in the middle of the woods. That prompted me to carefully examine this light. At first, it remained stationary and motionless, but then it started to move, caressing the top of the fir trees as it slowly moved away. It then became faster and faster and climbed higher. From where I was standing, I continued to observe it until it reached an altitude of about 200–300 meters (660–990 ft.), during which time its dark-yellow color slowly changed into a deep, dark red. Having reached this altitude, the light stood still for several moments, then started to move again, heading straight toward me. This happened at a sudden, enormous burst of speed with the light growing considerably larger as it approached and its color changing yet again, this time to a milky white. The ball of light suddenly stood still again and I patiently waited for whatever would undoubtedly come to pass. It should also be mentioned that the light object had continued to climb during its flight and had finally reached an altitude of 2,000–3,000 meters (1.25–2 miles).

Below the ball of light, a virtual rain shower of sparks started pouring down like a gigantic display of fireworks, as if two electric power cables had been touching for a long period of time. This phenomenon was accompanied by an extremely loud noise. Afterward, a distinct boom could be heard. At that point, its direction reversed and it went back the way it had come and then climbed higher and silently glided northward before becoming immersed in a mass of hanging clouds. Soon thereafter, it disappeared from view.

About 30 minutes later, another ball of light appeared, stood still above the fir tree crowns, as if searching, then turned and flew away to the east. I was able to follow it as a red ball of light until it finally disappeared high above into the clouds. (The maximum altitude according to the extraterrestrials was 2,200 meters [1.4 miles]).

I declare that my statements fully correspond to the truth and that I was neither daydreaming nor suffering from hallucinations of any kind.

As a supplement, I am adding a small excerpt from the contact conversation in which this night demonstration was announced by Semjase.

Excerpt from the *Contact Report 48 on Sunday, March 14, 1976 – 12:04 a.m:*

BILLY: I'm pleased that both of you are visiting me. Do you have something special in mind?

SEMJASE: Yes, Quetzal has several things to discuss with you.

QUETZAL: It is important, that you do not speak about these matters.

BILLY: If that's your wish, it's fine with me. You certainly gave me a good chase up the mountain.

QUETZAL: It's a good place here. In the future, Semjase will change the location of the landing place from time to time. Everything has become quite unsafe because various elements have taken a negative interest in our affairs, as you have already discovered.

BILLY: Unfortunately, I also had to be brought here in a car today, as the gas cable tore on my vehicle yesterday. My colleague brought me here and now he is waiting all alone in an open field about two kilometers from here.

QUETZAL: That is very kind of him; he is quite helpful. Extend to him my thanks. He has not made these efforts in vain. When I leave, I shall show him my ship. Furthermore, I shall give him a small demonstration by conducting an electrical energy elimination that he will observe quite well. This is a process in which energy is concentrated into a ball by drawing electricity from the atmosphere, which I then eliminate through a burning process. He will have to be patient though, as I am not allowed to do this below an altitude of 2,500 meters (1.6 miles) because the burning energy falls to the earth and is very hot. I shall ascend very slowly so he can carefully observe everything.

CHAPTER 8

Multiple Sightings by Independent Witnesses

Besides the day and night demonstrations, several people have derived great pleasure from the various sightings of extraterrestrial spacecraft. Daytime sightings of Pleiadian ships are of such exceptional rarity that I only have two such incidents to report. There is a special reason why the Pleiadians and their allies avoid being spotted with their ships during the day, if at all possible. The following informative report by Kalliope gives us further details about this. Not included, of course, are all the cases in which Billy was granted permission to photograph and film the Pleiadian ships during broad daylight for demonstration purposes. On the other hand, a relatively large number of night sightings have been reported, of which I will only mention a few. I will also take this opportunity to discuss an exceptional night sighting that was not staged by the Pleiadians. A peculiar event occurred when the extraterrestrial spacecraft was seen both in Hinterschmidrüti and Munich as well as in other places. Billy received an interesting explanation from Taljda on this very peculiar and striking night phenomenon.

Daytime Sightings
A Remarkable Experience – *Report by Kalliope Meier*
On June 28, 1976, my husband, Billy, came to us in the living room and to our great surprise, requested that we[45] all accompany him to a place outside Hinwil because he had to go to a personal contact. Complying with the invitation, H. Schutzbach drove us in his car to the high pasture near Oberdorf Riet (Betzholz-Hinwil) to wait there for my husband to return. Billy, who had driven ahead on his moped, drove a few hundred meters further directly to the contact site where he met with Quetzal, Semjase and her sister, Pleija.[46]

While we were waiting, we sat in the shade of the only tree on the high pasture and carried on a lively conversation to pass the time. A good half-hour must have gone by when Atlantis, six years old at the time, called out to us. "Look, something is flying there!" To our great amazement, we saw a large silver-gray object rise over the Pilgerholz Woodland at a distance of about 300 meters (990 ft.). Glistening brightly in the sunlight, it rapidly gained in altitude and then took a westerly course of flight.

H. Schutzbach had borrowed Billy's camera for all such eventualities so he could take pictures if any opportunity should arise. Incidentally, H. Schutzbach had yearned with an innermost desire for many months to see and photograph Semjase's spacecraft for once by daylight, which is why my husband asked the beamship pilot a number of times for such an opportunity, which was to be made possible quite unexpectedly on that day.

H. Schutzbach was the one in Billy's work group who could accompany him everywhere from the very beginning, as he was the hobby photographer responsible for the entire special field of photo documentation. For this reason, he became a "man of confidence" and was permitted now and then to go much closer to Semjase's ship than all the other group members. However, it turned out that he was unable to endure or cope with Semjase's field of radiation (without shielding). He spoke several times of feeling as if he were in paradise when within this field of radiation and after emerging from this "paradise-like frequency," his world crumbled. On that occasion, he had finally felt what true love and true peace were. As he was unable to permanently maintain this condition, the world for him had crumbled.

This sensibility prompted my husband to warn H. Schutzbach about wanting to see Semjase's spacecraft by day. In view of his insistent requests, Billy repeatedly explained to him that he ought not indulge too far in his desire. Furthermore, he would "flip out" like many other people to such an extent during a day sighting that H. Schutzbach would not be in the mental condition to take even a single, good snapshot.

Then, as the 7-meter (23 ft.) ship of the Pleiadians actually appeared over the Pilgerholz Woodland in broad daylight, my husband's prediction was fulfilled precisely. H. Schutzbach ran around uncontrollably, let his photo camera drop to the ground, and did not know how he should conduct himself. As he finally calmed down, but still obviously under great strain, he tried to take a few pictures while trembling so badly that he could not hold the raised camera steady in his hands. In the meantime, the object had moved far away and when H. Schutzbach was finally able to operate the release, the ship was so far away that it could only be seen as a small point. As it later turned out, only one single picture of these blurred snapshots was halfway useful.

The spectacle with the spacecraft lasted about 10 minutes. During this time we observed the silver-gray object ascend and fly off, growing ever smaller as it moved away in a southwesterly direction. All at once, the rapidly shrinking point veered to the right and then at tremendous speed shot off so quickly that it suddenly disappeared from sight. I personally was deeply impressed by this extraordinary experience. Everything within me was in turmoil. I pondered this all the way home. Even today, I still think of that day with fondness.

My First UFO Sighting – *Report by Elisabeth Gruber*

In the spring of 1982, I spent a few days at the Center in Hinterschmidrüti with my family. Early in the morning on April 23, 1982 somewhere around 9 o'clock, I was busy sweeping the area between the residence and the chicken yard when Billy unexpectedly stepped out of the kitchen. His attention was concentrated upwards to the sky. Having an idea why, I tried to follow the direction of his glance, and accompanied him with each and every step. He forthwith addressed me with the following words, "Look, that's Quetzal flying there with his ship." Billy showed me the flight direction with his outstretched arm and gave me additional information indicating the position of the spacecraft.

A thrill of joy shot through me. Indeed, I could quite distinctly and clearly see a disk-shaped ship flying along in the morning sky. From where I was standing, the diameter of the ship looked to be about 70 centimeters (28 in.), which was of considerable size when taking the distance into account. Furthermore, it often seemed to change its position, as it once almost looked like a wooden beam and then assumed the shape of a disk again.

It occurred to me that this spectacle would also be a special experience for my husband, and so I tried calling him. But the good man is never there when he is needed. I regretfully had to acknowledge that he was beyond the reach of my voice. It turned out that he had been busy several hundred meters away from the residence.

At the same time, Billy called Bernadette, who was in the bathroom. When she asked what was the matter, he told her to quickly come outside because Quetzal's ship could be seen.

Billy and I observed that Quetzal had considerably increased the speed of his ship. Immediately, Billy showed me the reason for this maneuver… namely, an airplane flying in the same direction was spotted in the sky. From all appearances, the airplane seemed to be pursuing Quetzal's ship. His ship became smaller and smaller very quickly. When Bernadette finally appeared on the scene, it could only be recognized as a small spot of light at a very great distance. Billy pointed out the ship's location and together we watched the object move away at tremendous speed until it could no longer be seen. Billy explained to us afterwards that he had been out in front of the house when he telepathically received greetings from Quetzal and received the message that he was flying over the house and his ship could be observed in the sky. Billy further told us that he had seen Quetzal's spacecraft[47] fly over the house. He went through the kitchen to the backyard to continue following the flight of the ship.

This is how I had the very rare pleasure of such a sighting, which was even greater joy for me because a daytime appearance had only been granted twice before by the Pleiadians.

This unique experience will always remain an unforgettable memory for me.

Nighttime Sightings

Lights In the Sky – *Report by Gilgamesha Meier*

In the year of 1975, when I was only eight years of age, I had an experience that I shall not forget for the rest of my life. I remember it very precisely as if it were yesterday.

My mother told me to go to bed between 8–9 p.m. So I went off to my room but I simply could not sleep. I was still far too excited and nervous from the entire day.

At this time, my parents, Kalliope and Eduard Meier, were sitting in back of the house. We were still living in Hinwil on Wihalden Street 10 in a house that was lovely to me. So I listened attentively for quite some time to Pop's and Mom's conversation. When Pop suddenly said to Mom that she should take a look at the horizon, she did so at once, just as I did. It almost took my breath away as I saw something in the sky that impressed me so much that I shall not forget it as long as I live. Sixteen UFOs were flying along the horizon. At the distance from which I saw them, the white or almost yellow balls had a diameter of about 18–20 centimeters (7–8 in.). I had very mixed feelings as I had not yet realized what I saw flying up there in the sky. Not until a while later did I discover on my own that those flying objects came from other planets. From that moment on, I have known that there are also other beings living in our universe.

I am very happy that they exist and it is nice to know that they are standing by and willing to help us in their own way, even if many people do not want to accept this truth.

What is Sneaking Around There at This Late Hour? –
Report by Engelbert Wächter - abridged

… because it was also a great honor for me to drive our "boss" around through the area possibly under the cover of night and fog. After the last preparations had been made, Billy and I drove away from the house around 7:30 p.m.

I had often accompanied Billy to his contact sites as a companion or driver. This time I drove along at a moderate speed, following instructions Billy continuously received by telepathic means from Semjase and then relaying them to the driver. Besides the directions indicating the way, only little or nothing at all was said. In the beginning, we traveled in the general direction of Tablat-Saland, along the "lowlands" on good, broad roads.

Shortly before we reached the buildings of Wittwe AG, a prefabrication company in Saland, we suddenly took a hard left and drove uphill on a very narrow roadway. Shortly afterward, we passed a small farming village. The good Ford continued its tortuous path uphill and its dependable purring was only interrupted by Billy's brief indication of directions. To the right, left, straight-ahead, right, etc. So around 7:45 p.m. we reached a sort of high valley (Säcklen) which, as I was able to make out on this "cow night," bordered on the even darker edges of the woods to the left and right. The headlights of our car skimmed ghostlike over the bushes and along the roadway. Then the lights got lost in the murkiness far ahead.

"Pull in here," said Billy, sounding really chipper and full of pep.

"Yes, here. Stop! You can just turn." He did not say a thing about parking, so I got ready to drive off in the opposite direction.

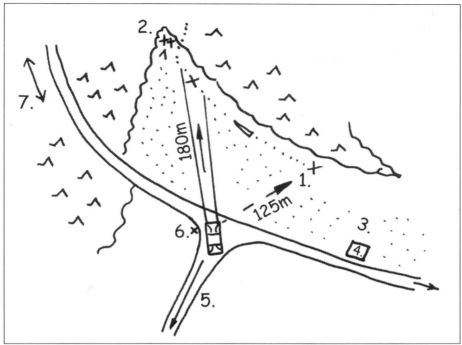

Fig. 8-1
LOCATION MAP OF THE EVENT
1-Menara and Quetzal; 2-Woods; 3-Pasture land; 4-Small barn;
5-Billy's walking direction; 6-My location, waiting place;
7-Way of arrival and departure

"Stop – stop!!!"

That is just the point! With Billy, you often do not know what to expect! It could happen that a driver who is left in the dark about matters would not quite know what to do or not to do. I automatically assumed that we had somehow taken a wrong turn; it would not have been the first time…

But we had not taken a wrong turn and destination XY had been reached.

Impressive as ever, Billy swung out of the car and glanced towards the woods, following the stirred-up jingling apparently coming from a nearby cattle pasture. Glowing small lights became visible and disappeared again. Well, all right, cattle eyes also happen to shine in the night.

While I was trying to neatly park the car so we could drive away without difficulty at the end of the contact, Billy briefly said good-bye, but not before casting a confirming glance at the stars… at his stars. Without a sound, he disappeared under the cloak of night turning ever darker. I could still see him for several meters, and then I was alone.

An almost eerie stillness enveloped me, which was interrupted now and then by an increasingly calmer jingling. Suddenly I felt the cold, which mercilessly reached for me through my thin jacket.

So I got back into the car, let the cassette tape play and provided a little warmth with the heat blower. Then I leisurely lit a cigarette, enjoyed its taste and kept watch like a lynx for possible pursuers. But nothing stirred. About thirty minutes must have passed before I stepped out of the car again to stretch my legs that had become icy-cold during this guard duty.

Then I unexpectedly had the feeling or the notion of having seen something glimmer to the right of me, halfway between the roadway and the edge of the woods. I placed my entire attention on full alert, quietly hastened back to the car and searched among all the junk in the glove compartment for the Russian hatchet (throwing ax). I carefully laid the hatchet on the seat, left the doors open with the light switched off and fully concentrated on the "hot spot" again.

Then I heard heavy steps rustle through the wet and almost 20-centimeter (8-in.) high grass. From all indications, it could only have been the steps of a grown man. Now and then a strange sort of light began to glimmer. The rustling steps became louder, and sounded as if two croppers were taking turns at cutting the wet grass some distance away. The light reflections were now easier to recognize in the light of the stars. A real feeling of warmth enveloped my heart with the thought that … but that is certainly impossible … How do I come up with such ridiculous thoughts – and where is this strangely peaceful feeling coming from? Could it be…?

Oddly enough, I had absolutely no feeling of uneasiness or sense of danger. So it could not have meant danger for Billy or for me. Certainly not! It was probably just the farmer wanting to look after his cattle. But that strange looking rain gear? Odd — and at this time of night?

As a precautionary measure, I checked the position of my weapon again while the brisk steps moved along close by the edge of the woods.

You just wait, farmer boy, I'll give you a proper fright. You see, it was suddenly clear to me that the halogen headlights were quite capable at this relatively short distance of abruptly illuminating a "night bird" like this one in the brightest of light. Quickly checking the direction of the car to determine the aim of the flood-light surprise — another double-check glance into the night. Man, – this happened within seconds of the highest tension. I cautiously seated myself behind the instruments and looked again through the windshield. Can I see anything at all through this glass? You bet I can see… It just began to glimmer again. This all happened within seconds and with extreme intensity.

Wonderful how this unsuspecting "bird" is groping his way right into the snare of my light. Only a few more meters to go. I feverishly fumbled for the ignition. The key was inserted. My halogen-light is nothing without turning the ignition key. The glimmering man was drawing ever closer to the destination point I had set. Only a few seconds now. The ignition key was already warm and moist. Now! By turning the ignition lock and switching on the halogen-light at the same time, I "opened fire" with a virtual flood of light.

A broad beam of white light flowed around a man clothed in a silvery shining "cloak." His step only faltered for a moment. Another two or three steps and he reached the border of darkness. Away! And that was supposed to be a farmer? I quickly let the motor roar, shifted gears, and then turned the car so I could capture his appearance in the headlights again. I just managed to catch a glimpse of the man retreating into the woods. Several branches cracked, and the spook was over. Only a few minutes later, Billy suddenly, as if coming out of the ground, stood in front of the car. He grinned at me, amused, and then startled me by asking if I always took pleasure in frightening harmless hikers. Had it not been for my neck, my lower jaw would certainly have dropped to the ground.

When I asked him how he knew all of that, he only smirked. As for me, I did not know what to think. Billy then continued the conversation. "Have you truly no idea to whom you gave such a fright?"

Of course I had a vague notion. But knowing the great precautions our Pleiadians friends take when moving about on our planet, I did not dare utter a word. I also have become very careful with my remarks, especially with respect to our friends, because how easily could...

Well now, "it" truly was our friend Quetzal and Billy had monitored the situation on the screen.

In addition to this, the following is an excerpt from the Semjase *Contact Report #139 of October 9, 1980:*

SEMJASE: ... One moment, Quetzal is calling me over the communicator.
QUETZAL: I just had quite a scare.
BILLY: That's quite clear to see, but look there, girl, the guy is grinning again. What's the matter with him?
SEMJASE: One moment and he will tell us.
QUETZAL: (Visible on the communicator screen.) Like any other hiker, I was walking through the night to get to Menara. I had reached the high edge of the woods unchallenged, just several meters away from the pasture fence where Menara was waiting for me by the cows, when I was suddenly standing in the glare of two light beam devices. Looking around, badly startled for a moment, I saw two auto headlights belonging to Engelbert's vehicle, as was determined by my analyzer. He must have observed me despite the dark night and thought that some stranger was roaming around who could possibly waylay our friend. That is my assumption.
BILLY: Quetzal, didn't you pull off your silvery shining cloak?
QUETZAL: No, my friend, I did not find it necessary, as I assumed that Engelbert could not observe or see me in the darkness.
BILLY: Then you thought too little too late, my son.
QUETZAL: That is correct. On the next occasion, I shall take better care.
BILLY: Well, the world won't go under because of it. Engelbert certainly had his fun watching you run into the hammer even if he supposedly did not do this on purpose, he had no way of knowing that it was you and not some wretched night scoundrel or other earthling.
QUETZAL: Certainly not, and that is why I did not feel assaulted or otherwise threatened. It was simply a momentary scare, which made me uncertain. In any case, you should explain the facts to him and extend to him my greetings. Good-bye.
BILLY: So long — it really got to him. I would have liked to have seen his face.
SEMJASE: That surely would have been quite a funny sight.
BILLY: Quetzal must have been more than 100 meters (330 ft.) away when he ran into the headlight beam. Why he did that at all is still not clear to me.

And can anything happen to you from the vibrations of the earthlings at this distance? According to my knowledge, you can come within 90–100 meters (297–330 ft.) of the earth people without protective equipment and not expose yourselves to any type of vibrational danger.

SEMJASE: The last part of your assessment is correct, but in the second part, you made a mistake in reasoning. Quetzal, with certainty, did not run into a beam of light from a headlight but must have suddenly been caught by it in the midst of the darkness.

As I, Engelbert Wächter, and Billy drove the car off the branched road and started home, the halogen headlight skimmed along the edge of the woods. The beam was indecently bright and Quetzal, who had reached the dark-skinned beauty, Menara,[48] was once again immersed in bright light. Standing peacefully beside each other at the pasture fence, they vanished from the beam of our homeward bound car into the darkness.

Dear readers, there are not enough words to portray my feelings about such an experience.

My First UFO Experience – *Report by Brunhilde Koye*

On the evening of April 8, 1983 at about 8:30 p.m. in Hinterschmidrüti, I took another close look at the sapling I had just tied to a windbreak rod to see if it would now grow straight. A strong foehn[49] was blowing the entire afternoon. Even as dusk was starting to fall, my scarf fluttered around my ears. I felt happy and content and watched the clouds as they quickly drifted along their way. When suddenly, what was that? No, there were no stars in the cloud-covered sky. But look there! A large light came towards me like a gigantic, shining floodlight. High above the watchtower in the east, it moved slowly and quietly westward toward our Semjase Silver Star Center.

At first, I stood there frozen. I could not form a thought as I gazed into the sky. I shook my head and slowly realized that my thinking ability had started to function again. I kept hammering the words into my head, "I don't want any evidence, I don't need it, because I have long been convinced of the existence of extraterrestrial spacecraft!"

After toying with these thoughts, I heard steps and saw Billy. He walked in an easterly direction from the residence to the garage. He was carrying his binoculars and was accompanied by Thomas. I was then quite certain that I had not been dreaming. No, what I was experiencing was pure reality. All of a sudden, I reached into my pocket and inadvertently came across my car key. I remembered that I had brought my binoculars along in the car. I quickly fetched them and was soon standing next to Billy and Thomas, focusing on the "heavenly object."

What I saw overwhelmed me. My heart was throbbing in my throat and my voice seemed to fail me. Indeed, it was a spacecraft! I very clearly recognized a large hull with a lot of light around it. The vessel-like form then changed into a triangle. It gave me the impression that it was as easily manipulated a mass as an air-filled balloon. Furthermore, there were many smaller lights arranged around the core of the object. Together, they formed the shape of a triangle. The lights moved now and then from the inside to the outside of the vessel-like form as if they were flying around their mother ship.

Bright white

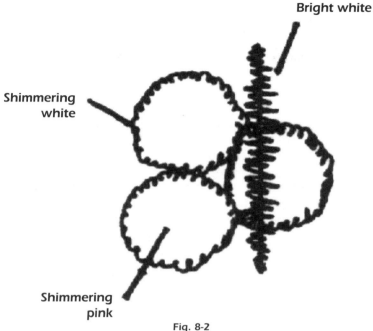

Shimmering white

Shimmering pink

Fig. 8-2
Sketch is by eyewitness, Thomas Keller

All at once, the luminous structure extended in length. The light grew weaker and weaker. It looked as if it were gradually moving back to the East. I heard voices behind me. Karen asked me for the binoculars. I gave them to her, but before I got my hands on them again, the luminous object had become tiny. Billy said that I would probably not find it again, and he was right.

I shall certainly never forget this unique spectacle. I am now indeed grateful for the "evidence."

Extraordinary Event on April 8, 1983 at 8:15 p.m. –
Report by Thomas Keller

I was just going to fetch additional tools for our mason-work when Silvano[50] suddenly said to Billy that a large light was in the sky. At once I went back to see whether it was the same light which had caught my attention a few minutes earlier but,at the time, it had not really "registered" within me. Billy ran quickly into the house to fetch his binoculars. We found a suitable place to view the thing. After a brief inspection, Billy suddenly said, "Phenomenal! Take a look through here." And I peered through.

What I saw caused me to hold my breath.

A form without solid contours could clearly and distinctly be seen in the sky. It continually changed its shape and its colors also slowly changed, blending into a great variety of shades. Upon Billy's request, I ran into the house to call the others so they could see it also. Quickly running back to Billy, I was allowed to look through the binoculars again. This time, the object was a bright, gleaming rose color (such as the "living clouds" in one of the "Spaceship Enterprise" episodes). I could note one of the forms and, with certainty, was able to make a rough sketch, although it was actually quite difficult because of the continuing changes in shape.

The "thing" seen with the naked eye was about five times as large as Venus. Clearly recognizable to us, as well as to Billy and several others who had joined us in the meantime, was its vertical, cone-shaped form that remained visible the entire time. According to Billy's estimation, the object was around 18,000 meters (11 miles) above the ground at a distance from us of about 35,000 meters (22 miles).

As we later lingered in the kitchen discussing it, Louis confirmed that he had observed the luminous object for a little more than 45 minutes. Engelbert only glanced at the "little object" for a short while, but then turned away. For him, it was nothing special. He had seen much more spectacular displays before. On the following day, Billy mentioned during work that Taljda had confirmed our sighting. She explained that it had been a ship with a diameter of 350 meters (1,155 ft.), the origin of which was far away from the earth, but which was something Billy could better explain.

As for me, I shall hold this extraordinary experience in fond memory and think of our friends in Druan[51] with genuine affection. *(See the following contact report.)*

Contact Report to the aforementioned event of Saturday, April 9, 1983 at 11:16 a.m.

BILLY: You reacted very quickly to my call, although it really wasn't so very urgent that it couldn't have waited until tomorrow.

TALJDA: It was not just your call that prompted me to visit you, but rather an important matter which has made it necessary to supply you with a bit of information. It could very well be that contacts are ahead of you in the next few months with other human beings from stars beyond your solar system.

BILLY: I see! Then you have come in a matter on behalf of both our interests. As for me, I had a question primarily concerning something quite peculiar that we were able to observe yesterday, on April 8.

High in the eastern sky, I noticed a glaring light at 8:14 p.m. about three to four times as large as Venus. At first I thought it was the evening star, Venus, before it dawned on me that we can only see Venus in the Southern and Western hemispheres. After that, I took a somewhat closer look at the glaring light and noticed that there were strange color shifts within in it that passed through all colors of the rainbow spectrum and also resulted in changes of form. Consequently, I rushed into my office and snatched my binoculars through which I was able to discern and observe a peculiar light structure about 1 meter (3 ft.) in size. It looked like a mirage to me, the form of which continuously changed and also seemed somehow transparent, just like a Fata Morgana[52]. I estimated the altitude of the object to be about 35,000 meters (20 miles), whereas its distance from our observation point must have been about 18–20 kilometers (11–12 miles). During my observation, I also detected various small objects emerging and flying away from the right side of the large object. Furthermore, I also saw various dark points and spots on the large object, something like protuberances or similar. I had seen similar things before on Ptaah's giant spacer[53] and that is why, in my opinion, it must have been a spacecraft that could only be seen as a Fata Morgana or simply as a reflected image. I therefore analyzed the glistening points flying away on the right side of the object as beamships, but assumed that the dark points and spots must have been hangars and the like, and the protuberances similar to the top structures of Ptaah's ship. If I calculate the size of the object's light with its distance, I come up with a ship of such expanse that it must have a diameter of about 320–340 meters (1,056–1,122 ft.).

TALJDA: Before I came here, Quetzal warned me about you, as we definitely observed that the event, in the manner you mentioned, did not go undetected by you and your friends.

BILLY: Oh! And why did Quetzal warn you about me?

TALJDA: He heard your conversation with Thomas and told me that the statements and dimensional estimates you made to Thomas were very close to reality. The object sighted by you and your friends was indeed a spacecraft that you were only able to see as a reflected image. The ship was hovering directly over your Center to study the location, as well as to study those human beings who are of the greatest importance on earth to those of us bound to the mission. For security reasons, as we have already made known to you, the flying object was screened against visibility with a form of technology completely different from ours, which produces reflected images that become visible in the atmosphere many kilometers away. As you already know, other human space travelers might not use exactly the same technology as we do. The Druans have shielding technologies that are completely different from those we possess. But now a word about your estimate… the reflected image of the spacecraft sighted by you and your friends was 26,000 meters (16 miles) away from where you were standing, while the altitude of the reflected image was 36,000 meters (23 miles) and the ship's diameter was 350 meters (1,155 ft.). Your calculations were thus more than astonishingly good, which astounds me despite Quetzal's early warning. Your other calculations of your observation also demand my admiration.

BILLY: You said something about Druans.

TALJDA: The flying object was a spacecraft from the planet Druan, the human life forms of which are called Druans. They are a highly developed and extremely peaceful human race and are capable of bringing innovations to our own technology. The planet Druan is located in the NOL system, which belongs to a galaxy the expanse of which is about 1.7 times larger than ours and is about 310 billion light years from this SOL system.

BILLY: In 1975, I was even a bit further away than… only a stone's throw. On my great space journey, you know. That's why a few million light years do not astound me or impress me any longer. Everything, in the end, becomes a habit.

TALJDA: Certainly, but that is not why I am giving you this information.

BILLY: You have no sense of humor at all.

TALJDA: Oh! That is also what Quetzal warned me of. Your often peculiar sense of humor.

BILLY: Right. It's a real nuisance, but you also said that I may be receiving visitors, probably from those dear Druans?

TALJDA: That is what I said. The Druans will be here on earth for at least five to six months for expeditionary purposes. However, according to our experience, their visit could instead be extended to several years. During this time, their spacecraft and their escorting flying objects will often be seen by earth people, but only in Europe during the first few weeks. After that, the Druan ship will also be sighted over other continents of earth. If earth people keep their eyes open, they will be able to observe the spacecraft quite frequently.

BILLY: That'll stir up things for me, especially with the clever and scientifically super-clever explanations such as balloons and the like. What does the object actually look like if one disregards the distorted reflected image?

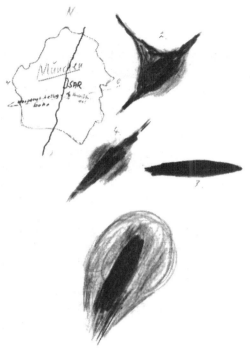

Fig. 8-3
Sketch of the sighting by Hans Zimmermann

TALIDA: Like a disk-shaped object, but a completely different form is reflected outwards by a specific protective screen that is comparable to the cone and facets of a mountain crystal.

BILLY: And which also produces the corresponding picture in all colors of the spectrum?

TALIDA: Apparently, you are not unfamiliar with such things.

BILLY: A simple prism principle about which one learns here in kindergarten, for example, by letting glass pearls with polished surfaces sparkle in the sunlight.

TALIDA: You never seem to be at loss for an answer.

BILLY: Exactly, that's why I'm equipped with organs of speech. You still haven't told me anything about the possible contacts.

TALIDA: That, naturally, escaped me. It is possible that a responsible person from the crew of the Druan ship, perhaps even several of them, will establish contact with you. In any case, they became interested in such a contact after we communicated with them and talked extensively about our joint mission on earth.

BILLY: And what could they possibly want from me? As an earthling, there's really nothing I can offer them.

TALIDA: You are too modest…

Note: Further sightings were reported, especially in Germany and Italy, which clearly referred to the same Druan ship.

Stay Informed
by Steelmark

Steelmark regularly sends out new information and updates on the Billy Meier Contacts. To be added to our contact list, fill in the information below and mail this pre-addressed card back to Steelmark.

Name: _____

Address: _____

_____

City: _____ State: ____ · Zip: _____

E-mail: _____

ASTF 3-04

Stay Informed
by Steelmark

Steelmark regularly sends out new information and updates on the Billy Meier Contacts. To be added to our contact list, fill in the information below and mail this pre-addressed card back to Steelmark.

Name: _____

Address: _____

_____

City: _____ State: ____ Zip: _____

E-mail: _____

ASTF 3-04

more Information

more Information

Postage
Required.
Post Office
will not deliver
without proper
postage.

Steelmark LLC
8086 South Yale
Suite 173
Tulsa, OK 74136

Postage
Required.
Post Office
will not deliver
without proper
postage.

Steelmark LLC
8086 South Yale
Suite 173
Tulsa, OK 74136

Panik und Rätselraten in Nürnberg –
Tausende haben es gesehen

Wilde Verfolgungsjagd
am Himmel

Es kam aus dem Nichts, war plötzlich da: Silbern schimmerte das unheimliche Dreieck am Himmel über Nürnberg. Es bewegte sich kaum, aber irgend etwas blinkte.

Wie gebannt starrten Tausende von Menschen hoch zu diesem glänzenden Ungeheuer. Hunderte riefen bei der Polizei, beim Wetteramt, bei Sternwarten an. „Über uns fliegt ein riesiges Ufo. Machen Sie was! Wir haben Angst!" meldeten sich den ganzen Tag über besorgte Männer, Frauen und Kinder.

Aber auch offizielle Stellen waren völlig ratlos. War es ein Spionage-Satellit, ein militärischer Versuchsballon oder sogar ein Flugschiff von einem anderen Stern?

Als das Ufo auch noch am nächsten Tag deutlich zu sehen war, nahm ein Team des Bayerischen Fernsehens die Verfolgung auf, mit einem Lear-Jet. Am Steuerknüppel der Nürnberger Flughafen-Direktor Helmut Müller-Gutermann. Der Pilot: „Wir verfolgten das Ufo bis in 12300 Meter Höhe. Aber wir kamen nicht nahe genug heran."

Mit seinem zwei Meter langen Teleskop konnte der Leiter der Nürnberger Sternwarte, Eckard Pöhl, mehr sehen: „Das Ding war wie eine deformierte Pyramide mit etwa 150 Meter Durchmesser, die Spitze nach oben. Der Rest sah aus wie eine durchsichtige Plastikfolie."

Das Rätsel löste schließlich am Freitagvormittag der Leiter der Flugsicherung Manching Gertwin Hühnerbein: „Wir sind sicher, daß das ‚unbekannte Flugobjekt' ein Stratosphärenballon ist, wie er üblicherweise für Messungen eingesetzt wird." [a]

Fotos: Walter Schwarz

Fig. 8-4A
(See English translation on the following page)

"Die Aktuelle" Munich, #18 from May 2,1983

Panic and Speculation In Nurenberg

Thousands Saw the Wild Pursuit in the Sky

It came out of nowhere and was suddenly there. The eerie triangle shimmered like silver in the sky over Nuremberg. It hardly moved, but something kept blinking.

Thousands of people stared spellbound at the glittering monster. Hundreds of people called the police, weather bureau and astronomical observatory. "A gigantic UFO is flying over us. Do something! We are afraid!" Such calls were received by worried men, women and children over the entire day.

However, the official authorities were also fully perplexed. Was it an espionage satellite, a military test balloon or even a flying ship from another star?

Since the UFO was clearly visible on the next day as well, a team from the Bavarian television network took up pursuit of the object with a Lear Jet.

At the control tower was the Nuremberg Airport Director, Mr. Helmut Mueller-Gutermann. The pilot: "We pursued the UFO up to an altitude of 12,300 meters (8 miles), but we could not get close enough."

With a telescope two meters in length, Mr. Eckard Poehl, the Director of the Nuremberg Observatory, was able to see more: "The thing looked like a deformed pyramid with a diameter of about 150 meters (495 ft.) and with the tip pointing upwards. The rest looked like a transparent plastic foil."

The puzzle was finally solved on Friday morning by Mr. Gertwin Huehnerbein, the director of air traffic control in Manching: "We know for certain that the 'unknown flying object' was a stratosphere balloon which is generally used for taking measurements."

Fig. 8-4B
(Translation of previous German article)

Rätselhafter Flugkörper über Köln gesichtet

wy Köln. Ein rätselhaftes glühendes Flugobjekt hielt in der Nacht zum Dienstag Polizei und Einwohner in dem Kölner Stadtteil Holweide in Atem. Angefangen hatte der außergewöhnliche Polizeieinsatz mit Anrufen aus dem rechtsrheinischen Vorort. Mehrere Bürger sahen ab 23.10 Uhr einen unbekannten Flugkörper und alarmierten die Beamten.

Die Funkstreife „Arnold 19/20" ging in Holweide auf Beobachtungsposition. Die Beamten meldeten: „Am Himmel ein glühender, kreisförmiger Gegenstand mit leuchtendem Kranz." Höhe und Größe der ungewöhnlichen Erscheinung waren nicht auszumachen.

Die Polizei ermittelte bei der Flugsicherung des Flughafens Wahn. Dort war weder ein Flugobjekt angemeldet, noch war eins auf dem Radarschirm zu entdecken. Die Beamten erkannten durch das Fernglas ein ballonähnliches Gebilde mit einer Lichtquelle ziemlich genau in der Mitte. Ein geometrisches Muster – horizontale und vertikale Linien – habe sich über den ganzen Flugkörper gezogen und deutlich von dem kreisrunden Objekt abgehoben.

Das helle strahlende Licht fiel den Polizisten auf. Sie schlossen aber aus, daß es sich um einen Stern handeln könne. Gegen 1 Uhr war der Spuk vorbei. Aufziehende Wolken verdeckten das Ufo. Bei der Kölner Polizei wurde das Erscheinen des unbekannten Flugobjektes im Computer gespeichert. In Form, Farbe und geometrischer Zeichnung soll das Ufo dem Flugobjekt ähneln, das vergangene Woche über Nürnberg gesehen wurde. Einen Wetterballon mit rund 80 Meter Durchmesser vermutete man dort hinter der Erscheinung.

Fig. 8-5A
(See English translation on the following page)

Kölner: Ein Ufo über der Stadt

KÖLN (dpa)

Ein rätselhafter glühender Flugkörper („Ein Ufo!") hat in der Nacht zum Dienstag Polizei und Einwohner in Köln in Atem gehalten. Nach Anrufen von Bürgern bestätigten Polizeibeamte: „Ein auffälliges, strahlendes Licht, ein kreisförmiger Gegenstand mit leuchtendem Kranz." Die Nachforschungen blieben allerdings erfolglos.

Fig. 8-6A
(See English translation on the following page)

Mysterious Flying Object Sighted Over Cologne, Germany

wy Cologne. A mysteriously glowing flying object captivated police and inhabitants of the Holweide district of Cologne in the wee hours of Tuesday morning. Unusual police action started with calls from a suburb situated on the right side of the Rhein. Several alarmed citizens saw an unknown flying object after 11:10 p.m. and called the authorities.

The radio patrol car "Arnold 19/20" went to the lookout site in Holweide. The authorities reported "a glowing, circular object in the sky with a radiant corona." The altitude and size of the unusual appearance could not be determined.

The police conducted investigations at the air traffic control tower at Wahn Airport. No flying object was reported or could be detected on the radar screen. With binoculars, the authorities recognized something similar to a balloon with a source of light almost exactly in the middle. A geometric pattern – horizontal and vertical lines – ran across the entire flying object and clearly raised above the circular object.

The police noted the brightly shining light but ruled out the possibility of it being a star. At about 1 a.m., the fuss was finally over. Gathering clouds covered the UFO. The Cologne police stored information on the appearance of this flying object in their computer. The UFO was said to be similar in form, color and geometric configuration to the flying object spotted over Nuremberg a week earlier. The object was presumed to be a weather balloon with a diameter of about 80 meters (264 ft.).

Fig. 8-5B
(Translation of previous German article)

Kölner Stadtanzeiger, on May 4, 1983

Residents of Cologne:
A UFO OVER THE CITY

Cologne (dpa) A mysteriously glowing flying object (a UFO!) captivated the police and inhabitants of Cologne in the wee hours of Tuesday morning. Following the calls of citizens, the police authorities confirmed "a peculiar shining light or circular object with radiant corona." The subsequent investigations however were unsuccessful.

Fig. 8-6B
(Translation of previous German article)

EXAMPLES: "Mein erstes UFO-Erlebnis," (My First UFO Experience) by Bernhard Koye and the enclosed newspaper article from "Die Aktuelle" Munich, #18 of May 2, 1983.

My First UFO Experience – *Report by Bernhard Koye*

It was Tuesday, April 19, 1983 at about 9:10 p.m. in Munich, when our dog very urgently wanted to go outdoors. But as I was only half dressed and our guest, Hans Zimmermann, was busily reading contact reports, my mother, Brunhilde Koye, decided to take the dog for a walk.

At approximately 9:25 p.m., Mom stormed into the apartment and called out excitedly and quite urgently, "Get dressed, get dressed!" Mr. Zimmermann and I hurried, slipped into some pieces of clothing and hastily left the house, hard behind Mom.

What had happened? As Mom explained to us, she was walking our dog, Wastl, along the Isar, when she suddenly caught sight of a glowing object in the nocturnal sky. And that is exactly what she wanted to show us, provided it was still there. Well, we were lucky! As we had a broad view of the sky from the driveway of our house, we ran there and saw the object, still visible in radiant splendor. Naturally, by using my Mom's binoculars, more details could be recognized.

After a while, we changed our position and walked through the nearby park to the bank of the Isar and continued our observation from there. In this place, we enjoyed the sight of the glowing object even more than before. It appeared to be very large. Mom suddenly remembered her first UFO experience on Friday, April 8 in Hinterschmidrüti. She could possibly have seen the very same Druan spacecraft then, because it had about the same features. Now, it gradually moved away from us, slowly ascending diagonally in the air. It was a very moving experience for me and I spontaneously took hold of my mother's hand.

About 9:50 p.m., a strong gusty wind arose, blowing exactly from the direction of the departing spacecraft and — so it seemed to us — setting only the tree-tops within a circumference of about 200 meters (660 ft.) in turbulent motion. We watched everything as closely as we possibly could with the help of the binoculars. Mr. Zimmermann made a special effort because he wanted to make a sketch of it.

At 9:58 p.m., clouds suddenly gathered in the sky and the luminous object faded away behind them in only a second's time. We stood there another minute, but it did not emerge again from the clouds. However, as I took another look around on the way home, it flashed very briefly one last time, like the light of a distant lighthouse, before it vanished for good.

What a dog can be good for after all!

Footnotes

45 ▪ Myself, my children, Gilgamesha, Atlantis and Methusalem, Amata Stetter and Mr. H. Schutzbach.

46 ▪ Pleija is Semjase's precocious sister. According to Billy, Pleja is a vibrant, adventurous creature with long, black hair. While visiting with Billy, Pleja took a spin on his moped as Semjase watched on nervously.

47 ▪ From Billy's point of view, Quetzal's ship appeared to have a diameter of one meter (3.3 ft.), when in actuality, the ship had a diameter of 7-meter s (23 ft.), thus indicating how high it was hovering over the house.

48 ▪ Menara is a dark-skinned woman from the Lyra System. She belongs to one of the races befriended by the Plejaren who were stationed on earth for eleven years (1975-86). She often acted as contact person in place of Semjase and Quetzal.

49 ▪ Foehn is a positively charged "falling wind" from the ionosphere — causing the brain to secret unusual amounts of seretonin — causing people to act strangely. In California, a similar ion wind is called the "Santa Ana" or "Satana" winds.

50 ▪ Silvano Lehman is a Core Group member of FIGU Switzerland and lives on the farm or the Semjase Silver Star Center, in Schmidrüti, Switzerland.

51 ▪ Druanians are a highly developed and extremely peaceful human race and are capable of bringing innovations to our own technology. The planet Druan, is located in the NOL System, which belongs to a galaxy whose expanse is about 1.7 times as large as ours, and this galaxy is about 310 billion light years from this SOL System."

52 ▪ Fata Morgana is a mirage seen especially in the Strait of Messina formerly attributed to fairy agency.

53 ▪ A very large spacecraft used by the Plejaren.

CHAPTER 9

Why Have the Extraterrestrial Flying Objects Not Landed Publicly?

In connection with extraterrestrial intelligences, it is sometimes incomprehensible to us why they exhibit such peculiar habits during their visits. Some of them zip around carefree in the open, while others take all possible precautions to conceal their presence from our view, as the Pleiadians do, for example.

There are extraterrestrial visitors who never land directly on the earth's surface, or at least do not leave landing tracks behind, but others leave clearly visible and measurable tracks wherever they land.

They establish and cultivate contacts with earth people in a way that seems peculiar. Most extraterrestrials avoid any contact with us, so personal encounters with them are purely coincidental or of short duration. In rare cases and under very specific conditions, they choose to contact individual persons for longer periods of time. However, the great majority of contact persons merely receive impulse-like transmissions without knowing how these thoughts originated, and assume it is from their own subconscious. Very few on our earth have actually experienced genuine personal contact with extraterrestrials. Furthermore, personal contacts always take place unofficially, privately and in secret. That is why the burning questions for many interested persons are, "Why do the alien visitors only cultivate personal contacts with a select few and why do they not show themselves to the broad public? Why do they not land on the Red Square in Moscow, on the green lawn of the White House in Washington, on the grounds of the international airport in Frankfurt, or perhaps even better, in the garden of the United Nations Palace in Geneva?" To prevent a shock effect, they could use a worldwide communication network to announce their arrival in advance. Why do they not make use of any of these possibilities instead of continuing to play a cat and mouse game with us? If the extraterrestrial visits are truly taking place here on earth — as the argument goes — then what could be more natural than establishing contact with the government of a superpower, with NASA or with the United Nations. They could make arrangements with influential personalities. Why do they not shake hands with Russian or American statesmen like Putin or Bush, etc., with the friendly words, "Hello, here we are. What can we do for you?"

Such spectacular action would undoubtedly be the most convincing and effective proof of the existence of extraterrestrial intelligences, a subject very much doubted by the majority of earth humanity. The extraterrestrials know this as well as we do. But to this day they still avoid making an official landing, if at all possible. Their way of action may not be immediately comprehensible to us but, after careful consideration, a few very plausible reasons arise. To better understand the matter, let us imagine ourselves in the following situation: Assume that we are the crew of a military helicopter and have been ordered to observe an unexplored region in the primeval Brazilian forest and, if possible, to assume personal contact with the natives by landing in the middle of a village. What if we learn the inhabitants of this primeval forest still live in savage barbarism, beat each other's brains out and regard every stranger as an enemy?

Based on this stance of suspicion and aggression, we would expect the tribal chiefs to resist any contact with strangers for fear of losing their prestige and positions of power. Without long years of preparation, a public encounter would be a daring venture involving great risk. A few of those who are unable to be taught might panic and probably try to shoot down the helicopter, (although they would not have the chance with their blowpipes and poison arrows.) Others would consider the visitors to be heavenly gods instead of friends and helpers. Radical elements would possibly plot to seize control of the totally unknown flying object and its crew in order to take over the leadership of all tribes with the assistance of these wonder-machines. Under such circumstances, a landing would certainly not be advisable unless done in a forcible manner, using all the weapons of a modern fighter helicopter.

Due to the vast technical superiority of such weaponry, a landing among these savages could indeed take place. But what would be the sense of doing so if the helicopter crew intended to cultivate contacts on an absolutely friendly basis in order to stimulate progress — not by using brutal force, but through teaching?

The situation is similar for extraterrestrials, whose spiritual evolution is substantially higher than ours and who come to earth with good intent in order to help us in our spiritual development. For the Pleiadians and other extraterrestrial races, there are compelling reasons why they do not land publicly and do not contact governments, preferring instead to deal in great secrecy with a few select persons who have absolutely no political, military or financial authority.

However, we should also ask ourselves whether it is possible for extraterrestrials to set foot on our planet without endangering their health. We must consider that not all human life forms in the universe have exactly the same physical constitution as we have on earth, since the conditions of life on their home planets can be quite different from ours. This may be due to atmosphere or gravity. Consequently, there are those who would suffocate in our atmosphere. They would not be able to leave their spacecraft without a space suit because our atmosphere would be deadly. A further problem is the possibility of mutual misunderstanding. It would be downright impossible for communication to take place if the extraterrestrials only communicated telepathically or used languages that are unknown on earth.

On the other hand, there are plenty of other extraterrestrials who would certainly be capable of landing publicly and establishing contacts at the highest political levels. The reason why they have not done so is because earth has not met their necessary requirements at the present time. Here are a few reasons why:

- In 1976, the Pleiadians tested many people of earth, especially the ufological circles, to determine their love for and recognition of truth. The results were devastating and brought the bitter realization that earth humanity is quite obviously not mature enough for a public landing. According to Semjase:

SEMJASE: The spirit of many earth people is still small and confined by religious slavery. In their limited minds, some of them (after the landing) would honor us extraterrestrials as heavenly gods, just as they did in earlier times.

In fact, whenever and wherever extraterrestrial intelligences have landed on earth, they have been honored and worshipped as godly beings. In this manner, earthman turned over all responsibility for his own destiny to the presumed astronaut gods.

As can be learned from the Contact Report of October 2, 1976, the ufological circles received the worse grades imaginable by Semjase and I cannot refrain from quoting an excerpt:

SEMJASE: ... These circles, which are guilty of turning the fact of the existence of the Pleiadians into an object of ridicule in the broad public, have caused us to be regarded as figments of fantasy and hallucination. This does not mean that all UFO groups work in this manner, but most of them do. The misguided ones search for fantastic explanations in technical, paranormal and purely spiritual realms. The most impossible theories arise from their foolishness and ignorance. These misled ones primarily focus on technical possibilities and ways of constructing our ships. They pay no heed at all to our mission or the values connected with it. This is typical of the people of earth, as they nearly always aim for material (worldly) gains and fully overlook basic values ... namely, spiritual values. They dream up the most incredible fantasies and even claim that beamships are operated by spiritual powers and are constructed according to spiritual blueprints. This is also a malicious, misleading claim, just like the idea that we would move within paranormal spaces.

The greatest insanity along these lines comes from those who concern themselves with incomprehensible matters which they do not understand in the least. They are known as parapsychologists, etc. It is this very group that carries out malicious and misleading subversive activities that effectively hinder the finding of the truth. Those scientists and pseudo-scientists who, for purely material reasons, occupy themselves with the search for possible clarification and explanations of the existence of our flying devices and even for proof that we exist, only exceed the errors of the parapsychologists. Still, the parapsychologists' actions are only illusions because, in truth, they are possessed by illogic and they are still caught in very materialistic, earthly and misleading forms of thought; therefore, they are incapable of acquiring any knowledge. They condemn everything as lies and deception, whereby they feel satisfied in their great delusions of grandeur. Among their kind is also the one you call ...,[54] whose stupidity and primitive behavior should not upset you. This person possesses no lasting valuable spiritual knowledge — as little as those who still move in fields of hierarchy-worship or the acknowledgement of such. They claim that we simply know nothing of spiritual matters. In fact, their statement only proves their spiritual poverty. These people have not yet discovered for themselves the genuine concepts of reality and truth.

The result of all this is, earth people today are not able to regard us and the existence of our ships in an honest, open and real perspective. The ufologists, who were selected to spread the truth and prepare the way for the arrival of extraterrestrial intelligences, have instead lowered themselves to the level of a primitive, pseudo-scientific sect and promote their own unintelligible and dirty nonsense of self-construed theories and lies. Because of them, earth people throughout the globe have distanced themselves further and further away from truth instead of being led to the truth. This fact proves that earthman does not have sufficiently fair and truly knowing powers at his disposal, which could prepare for the coming of extraterrestrial intelligences through purposeful enlightenment.

Note: As already mentioned, Semjase's criticism does not pertain to all ufologists.

- An official landing of a Pleiadian or other extraterrestrial spacecraft may not be staged on earth without sufficient preparation of the population. Otherwise, it would only be irresponsible and also purposeless. Therefore, earth humanity may not become acquainted with the existence of extraterrestrials while in its present clumsy evolutionary stage. If earth humanity were confronted all at once by the presence of extraterrestrials, we would all have to acknowledge them as a blunt reality, and unless previously prepared, the population would panic and the landing would provoke a catastrophe, the extent of which was not before seeable. Semjase was also of the opinion that we would have to count on a panic and those uncountable millions would become fully hysterical and "mentally ill." In this connection, one only has to think of the fictional invasion of the Martians from the radio program, "War of the Worlds" by Orson Welles, which was broadcast in the USA in 1938 and caused panic among numerous earth citizens.

According to my opinion, it would be extremely embarrassing for most of our contemporaries if they were to unexpectedly learn the untainted truth "with a bang," using the sledgehammer method. Their traditional view of the world would shake and inevitably collapse like a house of cards. They would possibly also discover what has been going on behind the scenes on our globe and how the populace has been deceived and considered to be stupid since time immemorial by power-hungry, money-craving powers. Since many people would be unable to endure this sudden revelation, they would most likely attempt to hold accountable the leaders who are mainly responsible for such deception. This would not happen without riots and bloodshed. Putting it plainly, there would be a bloody revolution against those in power and, hence, an outright civil war.

- In case a crew of extraterrestrials were determined, in spite of all reservations, to land publicly on Terra, the next difficult question to clarify is, which country should be honored with their visit? Which nation may be granted this privilege without angering the other nations? The way things are here on earth, the diplomatic skills of the alien visitors would never be good enough to prevent a flood of jealousy and envy from all those who were not chosen. This dilemma could presumably only be prevented if we had something like a single government here on earth. At the present time, there is no existing institution or higher authority so powerful that it could speak for the entire civilization on earth and represent the interests and well being of the entire planet. A unified, global government is for this reason, among many others, necessary for us. But the time for this has not yet come because which government today would be willing to hand its power over to others?

Some people, who do not have the slightest doubt that extraterrestrials are far superior to us in every respect, wonder why these visitors do not say hello by appearing in public. Naturally, in view of the technical superiority of their weaponry, they have no reason to be afraid of us. What they fear, and rightly so, is the large probability of being exposed to an embarrassing situation if a spacecraft crew should dare step on our territory, with or without permission. According to the statement of the Pleiadians, our governments are presently still too untrustworthy to make a friendly arrangement with foreign planetary inhabitants. In any case, fame-addicted, money-craving and power-hungry people are not in demand as partners — and commands to attack UFOs build little confidence, just to mention one example. According to Semjase's information, military circles or criminal elements would try to capture an extraterrestrial spacecraft under the guise of friendship and peace. Of course, that would be the coup of the century, because whoever possessed this brilliant technology could rule the entire world. And anyone who knows the methods of our secret services to some extent can imagine everything these secret agents would do with whatever technology they find useful. Should the alien guests be so careless to leave their spacecraft unarmed and without security, they could consider themselves lucky if they escaped unharmed. At any rate, who would let slip away the unique opportunity to gather as much powerful knowledge as possible? As we know from the Pleiadians, the extraterrestrials are not allowed to reveal their progressive technology as long as a civilization like ours misuses every new invention for power, political or war-like purposes. We can assume that the alien visitors strictly heed these regulations and would decidedly rebuke all requests or demands, as described. Otherwise, the resulting complications can be pictured by anyone — any additional commentary is superfluous.

Naturally, the extraterrestrials will see to it that they do not expose themselves to such a dilemma.

The Pleiadians, in accordance with their noble intentions, do not want to make use of their power. If possible, they would avoid any situation that might force them to use their weapons to protect themselves from unpleasant conflicts and dangers. If they were threatened by us or in any way attacked by weapons, they would have no alternative but to use all available weapons for their defense. They would by no means be uninjurable or even immortal in a battle, as presumed by many.

Furthermore, there exists a law of Creation according to which every human being, regardless of his race or origin, has the right to physical, psychic and consciousness-related freedom. No human being is allowed to be forced, but should be completely free and unrestrained to decide his own course of action in all areas of life, everywhere and at any time, and the same naturally holds true for the entire human race.

This principle of non-interference is very well known to the extraterrestrials. It is of such great importance that they avoid, if at all possible, the violation of even an iota of this principle. Now, perhaps we wonder what this has to do with our topic. Well — it would be nothing less than a form of influence if the fact of extraterrestrial existence were forced upon earth's inhabitants. This is because knowledge about the existence of alien planetary inhabitants has still not penetrated deep enough into the consciousness of earth people.

According to the Pleiadians, another effect not to be underestimated is the resultant sense of mystery that is lost. In other words, earth people would rapidly lose interest in extraterrestrials if their existence were 100 percent confirmed overnight by a public appearance. Such is the nature of earth people that they need the magic of mystery and of the unexplainable if their interest is to endure on a long-term basis. In contrast to earlier times when it was permissible to convince people of a matter by means of miracles, today it is advisable to find truth through one's own thought processes instead of with demonstrations that can be seen and heard with one's own eyes and ears. There are many things between heaven and earth which exist despite the fact that they can neither be seen nor heard.

The Pleiadians and their allies who have been working for years in various matters of the earth people, are more or less subject to the recommendations of the High Council, who cannot advocate a public landing until the requirements for such have first been fulfilled. But we have not yet reached the necessary evolutionary level for this to take place. Furthermore, we are socially incapable of being integrated as a partner with equal rights in a cosmic confederation. Our own efforts and growth will determine when a landing on a grand scale can take place. Until then, it is probably wiser and more meaningful if the foreign visitors cultivate contacts only with a few select individuals. With their help, the knowledge about extraterrestrials and their arrival can slowly but surely penetrate and grow within the consciousness of earthman and prepare us for the event. The more open-minded we are in this matter, the faster we will develop a positive attitude and the sooner the extraordinary event of a public landing can take place.

Incidentally, in the year 1979, the Pleiadians declared themselves willing under certain circumstances to establish contact with a government of earth, but only through their mediator, Billy. The secret service of the chosen country then took over the role of mediator. Unfortunately, the event could not take place because of the irresponsible attitude of a few high government officials who were either too cowardly or simply unwilling to accept the conditions set by the Pleiadians. The enormous benefits that a few power-mad and greedy politicians let slip away due to their negative decisions, their unreasonableness, nearsightedness and self-glorification, we cannot even begin to measure.

Footnotes

53 ▪ A very large spacecraft of the Pleiadians

54 ▪ The name of the culprit was deleted from the contact note as a means to legally protect Billy.

CHAPTER 10

Billy's Photos – Disputes and Rectifications

Glad to have received permission from his extraterrestrial friends, Billy produced hundreds of color slides and a total of eight short films. These sensational photos and fantastic film clips show various extraterrestrial spacecraft, landing tracks, impressive flight maneuvers and diverse demonstrations by day as well as by night.

Without exaggeration, I claim that Billy's photos are not only the best but also the most comprehensive of this kind that have ever been compiled by a single person on earth. They are by no means accidental snapshots, as are a great many other UFO photos. Moreover, every photo was planned and nothing was left to chance. The entire film material of FIGU, most of which was photographed by Billy and a few by his friends and acquaintances, could be produced only after express permission had been granted by the extraterrestrials. In each case, Billy had received telepathic instructions on the location and time, where and when photographs and filming would be permitted. Except for the pictures of outer space, almost all of the photographs were taken in the Zurich Highlands on the meadows and fields in the general vicinity of Billy's residences in Hinwil and Hinterschmidrüti, although somewhat less frequently at those two locations directly.

The actual purpose for taking the photos was not to satisfy a hunger for sensation and publicity as some have assumed, but to compile the best possible record to support the credibility of the contacts. Pictures not only serve as valuable viewing material and as helpful support of the text, but they also primarily have served from the beginning as an important support for its truthful content. And not lastly, the film material could be used as enticement, so-to-speak, for interested people who are supposed to be led via ufology to the spiritual background. Spiritual values, I would like to emphatically stress, are actually much more important than all ufological matters combined.

Complications with Photography and Filming

The photographing and filming were more or less complicated by the following circumstances:

- Billy, a one-armed man, was handicapped to a certain extent.

- He did not have the best of cameras for financial reasons. Billy also used the camera easiest for him to operate, which was an OLYMPUS -35 ECR with a focal range of 1:2.8 — f 42 mm and an exposure time constant of 1/100 seconds. All photos were taken with this camera.

- The influence of the types of radiation that do not exist in normal photographicwork proved to have unpleasant effects. But there is a fundamental difference between taking photos of earthly flying objects and of Pleiadian spacecraft.

- In the first years of the 11-year contact period (from January 28, 1975 to January 29, 1986), the Pleiadians had a spacecraft in operation called a beamship (ray ship). Its propulsion system did not release harmful radiation but it emitted an undesirable form of magnetic radiation into the environment. With the most modern-type ship that Billy was permitted to photograph and film in 1981, an especially intense magnetic radiation appeared in the area around the ship.

- Also to be considered when taking photographs was the invisible protective shield that diverted all flying objects, meteors, interstellar matter, etc., away from the ship to a distance of 90 meters (297 ft.). Only when this protective shield was turned off could close-up shots be taken from a distance of less than 90 meters without damaging the photo material. *(See ~ Photo #61)*

- Taking pictures of the outdoors from within a Pleiadian spacecraft proved to be quite futile without a supplementary apparatus because energy radiation was also noticeable here, and the quality of the photos was impaired to a great extent. Therefore, the Pleiadians constructed an apparatus enabling Billy to at least take pictures usable to some extent. Without this device, Billy would have been unable to carry out his job as photographer during his great space journey.

- Finally, any extraneous radiation, which appears in diverse forms while flying through outer space, should be mentioned. Even radiation that comes from outside our SOL system can have certain effects. This was evident from our pictures of the night demonstrations in June of 1976, as was clearly established by the Pleiadians' own examination.

Beside all the above named detrimental factors, there were also unfavorable effects for the photo material, as well as to the quality of the end products, be they photos, slides or films. So it was inevitable that Billy had to "swallow a few bitter pills," especially in the beginning when he had practically no idea of the radiation effects. One day, the photo camera unfortunately "exploded" in his hands, completely destroying the exposure meter and viewfinder. It has been proven time and again that good, clear close-up photographs were conditional and possible only to a limited extent. This is why Billy's photo collection has a certain rarity value, and not without good reason.

Other trouble arose a few years later in 1981 when Billy was on his way cross-country. He was traveling with his small house trailer and a mini-tractor that served as tow truck in order to film the Pleiadian ship with its many spheres (jokingly called by us the "wedding cake ship") with his video camera, and to make picture slides. When the "wedding cake ship" came too close, its magnetic field caused considerable trouble because it totally magnetized Billy's tractor. As a result, the starting mechanism no longer functioned, so the vehicle could not be started. The ship's pilot, Semjase, was unable to repair the damage herself, so Quetzal, whom she had summoned in great haste, had to come to the rescue. But the repair also caused problems for Quetzal. He had to tinker around for quite a while with work tools and mechanical equipment before he finally succeeded in getting the vehicle running again.

Unfortunately, that was not the end of it. A further inconvenience ensued — all the video film cassettes, valued at about 550 Swiss francs, received an overdose of magnetic radiation and became completely unusable. With an exact diagnosis of the circumstances, Quetzal determined that, according to his calculations, a protective lead mantle of 6.11 mm thick was needed to protect the film material 100 percent from the magnetic radiation. From then on, Billy had to keep his videocassettes in a lead box and could not take them too close to the "wedding cake ship." He also had to be very careful while taking pictures with the camera. The close-up snapshots of the "wedding cake ship" in the parking lot of the Center in Hinterschmidrüti were clear and distinct because the camera was behind an especially thick pane of glass. (See ~ Photo #21)

A few of Billy's hazy and blurred pictures can almost always be attributed to some type of radiation, except for the pictures taken in outer space. Photos damaged in this way display color changes, haziness, distortions, reflections similar to a Fata Morgana, subtle lateral shifts and changes in distance. An object (i.e., a tree) could seem to be laterally shifted or be at a changed distance due to a radiation effect if it came too close to a Pleiadian ship. The effect can even cause a photographed ship to look transparent, like a ghost picture. With close-up photos, it can also occur that the ship's contours appear to be partially asymmetrical or to have wavy lines. These extraordinary effects indeed appear in a few of the photos, especially if the security distance had not been observed. To judge photos that have been damaged by radiation, it is of enormous importance that the true causes are known. False conclusions are otherwise unavoidable. (See ~ Photo #61)

- Besides these difficulties, it was almost impossible to take any photographs during the day in the vicinity of inhabited settlements or solitary farms without being noticed by unwelcome guests who wanted to witness the spectacle. Occasionally, some people also bothered Billy out of pure curiosity... those strolling about, runners through the woods, lumberjacks, foresters or hunters. This type of disturbance was undoubtedly the greatest obstacle to Billy's photo and film work.

Advantages and Help

Despite the given difficulties, Billy's photos are nonetheless unique throughout the entire world in both quality and quantity. Understandably, many people have already tried to figure out how Billy managed to take an entire series of such spectacular photos as if on a production line. The answer stems from the fact that a number of opportunities were made available to Billy by the Pleiadians, advantages that an "ordinary earth citizen" simply could not have. As already mentioned, we are not dealing with impromptu snapshots but with selective pictures that usually were planned in advance.

Secondly, the time factor also plays a role that should not be underestimated. Billy, as a rule, always had enough time to make the necessary preparations, which is simply not the case with photos of sheer coincidence.

Furthermore, the Pleiadians practiced their demonstrations so that their spacecraft were always in position in front of the camera at an adequate distance, and often hovering, so the spacecraft simply could not be missed while the pictures were being taken.

The ability of the Pleiadians to shield their spacecraft against optical and acoustical detection and radar registration made it considerably easier for them to land at any place they chose, or any time of day or night, without risking detection. This is naturally very advantageous, especially as they avoid discovery under all circumstances. The Pleiadians firmly adhere to the motto: "The fewer spectators, the better. But the best is no one at all."

Only because of the sector shielding was it possible for Billy to take photos or to film over an extended period of time in broad daylight near inhabited settlements without having to fear a virtual onrush of people. With sector shielding, the spacecraft is completely shielded so it cannot be heard. At the same time, the camera is aimed toward the spacecraft along a narrow sector of visibility, while the ship itself remains absolutely invisible to all viewers outside this sector. On certain occasions, when the Pleiadians do not want to be detected under any circumstances, they apply a shielding hood by laying a "bell" of energy over all objects to be hidden from view. Without this excellent screening, Billy would have had to forget about the picture taking from the very beginning.

Despite this sector shielding, undesirable disturbances still occurred from time to time due to the unexpected appearance of curious onlookers and other outside spectators, which often tested the patience of Billy and his extraterrestrial friends. To be able to work in peace during the day with no disturbances, a blockage of the area in question by legal means would've been necessary. For known reasons, this solution, simple in principle, remained no more than wishful thinking.

Basically, the Pleiadians were thoroughly capable of keeping unwanted outsiders away from the scene of the event and of excluding other intrusions. But, as a matter of principle, they were not permitted to use such compulsory measures.[55] In order not to be detected, they had no alternative but to disappear like lightning, which actually happened several times, one right after the other. To perform this fantastic feat of disappearing from view without a trace and reappearing just as quickly, the Pleiadians make use of a teletransmitter machine. I have already reported on the procedure of this transmission or teleportation in *Chapter 5*.

Different Opinions, Speculations, Misunderstandings, and Slanderous Statements About Billy's Photo Material

As Billy's photo material, which baffled even experts, became known in the course of time through various newspaper articles, they spread like wildfire a stir as this one — at least not in ufological circles and UFO research groups throughout the world.

These photos eventually caused an avalanche of pro and con opinions — some people acknowledged the photos with amazement and admiration, others rejected them categorically as clumsy falsifications. Tempers ran high, especially in ufological circles, and evoked a multitude of antagonists who attacked Billy with negative articles, smear letters and specifically prepared alleged documentation and bulletins. These attempts to make him appear as a liar and swindler before the entire world continue even today.

Although in the meantime, some opponents of earlier times allowed themselves to be taught the truth after they possibly learned from the scientific analyses that no underhanded practices and falsifications were detected; others still persist in hostility even contrary to their better knowledge. For this reason, we are never really certain when and where a new slander campaign will be started against Billy and his group. And because such attacks are often based on false information pertaining to Billy's photos, I would like to bring a little light into the dark and confusing labyrinth of false assumptions and misunderstandings by using concrete examples. In doing so, I am aware that I am saddled with a Sisyphean[56] task, in view of the difficulties that will arise after presenting evidence in several cases. On one hand, the subject matter is difficult to understand and explain. On the other hand, the phenomena and circumstances in some cases are so unfavorable that they seem to favor the counter-arguments of our adversaries more than Billy's. However, I can present several bits of conclusive evidence that will at least find credibility among those readers who are striving to form an objective opinion of those phenomena without prejudice. *(See ~ Chapter 11: Scientific Analyses and Other Evidences)*

A Succession of Thefts

In this connection, I must not forget to mention the serious and continuing matter of thefts. According to Billy, out of about 100 slide films used to make 36 slides, the quality of a little more than half of them turned out quite well. But out of approximately 1,500 photos, only 700 remain in his possession today. More than half of all the photos have disappeared without a trace.

The photos of outer space that were taken on a five-day journey through our universe are not included in this count. In this regard, the situation looks even gloomier. As Billy assured me, most of these photos had undergone considerable damage in quality as a result of radiation from the cosmos and, therefore, were basically worthless. Nevertheless, the quality of the remaining photos of outer space could be termed as moderate to good, partially even as very good. Be that as it may, Billy, no longer possesses a single photo of his outer space travels, as unlikely as that may sound. After a counting in which I personally took part, more than 100 photos literally vanished from the collection overnight. A rather sad result, I must say. The whole matter also seems paradoxical to me. On one hand, Billy is depicted as a master of falsification who is capable of conjuring up one series of spectacular photos after another. But on the other hand, his photos are apparently so valuable that some people are foolish enough to steal them, even if they are supposedly only "crude falsifications." Apart from the thefts, it is more than astounding to find that certain groups, some with an enormous expenditure of time and money, have undermined Billy's credibility, labeled his contacts as "the greatest swindle in the history of ufology" and then spread this horror story world-wide.

Manipulations

According to Semjase, certain circles spared neither trouble nor money to falsify some of Billy's photo material to make them look forged. They did this with a vengeance of such perfection that hardly anyone took note of it at first glance. Only after careful examination did these manipulations surface.

The Pleiadians informed Billy that falsified photo material had been circulated in order to denounce him as a swindler.

Obviously, experts had not executed all of the forgeries because a number of inaccuracies were discovered. How would one explain otherwise that the thin thread that was later added to a UFO photo (as an alleged suspension of a spacecraft model) not only appeared in the wrong place but also in several places? It might also be possible that some distortions occurred through computer enlargements and created the impression that a flying object model had been suspended on several threads. Obviously, there are a number of possibilities, which give cause for erroneous or purposely false conclusions.

In connection to this, I must point out yet another inaccuracy, which clearly indicates that foreign powers have secretly had a hand in this. In other words, Billy never knew whether the developer had returned the true original photos and negatives, or only copies of them. As far as can be determined, only copies were handed back to him.

Double Exposure

I would like to begin this section with a written statement of a known UFO researcher, as follows: "Mr. H. J.[57] told of his experience of March 19–20, 1975 because on the following day, (Billy) conducted an experiment in the vicinity of Bäretswil with the same group and several children. At that location, he photographed those who were present, using a film frame on which a model had already been photographed earlier. He told those present that he wanted to photograph a space vehicle which would invisibly hover over them." The UFO researcher from Vienna "sang the same song" and wrote the following in a UFO journal after his visit to the aforementioned Mr. H. J.: "(Mr. H. J.) showed us double-exposed photos in which he was seen in a group with a UFO hovering overhead which, when taken, only Meier and the camera could see."

What is special about this "double exposure," several of which do indeed exist? There was a special reason for conducting that experiment. Billy wanted to prove to several notorious skeptics, Mr. H. J. being one of them, that the Pleiadians effectively master and use sector shielding to make their ship invisible to undesired onlookers while it was being photographed or filmed. And it was precisely for this reason that Billy requested a group of persons consisting of four men, two young women and two small children, to meet on April 20, 1975 (mistakenly dated as March 20th) at 10 o'clock in the morning behind Jakobsberg-Allenberg in the vicinity of Bäretswil, in order to provide the skeptics with concrete evidence. (This measure was an exception to the proviso of the Pleiadians that Billy was not permitted to bring any strangers along.) One gentleman had procured a Kodak slide film and handed it over to Billy in plain view of all those present. After Billy loaded this film into his camera, he moved a short distance away but still within view of the group and started photographing the Pleiadian ship. The spectators could easily observe Billy going about his work, but Semjase's spacecraft, which was hovering overhead, remained invisible to them because of the sector shielding — precisely as Billy had previously told them on a number of occasions.

After taking the pictures, Billy gave the exposed film to the aforementioned Mr. H. J. who then sent it to the Kodak Company for development and was the first to receive the developed pictures before passing them on to Billy.

Up to that point, everything seemed to have gone according to plan. But… yes, Semjase had intervened by intentionally manipulating the exposed slide film before it was developed so that half of the film was completely destroyed. And in the remaining half, the photos were very blurred. It happened that among them were apparently a few double exposures. *(See ~ Photo #62)*

Naturally, we ask ourselves why Semjase had done such a thing. Well, the explanation, which may be misunderstood by many earth citizens, is another indication that the Pleiadians often have a very different way of thinking than we do. Because of their higher evolutionary level, they act quite differently from what we would expect. Due to Billy's course of action, which appeared completely illogical to them because he was not permitted to bring any other persons along, Semjase lost control over her own course of action, even though she did allow the photographs to be taken. She later attempted to destroy that part of the film on which the spectators had also been exposed, but only partially succeeded in doing so. Semjase mistakenly caught the wrong half, so the photos of the spectators did ultimately end up in Billy's hands, resulting with some of them being of a very poor quality and double exposed. To better understand this rather complicated case, I would like to add the contact conversation between Asket, Semjase and Billy.

Excerpt from *Contact Report #32 of September 8, 1975:* After Billy had roughly described the peculiar incident to Semjase's girlfriend, Asket,[58] the following conversation developed:

ASKET: Is that so, Semjase?

SEMJASE: Certainly. I did not know at the time that he (Billy) could consciously behave illogically and, in this manner, break all logic. (Asket bursts out laughing.) Asket, you are laughing hysterically.

ASKET: (somewhat calm again.) Semjase's situation has amused me. The illogical course of action must have really disturbed her. (To Semjase:) What did you actually do then?

SEMJASE: It is incomprehensible to me. I undertook various illogical courses of action. It is really incomprehensible to me.

BILLY: She partially destroyed the film with some type of radiation before it was developed.

ASKET: But why? If for some reason you did not want to permit the photos, why did you even appear at the place of the event at all, or already being there, why did you not simply leave? It is quite illogical that you allow photos to be taken of you, only to destroy them afterward.

SEMJASE: But I said that it is incomprehensible to me. I really lost control over my actions. It is really incomprehensible to me.

BILLY: Do not get upset about it, Semjase. You apparently lost your head and suddenly thought with your feet. This can truly happen to anyone. But what were you really up to in doing so? Something is simply wrong here, is it not?

SEMJASE: Certainly, you are right. For certain reasons, I did not want the group of spectators to be included in the photographs, but I still allowed the ship to be visible to you and on the film, which I then later tried to destroy and committed another mistake in doing so. In my incomprehensible state of excitement, I furthermore projected the landscape picture, which I happened to see from my ship at that moment in front of your camera. You took no note of this. You were in a great hurry taking photographs and overlooked this. This projection was similar to the one you were permitted to film with your three friends.[59] Consequently, there must actually be two different pictures to see on your negatives or slides that flow into one another (double exposures), at least in several of the pictures. I furthermore emitted a bundled light source simultaneously with the projection to overexpose your film, in which I did not succeed, either. For some incomprehensible reason, the light source only produced the effect of a double exposure, which did not destroy the pictures but only damaged their sharpness. And lastly, I wanted to do even more and emitted an eliminator shortly before the film was developed in order to destroy the film. In my state of excitement though, which I simply cannot understand, I programmed it in the exact opposite sequence, which destroyed the wrong half of the film. These are the facts of this incident.

ASKET: Your way of dealing with this matter was really quite illogical and may have resulted from your encounter with an unaccustomed illogic in Billy, which caused your confusion. This led to a short circuit in your own logic and triggered a real chain reaction of illogical deeds which could only be stopped by allowing them to run their course.

SEMJASE: Surely, it must have been so, but I do not understand how I could act so irrationally.

BILLY: That is quite simple: A person who only thinks logically can no longer even imagine being illogical. If they are then faced with such a situation, they can no longer reconcile it with their own logic and they fall into a state of confusion. This confusion triggers illogical conclusions that lead to the same deeds and they, in turn, must run their course to the end before the rational logic can break through again.

ASKET: That is very precisely explained.

SEMJASE: Certainly, now I understand. It is very difficult, though, to work one's way into an unusual and unfamiliar thinking mode.

BILLY: You are probably right, Semjase. I believe that it would be very good for you and perhaps for others, if you venture into this thinking mode and examine it. Logic alone can be very dangerous if illogical forms can work their way in. I am of the opinion that logic and illogic have to work together to be able to exist. The one complements the other.

ASKET: That is again very precisely explained and it is, in fact, so.

SEMJASE: For the first time this has made sense to me through our conversation. I still have more to learn about these things.

ASKET: You have a good teacher, as the men of earth say.

SEMJASE: Surely, I have already learned many things from him, and his teachings are very lasting.

Actually, it is quite peculiar how different the opinions about one person can be. In any case, Billy's intentions were good but missed the target. Everything imaginable backfired on him. In light of the double exposures caused by Semjase, his critics accused him of doing the work himself, and so he finds himself unexpectedly in hot water once again. We shall hear still more of such problems.

In the following paragraphs, I will give you a closer look at the most frequent and well-known controversies which have been expressed by various parties with regard to Billy's photo material. Journalists, correspondents, so-called UFO researchers, etc., present their arguments when they launch their critical attacks against Billy.

Criticism of the Close-up Shots

See ~ Photo #63
Landed beamship on February 27, 1975 in Jakobsberg-Allenberg in Bettswil near Bäretswil.

Criticism: A suspiciously cropped photo

* The photographer intentionally cut off the lower half of the UFO to prevent the   model from being identified. *(See ~ Photo collection from "Analysis of Major Ret. Colman S. VonKeviczky" on page #12, listed in Resource Literature)*

* The lower half of the photo was intentionally cut off as if to prevent showing what has been described by many as anthills on which the UFO model is resting. *(See ~ "The Meier Incident, 'The Most Infamous Hoax in Ufology' " by Kal. K. Korff, listed in Resource Literature)*

Response:

According to Billy, the three landing legs underneath the ship touched the ground and were visible in the original negative. Someone then cropped the bottom half of the photo, cutting out the landing legs, and then enlarged the rest of the picture to its normal size. (This was accomplished by projecting the image on a wall.)

Criticism: A crudely constructed UFO model

* Photo #63 confirms that the crudely constructed aluminum body of the UFO model was built of heavy cardboard. Its thickness and lousy cut are clearly visible around the edge where the two cones have been laid on top of each other. The upper cone bends downward and the glued edges on the left and right sides are curved upward. *(See ~ Photo collection from "Analysis of Major Ret. Colman S. VonKeviczky" on page #12, listed in Resource Literature)*

* The cardboard that the model is made of is somewhat wavy, which can be determined by placing a ruler along the edge.

Response:

This photo belongs to the oldest pictures that Billy was permitted to take of a Pleiadian beamship. The mishap occurred as a result of getting too close to the spacecraft. This close proximity destroyed the exposure meter and viewfinder of his Olympus camera. It also created the wave-like contours in the photo. These effects could obviously be attributed to an intense radiation of the beamship.

Criticism: A landed spacecraft

* If we take a look at the band going around the spacecraft in the original photograph, we can see that it is remarkably similar to the belts worn by farmers in the region where Meier lived. It is also terribly similar to a type of rope used in this region to hang a bell around the necks of animals.

Response:
No comment.

Trash Can Photos
Criticism: Interpretation of one of the scorched negatives found

- Consider that the photo object seems to depict a somewhat modified Swiss farming hat. For a better understanding of this, I shall expand the accompanying text to another photo of this kind, which does not appear here: This is the interpretation of one of the various burned photos which were found in the area around the Meier farm. Apparently, this snapshot did not look good enough. According to reports, it was never passed on to Wendelle Stevens. It is supposed to show a Pleiadian ship that had presumably landed in E. Meier's yard. *(See ~ "The Meier Incident, 'The Most Infamous Hoax in Ufology'" by Kal. K. Korff, listed in Resource Literature)*

Response:
Various rumors have been circulated about the "trash can photos," masses of which have allegedly been "discovered" in Billy's trashcans. In reality, the following is what actually happened: One day in 1975, Semjase loaned Billy a model of her beamship for a short period to take a few pictures of it and then to be returned. On the basis of these snapshots, Billy planned to have a model-builder construct his own model spacecraft, but this plan never came to fruition. A serious mishap occurred to the negatives of these model photographs — they slipped off the office tabletop into a wastepaper basket and were not found until after the entire contents had landed in a fireplace. Kalliope, Billy's wife, discovered the more or less burned negatives in the ashes and handed them over to one of the group members to be restored, if possible. To what extent they succeeded is beyond my knowledge. Personally, I know only of one such usable photo of Billy's model pictures. And of the partially restored photos, only those of the poorest quality ended up, to everyone's misfortune, in the hands of the wrong people — those who are not especially friendly minded towards Billy. *(See ~ Billy's "Model Factory," Photo #65)*

It was the only usable photo of all model pictures.

Criticism: Semjase's spacecraft
The part of Semjase's spacecraft photographed in the snow is no longer than 1.5 meters (5 ft.). The slightly vibrating model is uniformly out of focus! A 7-meter (23 ft.) long vehicle in its entirety appears in a close-up picture somehow different from this slipshod work! The furrowed edge of the cone does not indicate an alloy of copper, nickel and silver of the vehicle, as Billy explained, but rather a sloppy razor cutout of cardboard. *(See ~ Photo collection from "Analysis of Major Ret. Colman S. VonKeviczky" on page #12, listed in Resource Literature)*

- Semjase's spacecraft after a landing in the snow. According to a number of statements in the writings published by Mr. Meier, this spacecraft is 7 meters (23 ft.) in diameter. Photographic analyses have shown that the object is more within the range of 1 meter (3 ft.). Since the ship was also out of focus when the picture was taken, it cannot possibly be the size Meier says it is. Otherwise, only the parts of the spacecraft nearest the camera would be unfocused whereas the opposite side would be focused. *(See ~ "The Meier Incident, 'The Most Infamous Hoax in Ufology' " by Kal. K. Korff, listed in Resource Literature)*

Response:

In the photo index of FIGU, this photo is clearly declared as a snapshot of a model, which everyone can read for himself in the photo legend where it says: "photo of an artificial beamship landed in the snow. Side view from below. The photo was made of a model of approximately 70 centimeters (28 in.) brought along by Semjase." We made continuous reference to a model and not to a 7-meter ship. There is certainly no mention of fuzziness in this photo; instead, it is shown to be laterally inverted and also twisted 180 degrees. *(See ~ Photo #65)*

Criticism: Rumors of stored models

- Ever since Billy's spacecraft photos have existed, rumors have circulated that Billy merely photographed models that he had made himself and which were discovered in his attic and in the garage.

Response:

- In my opinion, this criticism is an unparalleled sign of incompetence by the researchers of the Meier case! Consider the dishonest and matter-of-fact way such criticisms and lies have been accepted from people who are second-hand sources and have made no investigations. These false charges have been used against Billy on every possible occasion without considering that in doing so, his honor as a fellow citizen was maliciously and deliberately dragged through the mud. But it is so easy to say, "Billy built models." There's really nothing to it. For example, it is considerably more difficult to prove such claims in a court of law. As a matter of fact, such hateful people are actually to be deeply pitied, considering the burden of guilt they now carry. This applies to all persons who intentionally withhold, twist, falsely present and spread or attack the truth in any manner; they hinder the spiritual development of mankind — in fact to a very considerable degree!

- As stated, Billy received an approximately 70-centimeter (28 in.) large metal model from Semjase, as a loan for a short period of time, to photograph, which he had to return immediately thereafter. After the sad story of the burned "trash can photos," understandably enough, no one wanted to grist the mill even more. In other words, no one wished to follow the original plan to build a Pleiadian ship true to scale. So the plan had been abandoned by FIGU.

I can already hear the objections why such a beautiful model of a Pleiadian ship is still hanging in Billy's office. Well, this is one of two artificial models (42 centimeters [17 in.] in diameter) that American students built in Hollywood and presented to Billy as a gift. The American research group did not need it any longer. The photographers of the mentioned researchers tried to duplicate Billy's spacecraft photos by using the model. While one helper hung the model by a thin thread and let it "hover" in the air at the end of a long rod, the other shot a series of "model pictures" with Billy's camera. In fact, they did so from various distances and angles with variable values of aperture and exposure times. By using these model photos, the computer experts could prove the difference between Billy's genuine pictures and the fabricated ones quickly and clearly.

- Billy would truly have had to work in a film studio factory to have been able to produce models of everything that appears in his picture series. Besides seven different types of spacecraft, he would have had to manufacture numerous other replicas, all requiring a tremendous squandering of material, work, time and money.

- Whoever knows Billy's living conditions at his residence in Hinterschmidrüti will have to admit that it was impossible to secretly produce any models without relatives, family and house guests catching on to the swindle. After all, he does not live on a lonely farm or in a remote mountain hut as a hermit, but rather, he lives where his activities can be closely observed at all times.

- To work with models in the open country, where anyone has almost free access, would risk the danger of being caught unaware by curious passers-by, at least in the region of the Zurich Highlands. In fact, the photos of real Pleiadian ships were taken at locations where no objects exist to hang a model on, as can easily be proved.

- Without special helpers, which Billy did not have, he could not fake spacecraft photos anyway.

- Kalliope was skeptical of the entire matter from the very beginning and reacted every way but enthusiastically. Her family life was tremendously involved due to necessity, and naturally, she observed all of her husband's activities with great attention. For this reason alone, Billy could not have afforded to risk dishonest manipulations.

- According to Billy's own statements, he never built spacecraft models himself, nor had them produced by any other persons. Nor did he make use of any models suspended from mounts, by thin threads or even from helicopters or gas balloons. Billy, as well as Kalliope, can confirm this statement at any time in lieu of an oath before a court.

- The statements made by witnesses about Billy's photos, and the results of several photo and film analyses, clearly speak in favor of Billy. All the alleged claims by one person or another that Billy was seen building the models and then hiding them somewhere in a building — do not correspond to reality and must, therefore, be classified as misunderstandings, translation mistakes or intentionally spread untruths.

In connection with the models, I would not want to omit the presentation of a letter to you that a critic sent to Billy, the content of which is actually quite amusing to me and certainly helps to loosen things up a bit. (Mistakes were intentionally not corrected!)

A "Lovely" Letter to Billy

Mailed at the train station of CH-8174 Stadel near Niederglatt without name of sender:

"March 1st, 1983
Mr. Eduard Billy Meier,
8499 Schmidrüti, ZH

In "Blick" (a Swiss newspaper) of March 11, 1981 (issue), you reported about a UFO that supposedly landed in your yard on October 22, 1980 at 10:10 p.m.

The published photo of this is naturally a special mockup and has nothing to do with authenticity. Today, the UFO is unmasked and is now called UAP. (Unidentified Atmospheric Phenomena) You are not the only one who claims to have seen UFO's. Greater and smaller nuts are on our planet in great numbers and I cannot condemn you too much for your yarn spinning.

However, if someone spins yarn like Erich von Däniken, claiming that people originated from ape and gods, then he does not belong on our planet.

A professor told me one time: Either Däniken believes what he writes, then he has a very deep spiritual level. Or he does not believe what he writes, making what he does simply a business, then he's just an old fart.

I believe he (the professor) is right.

Now, it is not so bad with you. You only received a great portion of stupidity on the earthly road of life. The dumb must also live. But now please stop spinning yarn in respect to UFO's. What can be seen now and then on the horizon are UAP's and those are earthly steam formations that appear for awhile and dissolve again.

I wish everything good for your lifetime though and hope that you become increasingly more intelligent.

With best regards to Hinterschmidrüti ..."

Criticism: Photos #64 or #14
Preface:
Demonstration flight with Semjase's spacecraft around a giant fir tree[60] that was later eliminated by Semjase without a trace.[61]

- Hardly any other photo has been used so often as a perfect example of a Billy Meier hoax as this one. In ufological circles, for example, the rumor has been spread for years that it is a man-made model painted silver that had been looped around a sapling with the aid of a fishing rod.

I have already expressed my view about the accusations of the use of models, but in clearing this case, another condition needs to be mentioned. As a one-armed man, Billy would definitely have to have help to operate the fishing rod, which he never had — not in this instance or any other. Despite intensive investigations, no one has been able to find a single assistant of Billy's to this very day.

Incidentally, the opinion has been expressed time and again that the spacecraft does not appear large enough in the photo to provide sufficient space in the cockpit for three pilots. In connection with this, I would like to quote from a report, which Mr. W. M. from Vienna published in 1979:

"Meier's film shows a small sapling with a UFO passing over it. We determined that the maximum distance from the camera to this tree was only about 7 meters (23 ft.). If the angular height is then reconstructed, a tree of only 60 centimeters (24 in.) is the result! Meier's UFO, which was supposed to have been about 7 meters in diameter, could only have been at the very most the size a soup plate."

Response:

If one of our spruce trees is taken as a standard of comparison to judge the size of the photographed spacecraft, a miscalculation could indeed occur. In this case, we are not dealing with a normal fir tree but with a giant fir. Its crown is at least as large in diameter as the shown spacecraft of 7 meters. The cockpit is large enough to accommodate three pilots without the fear of bumping their heads on the ceiling.

After visiting the location, my viewpoints changed and became entirely different, as follows:

- If we consider a suspended model the size of a soup plate (26 centimeters [10 in.] in diameter) in front of a sapling 60 centimeters (24 in.) in size, then the distance between the camera and the tree would indeed be only a few meters.

- In reality, the distance was approx. 70–90 meters (231 ft.–297 ft.), depending on the photographer's position.

- The references listed below are an indication that it cannot be a close-up photograph:

- The fir branches hanging into the picture's right foreground provide the first clue. If these somewhat blurred and substantially larger branches are compared with the crown of the giant fir, the difference in range becomes quite apparent. The distance from these fir branches to the photographer's position is more than 7 meters. *(See ~ Photo #14)*

- If the branches of a 1–2-meter (3.3 ft.– 7 ft.) large sapling in a close-up photograph a few meters away are compared with the crown of a giant fir, a world of difference can be seen.[62]

- People who know about trees (foresters, gardeners) have all agreed that the controversial giant fir is definitively a full-grown fir (spruce) and never a small fir sapling.

- Furthermore, I would like to point out that measurements were taken by the American research group at several landing sites and were checked against these photographs. These investigations proved that both the diameter and the distances corresponded exactly to Billy's data at each site.

- In conclusion, I would like to mention the extensive scientific analyses, all of which confirm that Billy did not work with models.

And now for the other objections:

Criticism: Published statements

- "According to published statements, the Pleiadian spacecraft was photographed while it was circling around the tree. According to documents of Swiss meteorologists, the wind velocity on the day these photographs were taken was approx. 25 kilometers/hour (16 miles/hour). If the cloud formations of these photos are carefully examined, it becomes quite apparent that they must have been taken over a far longer stretch of time than a few seconds, as claimed. Furthermore, we visited the original terrain where these photographs had been fabricated and no evidence could be found that a tree had ever been there at all!" *(See ~ "The Meier Incident, ' The Most Infamous Hoax in Ufology' " by Kal. K. Korff, listed in Resource Literature)*

"As for the truthful content of the pictures in this series with the tree, the continuous change in the camera's angle proves that the photographer (Meier) always moved away somewhat instead of standing still in one spot. He quickly shot eight consecutive photos as he claimed — eight photographs that allegedly show a UFO as it is said to circle around a tree." *(See ~ Photo collection from "Analysis of Major Ret. Colman S. VonKeviczky" on page #12, listed in Resource Literature)*

Response:

- According to Billy, he shot two different series of this giant fir in Oberbalm. In fact, the first series were tripod photographs taken from a fixed standpoint, whereas the pictures of the second series were shot from various angles of view and distances. The fact that the time intervals from one snapshot to another were not seconds but minutes most likely needs no further explanation. And the fact that cloud formations can quickly change depending upon local wind activity is also well known to every photographer.

- As I described in *Chapter 6: Mysterious Elimination of Fir Trees,* Semjase liked to select the striking features of solitary giant firs to show the maneuverability of her disk-shaped spacecraft, and to give the best possible graphic expression through the contrast of the spacecraft's metallic luster and the dark-green giant fir.

- I have further explained why a total of five fir trees had to be eliminated. The fir tree from Oberbalm is one of these. It was made to disappear without a trace by Semjase and neither loosened earth, the remaining part of a root, nor anything else that would leave any clues to the existence of this tree. Furthermore, all memories, written records, photos, etc. were also eliminated, with the exception of those in Billy's possession, which were spared at his own request. This means that no person except Billy can remember that this giant fir ever stood in this meadow — not even the property owner who had cut the lower branches off for years to use as firewood. This mysterious story naturally sounds quite unbelievable to our ears and is thus readily classified in the realm of fable. But innumerable things happen between heaven and earth, which our school wisdom does not include nor give us any reasonable explanations. In this specific case, the Pleiadians gave us no further explanations about the functioning of these mysterious eliminations of memories, records, etc. Phenomena of this kind simply go beyond the comprehension ability of an "ordinary earth citizen." We have to accept it whether we like it or not. Based on our present evolutionary level, we are not yet capable of explaining such phenomena, not to mention duplicating them. It is understandable why this alleged "fairy tale of the fir tree" seems so unbelievable to us. But the fact that the Pleiadians from the planet Erra are 3,500 years ahead of us in technology, alone, the story is perhaps not as utopian as some erroneously assume.

Billy's Photos of Outer Space

An especially sad chapter undoubtedly refers to Billy's photos of outer space taken during his extensive space journey in July of 1975.

As explained at the outset, only a fraction of all photographs had the quality needed to make their processing worthwhile. Of the useable photos, all of them were quite good and, of course, had the most unique motif in the world. Billy did not enjoy viewing these photographs for very long because absolutely all of the outer space slides were stolen. Today he no longer owns a single one of them. Even more wearisome, they provided material for open acts of hostility in all possible variations and, thus, caused a lot of problems.

A substantial reason for this opposition stems from the attitudes of many who could not understand why Billy, of all people, and not a known NASA scientist, was chosen for such a tremendous undertaking. And the new data taken from Billy's descriptive notes for the individual photos, plus all the news about how the trip to outer space took place, other procedures, etc., were simply too much to understand all at once, too fantastic — and can be summed up in one word, "incomprehensible." Unpleasant matters were associated with this lack of understanding and, of course, gave the impression that each and every one of these photos had been faked. As a result of erroneous translations, which caused gross misunderstandings, interpretations of the photos were incorrect, as illustrated by media comments concerning the Lyra Ring Nebula, about which you will find detailed information under the heading, "The Eye of God" (JHWH Mata).

Moreover, it happened that Billy's photos of outer space were shown on television without naming their origin. Several pictures in circulation were used to make deceptively similar, though somewhat altered, reproductions in order to represent future earth technology. Worst of all was the fact that some of the motives had already been known for years in trick or science fiction movies, before Billy traveled through outer space and had made public the photos relating thereto. In Billy's case, whoever knew nothing of the facts undoubtedly must have assumed there was something fishy going on. But nothing "fishy" was taking place. First, some facts were not known until later — not even to Billy — and second, the skeptics did not know soon enough, or not at all.

The true background is that the Baavi Intelligences[63] had a mission to transmit several very special pictures, identical to Billy's space photographs, to certain sensitive earth artists in an inspirational manner; for example, to artists who specialize in futuristic illustrations, science fiction authors, and the like. Unfortunately, these inspirations were transmitted before Billy's space photos were publicized, that means with full intention — if one disregards a mishap in this matter,.

According to the opinion of the extraterrestrials, earth people are to be prepared for coming events. This is to be accomplished in a very graphic manner through the publication of such "inspirations" in the form of pictures. However, the criteria used to select the photos is unknown to me.

Billy thus had to swallow the accusations that his photos were not genuine and that he had merely copied them from existing paintings, magazine photos and illustrations of every kind, or were photographed from television programs. For our extraterrestrial friends, the entire misery must have been like a bracing cold shower. Their well-intended efforts produced the exact opposite effect. Certainly, the actions of the Baavi Intelligences can be correctly understood only if we try to put ourselves into their totally different manner of thinking. Lying and cheating are foreign to them. They freed themselves of these vices quite some time ago. They were only reminded of it again after they discovered that lying and cheating on earth is the usual practice. Thus, viewed from their lofty standpoint, no one can blame them for completely misjudging the earth peoples' behavior. Had they imagined how negative the reaction would be to their plans, they would certainly have refrained from carrying them out and would have left their premature "inspirations" alone.

According to several slides, which I have taken from a documentation of "THE BILLY MEIER FRAUD," I would like to comment on a few concrete objections in detail. I will begin with one of the most difficult of cases, which did not happen on his great journey through outer space, but several years later on a journey through time.

Photos of an Earthquake in the Future of San Francisco

Billy's disaster photos of the future earthquake in San Francisco continue to be among the most unbelievable examples of his entire photo collection and have met with the greatest hostility. This is also understandable. It sounds unthinkable for anyone to produce photos of future events, and because adverse circumstances were also involved, the whole thing appeared quite improbable. It will also be very difficult for even a tolerant skeptic to accept the following explanations. However, my task is not to completely convince anyone of this, even if I may wish to do so. I can do no more than describe the facts as objectively and truthfully as possible. Now the actual fact is that Billy was permitted to take a journey through time to the future of San Francisco with Quetzal on March 18, 1978 in a spacecraft borrowed from Menara. They viewed the ruins of the destroyed city after a devastating earthquake and photographed it. Unfortunately, the same pictures of this catastrophe had already been published in the September issue of *Geo Magazine* in 1977. And this publication came out about half a year before Billy's journey through time. Every outsider must have assumed that Billy had duplicated his San Francisco pictures from the article in the *Geo Magazine*, as no other explanation made sense. This suspicion finally intensified even more because Quetzal reacted quite angrily by confiscating all photos connected with this matter, so that it was and still is no longer possible to make any comparisons with the pictures of the *Geo Magazine*. If one has no knowledge of the aforementioned "inspirations" of the Baavi Intelligences, the next question must be, how did the artist come up with the disaster pictures of the *Geo Magazine*? Billy asked about this and Quetzal explained the circumstances of this embarrassing situation. As expected, the Baavi Intelligences transmitted via inner inspiration the disaster pictures of San Francisco in full detail to the highly sensitive artist of *Geo Magazine*. In the process of the publication, a mistake was made. The article in *Geo Magazine* was not scheduled for publication until autumn of 1978 but, instead, was issued by mistake an entire year too early — several months before Billy's journey through time.

Quetzal meant well when he confiscated Billy's photos. He simply wanted to protect Billy from further attacks.

As far as the details of the pictures are concerned, several members of the core group discovered a few minimal differences between Billy's original photographs and the inspired illustrations transmitted by the Baavi Intelligences to the artist for *Geo Magazine*. Further details about this are superfluous. Billy's originals are no longer available for comparison. These are the facts relating to the controversial San Francisco pictures, and there is not much more I can say about it.

The Eye of God (JHWH Mata)

See ~ Photos #66–#67

Criticism: Photograph of the "Eye of God"

The Eye of God was photographed during Billy's space flight with Semjase into the DAL Universe. They came closer to the Creator here but only had the chance to take a snap shot of one of his eyes. *(See ~ Photo collection from "Analysis of Major Ret. Colman S. VonKeviczky" on page #12, listed in Resource Literature)*

He (Meier) claims to have photographed it (The Eye of God) in the center of the DAL Universe; an interesting point to be made here, as the cosmos is unlimited. This photo was clearly identified by ufologist Tom Gates, an astronomer, as nothing more than a distorted picture of the Ring Nebula in the constellation of Lyra. Meier claims he took close-up pictures… and even one of God's eyes. (Astonishingly enough, in response to the question why he did not photograph both eyes of God, he answered that it was not possible, because his other eye had winked[64] at his Pleiadian companion, Semjase.) *(See ~ "The Meier Incident, 'The Most Infamous Hoax in Ufology' " by Kal. K. Korff, listed in Resource Literature)*

Response:

- The photograph is the Ring Nebula in the constellation Lyra, which is located in our galaxy and known to the earthly astronomers as *M57*. We have never claimed anything else.

- Photo #67 presented here is a very poor copy. The ball appearing in the center is not recognizable at all, which is unfortunate because this very feature gives the entire formation the appearance of a giant eye gazing out into space. Billy's photograph thus varies considerably from that of our astronomers.

- According to Semjase, this Ring Nebula *M57*, which the Pleiadians call "JHWH Mata," the "eye of god," was created in artificial manner by the deliberate destruction of a giant star. In connection with the perpetrator of this destruction, the JHWH was an extremely barbarous and power-hungry man who had unlawfully assumed the title of JHWH. This title means, "king of wisdom" or "god." The title bearer indicates a human being of great knowledge and wisdom who towers above his contemporaries like a king, provided he has actually earned the title and not unlawfully taken it on.

  Therefore, it is completely absurd to compare the Ring Nebula *M57*, which the Pleiadians call 'the Eye of God', with the almighty power of Creation of the universe.

Space Colony or Universe Barrier?

See ~ Photos #68 and #69

Criticism #1: Who owns the copyright?

In this collection is a slide with the heading:

"WHO OWNS THE COPYRIGHT? Billy (Meier) or Dr. O'Neill?"

- In the upper left side is Billy's photograph of the universe barrier that he personally saw and photographed during his great journey through space in 1975. In the lower right-hand corner, an illustrated color picture of a future space colony. *(See ~ Photo collection from "Analysis of Major Ret. Colman S. VonKeviczky" on page #12, listed in Resource Literature)*

Criticism #2: The photo and the illustration

- The concluding piece of incriminating evidence comes from Billy Meier himself. He claims that this is a drawing of the connecting tunnel into the DAL Universe. According to Meier, the diameter of the tunnel is 75–80 kilometers (47–50 miles) and its length is 1.3 million kilometers (806,000 miles).

- Compare Meier's drawing with this illustration made according to a design by Dr. G. O'Neill and NASA showing how a possible space colony could look. One can see that they (the two pictures) are identical. This illustration appeared in the Smithsonian Magazine in February of 1976, on pages 62–69. *(See ~ "The Meier Incident, The Most Infamous Hoax in Ufology" by Kal. K. Korff, listed in Resource Literature)*

Response:

- The picture in the upper-left side is not a drawing but an original photo that Billy took during his journey through space. It shows a "tunnel" passage that was technically created so that the large Pleiadian spacecraft — under the command of the JHWH Ptaah — could cross over into the neighboring DAL Universe at the border zone of our DERN Universe.

- The picture on the lower right-hand side is a poor reproduction of a color illustration produced by a future-visionary painter. This painter was inspired by the Baavi Intelligences. Completely misrepresented afterwards, the lower front part has been changed into a space colony.

- It can be proven that this photo by Billy was taken several months before the illustrated picture appeared in public.

- According to Semjase, the original illustration was professionally done, whereas the reproduction in circulation, shown here, contains a number of defects that even a layman can easily detect. In Billy's original photo *(See ~ Photo #69)*, the tunnel entrance of the universe barrier corresponds to reality, thus, is in the shape of an egg, whereas in this poor imitation drawing it is round like a circle and the rays are also not identical. However, the greatest difference between them can be seen in the foreground. In Billy's original photo, a wavering and iridescent energy can be recognized, whereas a landscape had been substituted in the illustration. Ultimately, the entire reproduction was referred to as a futuristic vision of a space colony. There can be absolutely no question of identity in this particular case!

Docking Maneuver Between the American Apollo 18 and the Russian Soyuz 19 Space Capsule on July 17, 1975:

See ~ Photos #70, #71 and #72.

Criticism #1: USA Apollo 18 and the USSR Soyuz 19 photos

- On July 17, 1975, the USA Apollo 18 and the USSR Soyuz 19 space capsules were docked in space. The historical event was clearly photographed by Semjase and Billy with a Polaroid camera through the window of Semjase's spacecraft. Neither the USA nor the USSR reported a collision course with a UFO during the mission. The conjecture was made that Billy explained this by saying that nothing was reported from either side for reasons of security. Semjase's spacecraft has no windows at all. In other words, did Billy, in the end, forget to paint windows on the side of the vehicle?

- In every photograph, the curved window frame looks almost identical to the frame of a TV screen, whereas the window in the slides appears to have a straight frame. *(See ~ Photo collection from "Analysis of Major Ret. Colman S. VonKeviczky," listed in Resource Literature)*

Response:

- According to Billy's own statements, he never took any of his UFO snapshots with a Polaroid camera.

- According to Semjase, five other extraterrestrial spacecraft (one Pleiadian and four others) were also in earth orbit at the time. They all observed the docking maneuver from a close distance — but were shielded so well that neither the Russian nor American astronauts noticed anything at all.

- As already mentioned, no actual Pleiadian ship was photographed in photo #64, but merely a model — the same one Semjase had previously loaned to Billy. A Pleiadian ship of this category has clearly visible color "windows" on the outside wall of the pilot's cockpit (at the bottom of photo #63), and are located in the upper part of the ship. The picture of the model shows only the lower part, which is pointing upward instead of down as a result of a 180-degree turn. This is another example of how quickly misunderstandings and misinterpretations arise. As for the rest, I have already pointed out that the ship's windows are actually not "windows" at all in the usual sense.

   Billy took his photos of outer space with a "photographer view screen" which has a curved frame and was made by the Pleiadians for this very purpose. That is why the curved window frames are seen in these pictures of outer space.

Criticism #2: Identifying falsifications

In a German magazine, the following points were intended to prove that Billy's photos of the Apollo-Soyuz docking maneuver were faked.

- The solar wings on the spacecraft Soyuz 19 were arranged in a rectilinear, elongated and horizontal position to the capsule and not folded, as in the picture from E. Meier (Billy). Evidence for this are the TV pictures broadcast live all over the world as the two units approached one another.

Billy Edward Meier, 1995 – Passive Member Meeting at the
Semjase Silver Star Center in Switzerland

1   East view of the Semjase Silver Star Center. Freddy Kropf climbed up to the very crown of a tall fir at the edge of the woods by the Whirring Meadow and from there photographed the Center. *Date: May 7, 1989. Photographer: Freddy Kropf*

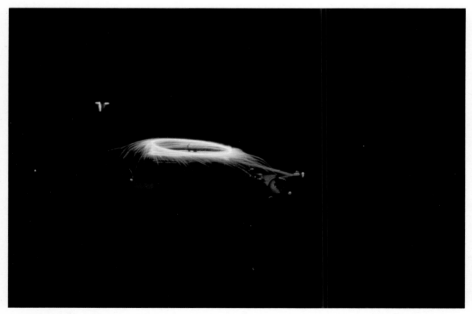

2   Burning of static electricity conducted by Quetzal in the Center's parking lot for demonstration purposes. Billy is standing in the middle of the energy belt.
Date: September 8, 1981. Photographer: Quetzal. Location: Semjase Silver Star Center.

3 Witnesses of the described demonstrations. Last row (left to right): Bernadette Brand, Engelbert Wächter, Freddy Kropf, Brunhilde Koye, Madeleine Bruegger, Silvano Lehmann, Methusalem Meier, Atlantis Meier, Billy. Front row (left to right): Guido Moosbrugger, Elisabeth Gruber, Christina Gasser, Edith Beldi, Jacobus Berschinger, Eva Bieri, Atlant Bieri, Kalliope Meier, Gilgamesha Meier. *Date: January 6, 1991. Photographer: Bernadette Brand. Location: Semjase Silver Star Center.*

4 Demonstration flight of Semjase's newest beamship taken on March 29, 1976, which shows various changes to her previous ship such as higher dome construction as well as ring construction. The newly added technical structures enable the ship to travel through time and to penetrate into other dimensions. *Photographer: Billy. Location: Hasenböl-Langenberg, (Fischenthal).*

5 Semjase, sketch by E. Eichenberger and Billy according to Billy's description. *Photographer: E. Eichenberger. Location: Semjase Silver Star Center. (See an an updated sketch of Semjase in Chapter Two.)*

6 Start and departure of Semjase's beamship after the first contact. *Photographer: Billy. Location: Frecht/nature preserve. Date: January 28, 1975*

7   Beamship and reconnaissance ship during a flight demonstration at sunset. *Photographer: Billy. Location: Ober-Zelg, Bettswil. Date: March 3, 1975*

8   Two beamships photographed from the window of a third beamship (Semjase's), but already at an enormous altitude; landscape is no longer visible. *Date: June 25, 1975. Photographer: Billy. Location: Berg-Rumlikon.*

9 Demonstration flight of Semjase's newest beamship. taken on. *Date: March 29, 1976. Photographer: Billy. Location: Hasenboel-Langenberg, (Fischenthal).*

10 Semjase's beamship during a demonstration flight. *Photographer: Billy. Location: Fuchsbüel-Hofhalden. Date: February 27, 1975*

11 Close-up picture of the underside of Semjase's beamship during a demonstration flight. *Date: February 27, 1975. Photographer: Billy. Location: Jakobsberg-Allenberg/Bettswil.*

12 Semjase's beamship is high above Ober-Balm. In the background, the Lake Pfäffikon is clearly visible. *Date: February 28, 1975. Photographer: Billy. Location: Ober-Balm.*

13 A demonstration flight of Semjase's newest beamship. _Date: March 29, 1976. Photographer: Billy. Location: Hasenböl-Langenberg, (Fischenthal)._

14 Demonstration flight with Semjase's beamship around a 14-or 15-meter tall giant fir. Lake Pfäffiker is in the background. (This tree was later eliminated by Semjase without a trace.) _Date: July 9, 1975. Photographer: Billy. Location: Fuchsbül-Hofhalden/Oberbalm, Wetzikon._

15 Demonstration flight of Semjase's new beamship. *Photographer: Billy. Location: Bachtelhörnli-Unterbachtel. Date: March 8, 1976*

16 Cropped Enlargement: Demonstration flight with the consequence that Semjase was harassed and badgered in her ship by a jet fighter (Mirage) of the Swiss Air Force. *Date: April 14, 1976. Photographer: Billy. Location: Schmärbueel-Maiwinkel.*

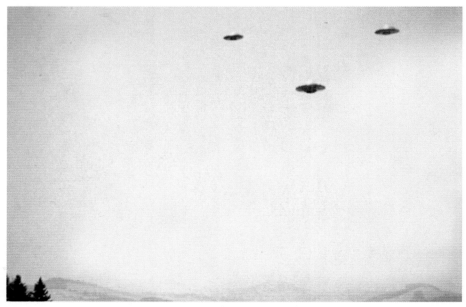

17 Demonstration flight of Semjase's new beamship and two reconnaissance ships of a newer construction. *Date: March 8, 1976. Photographer: Billy. Location: Bachtelhörnli/ Unterbachtel.*

18 Demonstration flight of Semjase's new beamship and two reconnaissance ships of a newer construction. *Date: March, 1976. Photographer: Billy. Location: Bachtelhörnli/ Unterbachtel.*

19 Telephoto shot from treetop to treetop, taken by Billy while sitting on a second ship at an altitude of about 40 meters. *Date: April 3, 1981. Photographer: Billy. Location: Auenberg/Egg.*

20 Semjase's newest beamship at a photo demonstration. (Commonly known as the "wedding cake ship.") *Date: March 26, 1981. Photographer: Billy. Location: Säckler, Dürstelen.*

21 Semjase's newest beamship hovering above the Center's parking lot.
Date: October 22, 1980. Photographer: Billy. Location: Semjase Silver Star Center.

22 Telephoto shot from treetop to treetop, taken by Billy while sitting on a second ship at an altitude of about 40 meters. *Date: April 3, 1981. Photographer: Billy. Location: Auenberg/Egg.*

23 A 7-meter ship next to the main street in the direction of Rotenthurm, hovering behind an automobile (Mercedes) with a tree branch above in the center of the picture. *Date: August 2, 1981. Photographer: Billy. Location: Altmatt/SZ.*

24 A 7-meter ship directly in front of an automobile hovering by the main street in the direction of Rotenthurm, (in the above left, a tiny portion of the second 14-meter ship can be seen.) *Date: August 2, 1981. Photographer: Billy. Location: Altmatt/SZ.*

25 A 14-meter ship hovering behind a tree by the main street in the direction of Rotenthurm. To the above left, a telemeter disk zipping around at a tremendous speed is visible. *Date: August 2, 1981. Photographer: Billy. Location: Altmatt/SZ.*

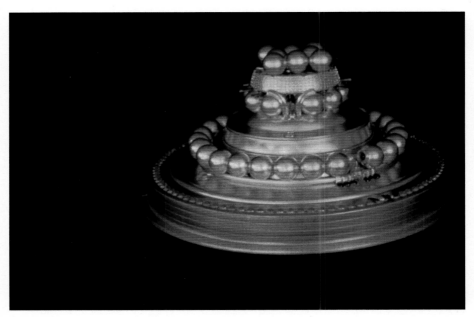

26 A self-illuminating beamship during the night over the Center's parking lot. *Date: August 5, 1981. Photographer: Billy. Location: Semjase Silver Star Center*

27 A visit at the Center by a dwarf human race from the Andromeda Region. Shown here is their pure energy spacecraft, which constantly changes form. One of the energy ships over the east horizon of Rüteli, shining brightly and glistening through the trees. *Date: April 19, 1979. Photographer: Billy. Location: Semjase Silver Star Center.*

28 A visit at the Center by a dwarf human race from the Andromeda Region. One of the energy ships below the crest of the rise of the Menara-Landing forest in a north westernly direction from the Center, while another energy ship is glistening high up against the sky. *Date: April 19, 1979. Photographer: Billy. Location: Semjase Silver Star Center.*

29 A visit at the Center by a dwarf human race from the Andromeda Region. Two energy ships above the parking lot, whereby only the radiating corona of the one to the right in the picture can be recognized. *Date: June 22, 1979. Photographer: Billy. Location: Semjase Silver Star Center.*

30 A visit at the Center by a dwarf human race from the Andromeda Region. One of the energy ships directly above the parking lot. *Date: June 22, 1979. Photographer: Billy. Location: Semjase Silver Star Center.*

31 Konrad Schutzbach (right) and Billy while filming and measuring the landing tracks of Rala's and Menara's ships. *Date: June 29, 1976. Photographer: Hans Schutzbach. Location: Ambitzgi, Wetzikon.*

32 Landing track of Rala's ship. *Date: September 29, 1976. Photographer: Hans Schutzbach. Location: Ambitzgi, Wetzikon.*

33 Landing track of Menara's ship from the parking lot of the Center, 3:41 a.m. (ice thickness: 10 centimeters). *Date: February 21, 1978. Photographer: Billy. Location: Semjase Silver Star Center.*

34 Landing track of Menara's ship from the parking lot of the Center. *Date: February 21, 1978. Photographer: Billy. Location: Semjase Silver Star Center.*

35 Landing track of Menara's ship taken during a flash visit at 9:05 a.m., during which Billy's wife had gone to Schmidrüti to take a child to school and was away for almost 10 minutes (ice thickness: 12 centimeters). *Date: November 23, 1977. Photographer: Billy. Location: Semjase Silver Star Center.*

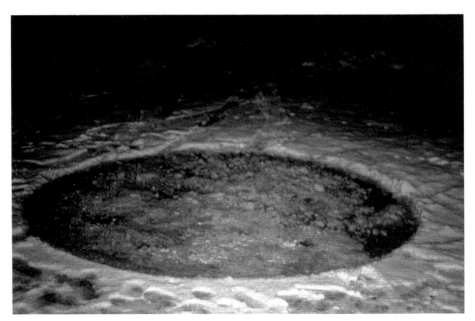

36 Close-up of landing track from Menara's ship taken during a flash visit. *Date: November 23, 1977. Photographer: Billy. Location: Semjase Silver Star Center*

37   Landing tracks of Quetzal's ship. (At top-center from left to right:) Methusalem Meier, Kalliope Meier. *Date: June 26, 1976. Photographer: Guido Moosbrugger. Location: Chrützlerboden, Oberchrützlen.*

38   Beamship tracks/impressions of the landing supports of Quetzal's beamship at 8:54 p.m. *Date: June 23, 1976. Photographer: Guido Moosbrugger.   Location: Chrützlerboden, Oberchrützlen.*

39 A beamship landed at 7:34 p.m. for the first time on the personal property of the Semjase Silver Star Center. Menara came with Semjase's ship and left landing tracks behind there, which is why it is called "Menara Landing." *Date: April 23, 1977. Photographer: Hans Schutzbach. Location: Semjase Silver Star Center.*

40 Landing tracks of Qutezal's ship. *Date: June 29, 1976. Photographer: Hans Schutzbach. Location: Pfaffenholz/Hinwil.*

41 Landing tracks of Quetzal's and Semjase's beamships. *Date: June 28, 1976. Photographer: Hans Schutzbach. Location: Pfaffenholz/Hinwil.*

42 Billy observes the fenced-in landing track. *Date: June 15, 1980. Photographer: Mr. Bertschinger, Sr. Location: Semjase Silver Star Center.*

43 Landing tracks of Semjase's beamship following the 135th contact in the night of at 12:55 a.m. *Date: June 14–15, 1980. Photographer: Billy. Location: Semjase Silver Star Center.*

44 Landing tracks of Semjase's beamship following the 135th contact. *Date: June 15, 1980. Photographer: Billy. Location: Semjase Silver Star Center.*

45 Billy's footprints from the open field to the street. There were only tracks from the middle of the field to the street, but none in the direction towards the starting point. The tracks emerged in this form because Semjase had dropped Billy off from her ship in the middle of the open field after a contact the night before (1/6/77), so that from the landing site, only tracks could lead to the street, but none to the point of origin.
Date: January 7, 1977. Photographer: Billy. Location: Winkelriet/Wetzikon.

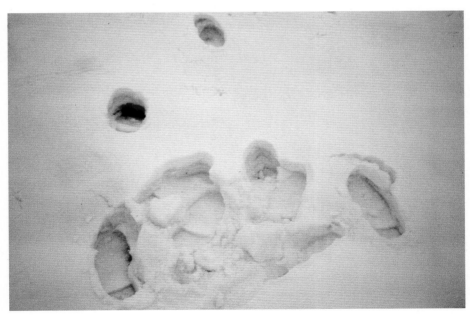

46 Billy's footprints from the open field to the street. *Date: January 7, 1977. Photographer: Billy. Location: Winkelriet/Wetzikon*

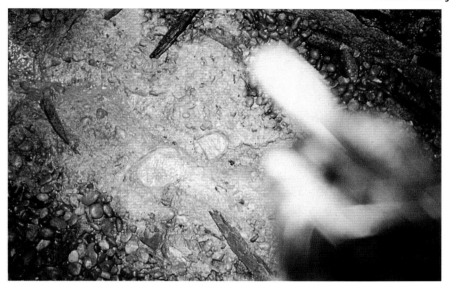

47 Footprint of a dwarf extraterrestrial, who was invisible to the naked eye, yet present in the cellar at the time of this photo. Helmet and shoulder piece of this dwarf is recognizable (lower-right corner), who became visible for 1/100th of a second during the exposure time and was thus exposed on the film. *Date: February 13, 1977. Photographer: Bernadette Brand. Location: Semjase Silver Star Center.*

48 Footprint of a dwarf dug out of the cellar of the Semjase Silver Star Center and poured into paraffin. *Date: February 2, 1977. Photographer: Mr. Bertschinger Sr. Location: Semjase Silver Star Center.*

49 Alena with Menara's laser pistol in front of Billy's office. *Date: July 6, 1977.*
Location: Semjase Silver Star Center

50 Alena with Menara's laser pistol in Billy's office. *Date: July 6, 1977. Photographer: Billy.*
Location: Semjase Silver Star Center

51 Billy on the house premises with the laser pistol borrowed from Menara.
Date: July 6, 1977. Photographer: Menara. Location: Semjase Silver Star Center.

52 Rear exit of a laser hole shot through the Semjase Tree. *Date: July 6, 1977.
Photographer: Billy. Location: Semjase Silver Star Center.*

53 A 3- to 5-meter tall fir tree, with a small beech scrub growing to one side, which was eliminated by Semjase at a later time (both clearly visible in the middle of the picture). *Date: July 1976. Photographer: Billy. Location: Langriemenholz/Hinwil.*

54 After the elimination of the 3- to 5-meter tall fir tree, at which time only the small beech scrub existed. *Date: July 1976. Photographer: Billy. Location: Langriemenholz/Hinwil.*

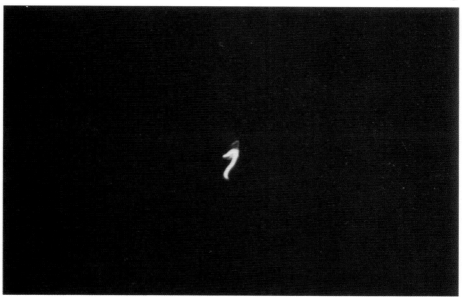

55 Demonstration flight of Semjase's beamship at night. Photo taken while the ship was ascending and flying away. *Date: June 13, 1976. Photographer: Billy. Location: Chalberweid/Ettenhausen.*

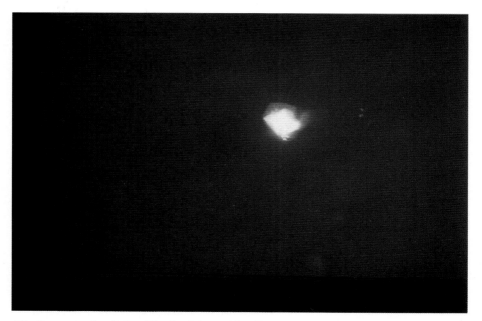

56 Demonstration flight of Semjase's beamship. *Date: June 13, 1976. Photographer: Billy. Location: Chalberweid/Ettenhausen*

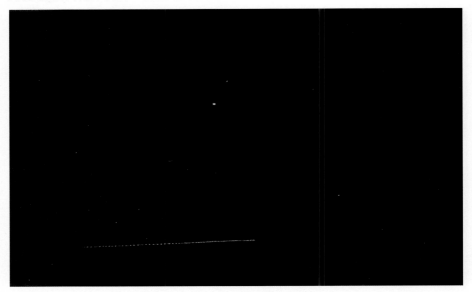

57 Telemeter disk of the Pleiadians flying by, taken beneath Venus, shortly before the night demonstration. *Date: June 27, 1976. Photographer: Guido Moosbrugger. Location: Winkelriet/Wetzikon.*

58 Semjase's beamship during the night demonstration, departure of the 7-meter ship. *Date: June 13, 1976. Photographer: Guido Moosbrugger. Location: Winkelriet/Wetzikon.*

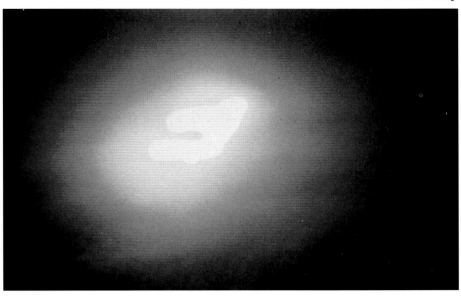

59 Semjase's beamship (recognizable in the original slide as a silhouette in the radiant light) during the night demonstration. *Date: June 13, 1976. Photographer: Guido Moosbrugger. Location: Winkelriet/ Wetzikon.*

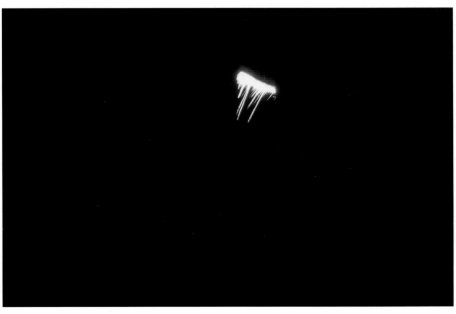

60 "Fine rain" (Conclusion of the night demonstration). *Date: June 13, 1976. Photographer: Guido Moosbrugger. Location: Winkelriet/Wetzikon.*

61 Semjase's beamship above Wihalden Street in the northern direction of Hinwil. The ship is half-transparent. The closeness of the ship and its vibrations most likely affected the quality of the film. *Date: May 20, 1975. Photographer: Billy. Location: Wilhalden Street 10/Hinwil.*

62 Demonstration flight of Semjase's beamship. Because people had been taken along to photograph without permission, Semjase lost control of her actions. Despite the fact that she initially allowed the pictures to be taken, she later tried to destroy them by radiating the sensitive negatives which she only partially succeeded in doing. Witnesses present: Hans Jakob and two of his daughters, Mr. Liniger, Mr. Leuenberger, Jacobus Bertschinger, two children of Billy (small children). *Date: April 20, 1975. Photographer: Billy. Location: Jakobsberg-Allenberg/Bettswil.*

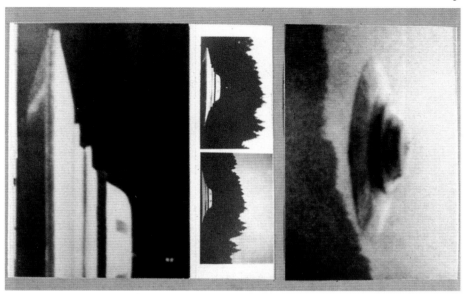

63 Hovering beamship (top frame); A series of landed beamships (middle and below) on February 27, 1975 in Jakobsberg-Allenberg/Bettswil. *(See ~ Photo collection from "Analysis of Major Ret. Colman S. VonKeviczky" on page #12, listed in Resource Literature.)*

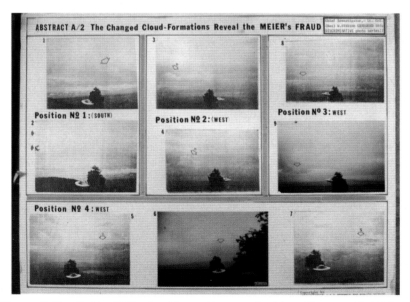

64 Demonstration flight with Semjase's beamship around a 14- to 16-meter tall, (46 ft. to 58 ft.) giant fir. Lake Pfäffiker is in the background. (This tree was later eliminated without a trace by Semjase.) *Date: July 9, 1975. Photographer: Billy. Location: Fuchsbüel-Hofhalden, Oberbalm, Wetzikon. (See ~ Photo collection from "Analysis of Major Ret. Colman S. VonKeviczky" on page #14, listed in Resource Literature.)*

65 Picture above: Semjase model turned 180 degrees and laterally inverted. Picture below: photo of a tub *(See ~ Photo collection from "Analysis of Major Ret. Colman S. VonKeviczky" listed in Resource Literature.)*

GOD's Eye o f the CREATOR upon "BILLY" MEIER and SEMJASE, during their ufonautical flight in the DAL-UNIVERSE.

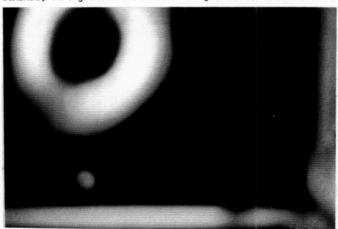

Sold to the members of "Billy"s FREE INTEREST–COMMUNITY FOR BORDERLAND – SPIRITUAL SCIENCES AND UFOLOGICAL STUDIES. SEM-JASE – SILVER – STAR CENTER, 8499 Hinterschmidrüti/ZH.

66 Ring Nebula of Lyra *(See ~ Photo collection from "Analysis of Major Ret. Colman S. VonKeviczky" Abstract G, listed in Resource Literature.)*

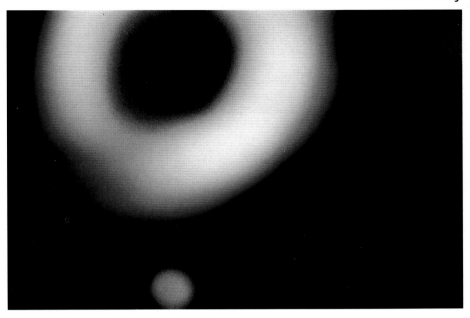

67 Ring Nebula of Lyra. *Date: 1975. Photographer: Billy.*

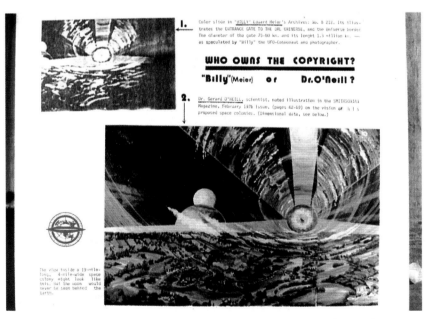

68 Space colony *(See ~ Photo collection from "Analysis of Major Ret. Colman S. VonKeviczky" listed in Resource Literature.)*

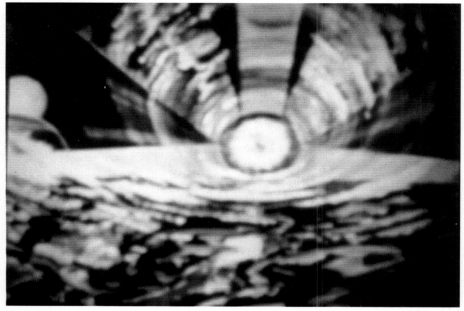

69 Barrier of the Universe. *Date: 1975. Photographer: Billy.*

70 Docking maneuver between the American Apollo 18 capsule and the Russian Soyus 19 on July 17, 1975. *(See ~ Photo collection from "Analysis of Major Ret. Colman S. VonKeviczky" listed in Resource Literature.)*

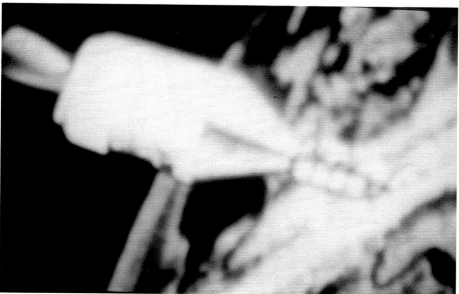

71 Docking maneuver between the American Apollo 18 capsule and the Russian Soyus 19. *Photo taken by Billy.*

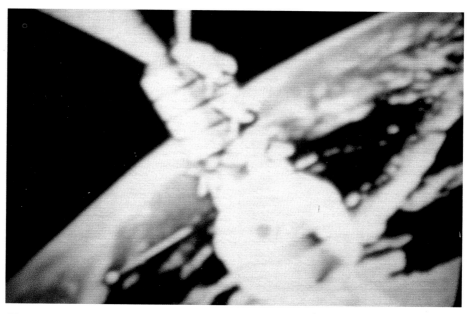

72 Docking maneuver between the American Apollo 18 capsule and the Russian Soyus 19. *Photo taken by Billy.*

73 Third assault against Billy. In the picture: Billy's jacket and his pistol. Place of bullet's exit in the jacket lining is plainly visible. *Date: Ascension Day of 1976. Photographer: Hans Schutzbach. Location: Sädelegg.*

74 Third assault against Billy. In the picture: Memorandum book, which Billy was carrying in his breast pocket, penetrated by the shot. Below the book is the tank plate, from which the shot ricocheted away. *Date: Ascension Day of 1976. Photographer: Hans Schutzbach. Location: Sädelegg.*

75 An attempt was made on Billy's life by an extraterrestrial group of Ashtar Sheran followers with an artificial lightning bolt as revenge for Ashtar Sheran who was eliminated in the DAL universe while conducting malicious acts of aggression. The lightning bolt hit Billy's thumb and was conducted into a stone situated below his hand, from which the lightning exited again with a small explosion. The explosion tore a piece of the stone away. While several meters to the side of it, the same bolt hit a birch tree for only a small fraction of a second beforehand, causing a 5-1/2 meter tall piece of the tree's crown to come crashing down. In the photo, Billy showed how he was standing by the aforementioned stone as he was struck by the bolt of lightning. *Date: April 24, 1990. Photographer: Freddy Kropf. Location: Semjase Silver Star Center.*

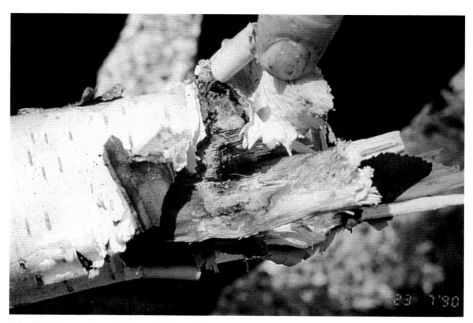

76 This is a portion of a trunk piece of a tree crown, which a lightning bolt struck and shattered. *Date: July 23, 1990. Photographer: Freddy Kropf. Location: Semjase Silver Star Center.*

- The Soviet spacecraft had no "spear-shaped" aerials on the outer end of the solar-cell wings. What's more, the actual aerials were U-shaped and considerably smaller in size than those in Mr. Meier's pictures.

- The aerials of Soyuz 19 were not longer than the width of the solar-cell arms, as in the picture from E. Meier. In reality, their breadth corresponds almost to that of the "paddle".

- The shadows on both objects, which Mr. Meier photographed, also do not correspond with the structure of the two spacecraft.

- Finally, the docking unit carried by Apollo to couple both crafts was missing altogether.

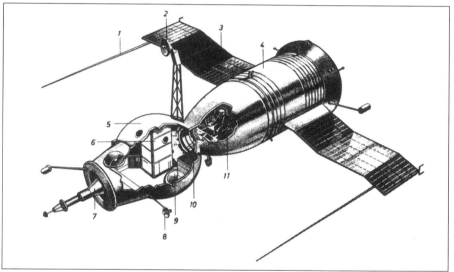

Fig 10-1
Taken from the book "Soviet Space Travel" with the kind approval of
Hubertus Hoose and Klaus Burczik, Review Publishing House

Response:

According to the magazine article, the objections raised by a spacecraft "authority" were based on an "investigation" the authority conducted using NASA material, television pictures and a Billy Meier photo.

Now one needed to know, of course, which photo was actually used as a means of comparison? The range of possible errors is quite extensive, especially with pictures of outer space.

As for my opinion: I am in the fortunate position of having almost a dozen Soyuz-Apollo pictures in my private collection to fall back on, though naturally, they are only copies of copies for reasons already mentioned. The originals would certainly be of a somewhat better quality. But the quality of several of these copies is still good enough to correctly see every single detail, which is most important here. These copies are, therefore, quite sufficient to refute the quoted objections, one point after the other.

As a good example, I would like to take a closer look at the last objection . It is claimed that the docking unit between the two space capsules, Soyuz-Apollo, is missing altogether in E. Meier's photo.

With the aid of the photos I have, I would like to make the following statement.

- In *Photo #70* (photo segments 1 and 2), the middle section between the two space capsules is so blurred and obscure that the docking piece cannot be seen at all.

- In photo segment 3, the docking piece is visible to a certain extent, but becomes blurred somehow with the background. A critic can thus be thoroughly convinced that the visible centerpiece is nothing more than a part of the background. Now, fine, if a critic only has the aforementioned material to work with, his conjecture about the missing docking piece becomes understandable and no one should take offense.

- However, had he gained access to the other photos, his criticism would not have been made in the first place. In this photo series, there are no less than three pictures in which the allegedly missing docking unit is actually found and definitely identifiable as such. (*See ~ Photos #71 and #72*)

Footnotes

55 ▪ Compulsory measures – By their Laws & Commandments, the Pleiadians are not allowed to interfere with the direct intentions of other civilizations.

56 ▪ Sisyphus — A mythical king of Corinth, condemned in Hades to roll a heavy stone up a steep hill, only to have it always roll down again when he approached the top. Sisyphean – endless and unavailing, a labor or a task.

57 ▪ H.J. was a former member of the earlier FIGU group.

58 ▪ Asket's race, the Timars (pronounced "timmarz"), emigrated to the DAL Universe about 50,000 years ago from our own universe, which is called "DERN."

59 ▪ Three people were projected onto a film, who in reality were not standing at that location at all. The pictures are very unclear and the people barely recognizable.

60 ▪ Giant fir tree, approximately 14-16 meters (50-53 ft.) in height

61 ▪ Semjase – The vanishing tree incident occurred on July 9, 1975 at 3:08 p.m. in Fuchsbül-Hofhalden by Oberbalm in Wetzikon.

62 ▪ Crown of a giant fir – For all comparisons of size and distance, a copy should always be available in the original size.

63 ▪ [Bah-vee] Baavi Intelligence have an association with the Pleiadians and are called on occasion to perform special tasks for them. They live in the same Tayget SOL System and dimensional plane, as do the Pleiadians.

64 ▪ Billy was teasing

Scientific Analyses
and Other Evidence

In our society, which for the most part is materialistically oriented, the motto still holds: "In principle, only what can be physically proven with measuring instruments, or unmistakably and repeatedly proven at any time with other aids, should be acknowledged as fact." This principle is especially true in all ufological matters and certainly is exactly the same with respect to the Billy Meier case. Why should it be different? Consequently, ever since Billy's phenomenal UFO story became public, new voices sporadically have been heard loudly demanding scientific evidence.

The American and Japanese research team also wanted to gain certainty in this way and did everything they possibly could to obtain material evidence, which was demanded by many people. After overcoming numerous obstacles, their endeavors were finally crowned with success. A layman can hardly imagine the tremendous amount of money, material, perseverance and good will it takes to actually conduct such a large-scale investigation. The most urgent problem is not in the matter as such, but in finding and convincing an institution to finance such a risky investigation because initially, no one is sure whether their great efforts will really be worth it in the end. Furthermore, researchers must consider that their credibility as scientists could be seriously endangered if superiors or colleagues discover their interest in ufological analyses.

Scientists must also consider their prestige. The difficulties faced when research teams try to win over renowned experts and well-known scientists for such endeavors are not trivial, even in the land of unlimited possibilities, not to mention that the Meier UFO case had already been proclaimed throughout the world as the greatest UFO swindle of all time. Incidentally, other important conditions must be fulfilled, such as the desire to be absolutely certain that no "marked cards" are used during the scientific investigation, and also that all work is carried out as thoroughly and conscientiously as possible without unfair influences. In all cases, it must be guaranteed that the results are exactly interpreted and published according to the facts. Logically, it would do the case little justice if a superficial investigation were conducted. It would inevitably lead to false results and misjudgments. On the other hand, what use are the best results if they are intentionally falsified? I do not base my arguments on merely assumed claims, but dishonest investigative methods or interpretations of physical evidence have been used and published in all possible variations in order to discredit Billy's proof material.

Nevertheless, Billy is fortunately able to present a series of reliable scientific analyses, photo and film analyses, sound and metal analyses, results of physical investigations of landing sites and the results of lie detector tests conducted on him and five witnesses. Quite understandably, we are very grateful to all persons and institutions that have contributed in some way or another to achieve these pieces of evidence.

Once in possession of such valuable pieces of evidence, one would expect that even obstinate skeptics would lose their footing, but this hope, unfortunately, went unfulfilled. That was when the then notorious skeptics started to really search for all possible or impossible counter-arguments in keeping with the saying: "It simply cannot be true, so it is not allowed to be true!"

A Few Examples of How the Skeptics Resist the Evidence

- Probably the most absurd claim asserts that the aforementioned analyses never took place and that the researchers involved, of course, never existed and that, therefore, the whole matter is nothing more than pure fabrication.

- Then there are people who do not contest the existence of the analyses and experts but who blame the researchers involved of malicious fraud, claiming the researchers only compiled the evidence desired because they had been bribed with a lot of money — similar to what is sometimes practiced in the advertising business.

- Other critics claim that these analyses could not be correct — that experts either made mistakes or were simply not competent enough to scientifically substantiate the results correctly.

One can sometimes really get fed up with everything we read and hear along this line, but one becomes accustomed to it in time.

Now, I no longer want to delay and would like to acquaint you with the most important results of the scientific investigations.

Statements Made by Witnesses About Billy Meier's Photos

Billy Meier brought his entire collection of UFO films to the photo shop "Baer" in Wetzikon (Zurich Highlands) to be developed into the black and white pictures. The shop would forward the color films to three different Swiss photo labs.

The proprietor of the photo shop, Mr. Baer, explained during an interview with two American UFO researchers, that:

- I never saw anything suspicious on the black and white film material, which I personally developed, nor was I ever requested by anyone to manipulate anything. A lot of people have suspected me of having done such a thing, but it is not true.

- I know nothing about UFO's, but the pictures are genuine. You can bring me before a court of law and I would make the same statement there as I have made to you.

- If Billy had had an accomplice, he would not have had to try different models for hours (camera models) to determine which photo and film cameras were the easiest to handle with one hand." (*Light Years* by Gary Kinder)

- Billy Meier had even invited Mr. Baer to accompany him to a contact and to photograph a Pleiadian ship on this occasion, if he wanted. Unfortunately, Mr. Baer did not consent to this special offer.

- Baer's successor, Mr. Kindlimann, was also unable to discover any kind of manipulation and gradually became convinced that everything correlated with the facts. (Light Years)

Results of Several Photo and Film Analyses

In the photo and film analyses made in the USA, there were also no falsifications detected. Several opinions on this:

- An expert for special film effects, Wally Gentleman, explained: "Is the knowledge of an expert found in this case or not? Because if the expert knowledge is not there, these photos have to be real." After studying the films, Mr. Gentleman concluded he could see "no way for a one-armed man to fake these film shots without the support of others. To produce these films, Meier would have needed to have a fleet of clever assistants, at least fifteen people…

- If somebody wanted to counterfeit only one of the seven films (short films), it perhaps would have been possible with $50,000 and in a studio where the equipment exists. The equipment would have cost another half a million." (*Open Letter* by Gary Kinder)

- Eric Eliason, an expert in photo evaluation, said in an interview with American author, Gary Kinder, "… I cannot think of anyone capable of falsifying these photos. If any kind of artificial preparation were added to the film afterward, the computer would have detected it. We have not found anything of the kind." (*Open Letter* by Gary Kinder)

- Dr. Michael Malin, Professor of Astronomy and specialist for the interpretation of photographs, made the following statement about the Meier photos: "I consider the photographs to be actually incredible. They truly appear to represent authentic phenomena." (*Open Letter* by Gary Kinder)

- "… I could not see anything obviously wrong with the pictures… According to what I saw, I can say that the matter is not a photographic fraud…" (*Light Years* by Gary Kinder)

- The physicist Neil Davis drew the following conclusion upon completion of his photo examination (photo sharpness, color density, double exposure, photomontage, models): "Nothing was found in the examination of the print which would cause me to believe that the object (spacecraft) in the photo is anything other than a large object photographed at some distance by the camera." (*Light Years* by Gary Kinder)

Analyses of Metal Samples

The head of an American research group once stated that, on principle, it was indeed possible to falsify photos or even films, but that it was absolutely out of the question to falsify metals or alloyed metals from extraterrestrial regions. In his opinion, providing an extraterrestrial metal fragment was the best piece of evidence we could offer.

In connection with this, Gary Kinder wrote that, somewhat to his amazement, Billy Meier had been "sitting" on metal fragments (given him by his extraterrestrial friends) for three years, which would have delivered clear proof of his authenticity. Unfortunately, the matter was not that simple. There were negative surprises at first. In 1979, the first metal analyses were initiated, and not even by Billy, himself, because the necessary money, as usual, was lacking. The first expert opinions were thoroughly depressing. No one in Switzerland or overseas was willing to invest the capital and work required for an in-depth study — especially not after it became known what this extraordinary examination was all about. Accordingly, only meaningless or derogatory opinions were expressed, as stated in the following "report:" A metallurgist of a Swiss company in Dübendorf examined one of the metal fragments and analyzed it as a simple "cooking pot" metal or a cheap cast metal alloy used to produce such things as tin soldiers.

After the American research group had finally succeeded in their long-term efforts to acquire two excellent specialists for the metal analyses, a totally unexpected turn took place. The specialists were Dr. Edwin Walker from Tucson, Arizona and Dr. Marcel Vogel, research chemist at the IBM test laboratories in San Jose, California. The latter is a pioneer in the technology of luminescence and has developed, among other things, liquid crystal, magnetic films and the floppy disk.

Both experts determined that the sample fragments were a metal alloy produced via a cold synthesis process. This process is still unknown to our technology on earth at the present time (*UFO Contact from the Pleiades* by Lt. Col. Wendelle C. Stevens, Ret.).

Mr. Walker experienced something in his research work that had never happened before in his 30 years of practice. While analyzing the composition of the metal, the Plexiglas encasing the metal fragment suddenly burst without any external influence, whereupon gaseous portions of the metal alloy were released (*Voice of the Aquarian Age, #29*)

In an interview with Jun-Ichi-Yaoi from Japan, Dr. Vogel made the following statement: "I can not explain this type of metal. By any known combination of materials, as a scientist, I could not put it together. With any technology that I know of, we could not achieve this on our planet! I have shown it to one of my friends who is a metallurgist and he shook his head and said, 'I don't see how this can be put together.' That is the situation where we are right now. And I think it is important that those of us who are familiar with the scientific world sit down and finally do some serious study on these things instead of putting it off as people's imagination."

The author, Gary Kinder, added to this, "I interviewed Dr. Vogel twice and he insisted that the metal sample, on which he had spent so much time analyzing, was truly unique." (*Light Years* by Gary Kinder)

Two of the metal fragments, which had darkened by oxidation, had quite a surprise in store for Dr. Vogel, which he formulated as follows: "When I touched the oxide layer with a stainless steel probe, red streaks appeared and the oxide coating disappeared. I only touched the metal like that, and it started to deoxidize and became pure metal. I've never seen a phenomenon like that before. It's just something that was unusual." (*Light Years* by Gary Kinder)

Dr. Vogel revealed other astonishing results of his research. Before the silvery golden triangular fragment (one of the four metal samples) had disappeared from Dr. Vogel's possession at IBM, he had placed it under his scanning electron microscope valued at 250,000 DM (1986) and turned on a videotape to record his analysis. The tiny specimen contained very pure silver and very pure aluminum, plus potassium, calcium, chromium, copper, argon, bromine, chlorine, iron, sulfur, and silicon. One microscopically small area revealed "an astonishing mixture of almost all of the elements in the periodic table. Each was exceedingly pure."

"It's an unusual combination," Dr. Vogel said later, "but regarding its type of structure, its appearance or form, I would not say that those alone would make them of extraterrestrial origin."

What astonished Dr. Vogel even more than the number of elements and their purity was the fact that the elements were separated from each other. "Each pure element was bonded to each of the others, yet somehow retained its individual structure. It's quite eerie if you look at the side-by-side combination of the metals," he said as he looked through the microscope and dictated his findings for the videotape. "One layer against another is very pure, but they do not interpenetrate each other. You have a combination of metals and non-metals together, very tightly layered. I don't know of anybody even contemplating the production of something like this."

In one small area in the middle of the sample (enlarged five hundred times), he found two parallel micro-grooves joined by furrows, precise hairlines somehow mechanically worked into the metal. But even more surprising to him was the major element present in that small area was the rare earth metal, thulium.

"It is totally unexpected," he said. "Thulium was only manufactured in pure form during World War II as a by-product of atomic energy technique, and only in minute quantities. It is exceedingly expensive, far more expensive than platinum, and difficult to obtain. Someone would have to possess high-level metallurgical knowledge even to achieve such a composition with this metal."

The magnification of the half-inch piece went from 500–1,600, and Vogel saw things he had never seen before. "A whole new world appears in the specimen. There are structures within structures — very, very unusual. At lower magnification one just sees a metallic surface. Now one sees a structure composed of various types of interlacing areas. This is very exciting." Vogel probed deeper and deeper into the metal.

"We are now at over 2,500-fold enlargement and one can see birefringent[65] structures. Very exciting! It is very unusual for a metal to have these bi-refringent areas. When you first take a section and place it under polarized light, it looks like metal, but at the same time … it is crystal!" (*Light Years* by Gary Kinder)

Remarkable as well is the unusual softness of the metal alloy of a Pleiadian spacecraft, in contrast to the traditionally hard metal bodies of our airplanes and spacecraft.

According to my opinion, the overall findings of the long-drawn-out investigations undoubtedly point out the extraterrestrial origin of the metal fragments.

Analyses of the Whirring Sounds

As we already know, the Pleiadian spacecraft can be shielded completely or in sectors both optically and acoustically. As soon as the protective shield is partially or totally opened, a strange and very intense whirring sound is heard.

Billy Meier was given three opportunities altogether to record such sound emissions on tape. (Twice in the area around Hinwil in the spring of 1976 and once in Sädelegg/Hinterschmidrüti on July 18, 1980. *(See ~ Chapter 6: Eerie Whirring Sounds)* (A copy of this recording can be downloaded for free from *www.steelmarkonline.com*).

These tape recordings were scientifically examined by several specialists and provided quite nice surprises. I would like to disclose a few of them to you at this point:

Two sound specialists explained to the journalist, Gary Kinder, that this sound analysis revealed something completely different from anything ever heard or seen before with the use of spectral- and frequency-analyzing devices. *(Open Letter* by Gary Kinder, *MUFON-UFO-Journal #28, April 1987)*

The computer engineer, Nils Rognerud, said, "I was very skeptical from a scientific viewpoint, but the sounds were unusual." *(Light Years* by Gary Kinder)

It was discovered that the sounds were a mixture of thirty-two simultaneous frequencies, twenty-four of them within the audible range and eight of them outside thereof — all of them were perfectly merged. *(See ~ Sound Analysis – p. 428.)* *(UFO Contact from the Pleiades* by Lt. Col. Wendelle C. Stevens, Ret.)

The sound engineer, Steve Ambrose, inventor of the Micro-Monitor, commented as follows: "These sound recordings have a number of surprising characteristics. How can these be produced? I am not speaking of how sound carriers can duplicate something of that kind, but how is it possible to get these strange things on a spectrum sound analyzer and on the oscillograph.[66] It's one thing to produce something that sounds like these recordings, but another thing to create something that sounds like them and also contains such stable and seemingly random oscillations. The sound pattern of the spacecraft was a unique recording that had an amazing frequency range. If it is a hoax, then I would like to meet the guy who did it, because he could probably make a lot of money in special effects." *(Open Letter* by Gary Kinder, *MUFON-UFO-Journal #28, April 1987)*

Ambrose knew many people in Hollywood involved in creating special effects, but these sounds, he said, were something none of them could ever have developed. *(Light Years* by Gary Kinder)

Jim Dilettoso,[68] who had examined the sound recordings with the use of a digital audio analyzer, said among other things, "To the ear they don't sound that unusual… but upon analysis, the tones continually rise and change, and partial combinations of them are getting louder and softer and doing things at such a rapid rate that even with a synthesizer being able to generate that many sounds, it would be an extremely complex matter (to produce this)." *(Light Years* by Gary Kinder)

Dilettoso wanted an independent confirmation. He sent the recording tape to Mr. Robin L. Shellman, a sound engineer with the United States Navy Sonar Sound laboratory in Groton, who made the following statement: "The equipment was set up to analyze for 50 or 60 Hz line frequencies, which are common electrical outlets. Meier could not have used any electrical AC source to produce the sounds. If the device that generates the sound were an electric motor or a machine, the line frequencies would be evident. But no such frequencies were detected." (*Light Years* by Gary Kinder)

"To reproduce a similar sound emission, a highly sophisticated electronic music studio would be necessary. This sound emission simply could not be realized with a number of synthesizers. For this reason, it would be too difficult to produce these sounds."

"This is certain that the noise could not be produced by a conventional type of machine known to earth technology." In 1980, it was estimated in the USA that a minimum of eight very expensive synthesizers and a highly sophisticated mixing system at a market price of $100,000 dollars would be needed to imitate those whirring sounds. (*See* ~ *Sound Analysis – p. 428.) (UFO Contact from the Pleiades* by Lt. Col. Wendelle C. Stevens, Ret.)

Further commentary is superfluous.

Physical Examination of the Landing Sites

In *Chapter 6*, reference was made to very impressive landing tracks that Pleiadian spacecraft had left behind at various locations in the Zurich Highlands. These solid pieces of evidence cannot simply be made to disappear from the scene, as too many witnesses actually saw the landing tracks with their own eyes and personally photographed some of them, as well.

Attempts were made to arouse suspicion in other ways, such as by writing that these landing tracks could not be considered conclusive evidence until they had been thoroughly examined. It must have been in Meier's interest to have these tracks examined. It was especially important because various comparisons with the (earth) environment would have established a connection by the increased radioactivity, magnetic radiation that could have been left behind by a spacecraft.

We recall the winter landing tracks of November 23, 1977. It happened in the parking lot in front of his residence. If faked, Billy would have had to melt the 10-centimeter (4 in.) thick, 3.5 meters (12 ft.) in diameter slab of ice within about 10 minutes, or the second landing track on his own property, a stone's throw away from the residential building.

How can it be explained that Billy could appear in the living room with absolutely dry clothes in spite of the prevailing weather conditions (thunder storm, gales and pouring rain) after an absence of about one hour? Quite simply, argued one skeptic, "Billy hid himself somewhere for an hour or so and maybe even took a little nap." Well, all right! But how did such jagged looking landing tracks get there in this nasty weather, or even better said, who made them? Besides, in this case, there were absolutely no footprints leading to the landing site or away from it. Furthermore, it is completely erroneous to assume that anyone would have chosen such miserable weather conditions in which to make these landing tracks, especially in this extraordinary form. Let's hear what a few other people have to say!

The witness, Herbert Runkel, said, "I am quite certain that Edi (Billy) did not fake these impressions. I often witnessed these landing tracks. I have exceptionally clear photographs that were taken at various locations and contain a great many details. I can assure you that the imprinted grass grew differently from the normal grass, even four years later."

Another witness by the name of W. Witzer from Stuttgart, who had the opportunity to inspect *Landing Track #2* after midnight on June 6, 1976, wrote in his report: "Having arrived at the landing site, we (he and a family F. from Kornwestheim well-known to him) immediately took a compass reading and, lo and behold, the compass needle was no longer pointing in the right direction."

Less fortunate was a scientist who wanted to register radioactive radiation at the landing site in Juckern with a Geiger counter during our absence (Billy and W. Witzer). This attempt was deemed to fail from the very beginning. The spacecraft that had landed there could not leave such radiation behind because of its different propulsion system.

Only in the beginning phase of 1975–1976 were the Pleiadian spacecraft equipped with powerful radiating propulsion systems, and that is why they are called "beamships." Such ships left measurable tracks behind wherever they came into direct contact with the ground. Certain residuals of this radiation can be traced after such a landing and, based on this fact, the American and Japanese research group conducted investigations with a gamma ray detector.

A thoroughly successful measurement of this kind took place in the nature reserve of Frecht near Hinwil, where Semjase and her beamship had appeared for the first time on January 28, 1975, and had also often landed there. The researchers could hardly believe their eyes when they first registered the test results of this contamination. Within one circular surface of 6.5 meters (22 ft.), the radiation level was no less than 100–400 percent higher than in the surrounding area, and not in a constant form but continuously rising and falling.

At other landing spots also, the dosage values showed an increase of 100–300 percent in a pulsating fashion. Surprisingly enough, an overdose of 300 percent was even detected on Billy's body and on several metallic objects (pendants). Nowhere else in the surrounding area could such excessive values be measured! (*Light Years* by Gary Kinder)

The results speak for themselves. I have no further facts to add.

Lie Detector Tests

During investigations, the American team used every possible research and test method suited to detect the truth and to confirm it.

For this reason, Billy and several members of his group underwent lie detector tests. Lies are known to mean "to tell the untruth with full intention," and it is assumed that a liar causes himself a type of stress that can be detected by measuring the reactions of the nervous system. As a layman, I cannot judge whether that is correct. Someone in a competent position nevertheless assured me that every liar exposes himself by an often only minimal and hardly perceptible change in his voice that can be mechanically detected and recorded with absolute certainty.

A lie detector of this type, which even hears a flea cough, perceives even the finest of fluctuations in the human voice with extreme precision, registers them and delivers the results for interpretation immediately. When compiling a list of questions, several questions should be worked in which can be assumed with great probability to trigger a type of stress situation in the one to be tested.

When Billy was tested with such a detector in 1978, he was asked — in the presence of a witness — a total of twenty-two questions that he was supposed to answer as quickly and precisely as possible, with no previous knowledge of the questions.

As for the effective value of such a test, there is certainly more than one way of interpreting it, but be that as it may, a "liar" would hardly subject himself to such a truth-detecting test on a voluntary basis. But this is only my purely personal opinion of the matter.

Here you will find the questions, which were taken from the book, *UFO Contact from the Pleiades*.

- Is your name Meier?
- Are we now in Hinterschmidrüti (Billy's current residence)
- Is this the year of 1978?
- Do you use a 35-millimeter Olympus camera?
- Do you actually take photos of extraterrestrial spacecraft?
- Do you know that they are extraterrestrial?
- Are you a Swiss citizen?
- Were you in India?
- Do you know a person by the name of Asket?
- Do you know this person to be an extraterrestrial?
- Did you use models for the pictures you took on March 28, 1976 in Bachtelhörnli (The photos were of the three spacecraft in flight.)?
- Have you ever used models for photos of spacecraft?
- Have you ever tried to pass photos of models off as extraterrestrial spacecraft?
- Were you ever in an extraterrestrial spacecraft?
- Have you already flown once in an extraterrestrial spacecraft?
- Do you receive your mail in Hinterschmidrüti?
- Was any of the equipment used by you anonymously donated to the group?
- Have you actually recorded sounds of an extraterrestrial spacecraft?
- Have you ever made photos from pictures or paintings and tried to pass these off as real objects?
- Are you now trying to deceive us with these photos?
- Are you satisfied that this test has been justly conducted?
- Do you have anything to add to your answers of the above questions? You can speak now.

Here is a list of questions for Billy's wife, Kalliope, Jacobus Bertschinger, Engelbert Wächter and Bernadette Brand that naturally had a different wording:

- Is your name…?
- Do you live in…?
- Are you a citizen of…?
- Do you know Billy Meier?
- Do you believe in Billy's contacts with extraterrestrials?
- Do you have any personal knowledge of or experience with such contacts?
- Do you think it is possible that the contacts take place in such a way that any earth people play the role of extraterrestrials?
- Has Billy taken photos of extraterrestrial spacecraft?
- What do you think, can these photos be made with a model?
- Do you have any knowledge that Billy has ever made photos with one of the models built by him?
- Were photos made of another model?
- Was this model from Billy?
- Was this model from Semjase?
- Have these models ever been passed off as genuine pictures of genuine beamships? (The photos which Billy made from a model received on loan from Semjase are meant in this case.) *(See ~ Photo #65)*
- Were these photos always referred to as pictures of the said model?
- Have you personally seen landing tracks of the spacecraft?
- Have you ever before seen the same or similar tracks on the ground?
- Do you have any notion of how Billy Meier could have made such landing tracks?
- Are you certain and convinced that Billy's contacts are real?
- Do you wish to make any statements, explanations or comments?

Result of all endeavors: After a careful analysis of the test results, no indication of conscious or deceitful intentions was detected on the part of either Billy or any of the other participants.

Confirmation of Astronomical Facts

It would far exceed the limits of this book if I were to explain all the advice, predictions and prophesies that Billy has relayed to us over the past fifteen years from his extraterrestrial friends or himself. I will therefore restrict myself to recounting only several astronomical facts, the majority of which have now been 100 percent confirmed by earthly science and space travel.

The Legendary Planet Malona, Malon or Phaeton

Like other legendary objects, Malona, also called Malon or Phaeton, lurks in the minds of many researchers of antiquity. According to the extraterrestrials, during prehistoric times, Malona was a direct neighboring planet of the earth that orbited around the sun in approximately the same path as Mars today. But at that time, we would have searched in vain for Venus where it is found today. I shall go into more detail about this at a later point. At that time, the planets of our solar system were situated as follows:

The planets of our SOL System were arranged in the following order:

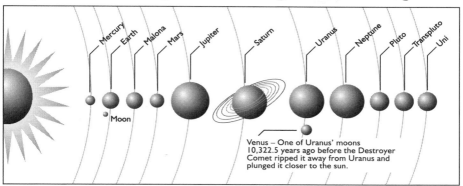

Fig. 11-1
The order of planets in our SOL System depicted approximately 75,000 years ago.

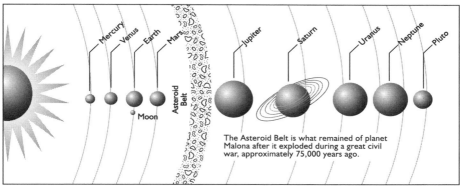

Fig. 11-2
Present SOL System

To this very day, due to their immense distance from earth, our astronomers have not discovered the two latter dwarf planets. The existence of Transpluto has been presumed for quite some time.

Malona served as a dwelling place for human life forms but was literally blown up through the fault of its own power-hungry inhabitants about 75,000 years ago as a consequence of armed conflicts. Contrary to the opinion of Phaeton researchers, who consider Malona to have been a gigantic planet, it was actually much more like a dwarf planet similar in size to our earth. A further assumption that the terrible tragedy was caused by a gigantic meteor that emerged from the depths of the cosmos and rammed Malona with full force and, thus, destroyed it does not correspond to the facts. The opinion that Malona was torn apart by the explosion of a gigantic atom bomb is not correct either. Instead, the Pleiadians teach us that the Malonans induced tremendous quantities of seawater into the crater of a volcano, which triggered the cosmic catastrophe. Apparently, only a few inhabitants were able to save themselves in their spacecraft by flying to earth and settling there. All others were unable to escape the terrible fate and became the victims of this monstrous explosive inferno.

This description naturally has nothing to do with the spirit forms of these Malonans. Billy described this circumstance as follows: "The rest of this planetary human race died in the fire of explosive destruction. Afterward, the released spirit forms floated away from the place of incident and set course for the next life-bearing planet, to become integrated there into the cyclic and orderly process of incarnation and evolution in accordance with the universal laws. This life bearing planet was none other than earth."

As an eternal warning of human unreasonableness and lust for power, most of the debris of the former planet now orbits the sun as the asteroid belt. This incident is also supported by the fact that many of the asteroids (planetoids) move in very long stretched-out elliptical orbits because they were hurled far out into space by the tremendously compressed forces of the explosion. A further indication of this is the apparent gap between Mars and Jupiter in the Rule of Interval by Titius and Bode *(See ~ Appendix C)*. In the region of the well-known asteroid belt, consisting of millions of tiny, dust-size particles and numerous irregularly formed boulders with a maximum diameter of several hundred kilometers are found. Most of them move in their eccentric orbit around the sun at a mean interval of 2–3 AU (AU = Astronomical Unit). *(See ~ Figure C-1 in Appendix C)*. A number of them occasionally cross our earth orbit as well and land in the vicinity of our earthly globe, as did Eros, which came within 0.15 AU of our planet in 1937.

If we now take a closer look at the abstract, Rule of Interval, we can determine two irregularities, the first is that Neptune should actually be in Pluto's orbit, for which I regretfully have no explanation. A second indication is the alleged planetary gap between Mars and Jupiter, which has already been clarified through the asteroids (planetoids) present there.

What cannot be seen from the Rule of Interval is the somewhat mysterious planetary shift, which resulted from the total destruction of the planet Malona. After Venus (originally a moon of Uranus) was locked into its present orbital path with the help of a giant comet known as the "Destroyer," Mercury was the inner neighboring planet of earth, and Malona the outer. As the cosmic tragedy was taking place, Malona was catapulted into what was the orbital path of Mars (approx. 2.8 or 2.9 AU) by the violent thrust effect of the first explosion. After arriving in its new orbital path, further explosions ripped Malona into numerous pieces, which now orbit around the Sun as today's asteroid belt. At the same time, the catapulted Mars came to a halt in the next inside orbital path, where Malona had been before. *(See ~ Figure 11-1)* The question, which still remains unanswered for me is why 75,000 years ago today's orbital path of Venus (0.72 AU = 108.2 x 10^6 kilometers away from the Sun) was not occupied.

Semjase's Explanations About the Planet Venus

The fact that Venus is not an offspring of Malona but a former moon of Uranus is quite apparent from the statements of the extraterrestrials. A giant comet (called "Destroyer" by the Pleiadians) tore Venus out of its orbit around Uranus about

10,000 years ago (10,321.5 years as of 1997). It was propelled on course toward earth, which gave rise to numerous cosmic catastrophes before the erstwhile moon of Uranus finally adopted its present orbital path between Mercury and earth.[68]

During a contact in 1975, Semjase revealed an entire series of data and explanations about the Evening and Morning Star, Venus:

SEMJASE: ...Due to the events at that time, the planet (Venus) was guided into a very peaceful orbit and therefore has one of the least eccentric paths. This is actually the result of Venus having passed close to the earth, which influenced the rotation time of the planet Venus. The gravitational force of the earth swung Venus around and caused it to rotate in retrograde.[69] As result of this very brief passage through earth's gravitational field, the rotation of the planet after breaking through could not be increased again and thus, acquired an extremely slow rotation time — the slowest within the entire solar system.

This is why a single day on Venus lasts 117 earth days and why the rotation time around its polar axis, with an inclination of 3 degrees, is 243 earth days.

The gravitational force of the earth robbed Venus of its own rotation energy 5,435 years ago (from 1997) and created great frictional heat. This frictional heat also created the physical conditions prevailing on Venus today. These physical conditions alone contradict all those charlatans and swindlers who claim that human life exits on Venus. This is completely beyond the realm of natural possibility. The environmental conditions of Venus and its atmosphere are absolutely hazardous for human life. The surface temperature of Venus, measured at a depth of 32 kilometers (20 miles), is still 457 degrees to this day, according to your Celsius calculations. This is also the reason that all water on this planet is vaporized and today forms a very thick cloud cover. In this way its thick atmosphere was formed. Pressure at the assumed sea level is three hundred and thirty-four times greater than the atmospheric pressure of earth. According to your scientific explanations, the atmosphere of Venus is hostile to human life forms because 87 percent of its volume is carbon dioxide, though the percentage fluctuates somewhat on occasion. Only 4.23 percent oxygen is present in the lower layers, while 95.47 percent is made up of nitrogen and inert gases. Water vapors are quite rare at the present time and the atmosphere is substantially greater than it is on your earth. The actual atmospheric pressure of Venus is one hundred and seven times greater than your earth's atmosphere. This fact also makes Venus hostile to human life forms. This high, slowly diminishing pressure would crush human life forms, demolishing them beyond recognition, and even metallic forms would suffer the same fate. For the orientation of you and your scientists, I would like to explain that we have found devices from earth on Venus that were completely crushed by the tremendous atmospheric pressure, even before these devices reached the surface of the planet. This refers to the exploratory probes of your nation, Russia, which were rocketed to Venus by the scientists of that land. The demolished apparati that we found looked as if they had been shot against a metallic wall with tremendous force.

Venus has a very weak magnetic field, and even the mantle known as the Van Allen Belt is also weakly developed. Consequently, neither offers great protection against the phenomenon known to you as solar wind. Furthermore, the very high temperature which impairs this belt must be considered. But the lack of water also has its consequences and is a factor in the planet's hostility toward human life.

Due to the event 5,435 years ago, the planet Venus is still in a phase of recovery and restoration. Slowly, over hundreds and thousands of years, the natural conditions for life will develop, and so the most primitive life forms will begin to develop, as they usually occur in natural manner, on all worlds becoming able to bear life. Therefore, it is even apparent to the foolish that Venus is a primitive planet in the sense that it is only in the initial stage of producing life.

As for the planet itself, it should be explained that it is very flat in the equatorial regions. The regions of structural relief are located far away from the equator. With regard to temperature, the day and night sides are almost equal, whereas greater differences in wind velocity are found in the lower and higher regions. On the surface, a complete calm prevails and only develops into wind in the higher regions. In even higher regions, the wind strongly increases and reaches velocities of 117 meters (386 ft.) per second. The lowest cloud layers are found at an altitude of 43.17 kilometers (27 miles) and can shift from time to time in atmospheric storms and so forth. This possibility is especially found in regions where winds flow downward to the planet's surface and accumulate at mountains that reach an average altitude of 2.3 kilometers (1.4 miles). The climatic and structural conditions are, by and large, the same all over Venus, although some differences can be seen. At the present time, it is a fact that human life on this planet is impossible if appropriate technical steps and aids are not used. Contrary to what various charlatans and swindler claim, no human life actually exists on Venus. But life is present in completely different forms, and no comparison can be drawn between them and human life forms.

The planet is still very wild. How could it be any other way after 5,435 years? Your earth moon is also an example of this. It is almost the very image of Venus when viewed below the thick cloud layer. Whenever other life forms or we go to Venus, which is rich in various minerals and other substances, survival is only possible by the use of special, protective suits which safeguard us from the dangerous atmospheric influences and its great heat. We also have to take into account the various forms of toxins and gas that envelope the planet in deadly vapors. The planet is subject to certain differentiations. We have to be careful of some places where the temperature rises above 500 degrees Celsius directly on the surface, and where the percentages of carbon dioxide, nitrogen, helium gas, argon gas and neon gas shift and atmospheric pressure fluctuates between the percentage points of 88 to 107. This covers the most fundamental explanations with respect to the hostile environment of the planet Venus.

At a different point, the Pleiadians from the planet Erra emphasized that, besides the earth, not a single heavenly body in our solar systemis inhabited by human beings, not even in spiritual form. Only the planets Malona and Mars were temporarily inhabited before their destruction.

The only exception to inhabiting the heavenly bodies in our solar system are the relatively few extraterrestrials who are staying in several planetary stations for the sole purpose of research. In the meantime, all of the physical data imparted to us by Semjase has been confirmed over and over again by the Russian and American space probes. It is also known to earth astronomy that Venus, in contrast to all the other planets, rotates extremely slowly on its axis. Beside that, it orbits retrograde around the sun. As taken from the book *Marathon in Space* by Reiner Klingholz,[70] the values given in this respect are as follows:

- Mercury = 58.65 days
- Venus = 243 days
- earth = 1 day
- Mars = 1.0 days
- Jupiter = .41 days
- Saturn = 0.44 days
- Uranus = 0.72 days
- Neptune = 0.67 days
- Pluto = 6.39 days

How these abnormalities of Venus came about is also unknown to earthly science. Rudolf Kippenhahn writes in his book, *Unheimliche Welten*, [71] p. 146: "As far as the extremely slow and unusual direction of rotation of Venus is concerned, our earth is suspected of having a hand in this. Every 583.9 earth days, Venus and earth come especially close to each other in their orbital paths around the sun. Venus is then in inferior conjunction and the distance between both planets is only 41 million kilometers (2,542,000 miles)." Kippenhahn's assumption comes very close to the truth, especially if one considers that he most likely has no knowledge of the historical event.

Confirmation of the Moons of Saturn

Excerpt from Contact Report #154 of October 10, 1981:

BILLY: That is clear to me, but while we are already discussing the stars, I have another question for you in regard to Saturn. As you know, the American space probe Voyager will pass by Saturn and send pictures back to earth. The scientists will certainly look surprised again, as they did with Jupiter. They will once more have to recognize from the photos that the not fully developed dwarf sun is orbited by more moons than has been assumed up to this time. According to my knowledge, it has been claimed up to this point that Saturn has only ten or twelve moons, although it actually has nineteen, if I do not count the Adonids. It would therefore be of interest to me whether all these moons will be discovered by the photo transmissions.

QUETZAL: This will be so — and even more. As you were already able to determine yourself on location on your great journey, there are nineteen moons that can actually be considered as such, orbiting around Saturn. These will probably be discovered in their entire number by the space probe. In all truth, there are not too many of the nineteen moons yet to be discovered. Since your journey, the earth scientists have discovered several additional moons in recent years, which apparently escaped your attention. Having discovered the moons around Jupiter, the scientists now anticipate finding a few more moons around Saturn, although a surprise is still in store for them.

BILLY: Do you think because of the Adonids?

QUETZAL: That is correct. These miniature planets called Adonids, as you said correctly, are so small that they cannot be detected or seen from the earth, at least not at the present time. The instruments needed for this do not yet exist. A large number of these miniature planets will definitely be detected by the probe and that will cause quite some confusion for the scientists.

> **BILLY:** I can imagine that there are quite a large number in orbit around Saturn — besides the few small wandering Adonids that only pass by the planet from time to time. I can well understand that they are not visible from earth. They only have an average diameter of between 10–50 kilometer (6–31 miles), if I still correctly recall what Ptaah and Semjase explained to me in 1975.
>
> **QUETZAL:** That is correct, but you should also know how and from where these Adonids have reached Saturn.
>
> **BILLY:** Naturally, Semjase said at that time that these small moons were larger pieces of the planet Malona, the orbital path of which was between Mars and Jupiter before it was destroyed and ripped into thousands of fragments through an explosion produced by the irrational people there. While the greatest part of the destroyed planet flew out into space, a larger group of fragments landed within the gravitational force of Saturn, which has been holding them firmly as the smallest of its satellites ever since. This also means that they aren't the actual moons of the unfinished solar planet but only immigrated foreign bodies the size of the Adonids, whereas the total number of Saturn's actual moons is nineteen.

According to a report in the renowned Swiss newspaper, Tages-Anzeiger, dated July 26, 1990, the American astronomer Mark Showalter discovered the 18th moon of Saturn, and now one additional moon is still waiting to be discovered by the scientists.[72]

Confirmation of the Statements Relating to Jupiter

Excerpt from the contact conversation, which took
place on October 19, 1978 between Semjase and Billy.
Billy wanted to know whether the American space probe, Voyager I, was able to obtain good results as it passed by Jupiter.

> **SEMJASE:** According to our calculations of its path and the flight path of the probe, it must come very close to the star and to various moons of Jupiter, which means that good results must be obtained if the apparati of the reconnaissance device function faultlessly.
>
> **BILLY:** Do you mean that the time has come for scientists to discover that the red spot of Jupiter is, in truth, a rotating and funnel-shaped hole in the wildly surging surface of this incomplete sun and that the funnel hole forms the center of a gigantic storm many thousands of years old? Does that also mean they will now find out that not only Saturn and Uranus have a ring, but also Jupiter, though it is far thinner and smaller than the other two around Saturn and Uranus?
>
> **SEMJASE** Definitely, even this will certainly be discovered. The probe will be steered so close to the heavenly body that it will have to record these things.
>
> **BILLY:** Aha! And will it then also be discovered that the ring around Jupiter largely consists of particles hurled out from the large volcanoes on its moon, Io, which are partially captured by Jupiter? But the greater part of all the material hurled out drops back onto Io again and practically covers all the volcanic openings, as well as the immense flat lands and mountains. That is why this particular moon, in contrast to the other moons of Jupiter, has no crater landscape. It is fantastically level in spite of its many craters.
>
> **SEMJASE:** You listened very carefully to my explanations on your excursion tours and have admirably kept them in memory. Are you able to remember other things? These facts, by the way, will certainly be discovered by the reconnaissance device.

BILLY: Fine! Of course, I still know a few things. I haven't forgotten everything that you and Ptaah explained to me. I can still remember well enough that the various large moons of Jupiter were of colors such as red, yellow, brown and white, as well as orange. I also remember you telling me that Jupiter was actually supposed to be a sun but that the mass had been too small for this star to actually develop into a sun. All the same, its entire composition basically consists of fluid helium and oxygen. I also still know that you and Ptaah explained to me that the surface areas were principally composed of potash salts and sulfur compounds extending deep into the surface and had then deposited as a very thick crust after the large water masses on this satellite had evaporated. Above all, I believe I recall you saying that the moon, Io, in particular, was once completely covered with water. If I recall correctly, you told me — I no longer know whether it was you or Ptaah — that the moon, Europa, would be the complete opposite of Io. Its water masses didn't evaporate and change but froze into a gigantic shield of ice. You also told me many other things and gave me explanations of which I still know a great deal. You told me that the respective moon that I referred to as a colossal chicken egg only measured about 200 kilometers (124 miles) in diameter. I believe it was the moon closest to Jupiter, the name of which I no longer can remember.

SEMJASE: You have an admirable memory in all things. The moon you just mentioned is known on earth as Amalthea. The moon, Io, you have commented on is, incidentally, the most active volcanic planetary body in the SOL System. But that was already explained to you at that time, if you still are able to remember.

BILLY: Naturally! I don't forget such things so quickly. You said at that time that this moon had far greater volcanic activity than the earth. Incidentally, I precisely remember you explaining that the kilometer-large cloud formation in the storm funnel of Jupiter traveled at very high velocity and rotated counterclockwise.

SEMJASE: Certainly, I explained that to you.

BILLY: I only wonder if my memory serves me right with regard to the volcanic activity on the moon, Io. If I recall correctly, you explained that volcanic eruptions take place with elementary force, causing enormous explosions that hurl their ejected material out like a nuclear bomb's mushroom plume to heights up to 180 kilometers (112 miles). They basically consist of dust particles, gases, ashes and a little magma that reach hurling velocities of up to 2,300 kilometers/hour (1,426 miles/hour) because a minimal counteracting force exists due to its lack of atmosphere. You also said that the greatest part of all the expulsion material falls back onto the moon, as I mentioned awhile ago. The rest, as you explained, is discharged into space where some are attracted by Jupiter and condenses very slowly within its ring into a large compound of sulfur ions. Is that right?

SEMJASE: Yes.

As these and other explanations reached the public, they merely served the skeptics as welcome opportunities to make fun of Billy's "fantasies" in the usual manner. In the meantime, a few skeptics may have sobered up. On the whole, all statements in the previous section have been confirmed by earthly science, as can be verified by anyone reading astronomy books of recent edition.

Of the seventeen moons of Jupiter, sixteen are known today. Also verified today are the individual rings of the gigantic planet Jupiter, and of Neptune, and at least eleven rings of the Uranus ring system.[73] Scientists have designated the red spot of Jupiter as a gigantic cyclone that rotates counterclockwise. Jupiter's moon Io undoubtedly provides the greatest surprise with its very lively volcanic activity.

An additional remark: An interested woman attested to and signed in her own handwriting the existing contact reports, referring to the aforementioned explanations, at a time when our earth scientists had no knowledge yet about the research results of today (1982).

Two Informative Letters

In 1975, Billy received a copy of a very interesting and informative letter by Mr. V. from Germany. Since this copy could unfortunately not be reproduced, as a result of poor quality, we had no other choice but to write down the contents word for word.

Dear Sir,

Please pardon the fact that I have presented you with this letter without knowing you. I received your address from a countryman who advised me to write to you, as you would surely be interested in my information.

I would first like to say something about myself so that you know with whom you are dealing. I am a 35-year old woman and a German citizen. For about four years, I travel as a hitchhiker around the world because I want to see and experience something once in my life. One thereby often encounters quite peculiar and unusual things that one normally would never experience. This is what happened to me seventeen days ago, which was quite peculiar.

It was in the Persian desert, down in Zahedan, about two miles outside the village on a bright morning. My friend, Peter, and I had pitched our tent there, extra remote, in order not to be bothered by the village inhabitants which is quite common in these regions. At about seven o'clock in the morning, we were awakened by a peculiar sound but were unable to see anything as we crawled out of the tent. The sounds were still there and came from behind a sand dune about 50 meters (165 ft.) away. Peter thought these were most likely workers who had something to do there. He was satisfied therewith and crawled back into the tent to sleep another one or two hours. I was interested and went to see what the workers were doing. I went around the large sand dune and suddenly stood before a woman, who was about the same age as I. Quite unusually dressed, she reminded me of the astronauts, whom I had seen in pictures.

The woman, who had been stirring around in the sand with an unusual device, was obviously shocked when she saw me. She immediately stopped working with the device. Being very astonished myself I went to the woman and asked here in the English language what she was doing here. The answer was that she was looking for something quite particular. She was digging something out which had crashed down here. She then simply continued to work and after a few minutes actually found the object she was looking for, a somewhat odd, spiral-shaped cylinder that she packed away in her unusual digging instrument. She then wanted to leave and said good-bye to me. Unusually attracted to her, I asked her to stay a moment, which she actually did after some hesitation. I introduced myself and asked her whether she lived in the area of Zahedan. She only laughed and said that this place was too unsuitable for her to live in and that she came from far away, and that her name was Semjaze or Semjase, if I correctly understood. We talked for a while about the people in Persia, and then she said that she really must be going. After we said good-bye, she operated her device. To my amazement, it raised quite suddenly from the ground and hovered in front of the woman, who moved away and disappeared behind another sand dune.

After recovering somewhat from my amazement, I ran onto the sand dune behind which the woman had disappeared. As I came to the top, I froze in amazement again, because what I saw could not possibly be true: About 100 meters (330 ft.) away stood something quite unusual that I had always laughed about up to that point if anyone told about it, namely a 'flying saucer.' I simply could not grasp it and believed that I had lost my mind. But it must have been true, because I saw how the woman with the device just disappeared inside underneath the flying saucer and how the door closed behind her. Totally soundless, the saucer suddenly lifted and flew somewhat in my direction. Suddenly, it seemed to me that an invisible hand pushed me aside and I fell and rolled down the sand dune. Somewhat numb, I got up again and saw how the flying saucer slowly climbed vertically. Then it suddenly shot off like an arrow and disappeared with a peculiar tone into the blue sky.

Frozen with amazement, I remained standing for some time before I went back to the tent. On my way, I felt quite peculiar and suddenly there was a voice in me which said "pardon" several times.

Afterwards, I naturally told everything to Peter, who only laughed about my story and said that I had the desert madness. We argued about it, which is why he left me several hours later, and disappeared forever. He at least told me that he wanted nothing more to do with someone crazy and thus went his own way. I am really not crazy and I know precisely that I really saw everything. I also remember exactly that the woman said to me during our conversation that she had a very good and kind friend in Europe. And I also know precisely that I saw her, as I saw her peculiar digging machine and the flying saucer. I am really not crazy and actually saw and experienced everything as I have written it to you.

In the meantime, I have a new friend and told him everything. He said that such things actually could exist and that you concern yourself with such matters. He read this once in a magazine and told me to write you my story as I have now done. I do not want you to mention my name in anyway if you tell my story to someone. It suffices that I am considered to be crazy by many if I tell of my experience. And if I ever go back to Germany, I do not want people to point at me and say that I am the crazy one who saw the flying saucer in Persia, the peculiar digging machine and the lady from the stars. Please understand this and do not mention my name.

I prefer not to give you any further information about myself or my home address. I already mentioned that it is quite enough that people call me crazy wherever I go and if I tell my story. In Germany, they might even put me into a madhouse if they knew exactly where I come from and when I return to my hometown. Please understand this.

I send you my kind regards and remain, yours truly E. Sch.

Antalya, Turkey, March 8, 1975

The following was written by hand across the second page of the letter typed above:

Dear Sir,

The enclosed letter from Turkey was erroneously sent to me due to apparent carelessness of the Turkish mail. I receive newspapers from Antalya in Turkey every month that are often poorly packed and arrive at my address half open. Quite obviously during the recent delivery this letter got stuck between the newspapers, and got stuck on the apparently still moist postage stamps when mailed, so it was forwarded to me in my newspapers. It is therefore no fault of mine that a large postage stamp was torn off when the letter arrived, which I nonetheless want to apologize for.

Since I am an honest person and do not open letters or other things that are not addressed to me, I am sending this incorrectly mailed letter to you. You can then have it correctly forwarded and sent to the given address.

Yours faithfully,

J. Krauer

Comment by the author: According to the contact report of November 17, 1989, Semjase's father, JHWH Ptaah, confirmed this encounter of his daughter with the German woman.

In the summer of 1976, Billy in turn received a letter in which the encounter with extraterrestrials of a German globetrotter was described and the contents of which also confirm that Billy's contacts correspond to reality.

Honorable ladies and gentlemen,

Enclosed we are sending you several copies of a letter of one of our friends who is traveling around the world as a globetrotter at the time. According to his request, we do not want to name any address. The reason for which you will find in the enclosed copies.

After a number of consultations with our minister, Pastor Dillmann, we have agreed to prepare the enclosed photocopies of the aforementioned letter and forward them to various addresses named to us by Pastor Dillmann, whereby we hope that the copies will be useful to you, although we ourselves doubt the statements made in the letter and are seriously concerned about our friend's state of health. Nonetheless, we would like to fulfill the request of our friend according to the advice of our esteemed Pastor Dillmann and are thus sending you the enclosed, the content of which you must clarify for yourself.

We were told that you concern yourself with such things as those mentioned in the letter so you certainly will know the meaning of all this. Along with the copies of the letter, there is also a copy of a sketch, which our friend enclosed with the letter. We can attest that he makes very good sketches with regard to physiognomies so that the drafts of both heads must be accurate. The object must correspond with reality if his information corresponds to the facts and doesn't stem from an attack of fever or the like which we suspect but are unable to check, because we haven't heard from him since the month of February.

Perhaps it will be useful to you if we mention all of the addresses received by Pastor Dillmann, to each of which we are sending a copy of the letter. Perhaps, you among yourselves may understand more about the peculiar statements of our friend.

Hoping to have been of some service to you and to our friend, we send our kind regards.

p.p. A. Albers

Trinidad, on January 2, 1976

Dear Friends,

On my world trip, I have now landed in Trinidad. You will find the nest on the Marmore River in Lianos de Mojos in Bolivia. I have been here for three days and have already seen very many interesting things. I have already filled many typewritten pages with my impressions and experiences. Yesterday morning I had an experience that almost knocked me off my feet. At first, I thought it was an hallucination or tropical frenzy before I was able to convince myself that I was completely normal. Perhaps you will feel the same when you read these lines of mine. You know me well enough, and know that I am no dreamer. Therefore, you simply have to believe me, even if it will certainly be difficult for you. Everything is so incredible and crazy that I still look for faults in my reasoning even today and still believe to be dreaming. But everything happened just as I am writing to you. Do not think that I am crazy or sick because I am neither one nor the other. However, let me tell you of my experience yesterday:

It was just 5 o'clock as I crawled out of bed and got dressed to make my way to the farther surroundings of Trinidad. About 10 minutes after getting up, I observed in the morning sky something that I simply could not believe. I have indeed heard of and read about flying saucers but have never thought about it nor believed in it. I always regarded such claims as wild notions. But then such a flying saucer flew over Trinidad very calmly and without a sound. It descended more and more and finally disappeared somewhere behind the bush. I thought I was dreaming and rubbed my eyes. What I saw simply could not be true. The saucer appeared to me from my standpoint to have the form of two large half round disks placed one on top of the other just like a discus looks.

I sat down at first and thought about it. Perhaps, I would be better off to return to civilization and have myself thoroughly examined by a doctor. But then I came to the conclusion that I should examine the case more carefully before deciding to take such a step. I took my compass and determined the exact direction where I believed to see the flying saucer go down. I then tied my bundle and marched off, continuing in the exact direction I had determined with my compass. It was precisely in the east. With great effort and sweat, I fought my way further and further through the terrain and rampantly growing bush. It seemed to me as if I would never reach my goal and I soon wanted to give up and turn back. I was already on my way for more than three hours and had not yet found anything. I therefore must have been suffering from a hallucination, because I should have stumbled across the flying saucer long ago according to my calculation if it had actually existed. I continued to work my way through the hindering brush breathing heavily and soaking wet from perspiration but already filled with the thought of turning back. Nevertheless, I didn't embark on my way back. Something kept driving me onward. It was as if passively I was simply drawn onward as if by a magnet. I could simply not defend myself against it. Then another half-hour must have gone by and I finally believed to have lost my mind when I suddenly saw something very large with a metallic luster shining through the brush. I stood there rigid and unbelieving at first, but then I overcame myself and fought the rest of the way through.

And again, I believed I was dreaming. A large discus of metal hovered in a large clearing only about 1 meter (3 ft.) above the ground, definitely about 14 or 15 meters (46 ft. or 50 ft.) in diameter. What was eerie about it was that neither sound nor any other tone could be heard. Nevertheless, this discus simply hovered above the ground in the open air. As if rooted to the spot, I remained standing only about 20 meters (66 ft.) away and stared disbelieving and not comprehending over to the flying saucer. I was incapable of thinking and could no longer take a step. I am accustomed to quite a lot and am downright hard-boiled from all my travels, but what I saw simply left me frozen. It simply could not and was not allowed to be true. Something like that simply could not exist.

I don't know how long I actually stood there and didn't move. I only know that something suddenly touched my arm and I turned around without understanding and as if in a dream. What I saw left me even more frozen. Two men were standing beside me in diving suits. I still know that I puzzled over it and asked myself why in the world these two were running around in the middle of the bush in diving suits. It did not dawn on me until later and I noticed many differences. The suits were visibly light and not cumbersome like many diving suits known to me. The silvery color also didn't correspond to the suits I knew. The two blond men also wore no helmets but had strange looking devices of various sizes and forms on their suits.

Still rigid, I was unable to speak a word although the men, who obviously belonged to the flying saucer, did not look mean and even laughed friendly. Suddenly, one of them said something but I could not understand a word of it. The second one then made an attempt, but with the same result. Their language seemed totally strange to me but with a melodious and amiable sound that relaxed me somehow and seemed to release me from my rigidness.

The two men of about the same size — were about my size, that is 174 centimeters (70 in. or 6 ft.) — took me by the arms and led me to their flying saucer which I, passively, allowed them to do. About 5 meters (17 ft.) in front of the saucer, they had erected some strange-looking things, under which also stood somewhat peculiar chairs or armchairs, in which we took a seat. I still was unable to utter a word. With a friendly smile, one of the men spoke to me again, but I still couldn't understand anything. His speech had an effect on the rigidness that had stricken me, it was now completely gone and I was quite calm. Then I was suddenly able to speak again. Astounded, I inquired in Spanish about this incident that was incomprehensible to me. Obviously, now they did not understand my words. I then made an attempt in English but with the same result. The same thing also happened with my native German language. We simply could not communicate. Then one of the men spoke with me again in his melodious and congenial language, while grasping his belt and switching around on some device hanging on it which was no larger than a package of cigarettes. While speaking, his language suddenly changed and just as suddenly I heard Spanish words, then French and right away German. I don't know why, but I was suddenly excited about it that the men must have noticed. The selection of the German language remained and the men were insistently speaking to me in my mother language. I still know precisely as they said at first, 'We can now communicate through our language transformer. Greetings unto you and be not afraid. We have come here in peace and shall depart in peace.' Those were the first words that I could understand and I shall certainly never forget their exact wording. It was so greatly impressive to me that everything was deeply imbedded in my memory, you can sincerely believe me.

After we were able to communicate, I was asked whether I was able to retain everything in my memory, if they — these two men — were to explain various things to me. I answered this question affirmatively and explained that I would write everything down in short hand at once, if this were allowed. I was a world traveler who earned my living by writing reports of my experiences. This was even very good they answered but wanted to know what short hand was. I was surprised about this question but answered it correctly for which they were grateful. I then gathered my shorthand pad and a pencil and began to record everything word for word that was spoken among us. That is why I can give you a literal repetition of our conversation that will certainly be just as amazing and staggering to you as it was to me. But let me tell you everything in proper order as I have recorded it.

Contact Conversation Between the Two Extraterrestrials, Kohun and Athar from Proxima Centauri, with the German Globetrotter H.F.

I am Kohun, said one of the two men.
I am called Athar, said the other introducing himself.
My name is H.F., I explained to both of them.
Do you live here in this rugged country? asked Athar.
No, I am a tourist here, as I am from Germany.
What is a tourist? asked Athar.
A visitor, was my answer.
Then Athar and I are tourists, said Kohun.
How am I to understand that? I asked.
Kohun answered: We are not from this world, which you call earth.
And how am I to understand that? I asked again in astonishment.
We come from the stars, answered Kohun, and we are not creatures of this world.
I suppose you want to pull my leg, don't you? I asked. I actually believed that what they said was merely a joke.
No, we come from the star system, Proxima Centauri, as you call this group of stars, was Kohun's answer. It is the closest solar system to this world — about 50 trillion kilometers (31 trillion miles or 5 light-years) away from here according to your method of calculation.

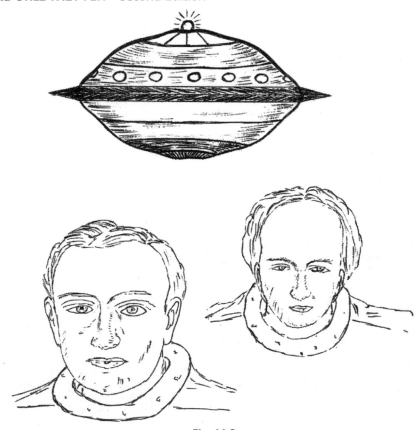

Fig. 11-3
Kohun, Athar and their Beamship

That can't be. That's a utopian notion, I said.

KOHUN: We aren't joking.

H.F.: Then you must be star men?

KOHUN: That we are, if you wish to call us so.

H.F.: I can't believe that.

KOHUN: It is the truth.

H.F.: That is incredible. What are you doing here?

KOHUN: We often come to earth. We are following the events here and observing the development of mankind. Unfortunately, they are very far behind in
their development as a result of religious deceptions and political intrigues. The
people of earth could bring great havoc due to their lack of development and
struggle for power, through which also very distant stellar systems could become affected. That is why we come to earth as observers to prevent the worst
from happening if need be.

H.F.: That sounds unbelievable.

ATHAR: We are telling you the truth.

H.F.: If you are really telling the truth, what could the two of you actually do, if
something were really to go wrong?

H.F.: Have no reservations, we are not alone. Besides us Centaurians, there are a number of different space races on earth, though they come from far more distant systems than we do.

H.F.: It all sounds so utopian. What actions do you plan to take against the present development on earth? You can't simply change something by force. That would lead to a world war. Where do the other star people come from?

KOHUN: I have already explained that we are telling you the truth. It is there-fore not utopian. We also do not plan to take any actions against the earth. We have no right to do that and especially not by force, which we are forbidden to use. You do not need to fear a war from our side. We have many friends on earth with whom we have contact and who are working for the well-being of mankind, according to our instructions, in a peaceful form. They are spread-ing the knowledge about our existence and our mission. You call these fellow men contact persons. They are working on behalf of our orders and therefore meet with hostility. They are accused of lying and of fraud, against which they unfortunately can rarely defend themselves. It is just as unfortunate that certain elements, mixing among the good contactees, merely practice fraud and make sport of it, and thoroughly jeopardize the task.

The most important of all contact persons is especially exposed to great hostility and his life has even been threatened. He is a man of highly significant value who has been educated to be the Prophet of the New Age. His mission is the most important of all. He, as the prophet, must once again bring the au-thentic teachings of the truth anew to the people of earth. These are the teach-ings you call the teachings of the spirit. These teachings are conveyed to him from the highest of all spirit realms in connection with space races from the Lyra Constellation, the stars of the Pleiades, and the DAL - universe. Besides these, a number of other space races are residing on earth or who come here regularly. Without a doubt, the greatest and most important tasks are carried out by the space races who come from the Pleiades. They are the most distant descendants of the earth people's ancestors. That is why the great mission falls within their realm of authority. These space races have three different stations on earth un-der the direction of a commander by the name of Quetzal, whose representative is a female being who is about 350 earth years old. She is called Semjase and is the daughter of the most powerful commander of the Pleiadian space fleet. The earthly contact person of the Pleiadian race is a man of about 40 years of age who lives in a country called Switzerland. We know his name as Billy. Altogether, there are six different space races stationed on earth (the number of whom has just been doubled) — and on the neighboring stars of Venus and Mars, where are only a very few in very small stations. The number of residents on Venus and Mars only come to about fifty. These planets are absolutely uninhabitable and are extremely hostile to life, as are all other planetary bodies of this solar system, a system in which only the earth is habitable (for the time being) and actually carries life as you know it in material and spiritual form, a fact that may soon be confirmed by your science, despite the contrary and lying claims of jokers and frauds who claim to have had or to still have contact with us even today.

H.F.: That is unbelievable; is that really all true?

ATHAR: We are speaking the truth.

H.F.: I simply can't believe it. It all sounds like a utopian horror.

KOHUN: Our data nevertheless corresponds to the truth.

H.F.: I guess I have to believe it, whether I want to or not. Your flying saucer alone proves to me that you must be right.

ATHAR: We call our flight devices beamships.

H.F.: May I know something about its propulsion?

KOHUN: We are not permitted to give information about such things.

H.F.: Too bad.

ATHAR: It would be a great help to us, if you could offer us your assistance.

H.F.: Gladly, how shall I help you?

ATHAR: We would like to entrust you with a task in connection with our existence.

H.F.: Should I write something about you?

KOHUN: That would be very useful for our cause.

H.F.: I can't do that. I am not crazy. No one would buy that story from me, and I would be declared insane. I can't take that chance.

KOHUN: As you will, then our efforts were in vain. You must leave us now.

H.F.: Wait, I didn't mean it like that. Perhaps I could give it try, if I were to remain anonymous.

ATHAR: How are we to understand that?

H.F.: Simply that I do not reveal my name.

KOHUN: That is not helpful for our cause.

H.F.: What should I do then?

KOHUN: You would have to go before the public as our contact person.

H.F.: I can't do that. I am not that crazy.

ATHAR: Then our discussion is ended.

H.F.: It is indeed a real pity, but you must understand my situation.

KOHUN: If this is your final decision, then our conversation has come to an end.

H.F.: I guess so, but I simply can't do it. Couldn't you at least answer one last question?

KOHUN: If it doesn't deal with our flight devices and apparati, it is alright.

H.F.: You just spoke of persons who call themselves contact persons but are not really such. I have read several names that I recognize. One of them is called Adami, or something like that, another one Genovesa and still another Michalek. Could you tell me something about them?

ATHAR: Why does that interest you, as you otherwise will only wrap yourself in silence?

H.F.: It is only a question. On the other hand, you have convinced me that you must really come from the stars. I would like to learn and further educate myself. I simply cannot go public in order to fulfill your wish. On the one hand, no one would believe a word I say. On the other hand, I'm simply not the suitable person.

KOHUN: You may well be right. It is also your right to know the truth. The names you mentioned are well known to us, though you mispronounced them: The first is called Adamski, the second, Genovese, and the third, Michalek. These are not names of real contact persons, but of malicious swindlers. Neither one nor the other of them has ever had contact with us or any of the other space races. As far as we know, they have also never even sighted one of our beamships. These three are not the only frauds of this kind. There are very many of them. If you hear at a later time such names as Zilar, Menger, Miller and Nelson or Castillio, Siracusa… then you can be sure that these are definitely the names of frauds.

ATHAR: Wouldn't you still consider to work for our mission?

H.F.: It certainly sounds enticing, but I really can't do it. Perhaps later. I would first like to talk to someone at length about these things, who knows of the entire matter and is well informed. Could you give me the name of anyone?

KOHUN: Turn directly to the most important man of all. You cannot simply take over this task at a later point because you must decide now. Either you know now what you can answer for and what your duty is, or we have to do without your help. We must be strict in this regard.

H.F.: Then I have to pass, because I cannot make a decision now. Too bad. I shall think about everything, and perhaps make an attempt to at least publish this one experience with you.

ATHAR: That would be a pleasure for us and would also be quite useful. But now, you must really go. We have other work to do. It is too bad that we guided you here in vain. Go in peace and be not afraid!

Dear friends.

I could write the entire conversation word for word up to this point, and in the end, everything no longer seemed so fantastic. After a few more friendly words, we took leave of each other and I walked for hours back to Trinidad, arriving there shortly before nightfall. I lay awake the entire night and thought about everything. I found that I had acted rather stupid. I would have perhaps learned much more from Kohun and Athar through a feigned promise. I was so confused at that time (yesterday) that I didn't even think of it. I only thought about people calling me crazy if I were to actually publicize something. I really don't know what I'm supposed to think of all this or whether I'm dreaming. That's why I am writing you and eagerly await a response from you soon. Perhaps I did the right thing or perhaps the wrong thing. Please speak to my father about it and to the pastor and ask them for their opinion, and let me know their answers soon. Also ask the pastor whether the conversation I recorded should really be made public or not. If he thinks I should, then please do so. I would like to request that neither my address nor your address be mentioned. I don't wish to be bothered after my return home. If you mention only your address, they would also inevitably stumble across me, which I would definitely like to avoid. You certainly can understand. So, if you publicize it, then no extra tours and no hastiness. I am anxiously awaiting a response with your opinion. In about one month, I should be in La Paz where you can reach me at the usual address. Until then, all the best and kind regards to everyone.

Your globetrotter friend,

Horst

CLOSING COMMENTS:
Mysterious Elimination of Fir Trees

See ~ Photos #53 and #54

The story of the vanished fir tree is a delicate matter that has already caused some skeptics to mount the barricades. How, they say suspiciously, do you intend to prove that the said tree ever existed? Even if it did, it could be that the mysterious fir tree was secretly dug up by Billy, during the temporary absence of about one dozen witnesses, without even leaving the slightest trace behind. *(See ~ Chapter 6)*

The following reasons clearly speak against this:

- The first objection that the tree was never there can be easily refuted. At least two photographs exist in which the young fir tree can be clearly seen.

- Furthermore, a picture exists of the same terrain, but without the tree. This is a good opportunity for comparison: One photo shows a young fir tree of majestic size with a reddish-colored beech shrub peeking out sideways from behind. In the other photo is not a trace of the young tree and the shrub appears quite alone. If we were to assume that Billy removed the young tree, he would have had to risk being discovered by witnesses. Furthermore, he would have had to prepare the blanket of soil in such a way that, within one to two hours, we would not notice the disturbance. Loose soil can indeed be trampled down, but no such unbroken blanket of grass can develop in such a short period of time.

- Finally, I would like to point out that the beech shrub foliage had only grown on one side… it certainly had not grown one-sided without a reason.

Eerie Whirring Sounds

See ~ Figure 6-2 in Chapter 6

I can make the following statements regarding the third demonstration of whirring sounds, which took place on July 18, 1980 in Sädelegg-Schmidrüti. As with many other demonstrations, several witnesses were present who can verify all the facts of the matter at any time, because…

- They observed Billy's activity throughout the entire sound recording session. *Figure 6-2* is the standpoint of several witnesses with their own recording devices.

- They were permitted to experience the loud sound emission on location live.

- They were able to produce their own sound recordings.

I would like to take this opportunity to again point out the other daytime demonstrations, such as: landing tracks, extraterrestrial dwarfs, extraordinary radio contacts, laser beam-pistol demonstrations, and an uninterrupted succession of beaming episodes, of which the latter, I believe, offer the greatest circumstantial evidence.

Naturally, the night demonstrations, as well as day time sightings, belong to the same category.

A Strange Beard Story

As a rule, it is sufficient if a man shaves for his morning toilet, so he looks clean and well groomed for the entire day. If he does not shave for some reason or other, be it out of pure laziness or a lack of time, this is not so bad in and of itself. However, this small negligence cannot be concealed over a longer period of time. Beard hair is known to grow incessantly, even during the period of sleep at night, and the bristly stubbles sprout on one's face the next morning at the latest.

These banal observations are certainly known to everyone and only serve as an introduction to the strange beard story that I heard from Jacobus Bertschinger.

This incident dates back to the year 1975 when the Meier family still resided in Hinwil. At that time, Billy did not have a full beard as he does today, and everyone was used to the fact that he shaved regularly. That is why Jacobus was even more astonished when confronted with the following incident. In the summer of 1975, or more precisely, on Thursday, June 17, Billy left his residence freshly shaven at 9 o'clock in the morning and did not return home until early the next morning.

At that time, Jacobus was in Meier's living room, impatiently awaiting Billy's return. He can remember all the details quite well, as he assured me. After Billy had entered the living room, two things were especially noticeable to Jacobus. First of all, Billy seemed to be extremely tired and exhausted, and he obviously could only hold his eyes open with great effort. Secondly, Billy had such a thick beard it seemed as if he had not shaved for an entire week. But Jacobus knew precisely that Billy had only been absent for a little less than an entire day and by no means long enough for such a clearly visible, long growth of beard. Therefore, Jacobus was completely correct in his assumption that something peculiar was going on. There was no other explanation. What would you say if a good acquaintance of yours appeared with a beard growth of several days, although you knew he had freshly shaved himself one day before? Perhaps you would think of a magic potion or some other unknown hair-growth tonic to explain the phenomenon. But both assumptions are not correct. The solution to the riddle had to be found somewhere else.

In reality, it was a matter of the following facts: Pleiadian friends had taken Billy in Ptaah's large spacecraft on a great journey throughout our universe. This extraordinary excursion, never before granted to an earth person, lasted as long as five earth days. The fact that Billy, despite a five-day absence, returned home twenty-two hours later is extraordinarily puzzling. But there is a single, plausible explanation and that is, "time manipulation!"

In addition to this, another curiosity manifested: According to Billy's statements, he did not sleep as much as a wink by day or night during the entire trip. The next spontaneous question is, how was it possible for him to go so long without sleeping? Billy explained that this was no accomplishment of his. Rather, he was given very special foods that kept him continually awake. Obviously, these Pleiadian foods have a much stronger effect than the stimulants of the amine group obtainable in our markets.

It is no wonder that Billy, after these five days and nights without sleep, satisfied his body's demand for sleep by lying down in a sound, deep sleep for thirty-six hours.

General Examinations

To thoroughly examine the truth of all the events, the American and Japanese UFO researchers stayed in the vicinity of Billy's residence for a total of three hundred days over a period of four years, keeping him, his friends and colleagues under observation literally day and night in order to uncover any eventual unfair doings. The positive results of these efforts finally culminated with the publication of the two pictures volumes in the USA, UFO Contact from the Pleiades, Volumes I and II, and an additional book in the English language, UFO Contact from the Pleiades by Lt. Col. Wendelle C. Stevens, Ret. Two years later in 1984, the German book, Ausserirdische und die Friedenssehnsucht der Erdenmenschen, appeared, written by Maarten Dillinger, who had also spent a long time researching this case.

Long weeks of in-depth study over a period of three years can be traced to the well-known author, Gary Kinder (USA), who was prompted by the hostility toward Billy in the USA to finally shed light on the case. His best-selling book titled *Light Years* crowned his zealous endeavors.

All of the investigations mentioned finally led to a unanimous conclusion that a one-armed man like Billy could never have produced such extensive and conclusive material evidence without help. Since Billy certainly did not have the necessary financial means, it was suspected that financially powerful backers lent him a helping hand. But the only question is, where can these alleged backers be found? Certainly not in Switzerland! These alleged "helpers" have been searched for in vain to this very day. Even Billy's greatest adversaries have not succeeded in tracing down a single accomplice.

As indicated earlier, Billy does not live like a hermit in a secluded mountain cavern, but lives with his family and a number of other center residents under one roof, so his activities are continually observed. What goes on in the FIGU Center is very carefully registered, and it is hardly imaginable that all the residents would allow themselves to be led "up the garden path" for so many years.

In this connection, the children should also be mentioned. By their very nature, they are often better observers than adults and realize much more than is generally believed. It may be assumed with great certainty that Billy's children would eventually have broken their unrelenting silence and innocently blurted out some crooked deal, if anything of the sort had actually happened in connection with the contacts.

And I say quite openly that Billy would have had to be on guard against his own wife. She was not 100 percent convinced about the entire affair and was very skeptical, during the first years in particular. At the beginning of official contacts, a colossal change took place in her family life and she had to become accustomed to it. From one day to the next, they were continually besieged by visitors, and Billy was always so overloaded with work that not much time was left for his own family. Would a wife take pleasure in seeing her family life restricted in this way?

Based on these very unpleasant circumstances, Kalliope kept a watchful eye on all the actions of her husband, so sooner or later she would have had to discover any fraudulent activities such as building spacecraft models or the like. But nothing of this kind took place. The assumption that she actively supported her husband in unfair intrigues is also completely out of place. As already indicated, the exact opposite was more likely the case, and that can be attested to by all persons who were personally acquainted with Kalliope.

The Most Important Links in the Chain of Evidence

In the chain of evidence given thus far, undoubtedly the most important links between the contact man and his witnesses have been left out. The credence of the entire story ultimately stands and falls with them. Therefore, the next question to ask is, why would Billy have chosen to play the megalomanic super contact man for decades, as is unjustly claimed? If this were true, and Billy's critics were correct, by now he would have eased himself into a snug position and literally risen from rags to riches, and all at the cost of his "flock of followers."

But whoever presumes this really has not the faintest idea about Billy's purpose or way of life. That is why I reiterate what I have already explained in *Chapter 4*. Besides his literary activity, Billy works untiringly and principally for the mission, for FIGU and the construction and maintenance of the Center, and all of this is done, mind you, on a voluntary basis with no compensation!

It is indeed true that his living conditions continued to improve from year to year, but Billy himself was substantially involved in this progress, as is known to all of those who personally helped in building the Center and who continue to do so. Among the pleasant aspects of this process is the fact that Billy, because of his work, is able to attract a group of zealous co-workers around him and to gather numerous friends and sympathizers from all over the world. Absolutely unique, of course, are all the advantages, which inevitably resulted from the friendly relationships with the extraterrestrial intelligences.

It would be entirely wrong to believe that these contacts merely took place for his personal pleasure. As explained in *Chapter 4* in greater detail, they are, rather, coupled with a very difficult and worldwide mission. We have now come to the reverse side of the coin, to the less pleasant aspects of the life of a contact person. In regard to the mission work, many people committed themselves to work together with him of their own free will. However, in the end, Billy has no alternative but to carry the heaviest burdens and the greatest responsibilities himself. It is a mistake to believe that Billy's motives are founded in ambition to become famous. On the contrary, he lives his life in seclusion. In this connection, it can be proved that Billy rejected a very enticing offer, the goal of which was to entrust him with the leading position of a planned, global organization for the promotion of friendship with the extraterrestrials. So what is all this talk about his alleged yearning for fame supposed to be? Unfortunately, the fact is that Billy is not allowed to lead the life of a normal citizen. He was and still is sporadically exposed to immense physical and psychic strains that can only be endured by sacrificing all of his energy reserves.

- Billy is often described as a liar and swindler with the threadbare argument that he has faked his entire photo material and that his remaining evidence is as good as worthless. All the scientific analyses are not even acknowledged as relevant.

- He has to tolerate the fact that journalists, reporters, authors or other adversaries confront him with hostility. They negate or play down everything positive about the Billy Meier Case, including the regular practice of the Peace Meditation. They bring untrue stories, "old wives" tales and other webs of lies before the public to make mincemeat of him in this way. Many of his accusers are not at all informed about the actual circumstances, but simply repeat everything they hear what other sparrows occasionally have whistled from the housetops.

- It has often been chalked up against Billy that he has never officially denied the accusations raised against him, because he would simply not be in the position to do so, therefore it could be assumed that they are actually correct.

- Regretfully, Billy must discover more and more that his writings are sold in foreign countries without his permission. They are, at times, incorrectly translated in part and, even worse, his writings are completely and intentionally falsified in every detail.

- Furthermore, there are people who fully acknowledge the outstanding material proof, but then declare his descriptions about his flights throughout outer space, time travels, philosophy and religion as mentally deranged claims, delusions or outrageous nonsense. To my way of thinking, Billy cannot be blamed for the fact that much of the phenomena related to his contacts seem inexplicable according to our present level of science and technology. They are not accepted due to a lack of understanding. It is common knowledge that every person who speaks of unusual facts, which are not scientifically recognized, comes in conflict with the prevailing spirit of the time. It has always been that way. Billy is also aware of this. Therefore, he is very cautious about treading such delicate ground in his writings, as he must assume in advance that these new ideas would challenge his opponents and possibly prompt them to "mount the barricades" to challenge him as if he were actually a swindler. Beside that, Billy would certainly have removed all incongruities from his contact reports in order to avoid misunderstandings, which removal, in turn, gives cause for malicious suspicions. (For example: In contrast to earthman, the Pleiadians speak about a sun system if a planet is orbited by at least three moons.)

- Paradoxically, Billy's opponents assign all possible and impossible miraculous abilities to him when it comes to defiling him as a charlatan. At the same time, they insult him as the dumb farmer from Hintertupfing. I must say that this is a dangerous game. If the persons concerned had even the faintest notion of how much guilt they will load upon themselves if they try to prevent the spreading of the truth, they would definitely keep their hands out of it. But, as a famous proverb says, "Ignorance of the law is no defense!"

- Whether he liked it or not, Billy had to cope with the fact that he was often let down by former group members and friends, always disappointed anew, and even betrayed by some of them. The very ones for whom Billy sacrificed most of his time and patience and whom he supported in word and deed, fired the most poisonous arrows at him. Not much less trouble and annoyance were the troublemakers within his own ranks who also wore down his nerves. But luckily enough, this nerve-racking condition has eased considerably over the years.

- However, I find it remarkable that Billy never deviated one iota from his predestined course, despite all adversities and health problems. He continues to strive with all his might to fulfill the task he accepted. This is ultimately for the benefit of us all.

- As thanks for all this, he has received worldwide hostility. He is never certain of his safety, which can be confirmed by the thirteen insidious attempts on his life during the past fifteen years. *(See ~ Chapter 12)* The cleverly devised attacks of the Giza Intelligences were also anything but harmless. *(See ~ Chapter 13)* It is actually futile to ask why such great endeavors are made to send Billy to "the beyond" if there is no truth to what he says. It is also not pure coincidence that all attempts on his life were miserable failures.

- Quite frequently, Billy's core group is often depicted as a religious sect and its members as compliant followers of a would-be guru who serve their boss with body and soul.

Well now, our listed counter-arguments should convey plenty of "food for thought" to even the most insistent skeptic, at least I would think so. Finally, every reader must decide for himself whether he considers Billy trustworthy or not.

Naturally, Billy's co-workers and witnesses also play an immensely important role. If the mission were simply nonsense, they would never carelessly jeopardize the good reputation they enjoy at work and in society just to support Billy. They know exactly that all those who do acknowledge Billy publicly, or support him, must count on the fact that they, at best, will be given condescending smiles by their contemporaries or classified as yarn spinners and meet with hostility. In this regard, I can speak from my own long years of experience. I know how unpleasant it is to be made fun of in public by the communication media, or if someone whispers that I have brain damage from the last World War and am, therefore, not quite right in the head.

Be that as it may, the simple truth is that approximately twenty witnesses have documented the authenticity of their experiences by writing them down according to the truth with their signature affixed. If need be, they would testify before a court of law if so desired. In my opinion, nothing more can be demanded of them. Even the best of statements can be disputed in principle, especially if witnesses are only known superficially and from hearsay. Therefore, a conscientious investigation of all facts and of the witnesses might still offer no final certainty for some. But no one should assume that the fruits of truth will simply fall into one's lap.

In this connection, Semjase tried to make it clear to earthman on several occasions that we in the Age of Aquarius are supposed to have outgrown the time of visible proof of the truth. Literally stated:

SEMJASE: Proof in today's Age of Aquarius is provided by human reason, the understanding mind and the infallible logic of truth. This can truly only be accomplished by hard spiritual thought work.

She also stated unequivocally that, thanks to Billy's mediation, we have received sufficient material for spiritual assimilation. The task of seriously examining this material is entirely up to us. The extraterrestrials are not permitted by law to convince earth people of the truth. But that is precisely the crucial point — and one which does not suit the plans of the great majority. People are by no means willing to accept this argument because it does not correlate with their wishful thinking for outside help and support in all possible variations. Hard spiritual thinking is stressful and is, therefore, too time consuming and troublesome for many to pull themselves together to do so, especially if there is no financial advantage involved. But as hard as it may sound, there is no getting around "hard spiritual thinking." That is as sure as the 'amen' in the church. For the consolation of all seekers, I will repeat: There is a universal law which assures, with absolute certainty, that everyone who makes serious endeavors in matters of the truth with patience and perseverance, and takes advantage of the invaluable help of the Pleiadians and their allies, will find this truth one fine day. However, some may find it a little earlier than others.

DECLARATION OF WITNESSES

The undersigned herewith confirm that they have never observed or known Mr. Eduard Albert Meier (Billy), residing in CH-8495 Hinterschmidrüti/ZH, of ever being involved in any unfair intrigues or manipulations in order to feign false facts … much less having ever been involved as assistants.

Furthermore, we know of no wealthy backers ever giving Billy material help in any way for the production of his ufological slide series and short films.

We also confirm that the reports of our experiences outlined in this book completely correspond to the truth. If need be, these statements can also be sworn to before a court of law.

Hinterschmidrüti, Semjase Silver Star Center on February 16, 1991.

Überdies bestätigen wir, daß unsere Erlebnisberichte, welche in diesem Buch geschildert werden, voll und ganz der Wahrheit entsprechen. Diese Aussage können wir gegebenenfalls jederzeit vor Gericht bezeugen.

Hinterschmidrüti, Semjase–Silver–Star–Center am 16. Februar 1991

Bertschinger, Jacobus	
Bieri, Eva	
Brand, Bernadette	
Brügger, Madeleine	
Gasser, Christina	
Gruber, Elisabeth	
Keller, Thomas	
Koye, Brunhilde	
Koye, Bernhard	
Kropf, Freddy	
Lehmann, Silvano	
Meier, Kalliope	
Meier, Gilgamesha	
Meier, Atlantis	
Meier, Methusalem	
Moosbrugger, Guido	
Runkel, Herbert	
Wächter, Engelbert	
Wächter, Maria	
Wächter, Conny	
Zimmermann, Hans	

Fig. 11-4
Signatures of witnesses

Footnotes

65 ▪ Birefringent – The splitting of a light ray, generally by a crystal, into two components that travel at different velocities and are polarized at right angles to each other.

66 ▪ Oscillograph – A device for recording the waveforms of changing currents.

67 ▪ Jim Dilettoso is the owner of Village Labs, Inc. in Tempi, Arizona. Mr. Dilettoso is a very skilled technical researcher regarding anomalous phenomena.

68 ▪ Mercury and earth – This is corresponding to Billy's information.

69 ▪ Retrograde – Moving backward

70 ▪ *Marathon in Space* by Reiner Klingholz (G. Westermann Publishing House 1990)

71 ▪ Unheimliche Welten by Rudolf Kippenhahn (German Publishing House GmbH, Stuttgart 1987)

72 ▪ Mark Showalter discovered the 18th moon of Saturn. (From the Voice of the Aquarian Age, #76, September 1990)

73 ▪ Uranus ring system (Based on 1990 scientific data)

Futile Murder Attempts on Billy

The fact that contactees and their followers are often met with hostility is nothing new, but intense hostility is especially true for Billy. In 1976 alone, four attempts were made on his life, then two more in 1978, one in 1980, four in 1982, one in 1989, and the last one in the spring of 1990.

The specific attacks by the Giza Intelligences in 1989 are not taken into account here. They will be discussed at length in the next chapter.

If anyone asks about the reason for these attacks, the only answer to this question is that Billy, as proclaimer of the truth, is a thorn in the side of many a person and organization of this world because he has boldly denounced their secret schemes and in doing so, exposed and jeopardized the outcome of their malicious intentions. Because there is resistance to the truth being made public, many attempts have been made to silence him in the hope of dispatching him to the beyond.

First Attempt:
A Shot Fired Through the Office Window

The first murder attempt took place on January 5, 1976 at about 7:30 p.m. in Hinwil while Billy was in his office The office windowpane suddenly rattled as a shot was fired at him from a small bore rifle. Billy perceived the whiff of air as the bullet whizzed by, a hairsbreadth from his forehead, then ricocheted from a hanging copper spiral next to the overhead light and finally struck the ceiling with slackened momentum, leaving a good-sized crack.

In the monthly bulletin, *Voice of the Aquarian Age, Issue #23* entitled "Everything Must Be Learned," Billy commented about this incident as follows:

> **BILLY:** It has been quite some time since I was contacted by someone who re-
> morsefully acknowledged responsibility for the shot in Hinwil. As I had already
> promised in Issue #7 of the *Wassermann-Zeitschrift*, I had no intention of report-

ing anything in this case and would remain silent if the male or female gunner were to contact me. I kept this promise until the guilty person, who now belongs to my circle of friends and has belonged for quite some time, came to me and admitted the deed and desired to publish her motives in the Voice of the Aquarian Age, but under the condition of anonymity. This should be understandable to everyone, which is why I am publishing what was placed at my disposal without naming the author.

The person concerned took great pains to present his/her thoughts in poetry form which, in my opinion, turned out quite well. That is why I am publishing the following work in its entirety without changing a single letter or making any corrections.

What I want to explain, as requested, is that the person in question will be forgiven by all who had and still have unfriendly feelings toward him/her due to that action. Therefore, I say the following: For my part, I feel neither hatred nor a desire for vengeance against the person writing the following poem. It would neither be humane nor justified. That is why I am asking all to understand my reasons and to act in the same manner as I. Neither I nor anyone else has the right to condemn or even revile a person for making a mistake. The matter is over and should be forgotten. The person has become aware of the mistake made and has acknowledged it and learned the correct lesson, which is why there is no longer a reason for reproach. Besides, I am still alive, and there was no damage of any kind because of this erroneous deed. The entire affair should be buried and forgotten after the following clarifications (poem) have been presented:

> Like a star twinkling in the dark of night
> Finally knowledge and wisdom within me alight.
> I found it one day through love and fortuity,
> 'cause something spurred me onward to Schmidrüti,
> where Billy resides in the Semjase Center
> and invaluable joy in my heart did render.
> Billy, a man of knowledge and wisdom,
> - ne'er more in life should I like t' miss him -
> gave me his hand and returned to me life
> making me joyous, blissful and blithe.
> Through him I came to know truthfulness
> and must never again err in lawlessness.
> Billy is the predestined prophet of this Age,
> a man of truth, the very best by far, and a sage.
> His knowledge is vast, mighty and grand,
> full of wisdom in Creation's laws he stands.
> But he fares the same as all prophets do,
> loathed and denounced by a plebeian slew,
> by cult religions, perjurers and fools as well
> trapped in the lies of their self-created hell.
> But for many a man as well as for me,
> he has lighted the path to life eternally.
> He fathoms the truth, knowledge and love,
> bringing wisdom and peace to all of us.

In truth, he is ever so kind and of humble vestige,
as he defends Creation in the valor of knowledge.
Though he is often cursed with great ferocity,
in his eyes are never found tears of animosity.
As the best, he tolerates lies and affliction,
if cursed, his reply is a smile of remission.
Never does he curse even his greatest foes,
though his eyes may reveal a troubled glow,
which attests to the grief he feels for the evildoers,
who live without knowledge and light in damnation.
And if a foe happens by and for love does beseech,
Billy offers his hand with a blessing and peace.
And this is far more than Christendom:
For it is truly of life and crowning wisdom.
And this I should know, since I too was a foe,
vicious towards Billy, in sectarian woe.
And I tried to destroy him and take his life
as I shot through his window, torn with strife.
Veiled by the night I maliciously lay in wait,
until my small bore rifle did ringingly detonate
to cut Billy down in the cold-blooded belief
that his teachings contained no truth in the least,
for I in the shackles of my belief was confined
and robbed of a healthy and rational mind.
But with no heed to danger and no mortal fear,
Billy brought his teachings he did persevere,
which led me to question and drove me to doubt,
which one day I sat down and wrote Billy about.
I soon went to him and the whole thing expounded,
but not one word of ill-will resounded.
Billy, who was ever so kind and showed only grace,
all this for the rest of my life I'll embrace.
Billy's deed let me recognize the truth that day,
and ne'er again shall I run in cult religions astray.
I chose the truth instead of religious obsession,
and live my life now in a truthful direction,
which I, through Billy, the prophet of this Age, have found
and for life and eternity am now homeward bound.
Thanks be unto him of earth and of all mankind
whom Billy our prophet, is filling with light.

Second Attempt:
The Mystery of the Loosened Lug Nuts

The second attempt took place on April 21, 1976 as Billy was on his way to Munich with friends in Jacobus' Volkswagen to present a slide lecture at a UFO conference. On his way, specifically right in the middle of the provincial capital of Bregenz in Vorarlberg, the wheels of the vehicle suddenly started to jump. An immediate check of the vehicle was necessary to see what was wrong. The cause of the break-down quickly came to light. To the fright of the passengers, it turned out that the lug nuts on all four wheels had loosened during the drive. The entire incident could be traced back to gross negligence on the part of the auto shop mechanic, but as later was determined by JHWH Ptaah, the loosened lug nuts were by no means the fault of the mechanic.

In the *Contact Report #65 on October 23, 1976*, Ptaah strongly warned Billy against undertaking additional lecture trips because his opponents were lurking in all corners and places to rob him of his life. With respect to the scheduled trip to Munich, he said as follows:

> **PTAAH:** We were able to prevent a malicious incident at the last moment again, when you were driving on the same route with your friends as you plan to take today. You remember that the wheels suddenly started to come off on your friend's vehicle. The lug nuts had been loosened. This was not due to the negligence of the workers at the repair shop, as you assumed, but rather a pre-meditated attempt on the lives of your friends and especially on your own life. I took the trouble to clarify these things myself, as it all seemed somewhat peculiar to me. The fact that the lug nuts were loosened on all four wheels at the same time was quite illogical and too much of a coincidence to be an accident or simple negligence. Therefore, I attended to this matter via a so-called viewing of the past. I discovered that during the night in question, a person who, unfortunately remains unknown, tampered with your vehicle and loosened the nuts in their screw threads before you drove away.

Third Attempt:
Billy's Heart was the Sniper's Target

Billy did not have to wait very long for the next attack. It occurred in the still dark and drizzling morning hours in Sädelegg on his way to a personal contact with Semjase accompanied by Jacobus, Hans and Konrad Schutzbach. Two unknown persons in a vehicle followed them. The incident took place as Billy and his three friends stood next to each other in a semi-circle out in the open country. From a bush about 25 meters (83 ft.) away, a bullet from a 6-millimeter magnum hit Billy in the heart region, hurling him the ground.

Luckily, Billy had dreamed of this attack three times and had taken appropriate precautions by hanging a plate from an armored tank made for this very purpose around his neck so that his heart would be completely protected. On this particular morning he also wore a heavy Canadian flier jacket and carried a notebook in the left breast pocket as an additional shield against the impact of the bullet.

Armed with a pistol, he set out on the dangerous venture, knowing well that no danger threatened his three companions. When the shot was fired straight at Billy's heart, the magnum bullet bored through the jacket and then through all the pages of his 3-centimeter (1.2 in.) thick notebook and finally stopped when it hit the metal plate.

Thanks to Billy's precautions and his levelheaded fearlessness, he once again escaped unharmed. To Semjase's surprise, he showed no sign of alarm about the entire incident. As a result of his speedy reaction ability, he was even able to shoot the sniper's hat off at a distance of about 70 meters (231 ft.), whereupon the sniper hastily fled. *(See ~ Photos #73 and #74)*

In September of the same year:

Fourth Attempt:
Neo-Nazis Shoot at Billy from Their Hovering Craft

This attempt took place in Winkelriet near Wetzikon after Billy had discovered tracks of a spacecraft and a moment later set out to look for it. According to Ptaah's explanations, the ship was of extraterrestrial origin from a foreign galaxy, but was no longer able to leave our earth as a result of irreparable damages to its interstellar propulsion system, which was destroyed beyond repair. The crew could survive only until their supply of breathing gas ran out. Unable to breathe our atmosphere, they were doomed to suffer death by suffocation. A secret neo-Nazi group had seized this space ship with its planetary power system still functioning perfectly. During Billy's search for this spacecraft, two neo-Nazi crewmembers observed his approach. They counted on Billy's curiosity wanting to give the unknown object a close look, and only waited for the suitable opportunity to shoot him down like a rabbit. Of course, Billy did not do them that favor. His intuition prompted him to drive to the spacecraft's landing site on his moped under cover of darkness. This precautionary measure insured that he would only be vaguely visible and the gunshot would be inaccurate. So when the shot was fired it whizzed into empty space. Still, the danger was not yet over. The craft then rose from the ground and airdropped small parachute flares to illumine the area to resume the attack. But Billy reacted immediately by hiding in a protective hollow, thus escaping the range of fire.

Fifth Attempt:
A Gunshot Shatters Billy's Peaceful Spring Evening

On May 21, 1978, some time after midnight, 17-year-old Silvano Lehmann, who was spending a week at the Center for the first time, was a direct witness of the fifth murder attempt (the first one in Hinterschmidrüti). I, myself, was also one of the witnesses. Silvano, Billy and I were standing in front of the Semjase Silver Star Center living quarters, discussing suspicious sounds that had lured us outside shortly before. The light of three garden lamps enabled us to see the nearby buildings quite well, whereas further away, the surroundings lay in the heavy shadows of the mercury-vapor lamps.

After awhile, Billy heard another suspicious sound and asked me to go take a look at the "tomcat in the house" to see if something else was wrong. I had barely entered the house when a shot rang out from the direction of the garage and shattered the stillness of the night.

Silvano jumped into the air with fright, achieving a record high jump as the projectile streaked past his body before it struck the ground immediately in front of Billy's feet and then ricocheted off with a howl.

According to Billy's order, Silvano went off to look for the sniper — armed only with two rocks, while Billy tore into the house to fetch his "barrel." I went to the east corner of the living quarters and stumbled across Billy and Silvano again. The three of us went toward the garage, the direction from which the shot had been fired. During our investigation, we were clearly able to determine that the culprit had been standing at the old cement mixer directly next to the garage. Due to the calm night air, the smell of gunpowder still lingered over the cement mixer, but no trace of the gunman could be found anywhere in the area.

Sixth Attempt:
The Car Goes Out of Control. Are the Men in Black Involved?

This attack occurred in the same year (1978) on the evening of December 4 at about 9 p.m. as Billy was giving his wife, Kalliope, her first driving lesson in Madeleine's car, a Sunbeam.

In Contact Report #118 on December 7, 1978, Billy was requested by Semjase and Quetzal to relate in detail the exact course of this event. He reported the following:

BILLY: Monday night, December 4 at 8:53 p.m., I drove my wife, Kalliope, up the hill near the garage in Madeleine's Sunbeam, when suddenly the motor roared as the gas pedal got stuck. Despite my efforts, I was no longer able to hold the rattletrap on a straight course on the icy roadway. Kalliope sat behind the wheel for the first time, which, I must say, created quite a problem for me on the passenger side regarding the steering. Though I tried to hit the brakes through my wife's legs, I was unable to do so, nor was I able to turn off the engine because I was lying half in front of the steering wheel and had to steer. In addition to that, I didn't want my wife to be flung into the windshield as the rattletrap skidded to the right on the ice just a few meters away from the corner of the house, and then crashed into the corner of the house at about 65 kilometers (40 miles) per hour. The motor continued to roar at full speed after impact, whereupon I turned the ignition off after recovering somewhat from the impact. I had been thrown against the steering wheel, injuring my right eye, and then against the front windshield, hitting my skull. Afterward, I inspected the car with Jacobus because we wanted to find out why the gas pedal had suddenly jammed and could not be released, causing the old heap to gather speed and take off like a torpedo. That's when we finally discovered the hidden defect: The gas pedal was jammed over the brake pressure cable, where it must have been forcibly pushed, causing it to malfunction. This jamming would have eventually worn through the brake lubricating pressure cable. And you know quite well what that means!

SEMJASE: It means that the brakes would have failed. I had Quetzal explain that to me.

QUETZAL: That is correct. I do not understand why you did not operate the clutch next to the brakes. You would have brought the vehicle to a stop that way. Of course, your wife was sitting behind the wheel for the first time, as you said. I understand. Now, your story coincides with my observation of the past, which corresponds with yours, at least as far as I am able to understand. As far as my observation of the past is concerned regarding the gas pedal and the flow of gas, a regrettable fact was established. From what I was able to see, three dark figures worked on it and carried out this dangerous manipulation for the sole purpose of destroying your life. These people cold-bloodedly accepted the fact that the lives of other persons would also be endangered. But with respect to this, my friend, we warned you months ago, and at our last meeting, that you should be very alert at night. Your enemies have been preparing very unpleasant things for some time. But you did not listen. The result of this is what you have now experienced. The incident could have easily cost you your life. ...

BILLY: ... tell me something about the three dark figures of whom you have spoken?

QUETZAL: The three men belong to the secret neo-Nazi group known by the name of the Schwarze Männer (Men in Black).[74] One of the three kept the Semjase Silver Star Center under surveillance from last Friday night to the early morning hours of Saturday, while the other two carried out the manipulations on the vehicle in which you and your wife had the accident. They drove away afterward in a large black vehicle.

Seventh Attempt:
Sudden Back Pain Foretells an Impending Attack

Most likely due to the regular night watch introduced at the Center, this seventh attempted murder did not take place until May 11, 1980. About 10 p.m., while sitting with Wendelle Stevens on a sofa before the house and enjoying the relatively warm evening. Billy was suddenly overcome by an attack of such intense back pain that he could not sit still and started squirming back and forth. He was quite familiar with this sort of back pain. It had always served as a warning signal of threatening danger. The movements triggered by the pain in his back saved his life. Suspecting imminent danger, Billy had scarcely said, "There is something wrong," to Wendelle Stevens when a projectile as wide as a finger whistled past his head and shot into the wall a few centimeters away, spattering him with mortar. A few minutes after the shot had been fired, Billy's daughter, Gilgamesha, found the completely deformed bullet that had ricocheted off the wall. Bernadette, who was sitting in her room and typing at the typewriter at the time, also heard the shot. According to her statement, it gave her such a shock that she sat motionless in her chair for a while.

Eighth Attempt:
Another Gun Shot Through Billy's Office Window

After almost a year of peace, four other assassinations were attempted within short intervals between the months of April and July of 1982. On April 5, 1982, Billy was working after lunch at the corner of the house in front of his office. In the stillness of the early afternoon, as the center residents were scattering in all directions pursuing their work, another shot was aimed at Billy. The bullet went through the protective glasswork of Billy's office foyer and ricocheted away without causing any further damage. Billy later discovered that the sniper had been standing close to one of the young, newly planted fruit trees where it was easy to hide and then make a fast getaway without being noticed.

Ninth Attempt:
A Shot Bores into the Trunk of the Semjase Tree

On the Sunday morning of June 6, 1982 at about 6 o'clock, Billy was sitting quietly thinking under the Semjase Tree, when all at once a shot cracked from the northwesterly corner of the house. The .22 caliber, copper-jacketed bullet hit the trunk of the Semjase Tree and got stuck in the bark. On that same afternoon, Ferdinand Pfeiffenberger removed the deformed projectile from the wood with a pocketknife.

Tenth Attempt:
A Shot Blast from the "Whirring Meadow"

On an afternoon in early July 1982, Billy was sitting with Uschi Büchli on the small wall made of drill bits across from the garage. At approximately 2 p.m., a shot zipped past Billy's head from an easterly direction, either from the "whirring meadow" or the mountain slope. At that time, there were no trees blocking the view of the garage and its surroundings.

Silvano and Popi came running up after hearing the shot and Silvano darted off to the easterly bend in the path but was unable to find anyone. As a result of this incident, our industrious workmen of Hinterschmidrüti mounted a floodlight on the roof of the garage.

Eleventh Attempt:
A Sniper Fires Six Shots Toward Billy's House

On the night of July 29, 1982, at about 11 p.m., Billy was with Uschi Büchli behind the main house when all at once a shot whistled into the ground in front of Billy's feet. Both stormed away — Billy to fetch his gun and to alert Jacobus, and Uschi into the house to take herself out of danger. While they were rushing to the house, another five shots were fired, which fortunately missed their target, as did all the others. Afterward, Billy and Jacobus patrolled the area around the residential building and inspected the entire area in the hope of finding the gunman so they could hand him over to authorities. This wishful thinking remained unfulfilled again. Instead, a regrettable incident took place that could have ended badly under certain circumstances. Shortly before midnight, Billy was surprised by a shadow. He reacted promptly by snatching his handgun and drawing the trigger. A moment later, he recognized his friend, Engelbert, as the shadowy figure. Like lightning, he jerked the gun aside but the shot had already been fired and the bullet whistled into space, passing by Engelbert, who unsuspecting had started his first round of the night watch.

Twelfth Attempt:
The Car Windshield Burst Asunder with a Bang

This attempt turned out to be quite obscure. It was not immediately apparent as an assault against Billy.

On September 30, 1989, Billy and Eva were on their way to take care of shopping. As they were crossing the main street from Hittnau to Saland in front of Widmer's Joinery and Sawmill at 11:35 a.m., the windshield of the Lada burst asunder with a bang, immediately exhibiting a hole. Billy thought a small-bore rifle made the hole.

In the afternoon, Billy and Eva reported this unknown person to the police in Pfäffikon.

As later clarifications revealed, the gunman was lying in ambush in the woods above Widmer's Joinery. He apparently knew that Billy would drive by this place. Unfortunately, there was no way of discovering who the sniper could have possibly been.

As all examples indicate, Billy must have become a very uncomfortable threat for a number of organizations or individuals; otherwise, how can the repeated murder attempts be plausibly explained? Incidentally, there is also further proof that a great deal more is at the bottom of the UFO Meier Case than just what Billy's opponents would like to publicize as Billy's self-importance, etc.

Thirteenth Attempt:
A Lightning Strike Created by Nefarious Extraterrestrials

This attempt took place on April 24, 1990. The event was unexpected and unprecedented because it was carried out by extraterrestrials.

In *Contact Report #236 on Thursday, April 26, 1990*, Ptaah and Billy reported about this disaster:

PTAAH: Good, then I can now speak about the matter I actually came here for?

BILLY: Yes, if it's so urgent and important, although I actually did have one further question that concerns me personally. I simply can't come to grips with it.

PTAAH: Then do not let yourself be rushed.

BILLY: Well actually, I don't want to make much ado about nothing, but what I have on my mind keeps me guessing. On Tuesday evening at 7:30 p.m., something happened to me which involves a few peculiarities that do not make sense.

PTAAH: These are the matters I wanted to discuss with you. First, tell me about the entire incident from your point of view.

BILLY: Do you mean the story about the lightning bolt?

PTAAH: Yes, my words are about that incident. But please tell me the entire event from your point of view.

BILLY: Well good. I was on my way with Eva the entire afternoon, taking care of errands that had to be run that day. It was Tuesday the 24th at about 7:15 p.m. We were on our way back to the Semjase Silver Star Center and very pleased that the weather appeared to be nice down in the valley in Schmidrüti because the sky was blue and the sun rays were shinning down. We saw this as we were driving along in Tablat. Unfortunately, the day hadn't been very nice with respect to the weather. It had been continually overcast with occasional rainfall. Shortly after passing through Tablat, to the left of the road the sun shone on a meadow thickly overgrown with blooming dandelions. It seemed as if the meadow were glowing in pure gold due to the sunrays. I was most delighted about this and drew Eva's attention to the beautiful spectacle.

After arriving at the Center, we unloaded the car and I then went to the fairy-tale pond (next to the parking lot in the Center) with Silvano to place decomposed stumps, roots and boughs around the pond and around a stone weighing one ton. We had placed the stone there at 4 p.m. on the previous afternoon. I was standing directly behind the large stone, leaning over it toward Silvano, who was standing a little lower than I down on the street and holding a tree stump toward me. I was about to grasp it. Bernadette and her son, Natan, were standing about 3 meters (10 ft.) to the left of Silvano and were watching us. At the very moment my hand was reaching for the stump about 15 centimeters (6 in.) over the outer edge of the stone, a flash of light hissed toward me from the left. The hissing was heard only for a fraction of a second and, lightning-like, changed into a loud crackling, as if two energy-laden electric cables were crashing into one another. At the same time, a bluish-white arc of light radiated from my thumb and a powerful bolt of energy was released into my hand. It instantly shot up into my shoulder, around the back of my head and down into my right leg and foot.. In the same fraction of a second, a lightning bolt tore out of the ball of my hand and struck the stone lying a few centimeters below it. A small stone splinter ripped off and shot away like a small glowing ball toward Bernadette. At the same time, about 35 centimeters (14 in.) below the upper edge of the stone, a short, splintering and cracking sound drowned out the electric crackling, while several rock splinters hissed around Silvano's body. The splintering crack occurred because that lightning-bolt exited from underneath the stone. A piece the size of half the palm of a hand was torn out and splintered at the depth of approximately one centimeter. I was able to see and comprehend all this within a split second because I was looking at my hand just as the lightning struck. The bolt into my hand was quite powerful, as well as the pain, which shot through me and has lasted until now. I was thrown backward and slightly to the left. This lasted only about a third of a second. The one-third second timing was exact, as I saw, about 7 meters (23 ft.) to the left of me, a bluish-white brightly shining ball about the size of six footballs flash down from the blue sky high above the Semjase Tree. At a height of about 2.3–2.5 meters (7.5 to 8.25 ft.) above the ground (almost exactly between the Atlas Cedar and the American Red Oak that grow on the bank of the Fairy-Tale Pond), the shining light formation burst in a glistening explosion. An ear-piercing, bursting and shredding thunder bolt ripped the air directly above our heads, while a shock wave pressed my left knee down hard against the large stone. Silvano got so frightened that he took a gigantic leap backwards, while Natan vanished into his room like lightning itself. To Bernadette, who was standing on the street only about 3 meters (10 ft.) to the left of Silvano, a small miracle happened — as an exception to the rule, one didn't hear her talking. The powerful thunderclap had simply robbed her of her voice. She stood there flabbergasted for a while and was quite obviously thunder struck.

As this thought shot through my mind, I had to grin despite the burning pain in my arm; also because of the grimaces on the face of Bernadette and Silvano. Both of them were momentarily aghast. Obviously, not only these two had a tremendous shock. In a short while, Eva came running out of her office and asked excitedly what the tremendous thunderclap was all about. Engelbert also explained later that he had literally shot up from the sofa on which he was comfortably sitting in front of the television set because of the smashing bolt. Now good, that's everything up to that point. Naturally, I have thought everything over a bit and have stumbled across several curious things that don't rhyme with the normal process of lightning bolts. First of all, I was standing directly under a 12-meter (40 ft.) tall Japanese Larch Tree that would certainly have been a better lightning rod or lightning receptor than I. I must say the same thing about the Fairy-Tale pond, which viewed from where I was standing, was only about 3.5 meters (12 ft.) to the left. The same holds true for the two birches and gray alders that are also about 12-meters (40 ft.) tall and were about 15-meters (50 ft.) further to the left of me and on the other side of the Fairy-Tale-Pond. Why didn't the bolt strike one of these tall trees? The glistening ball of lightning or the lightning ball shot down from high above the Semjase Tree, streaking toward the crown of the gray alder, in order to hissingly cut a sharp angle directly at the tip of the tree top. It then drove down between the Atlas Cedar and the Red Oak. All of that happened under a beautiful blue sky and during the last sunshine of the day.

That's a little too much all at once, if I take the curiosities into consideration. Something seems fishy to me about this whole thing. Something is simply wrong. Everything that happened was totally different from other similar incidents; for example, when a ball of lightning hissed barely 50 centimeters (19.6 in.) in front of my face during a thunderstorm and exploded. No one would have believed what happened to me if I hadn't been able to call on Freddy as my witness. He was standing only about 1 meter (3.3 ft.) to my left when it happened. At that time, everything was quite different from what happened last Tuesday evening. In 1977, when I was standing in the Center's kitchen during a thunderstorm, I looked out the window only to watch a one-meter large ball of lightning roll down over the roof and explode in a glistening detonation near the edge of the roof. It tore several sheets of metal off the roof. This time, everything was so different. Somehow, it looked to me like a piece of directed intrigue. It was, indeed, a ball of lightning that I saw. By the way, there was a witness. Before Bernadette became thunder struck, she also observed the ball of lightning as it shot from the sky and burst between the two trees. I also want to mention this because our earth scientists are still not clear whether balls of lightning really exist or whether they are merely fairy-tales or hallucinations. Now, I think I have probably said everything, except perhaps for the fact that I will still go to the doctor today. The pain has increased since it happened and there is also a slight burning of the skin. *(See ~ Photos #75 and #76)*

PTAAH: You told your story quite detailed and it corresponds exactly to the recordings of the control disk. It will certainly be good for you pay a visit to the doctor, just in case. Unfortunately, I cannot be helpful in this regard. I have absolutely no experience or schooling along these lines. Nevertheless, you should come with me after our conversation (into Ptaah's spacecraft) so I can at least determine whether you have suffered any damage.

BILLY: I have suffered no burns or similar things.

PTAAH: I would nevertheless like to convince myself you were not harmed. Besides, your assumption, or rather your assessment, is with good reason. The entire incident was not of natural origin, as it was supposed to appear. The incident was willed and guided. If I speak of unnaturalness, I mean that unnatural forces triggered and activated everything. Such is the case: The lightning that struck your hand was just as real a ball of lightning as the ones you observed earlier. Those were of natural origin, created by the electric energies of the atmosphere. The balings of these energies are created by natural means; however, the origin of this baling was caused artificially, as well as the lightning itself, and also the ball of lightning, and both were steered.

BILLY: The devil, too! I almost thought something like that. Perhaps it is true that the roaring thunderclap actually burst only about 110 meters (363 ft.) above us in the air?

PTAAH: That is not exactly correct, but your assumption is very close to reality. How did you calculate this distance?

BILLY: Quite simply: Light arc-lightning strike on my hand, times the distance per second of the thunderclap. According to my calculation, the time was about a third of a second… to be more precise, somewhat less than a third of a second. At a temperature of 0 degrees, the sound wave moves, according to my knowledge, as a longitudinal vibration at a speed of 331 meters/second (1,086 ft./second), which is equivalent to a distance of 993 meters (3,277 ft.) per three seconds. Therefore, the three seconds correspond to an approximate kilometer (3,300 ft.). That's how I calculated it. Naturally, it is clear to me that I can't be exact. I don't know the temperature that prevailed at the time of the incident. That is quite important for an exact calculation.

PTAAH: I should have expected this logical answer from you. Well good. The thunder was created from a height of 108 meters (356ft.) above the ground. It was not actually thunder, which as a rule…

BILLY: That's what I thought.

PTAAH: You cannot really know what I wanted to say.

BILLY: Yes, I can, my friend. I thought of something like that. The thunderclap was brief, exploding, splintering and tearing everything to shreds. The air was simply torn to bits — not by the lightning but, rather, by the thunderclap, which is unnatural but is precisely what I observed as I was struck by the lightning. I know damn well from experience that air is ripped to pieces in the tiny fraction of a second when the lightning is hissing around. Calculated according to Adam Riese and other clever minds, the air in front of my face should have been torn asunder the moment of the roaring tumult as the lightning bolt struck my hand and knocked me back. Nothing of the kind happened. But a third of a second later, the peculiar thunderclap rolled over our heads. This can't be compared with a natural, short thunderclap. The deafening thunderclap seemed to be more an ear-piercing explosion. It was like the time in the past when you had to atomize the atomic air ship of those crazy people, causing a hellish bang of an explosion, when the crazy lot dared to release an unmanned death machine toward us. Everything about the thunderclap on Tuesday reminded me of that time. Only one thing irritated me. On Tuesday evening during the thunderclap, I saw a glistening ball of light, which exploded directly in front of me, and the light curved onto my hand, but otherwise, I saw nothing at all. I saw nothing high up in the air where I should have actually seen an explosion, if my assumption is correct.

PTAAH: Contrary to my assumption, you do know it. Yes, what you suspect is correct and indeed very accurate. The thunderclap was an explosion caused by an unmanned flying device, which was destroyed by us. This device was programmed to kill you and, indeed, precisely in the same manner as you experienced everything. The lightning bolt which flashed into your hand was only the search-and-guide beam for a lethal ball of energy— the ball of lightning racing behind it. The search-and-guide beam alone would have been enough to kill you if it had struck you in the right place, such as in the chest or the back. Due to our intervention, which unfortunately came somewhat late because we simply were not fully in command of things, the attempt on your life was prevented, as the saying goes, at the very last moment. Unfortunately, we were not able to protect you from certain effects of the attempt you had to contend with. Astonishing for us was the observation that you were not the least bit frightened, in contrast to all the others who were present in the Center.

Well, it would not surprise me that you could not observe anything other than the blinding light arc on your hand and the ball of lightning because that strange flying device, directed and programmed to destroy you and was absolutely shielded from view or from any technical detection. The same was also true for the process of the explosion of the flying device. We were not able to shield the sound of the explosion, nor the pressure wave that reached you with somewhat weakened force. We were also unable to prevent you from being minimally exposed to a weak radioactive ray. In several weeks that radiation will have dissipated and will not endanger your health. This is actually the explanation I wanted to give you. This is also the reason for my visit and why I waited for you on the 23rd when Eva gave me a fright. I came here on that evening to warn you of all this.

BILLY: You're certainly good, man, oh man. You also know that...

PTAAH: We are really very inattentive, and in addition to that, you did not bring it to our attention. Luckily enough, it is not of great significance, since our...

BILLY: Good, but couldn't you please explain to me what the actual reason is for wanting to send me to the eternal hunting grounds again? Who is behind all of this and why did someone want to give me a ride to nirvana once more? Seemingly, some heroes are involved who are at home somewhere in the Milky

Way. Earthlings don't have the technical potential as you mentioned in your explanation. Or are the… behind all this? But no, they couldn't have such a possibility, or could they?

PTAAH: That is correct. But listen — you have very many enemies on earth. In fact, they are around the entire globe. There are those in Europe and in America, as well as in Asia and Africa. Africa and South Africa should especially be mentioned, as well as Japan and Asia. On all these continents and in all these countries are many swindlers, liars and deceivers who live in fear about their swindles, lies and fraudulent existence. These degenerate ones hate you and want to kill you with the power of their thoughts. All of these swindlers, liars and deceivers claim to have contact either with us or with other life forms from the wide expanse of universal space, or to spirit forms, etc., are all urging to push you out of your life and to kill you with their malicious and negative thoughts. Unfortunately, friends of yours are rendering them assistance. They fall prey to and believe the swindlers and liars who deceive your friends into lending a hand in any attempt to harm you. Your friends of course do all of this subconsciously, for blinded as they are by these liars, deceivers and swindlers, they can no longer recognize the fact that you, alone, on earth have the task of spreading the truthful teachings of Creation, of the spirit and the laws and commandments referring thereto.

Through the liars, swindlers and deceivers who call themselves mediums, contactees, channelers, healers, and whatever other lying names, the people of earth no longer realize that you are the one and only person able to spread the teachings of Creation and of the spirit among all the nations of the earth and among all human races. Therefore, you bear this most difficult of all difficult tasks incumbent upon yourself and you fulfill it in modesty. As thanks for it, you are cursed, although you bring deliverance for the entire earthly humanity and equally for all nations and races.

Very many who call themselves friends of yours deceive you wretchedly and try to profit from your knowledge and your teachings. Many want to raise themselves above their fellowman and play master and prophet, although they are without any knowledge of truth or understanding, and the ability and all knowledge about the truth and of the laws and commandments escapes them. So they become disloyal, curse and threaten you, and even go as far as to make attempts on your life, as was the case last Tuesday.

To blame for this, above all, are those who are openly or indirectly your enemies and indeed, also those who call themselves your friends. They deceive you and profit from your knowledge. To blame also are all those in Europe who are working in many ways against you and your mission. To blame are also Lee Elders and Randy Winters, Roberta Brooks, Fred Bell and many other members of MUFON and many other groups around the world. Also to blame are… who fall prey to liars, swindlers, and deceivers and have renounced you and the truthful teachings. To blame are also all those around you who lie about alleged contacts with alleged higher spirit forms. To blame are all those who are your opponents, because of the power of their rejection, the power of their lies, deceit and all their swindle, as well as the power of their malicious, negative and schizophrenic medium and channeling intrigues, they create tremendous deadly energies against you. They are gathered in electromagnetic balings around the earth and influence unstable, as well as negative and malicious persons against you.

Also influenced negatively are the tremendous powers of nature; for example, energies that produce lightning. That is how it happened that a malicious group had the audacity to try to kill you by this means and thereby destroy all the teachings of Creation, the spirit and the truth. They redesigned a flying device in such a way that it worked independently as a robotic unit to hunt you down. The simple procedure was — they gathered all negative vibrations of human beings on earth directed against you and stored them in a device of immense size that was manufactured for this very purpose. For over two years, these fallible ones were at work in this way before it attracted our attention, which only happened because we tried to find out why... renounced you. In doing so, we stumbled across three very persuasive persons who live in tremendous fear of being exposed by you as swindlers, liars and frauds. The thoughts of these negative persons were directed at you with such deadly intent that we saw fit to look for the reason in the storage planes, where we discovered tremendously destructive powers stored against you. From there, unimaginably large amounts of power were being drawn from somewhere. The need to get to the bottom of these occurrences was evident and we soon discovered the designers of this murderous deed. The remnant group of followers of the now deceased Ashtar Sheran,[75] who finally ended his existence in the DAL-universe (1983), felt obligated to avenge their former lord and master. They thought the most impressive way to avenge their dead lord would be to nip the teachings of truth on earth in the bud, so they planted malicious negative impulses in various friends of yours, who renounced you and became enslaved by these very swindlers, deceivers and liars, as in the case of... and several others. In order to stop the teachings of truth, of spirit and of Creation, as well as its laws and commandments, and to suffocate it all, they thought it would only be necessary to transport you from life to death. The deed was to be handled in such a way that a natural death was to be feigned. You were to die by a stroke of lightning. The idea was that a ball of lightning would be directed at you through a search-and-guide beam, whereupon the explosion and energy bomb would rip you to pieces. We unfortunately, were only able to partly block the deed at the very last moment.

For the fallible plotters to be able to realize their plans to such an extent, it was necessary for them to possess all the negative energies of your enemies by storing them in the mentioned.... With these powers, it was possible to gather and culminate natural electric ether energies into a small point over your Center to form the energy ball, and shoot it from the... and let it follow like a streak of lightning behind the search-and-guide beam in order to rip you to shreds with the explosion. For the persons around you and also elsewhere, it would have looked as if you had been struck and killed by a rare lightning ball coming out of a clear blue sky. This way, your enemies and renouncers, as well as sectarians, could depict your death as the wrath of God, just as planned and pre-programmed by the fallible ones. Fortunately, we now have them in our possession. Due to the advice of the High Council,[76] they have been relieved of all technology and banned to live for the rest of their lives on a planet, from which, with certainty, they will never return.

BILLY: What more can I say to that? How hateful must these persons be that they go to the very last. They are simply poor misguided persons who try to destroy everything in wild hatred. They are also megalomaniacs and as foreign to the creative truth as a person can possibly be. The fallible ones here on earth, as you call them, aren't as much as a hair better in this regard. Delusions of grandeur and addiction for power and total control is terribly pronounced among them and that is why they only too gladly believe and follow those who are false contactees and false prophets, as is now the case in Japan as well.

PTAAH: Not only in Japan, my friend. Now that politics have taken a turn for the better in the Eastern Block countries, western information related to inter-planetary spacecraft and all other fantastic stories along these lines are also spread there. Certainly, it cannot be avoided that many misguided swindlers, liars and deceivers and self-deceivers are also found in these countries. They spread fabricated stories about alleged contacts with life forms from earth-alien planets. Such loathsome actions have already begun some time ago and have already produced bitter and evil fruit around the world. Especially the deniers of extraterrestrial life, as well as the sectarian UFO groups all over the world, are the most gullible believers of such modern lying stories for the Eastern Block countries formerly closed to the West. Both the deniers and the sectarian supporters of extraterrestrial life try to gain an advantage from this. They want to create a new field of power for themselves by spreading lies and insane ideas and casting people under their spell. Both sides try to spread and represent an ideology that they erroneously believe is able to exist. Ideologists, however are…

BILLY: … condemned to failure every time and in every case.

PTAAH: That is precisely what I wanted to say. You already knew that at the age of nine. I remember quite well how, in 1946, my father told me that you said something like the following to him: 'In the entire universe, there is not a single ideology that could serve as a guideline, direction, to show the way of life for man. Only the truthful truth of Creation, of the Spirit and all of the laws and commandments in wisdom connected thereto are capable of doing this.'

BILLY: Yes, I can still remember that I said that to Sfath and that he looked at me and was speechless.

PTAAH: This is what he said to me at that time: That he was shocked that a boy at the age of nine was able to have such profound thoughts. He was not informed about your origin. When I informed him about it he began to comprehend, and his shock changed to respect and reverence. This was also the reason why he instructed you in many more things and in greater knowledge than his duty called for.

BILLY: For which I will be grateful for the rest of my life. I often think of him and wish I could see him again and thank him for everything.

PTAAH: You have done that more than enough, as he assured me. He even felt ashamed that you showed your gratitude in such a far-reaching, respectful manner.

I am sad to report that several more attempts on Billy's life occurred after the publication of the first printing of *And Still They Fly!* Please refer to my new *Chapter 15,* for more chilling reports depicting several new attempts to snuff out Billy Meier's life.

Footnotes

74 ▪ Men in Black (See – Chapter 6 – for clarification)

75 ▪ Ashtar Sheran – Is the pseudonym for the extraterrestrial leader Aruseak. (See – *Chapter 6* – for clarification).

76 ▪ Residing in the Andromeda Galaxy, the High Council is the name of the central authority of the Plejaren and their allies within the Cosmic Federation.

CHAPTER 13

Attacks of the Giza Intelligences

Who are the Giza Intelligences?

According to their ancestry, the so-called Giza Intelligences are of the same lineage as the Pleiadians who, during pre-historic times, lived in certain areas of the earth. After a period of peace lasting 18,000 years, power-hungry scientists tried to take control of all power, as they had already done in earlier times. Remembering that earlier fate of their ancestors, the people saw through these plans early enough and rebelled. The power-hungry scientists were left with no other alternative but to flee in their spacecraft into the wide expanse of outer space. Their exile took place about 15,000 years ago. The banished scientists settled in the neighboring system of Beta Centauri, created many offspring and developed a technology with incredible capabilities. Their government used all available means to promote an insane hatred against the earth people, with the intent of returning to earth as soon as possible to avenge their banishment and establish a tyranny. The product of their single-mindedness was a people of malicious and bestial nature. Spurred on by inhumane hatred, they were even able to raise their average life span to several thousand years. Each and every individual was trained in war actions and taught how to use intrigues to stir up discord and play one man against the other. Discipline within their own ranks could only be upheld by laborious efforts and cruel punishments. After 2,000 years, they reached a point where they were able to attack the earth, and 13,000 years ago, these people, filled with so much hatred, returned to earth in their large spacecraft under the leadership of JHWH Arus I.

A scientist of extremely bestial mentality, Arus I was rightfully called "The Barbarian." To assist him in his plans, he had appointed two hundred scientists in various specialized fields as representatives and sub-leaders. In a lightning fast attack, they invaded the earth and first conquered the country of Hyperborea, high up in North America, where a very mild climate prevailed at the time. (Incidentally, Hyperborea is now known as Florida, which assumed its present position after a polar shift.) From there, they battled their way to achieve great power over the earth. It would lead too far afield to mention the details in this connection, but the descendants of Arus I led a hard rule over the enslaved earth people. In their megalomania, the invaders let themselves be celebrated as God (in the sense of the Creator), demanded blood sacrifices and performed deadly retaliatory measures against the earth people. They caused great disasters, privation and misery among many nations of earth.

Of the three sons of Arus I — Arussem, Ptaah and Salam — it was Arussem who murdered his father with the intention of continuing domination over the people in the same malicious manner as did his father . But his two well-meaning brothers, Ptaah and Salam stopped Arussem. They put an end to the bloodshed and all other evils and ruled the earth in a just and humane manner. For Arussem and his followers, there was no place left on earth to live. They were exiled from earth 3,351 years ago. However, it was not too long before Arussem and his followers secretly returned to the SOL System and nested deep inside the earth underneath the Giza pyramid. Underground chambers were newly constructed into the main headquarters. There they further developed their ingenious security systems. From that point on, we refer to this negative and ancient splinter group of the Pleiadians as the "Giza Intelligences." They were forced to work from their underground chambers, using the most malicious methods and machinations. Their plans were those of intrigues, lies, cheating, false teachings, misleading, negatively influenced states of consciousness and much more.

They never gave up their goal of gaining world dominion, and considered any means to that end as right and fair. From that time on, they spread false religious teachings and selected certain earth people as contactees who were misled via secret influencing and misused as submissive servants. They did not shy away from abducting human beings and, if need be, from murdering them.

A practical example of this is given in an excerpt from *Contact Report #35 on September 16, 1975*, which Semjase transmitted to Billy telepathically:

SEMJASE: The Giza Intelligences, craving world dominion, are preparing a very malevolent crime to harm various other intelligences disinclined toward them and who question their credibility. They have put forth great efforts in recent times to influence earth people in a sectarian manner in order to commit an extraordinary crime against human life, and by which the existence of extraterrestrials was also to be made impossible and ridiculous.

For quite some time, a human couple on earth has been under the malicious influence of the Giza Intelligences to prepare the way for criminal and disgraceful things. The purpose of these intrigues was to misguide great masses of earth people with false teaching, so that the earth would no longer be habitable in about one decade. According to this false claim, earth people would perish in great numbers and everything would fall prey to death. They were told that not all earth people had to die. A rescue action would subsequently be arranged by the extraterrestrials. Willing persons would be picked up by extraterrestrial intelligences and brought to another better and more beautiful world where they would have a free and better life. This was announced through posters and other forms of advertisement. In order to recruit those who were willing, a gathering that served this malicious purpose was held last Sunday, September 14, 1975 in a place called Waldport in America. This is what happened: Those interested were told at the gathering that they could immediately be taken to a camp where they would be prepared for their alleged flight into outer space in order to overcome the problems of space flight and to acquire the knowledge needed for their new life on the other, supposedly better, world, and adapt to their new lives there. The only condition of this resettlement enterprise was that all earthly goods would be sold or otherwise disposed of and that no children would be taken along. Unfortunately, more willing persons gathered for this malicious enterprise than had been foreseen. In a rush, many of them heeded the calls of the solicitors and followed them to await the supposed event in that camp. The consequences of this well-thought-out criminal enterprise are absolutely clear to us. Various expectations were in store for these misguided people:

- The entire enterprise was to be camouflaged in the form of a new sectarian religion, by which all willing persons would be deceived and misled to prevent them from detecting the hidden motives.

- Weak and otherwise unsuitable persons were to be gradually sorted out and murdered.

- Several of those found to be suitable would be forced into slavery to do compulsory labor as working robots on earth for the benefit of the Giza Intelligences, who were in need of various earthly items they did not wish to acquire through their own work. Those who were found to be useful were to be carried off to perform slave labor away from the earth.

- Others were to found a new sectarian organization and work in a religious manner for the plans of the Giza Intelligences on earth.

These five points were worked out by the Giza intelligences and were supposed to be used. The earth people soliciting for this enterprise were unaware of the fact they were living in an implanted delusion.

The Giza Intelligences have discovered that Billy's group is working on this matter, so they will have to seek new ways of keeping their enterprise from being thwarted. Therefore, the danger that all the misguided people will be murdered does indeed exist. The life of an earth person is of absolutely no value to those with a mania for world dominion…

End of excerpt from Contact Report #35

Since we now know about the negative and completely degenerated mentality of this Pleiadian splinter group, we do not need to wonder that they would stop at nothing to disrupt and prevent, if possible, the construction of the Center in Hinterschmidrüti. Billy, of course, was included in this scheme as the leader and organizer. That was why he was to be abducted. The abduction did not happen, instead, the Giza Intelligences began the various attacks on Billy and the Center, which I shall now discuss in consecutive order.

Attacks of the Giza Intelligences

First Strike:
Covert Extraterrestrial Troublemakers
The first negative action of the Giza Intelligences in the campaign against Billy and his group took place early in 1976 in Hinwil. As in all succeeding attempts, this first one was planned very carefully and with insidious cunning. Incidentally, everything happened so shrewdly that even a cunning Mafia boss would become green with envy.

Other articles appeared in Swiss newspapers:

Waldport, 6th Oct. (AP)

MESSENGER FROM OUTER SPACE FOUND BELIEVERS

The authorities from Waldport in the American State of Oregon are now verifying information, according to which about twenty inhabitants have sold their possessions and moved away after listening to a lecture by a life form allegedly from outer space. Rion Sutton from the Criminal Department of the Sheriff declared on Sunday that he heard of a man who sold his fishing boat with a value of $5,000 for $5. The fisherman disappeared, just like the farmer who not only sold his property to friends but also left his three children behind. "A hippie is supposed to have given away his guitar," reported Sutton. "And it was his one and all."

"Those are really genuine flying saucers. The Johnsons are selling their house."

"Tages-Anzeiger" Zurich October 7, 1975

IN A CAMP, THEY ARE WAITING FOR THE FLYING SAUCERS

The unusual incidents started after about three hundred citizens attended a gathering in a motel in the coast village. There, someone, who claimed to be a messenger from outer space and about whom no one can give any closer information, declared that in the next ten years, people of earth would be taken to another world and therefore have a better life. Before they go, they must rid themselves of all their earthly possessions and leave their relatives. In Colorado, there is a camp in which the persons can wait for their better life until they are picked up by a flying saucer. Mel Gibson of the State Police of Oregon commented on the entire affair with the following words: "A strange story. I have been here for twenty years now but I have never experienced the likes of this before."

As far as the first "strike" was concerned, on the surface, absolutely nothing appeared to have happened. Nevertheless, Billy complained for quite some time that he was simply unable to concentrate on his work when in his office, which was not the case anywhere else. The trouble got worse and worse until he finally was certain something was wrong in his workroom. He was greatly irritated by his inability to correct the problem. He had not the faintest idea of how he should go about it. The matter gradually became too much for him. As a result, he trustingly turned to his extraterrestrial friends in the hope that they could unveil the truth of this troublesome situation by using their technical capabilities. But they also had difficulty in getting to the bottom of this enigmatic matter. After intensive, painstaking research, the answer was absolutely certain: Billy's workroom had become intolerable because invisible, negative rays were incessantly and ruthlessly bombarding him there.

Quetzal, who had tried to clear up the case, found three small one-centimeter-sized (.4 in.) amplifying stations hidden in three trees in a wooded area of the Hinwil Hausberg Bachtel.These stations were arranged into an equilateral triangle, with a distance of 2,300 meters (1.4 miles) between each one. They served as relay stations to receive very intense and dangerous vibrations from a central interference transmitter and dispatch them into Billy's office. The actual interference transmitter was suspended in a constant position high up in the earth's atmosphere.

Quetzal took remedial measures by rendering this cunningly devised system inoperative. Nevertheless, at that time he could not guarantee 100 percent whether or not such an incident would be repeated. But by now, additional measures have insured that nothing of this kind could happen again.

Second Strike:
A Disastrous Bacterial Infection

After more than a one-year break, another nasty surprise raid took place in Hinterschmidrüti, which goes to the account of the Giza Intelligences and their accomplices. According to investigations by the Pleiadians, the Giza Intelligences allied themselves with very malevolent extraterrestrials. They were refugees from the Pegasus Region who had been in our SOL System in their 50-meter (165 ft.) ship for a number of weeks. Due to their negative mentality, these Pegasus people were more than willing to work with the Giza Intelligences and to stand by them with help and advice in any way desired. As it turned out, they had enormous abilities well suited for carrying out hostile attacks. This entire episode began on August 10, 1977, as Billy was standing in thought in front of the Semjase Tree. He observed a super-sized insect, not at all native to Swiss latitudes, the dimensions of which were by no means natural. This odd creature without a doubt must have been intended for Billy. After it had circled him twice, he became suddenly ill and from that point on he felt sheer miserable. Furthermore, the same disease suddenly affected almost everyone in the Center. They complained of strong headaches and a general feeling of being ill, but their complaints were by no means as severe as Billy's. Naturally, no one knew at first what circumstances had led to this disease. Among the Center's residents another surprise prevailed and that was the unusual behavior of Semjase. She had telepathically made an appointment with Billy for a personal contact on the night of August 10 and had actually appeared in the Center for this purpose, only to take off immediately head over heels without any explanation.

At their next meeting, Billy learned the reason for this peculiar behavior. After Semjase had made her telepathic announcement, she appeared with her 7-meter (23 ft.) ship in Hinterschmidrüti, allowing it to be visible for a short while in the night sky, to the pleasure of several inhabitants of the Center. After that, at Billy's request, she intended to leave a sign of commemoration for FIGU, in which she did not succeed, unfortunately. The Semjase tree grows on the hillside of the FIGU center property. Billy once used this tree as a target when he fired a laser beam with the laser pistol which Menara had loaned him. This tree has a total of three distinct features which distinguish it from all the other trees:
(See ~ Photo #52)

- a laser beam had been shot completely through its trunk
- the tip of the treetop is missing
- a nefarious microbe nest had to be eliminated from the tree

For the third fact, the reason occurred as follows:

As Semjase hovered with her ship over the top of the tree, she registered such strong pain impulses from Billy that she flinched with fright and in a hasty reflex movement, she pressed the control stick down and accidentally collided with the treetop. With the sound of collapsing branches, the entire treetop was pressed flat. This visible change of form has remained unaltered to this very day. For residents of the Center who were there at the time, it was incomprehensible. They heard the noise of the cracking branches but were unable to determine its origin because Semjase's ship was shielded and remained totally invisible.

As already mentioned, Semjase was overwhelmed by Billy's emission of uncontrolled impulses of pain. An exact analysis revealed that Billy's serious illness resulted from something totally unknown at first. Under these circumstances, it appeared useless for Semjase to continue with the planned contact. Instead, she decided to work with Quetzal to search for the mysterious reasons of the problem. With joined forces, Quetzal was finally able to clarify the case. He was able to determine that the insect was an artificially made creature in the form of a praying mantis. The insect did not appear anywhere else in nature in this size. Its body housed an entire brood of infectious bacteria, which could be released through a spraying device. All in all, it was a shrewdly devised creation by the malevolent accomplices from Pegasus. They let the artificial insect — remotely-controlled, of course — infect Billy by flying around him two times while a small part of the pathogenic bacilli was blown out from the inside through a minute orifice. It functioned wonderfully. That was not all. The artificial praying mantis also fulfilled another order by planting a real working nest of microbes into the branches of the Semjase Tree[77], where the dangerous pathogens were able to breed and multiply. According to Quetzal, we were dealing with a disease unknown to us and which was on the verge of spreading over the entire earth by means of wind currents. It could have produced very grave consequences if effective countermeasures had not been taken in time. These measures were accomplished by the actions of Quetzal and several assistants who in great haste developed an effective counteragent to be sprayed throughout the entire earth atmosphere to finally eliminate the danger of a global bacterial infection. The measure was a decisive success. Billy and all the others with this type of illness were soon healthy again.

As a small compensation, Billy obtained permission from Semjase during the next contact to eliminate the harmful concentration of bacilli from the crown of the Semjase Tree.

Here is an excerpt of the contact conversation between Semjase and Billy of August 24, 1977:

SEMJASE: My ship has various types of weapons, as you know, such as a laser, for example, similar to the one with which you shot the hole in the tree.
I shall destroy the nest through surface burning. Look here, you can see it on the visual screen.

BILLY: Oh yeah — my, it's really wobbling. May I blow that thing out?

SEMJASE: You have never operated such an apparatus.

BILLY: I still would like to try.

SEMJASE: As you wish, but then I have to move quite a bit closer to the tree. Wait — so, now we are 30 meters (99 ft.) away from it. Here, through this visual device you can regulate the extent of the laser, that is to say, the radiation surface of the laser gun. You can move this disk by this sliding device, and determine the amount of radiation. This way you can specify and determine very accurately the entire focus of the burning. If you touch this small button, the energy is released from an opening on the underside of the ship as fine as a hair to destroy the target with a ray in laser form. You can regulate the strength of the burning, here — as you should not further injure the tree below. Now practice this for several minutes by going through the manipulations several times in your mind.

BILLY: Good, what are you doing there, girl?

SEMJASE: I am only checking a number of the ship's functions in the meantime, and it … be careful my friend — you have already activated the laser.

BILLY: Certainly, that wretched thing has vanished already .

SEMJASE: You did not follow my instructions, but simply aimed at the target, briefly adjusted it and released the energy.[78]

BILLY: Naturally.

SEMJASE: I told you that you first…

BILLY: Isn't it right? Come take a look first, before you get all upset.

SEMJASE: Yes indeed. That was very good. The radiation was only a bit too strong in circumference but it was very good. It is inexplicable to me how you could do that so well because you have never worked with such a device before.

Third Strike:
The Puzzling Collapse of the Concrete Wall

In the course of the extensive reconstruction work of the Semjase Silver Star Center, our group was to erect a spacious meditation facility according to data from the Pleiadians. For this purpose, we joined forces with all the men available from our group and others who were near us to erect a concrete wall approximately 5 meters (17 ft.) long, 2 meters (7 ft.) high and 1.5 meters (5 ft.) thick. We selected these unusual dimensions with full intention and consideration, because the side of the wall toward the mountain would have to withstand extremely strong pressure from mountain water. Having finally completed the job at 3:30 in the morning after many strenuous hours of work, all of us were ready to drop from exhaustion but were nonetheless pleased and content with our accomplishment. As a visible token of our joy, Herbert Runkel and I insisted on having a little fun despite our exhaustion by sticking a shovel in the ground and boisterously dancing around it several times.

But none of us would have dreamt that our unrestrained joy would only be of extremely short duration. We discovered a deplorable mess the very next day. Hard to believe, but the naked facts just cannot be changed. All our efforts and grinding work of the previous day had been in vain! The concrete wall, the completion of which we had jubilantly celebrated the day before, was no longer standing but lay flat on the ground and lay even about 1 meter (3.3 ft.) away from the wall. We simply stood there at our wit's end. No one came close to imagining how this misfortune could have happened; in fact, no one could even utter a word at first. A while later, after we had gradually recovered from the initial shock, we clearly established that our wall by no means could have fallen in a natural way. It rather looked as if it had first been raised a bit and had not been tipped over until afterwards. Magical forces must have been at work. Try as we might, a plausible explanation simply eluded us. Exactly one week later, the riddle was solved, not by us, but by an extensive investigation of the Pleiadians. Due to the personal contact on Sunday, September 4, 1977, at which Ptaah, Quetzal and Semjase appeared at the same time, Quetzal explained the incident and the motives behind it. The hostile Giza Intelligences had the malicious intent of sabotaging the construction of our meditation center and preventing its opening by all means available to them.

Nevertheless, they tried to make it appear as if earthly forces of nature had been at work. They were careful to let nothing draw attention to their activity or their existence. Otherwise, they knew and feared that the authorities or scientific or military groups would start a large-scale search operation to track them down and arrest them. The newly constructed concrete wall seemed to be an appropriate object with which to begin their destructive work. And as before, they contacted the malicious Pegasus people, who were again able to accomplish the work of destruction with their superior abilities and machinery. As a so-called reconnaissance patrol, a Pegasus spy was first sent into the Center to probe its layout and situation on the premises. As it later turned out, Billy and Renato had noticed this man the night before on the grounds of the Center. Billy estimated his height to be about 1.8 meters (6 ft.) His eyes, the size of beer coasters and fluorescent in the dark, definitely attracted special attention. After being discovered, he disappeared noiselessly by floating away over the ground without leaving any tracks behind. The actual assault finally took place the night of August 30, 1977 at 4 o'clock in the morning. The Pegasus people transported an oscillating vibrator to the Center and placed it in direct proximity of the concrete wall. One of the Pegasus people set the device into operation by using spirit power.[79] Everything was going like clockwork. The oscillating vibrator, which worked on a microwave basis, released an incredibly powerful vibratory wave by combining the highly oscillated waves into a bundled form, which ripped the wall out of its anchors within a few seconds, raised it somewhat and then hurled it to the ground.

According to Quetzal, the oscillations have an absolute deadly effect for any life form — it would cause a lightning-fast aging process to take place. Exposed to this, a 30-year-old man would look like an aged man within a short period of time.

Such a world-wide sensation, naturally, can barely be kept secret. As these Giza and Pegasus groups had to remain in hiding, it was reasonably certain that we did not need to fear attempts of this nature on our lives.

Luckily, that was the last action of the Pegasus group against us. Their game on earth was finally up and they could no longer do us any harm. Semjase's father, Ptaah, personally took care of the matter. He brought the so-called "logical force" into action, as it is so nicely called in the universal jargon. Stated more accurately, Ptaah had the malicious accomplices taken captive and returned them and their ship to their home where they would receive their just punishment. They certainly had other transgressions to account for, otherwise they probably would not have fled from their home world in the first place.

Fourth Strike:
A Life-threatening Supersonic Boom – *Account by Bernadette Brand*

On February 18, 1978, a wedding took place in our neighborhood of Schmidrüti and as custom still has it in many places of Switzerland, a three-shot salute was fired into the sky of the neighboring village in the early morning hours to mark this occasion. Two or three seconds after the third shot had been fired, a tremendous thunderclap roared over the roof of our residential quarters in Hinterschmidrüti and shook the entire building to its very foundations. Everything that wasn't nailed and screwed down jangled and rattled.

It seemed like a supersonic boom to Billy. He had experienced several of such booms in the past and once had almost been struck by one. Billy reported an experience he had many years ago when he was staying in an old hut not far from Zahedan in the Persian desert. Suddenly, an uneasiness drove him out of the structure. He left the area at once and dashed off. About 150 meters (495 ft.) away, he suddenly heard the howling of a low-flying jet plane. He looked around and saw a jet speeding toward him at low altitude over the ground. Only a few hundred meters from the hut, this devil of a bird shot diagonally into the sky, tore past the hut and then thundered with a hellish boom. Like a primeval thunderclap, the sound tore back over him and he saw the ramshackle building vibrate and collapse in slow motion, as if destroyed by a ghostly hand, whirling dust up into the air.

The tremendous thunder that was heard on Saturday morning, February 18, 1978 in Hinterschmidrüti sounded just like the supersonic boom caused by that jet fighter. Billy convinced us that exactly the same thing should have happened to the residence in the Semjase Silver Star Center as it did to the hut in the Persian desert.

The fact that this didn't happen was due to the following circumstance: Kalliope[80] had been in the hospital for several days after undergoing surgery. Because Billy was very worried about her, he was under observation by Quetzal and Menara, who witnessed the incident and were able to take immediate protective action. Thanks to their help, the worst was prevented at literally the very last moment. According to Quetzal, he was in his spacecraft at the time, accompanied by Menara, at an altitude scarcely above the Semjase Silver Star Center in an invisible state.[81] After the first and second salute shots were fired in the village, a remotely-controlled, triangular-shaped spacecraft of the Giza Intelligences suddenly came tearing toward the house from the south. It hovered briefly above the Center's living quarters at an altitude of about 60 meters (198 ft.) and then rose vertically into the sky after the third salute shot at a velocity of double the speed of sound, creating a dangerous shockwave. Quetzal, who immediately recognized this malicious intent, reacted within a fraction of a second and shot forward like lightning scarcely 10 meters (33 ft.) above the rooftop to intercept the gigantic blow of the sound wave caused by the triangular spacecraft now hovering at 50 meters (165 ft.). In doing so, there was great danger that Quetzal's ship would be destroyed or greatly damaged, which luckily didn't happen. The Pleiadian ship withstood the threat, and the colossal wake of the sonic boom at the breaking of the sound barrier was deflected, fan-like, off Quetzal's ship and raced away over the house. Nevertheless, acoustical waves did continue downward and were strong enough to powerfully shake the entire house.

Without Quetzal's courageous intervention, the residence would have surely collapsed and buried a number of people. Therefore, the following persons were saved from this mortal danger: Billy and his three children, Gilgamesha, Atlantis and Methusalem, as well as friends Elsi Moser, Margarete Rose, Jacobus Bertschinger, Engelbert and Maria Wächter with their two children, Conny and Rolf. As an appropriate response to this assault, Menara gave the Giza Intelligences a lesson, which they most likely won't forget any time soon. The triangular spacecraft that carried out the attack was a remote-controlled apparatus belonging to them. It was the only one of its kind they still possessed. On this occasion, it also met its fate — on the return flight to its home base, it was followed by Menara and eliminated after a brief, hot pursuit. In the end, nothing was left of.

Fifth Strike:
Negative Vibratory Impulses

Besides the four strikes already mentioned, the Giza Intelligences also tried to deal us another blow in quite a different way, one almost unparalleled by its insidious malice. For many years they had influenced all the members of our group, not only persons who were hostile towards us, by literally bombarding these people with negative vibratory impulses. Depending on an individual's ability to resist, those affected reacted in various ways. In most cases, malicious ideas were implanted on a totally subconscious level. No one was consciously aware of this fact, so no attempts were made to take the necessary precautions for defense. With these targeted attacks, the sinister wrongdoers achieved two goals at once:

- At first, not all of the group members managed to mobilize the necessary resistance power to master the situation. Therefore, the doors were opened within the group to dissension and quarreling. Of course, not all arguments were triggered by this means, but the squabblers could at least excuse themselves that the Giza Intelligences were to blame.

- Great harm arose toward our group because the number of our enemies throughout the world steadily increased as a result of such insidious and far-reaching influence. Of course, the persons and groups who were hostile toward us had not the vaguest notion of the criminal intrigues behind all this.

Sixth Strike:
A Deadly Shock to Billy's Psyche

In the afternoon of March 30, 1978, the malice finally reached an absolute climax. To deal the final blow to Billy's construction of the Semjase Silver Star Center and his entire mission, the Giza intelligences initiated a deadly attack on Billy's life. In fact, it occurred at precisely the moment when Billy's protective spiritual blockade collapsed as a result of his debilitating health. More details of this incident are too complicated to explain in only a few sentences. The assault took place in the form of a forced shock to Billy's psyche. The intensity was of such unimaginable magnitude that any other person exposed to it would have died from a violently induced heart attack.

It was the intention of these shameful deceivers, who knew all the tricks of the trade, to send Billy to the beyond in this way, although outwardly, it would have looked as if he suffered a heart attack and, therefore, had died a natural death.

To this day, the Pleiadians have no plausible explanation why Billy's death fortunately did not take place. How Billy was able to manage this is still an unsolved riddle. According to their calculations, such an assault should have been fatal for anyone as well as for Billy. With good reason, the Pleiadians were dumbfounded by this incident. Beyond that, they were dismayed to discover that they could do nothing to help Billy in such a situation in the future. He would always be solely dependent on his own powers. In view of his miserable state of health, this could mean his premature death and the destruction of the entire mission. After the Giza Intelligences were obviously determined to stop at nothing, a speedy repetition of this assault had to be expected. Therefore, the Pleiadians could not risk the fact that Billy would continually be exposed to this fatal danger without protection. According to a commandment of Creation, the free will of every human creature must be safeguarded, even if misused for negative purposes. But everything naturally has its limits and, in this case, they were clearly violated. Consequently now, also in accordance with a law of Creation, the so-called "logical force" was permitted. Drastic action was finally taken, which, according to our comprehension, was long overdue. A punitive response was initiated to finally end the macabre game.

In total agreement with the High Council, extensive and difficult preparations for this unique action by the Pleiadians were launched in May of 1978. Ptaah and Quetzal, along with their assistants, had their hands full tracking down the Giza Intelligences in their numerous hideouts and taking them captive. They defended themselves energetically with all means available. A large number of about 2,100 of these wicked ones had to be driven out of their tightly secured headquarters below the pyramids of Giza and taken into secure custody. All devices, as well as a spacecraft stationed there, were totally eliminated. All chambers were filled in with hard material (boulders, rocks, etc.) so that, with the exception of the upper passages, there is practically nothing left to give any hint of this former subterranean center of power.

After destroying all bases of the Giza Intelligences on earth and in the SOL System, the Pleiadians deported the criminal elements in a large spacecraft to an isolated planet in a distant galaxy in the Neber Region. They must live there until the end of their lives without any technical aids, which had been eliminated along with all the other equipment.

Seventh Strike:
An Extraterrestrial Will-o'-the-Wisp

In August of 1982, the seventh and last strike of the Giza Intelligences happened several years after their deportation, a total surprise and unexpected to us, after we felt completely secure against their attacks.

It started with very peculiar and inexplicable appearances of lights after nightfall at the Center. They were observed by Billy and partially by Mrs. Pfeiffenberger (former group member) on August 14 and 15. On Saturday the night of August 15, a very bright, gigantic and luminous object, which looked very similar to fog, appeared a number of times in front of Billy's office window. According to Billy's description, unusual movements emerged from it and finally formed a gigantic hand that moved as if grasping and searching toward the fence in front of the house. Oddly enough, this ghostlike apparition could not tolerate light and consequently avoided the direct glare of the yard lamp. It emitted extremely intense and malicious vibrations, which struck Billy with tremendous force.

The night before, two similar apparitions but with a reddish color had appeared next to the shed. About one hour later, Billy reported seeing a glaring green color surrounded by a glistening white corona from which a luminous red figure emerged. The entire atmosphere around it ionized and spread a far-reaching smell of sulfur. This entire episode lasted about 15 seconds and Billy added: "As I ran around the corner of the house, I saw the ionizing formation stop its hand-over-hand movements as if due to a sudden fright, only to become a violent whirlwind within seconds, like a hurricane or sandstorm or tornado. The raging whirlwind created an inward density as it raced backward toward the woods ... only to light up glaringly in the tree branches high above and disappear among the branches."

But what in hell's name was the meaning of that eerie and threatening spectacle, and who pulled the string behind it all? This time again, the Pleiadians were called to the scene of the incident and after complicated investigations were finally able to explain everything in detail about this difficult case. We learned from Quetzal that it was only Billy's self-control and his phenomenal powers of resistance that kept him and his group members from injury.

According to Quetzal's analyses, the strange light apparitions were produced by an energy bell, built and materialized in the Center, which could mobilize and release enormous negative forces to have disastrous effects on the Center residents. To be more precise, there were three levels of harm:

- If a person were struck with low concentrations of these negative forces, the person attacked would instantly deny all truth and the laws and commandments of Creation and develop into a fanatic sectarian without any hope of freeing himself of it in this lifetime.

- If someone were exposed to a very weak concentration of negative forces, they would become hopelessly insane.

- Were a human life form exposed to the full strength of a negative energy block of this nature, it would inevitably mean absolute death.

Since the negative energy bell could not be removed or rendered harmless overnight, the Pleiadians gave temporary security instructions and erected a special protective mechanism. This was done by attaching an additional device to their telemeter disk already stationed high in the atmosphere above the Center that radiated protective vibrations over the Center. It could only fulfill this function if a wide-brimmed hat with a minimum diameter of 34.2 centimeters (14 in.) was worn by anyone outdoors and in the open of the Center property after dark. We were directed to simply flee or to seek shelter in the Center in order to escape the danger area of the fog-like apparitions of light.

The next obvious question is, what does all this have to do with the sinister dealings of the Giza Intelligences? They had already been deported to a distant planet in May of 1978 and have been completely isolated ever since, without any technical aids and equipped only with the bare necessities of life until their death. According to the proverb, "It is the unexpected that usually happens," they prepared an unpleasant surprise for us. During the investigations regarding this matter, the Pleiadians stumbled across several facts that were completely unknown to them and caused great astonishment. It proved to be crystal clear that a splinter group of the Giza Intelligences had left the earth several centuries ago to establish their own people on planet SABAN. This seemingly desolate planet belongs to a small planetary system called KARAN, no less than 2.8 million light years away from earth. This group had never given up its malicious intent and ever since had remained in continuous contact with members of their species on earth, at least telepathically. It is quite apparent that the deported Giza Intelligences were receiving all imaginable help and support from this splinter group of allies.

To fulfill their evil intentions, the Giza allies had developed a devilish technology on SABAN that enabled them to send negatively polarized vibrations to the smallest of targets, even millions of light years away. These vibrations were programmed to attract similar negative vibrations of cult followers, religious fanatics, sectarians, etc. at the target area and to gather them into an enormous energy block of tremendously destructive force. But that's not all. From their planet, the SABANs were capable of finding and hitting a life form as small as a fly on earth. They took advantage of this ability, not only to bombard group members in the Center with negative impulses in this insidious manner, but also many other earth people who are in any way sympathetic to our group.

As for the phenomenon of the energy bell in the Center, the Pleiadians discovered relatively quickly that the actual origin was not found within the realm of earth but far out in outer space — where?… they did not know at first. Quetzal's analyses clearly established the existence of an unknown transmitter. It had created the disruptions at the Center, but enormous efforts and a vast number of assistants would be necessary to trace its exact location. In order to master this provocation as soon as possible, the Pleiadians started a gigantic search operation throughout the universe. They used an astonishing 11,000 spacecraft equipped with the most modern analyzing instruments, probes and so forth. This well-arranged mammoth action was crowned by sensational success. When one of the numerous search units located impulses from the transmitting station and followed this trace, they found the source of the emissions coming from the Giza splinter group on the planet SABAN. They had erected metallic domed structures there. Resistance of the SABANS during the intervention of the Pleiadian search troops was broken relatively fast, the bases were occupied and the inhabitants taken into custody.

I would like to cite the rest of the story with an excerpt from *Contact Report #179 on Friday, October 22, 1982*:

> **QUETZAL:** To eliminate the danger of these elements (of the Giza splinter groups) once and for all, we are forced to eradicate all the achievements (inventions and technologies) of their efforts which otherwise would cause great difficulties. However, the Sabans have fortified and secured their complex to the extent that our destruction could trigger a catastrophe reaching far into outer space. Through a timing device, the Sabans would set into motion an enormously far-reaching and fatal destruction on their planet if we simply destroyed their installations. Therefore, during the course of yesterday afternoon, we sent in special commandos to eliminate that danger. The timing device that would trigger the catastrophe had to be set into reverse, making it go backward until it reaches the starting point, causing it to deactivate. It had....
>
> **BILLY:** This would be a so-called time bomb, if I have understood you correctly. In addition, your explanation means that this time bomb couldn't have been simply deactivated, but that its ignition could only have been stopped and its danger only eliminated if the time, which has already started to run, was set back to its starting point. That is clear to me so far, but I don't understand why you couldn't have destroyed the complexes if you were already able to stop the lapsed time period.
>
> **QUETZAL:** Everything had been so cleverly constructed that a catastrophe would have been triggered if the time lapse had been interrupted and the installations destroyed. The only possibility of avoiding a catastrophe was to reverse the polarity of the time and make it run in reverse. Only then was the danger prevented and then its elimination process could begin. We had to be prepared to disintegrate the entire planet into energy because the planet had been thoroughly restructured to, truthfully, turn it into nothing less than an overkill bomb that would have completely destroyed everything within a radius of millions of light years if it were fully activated. We have already eliminated this danger, so the time lapse now runs in reverse and, according to your time calculation, will reach its starting point again next Sunday, October 24, 1982 at 2:11:08 p.m. We can then start the elimination of the device, which will require another 46 minutes. Up until then, the negative vibratory impulses will still continue and several group members will be imperceptibly influenced by them. You can be sure that everything is in order again and no further negative influences can occur after 3 o'clock on Sunday afternoon.

We could now finally breathe a sigh of relief. Thanks to the great help of our extraterrestrial friends, the unpleasant matter of the Giza Intelligences was finally settled. And in view of the fact that those wicked ones carried out all kinds of negatively degenerate activities during the past few thousand years on earth, the significance of remedial measures taken by the Pleiadians cannot be overestimated — truly a blessing for us and the entire humanity of earth!

Footnotes

77 ▪ The Semjase Tree (See – *Chapter 6 – Demonstration of Laser Beam Pistol*)

78 ▪ Billy fired the laser gun, which shot off a destructive beam of light.

79 ▪ Spirit power - Unlike the Pegasus people, the Giza Intelligences were incapable of turning the device on with spirit power.

80 ▪ Kalliope is Billy's wife. She is also called Popi.

81 ▪ A non-visible state means to be shielded against optical detection.

What Do the Extraterrestrials Want Here on Earth?

Where Do Extraterrestrial Spacecraft Come From and What Do We Know About Their Crews?

The question whether extraterrestrial spacecraft possibly originate from our solar system should first of all be clarified. Based on explanations by the Pleiadians, who are well informed about our planetary conditions, the following can be said:

- In prehistoric times, two other planets besides the earth were temporarily inhabited by human beings. These were the red planet Mars and the legendary planet of Malona. The latter, as explained in *Chapter 11*, was literally blown up and torn into innumerable pieces by its own inhabitants about 75,000 years ago as a result of armed conflicts. From that point on, most of the asteroids (or planetoids) have orbited in elliptical paths around the sun in the gap between Mars and Jupiter. This asteroid belt, serving as an eternal warning sign, should always remind us of how brutal force of rival groups can ultimately lead to total destruction.

- Except for earth, no other planet in our SOL System is populated by a human race, and this fact is related to the unsuitable conditions for life on the other planets. Some planets are in different phases of development, which means that several of them are no longer capable of providing the basic elements needed to sustain life due to their advanced age. Others are still in a certain primordial phase, and even if the lowest forms of life may have developed, millions of years will pass before higher life forms are able to exist on them.

- Contrary to statements claiming otherwise, neither half-spirit forms nor higher, pure spirit beings exist in any region within the entire solar system.

- Several stations exist in this SOL System, which were established by extraterrestrials as bases and starting points for many types of research expeditions. Our earth also accommodates extraterrestrial bases which are so well hidden and guarded that we have no chance of discovering these hideouts with detectors available to us today.

For example, a Pleiadian station in a mountain range in Switzerland did not simply exist since yesterday but, rather, has existed for three hundred years. A second station can be found in the Far East, and a third in the western hemisphere somewhere in the United States. *(See ~ Chapter 15 for an update regarding the status of all Pleiadian bases on the earth)*

The extraterrestrial races who were busy on earth during the eleven-year contact period (1975–1986) were either from the Lyra and Vega Systems or from the Pleiades. All others who now fly around our earth come from neighboring stars outside of our SOL System or live in far-off systems of the universe.

Extraterrestrial visits actually take place, and not only in science fiction such as books and films. They are not all human delusions. The fact is, such visitations are absolutely real and are not as far-fetched as they may seem, especially if we consider that 7.5 million human civilizations exist in our galaxy, the Milky Way. Some of these civilizations have mastered space flight at least to the extent that they can easily select our earth as a flight destination.

Earth people are neither the only human beings in existence nor the "Crown of Creation," because the specie "Human Being," according to Genesis, is by no means an exception in the endless realms of the universe. Quite to the contrary, no less than 79 pure human races were created by the almighty Spirit of Creation (exactly 40,353,607). The races have intermingled during the course of time, and the number of races has now reached a new total of approximately one thousand decillions (10^{63} — that is 10 followed by 63 zeros!)

As for the nature of these human individuals, I can only repeat what the Pleiadians already pointed out in *Chapter 2*... that other human life forms are neither indefinable monsters, ethereal angels nor spirit beings. (The term "extraterrestrial" has nothing to do with "ethereal.")

All humans beings throughout the entire universe are endowed with coarse-substance bodies of flesh and blood, as are we earth people, but with numerous anatomical differences. Incidentally, the skin color does not constitute a racial feature, as is commonly assumed here on earth, but race is distinguished by anatomical differences such as straight or slanted eyes, two or more arms, etc. Diversity among human beings in view of their outward appearance, skin color, life span, etc. is enormous. As far as outward appearance is concerned, we can by no means expect all of them to look like earth people. Nevertheless, about 95 percent of all human life forms have a purely human appearance, although some of them do not exactly correspond to our ideal of beauty. Several types would probably appear very strange or even ugly to us, but nevertheless, not monster-like. On the other hand, we would also make at least a strange impression on many other races, despite what we consider our physical beauty. In this respect, earth people occupy an exceedingly good position. This means they have well-balanced proportions and are surpassed in bodily beauty by only a few races. At some point, every physical development reaches its peak and can no longer be improved upon.

As far as physical size is concerned, we are totally justified to speak about dwarfs and giants. The size range is somewhere between the small 40-centimeter (16 in.) little people and the several meters-tall giants who are surpassed by the Titans, who reach a maximum gigantic height of 12 meters (40 ft.)!

The diversity of human body color is also enormous, as no less than $7^3 = 343$ different skin colors were created by our Creation, some of which we earth people have never seen yet. From this colorful palette, the color "green" is naturally not excluded. I only mention it because of the mocking manner in which the "little green men" are always cited in newspapers to make the UFO supporters appear ridiculous to the public.

Also phenomenal and astounding are the gigantic differences in regard to life span. Our present life expectancy on earth is rather low compared to that of the extraterrestrials. In fact, extraterrestrial intelligences exist who have a life span of several hundreds or thousands of years, or much longer. But immortality, in terms of a bodily lifetime, is out of the question as all coarse physical matter perishes and is subject to the continual cycle of becoming and passing away, of birth, life and death.

The laws of nature are constituted in such a way that even an ancient Methuselah must depart from life when his last hour has arrived.

Besides that, the extraterrestrials possess about the same attributes as we —positive and negative, and they are also more or less burdened with faults, depending on their evolutionary level, character and so forth.

From an evolutionary standpoint, human civilizations in our universe vary greatly in phases of development: Some are still vegetating along in the Stone Age and bash each other's heads in with clubs, while others have reached the same phase as we, or have even moved on to much higher levels. The reasons for this are easily explained, as follows:

- In accordance with the laws of nature, human races in the universe were not all created at the same time, but in time segments vastly apart from each other.

- Although in principle, all must walk the same path, there are considerable differences in how to walk along the path. Phases of development can also be experienced in different ways and be of variable duration. The destinies of nations and their individuals are basically determined by themselves and, consequently, so is their progress in both material and spiritual regard.

Based on the universally valid freedom of will, every man can decide for himself whether or not he wants to follow the laws and commandments of Creation, provided that no governmental provisions, authorities, and so forth, keep him from doing so.

In the immeasurable expanse of the universe, not only positively disposed, peaceful intelligences exist but also negative and malicious ones. Otherwise, how would it be possible that some of the technologically and scientifically highly developed peoples, who even master interstellar space flight, nevertheless behave like common barbarians. They use their superior war technologies, for example, to enslave weaker civilizations and conduct vicious raids throughout the universe due to pure thirst for power and greed.

Progressive races have largely reduced their aggressive drives or have them so strongly under control that they no longer instigate or take part in armed conflicts, unless they are forced to defend themselves against hostile attacks or to intervene for reasons essential to safety.

When human civilizations succeed in abolishing all acts of war and overcome most diseases and other evils, and adapt their lives according to the laws and commandments of Creation, they will lead a substantially more peaceful, blissful and successful existence than is the case with us. It is finally entirely up to us to determine how long it will take for the totally unnatural and degenerate circumstances on earth to disappear and forever belong to the past. Regardless of differences, all human beings throughout the entire universe share a common task in life. In other words, the meaning of life is completely the same for everyone! This most important and fundamental question of life can be addressed and characterized by asking: Where from? Where to? Why? Where does man come from? Where is he going? What happens after his death? And finally, the most important question of all — Why does man live at all?

Some human beings are surprised when addressed with such delicate questions, as they are not interested in philosophical challenges. They can be compared to a patient who does not come to terms with his health until he is stricken by an evil disease. As long as he is strong and able, he never gives a second thought to the possibility of illness. But confined to a sickbed, he may seriously think about those questions he had never before confronted. As a rule, every sick individual has no greater desire than to get well as soon as possible.

And what about people who lead a carefree and pleasurable life and whose wishes are more or less fulfilled and who are able to enjoy a life of wealth, prosperity and abundance? According to their thinking, there is no reason why they should think about such fundamental questions, as they enjoy good fortune and more or less possess everything they have ever desired. Why should they grapple with such far-reaching questions and burden themselves unnecessarily? But their opinions usually undergo a radical change when they suddenly feel abandoned by luck and, contrary to expectation, run into difficulties or serious trouble because of unforeseen circumstances.

In contrast, these aforementioned questions are understandably and permanently uppermost in the minds of the poor people who live in poverty and waste away on the verge of starvation, suffering from hunger day in and day out.

But such subjects could become a reality for everyone some fine day, even for citizens of an affluent society in times of political tension and social insecurity when unemployment spreads and monetary inflation increases. Under these circumstances, belts must be considerably tightened and people can only look toward the future in fear and anxiety.

Actually, it is regretful and shameful that people would have to face a crisis before finally starting to think about their purpose of existence. Fortunately, the positive vibrations of the Aquarian Age are enabling more and more people to carefully consider the actual meaning of their lives without having to first experience some type of crisis. And in my attempt to briefly describe the meaning of human life as best as I can, I will keep my explanations in line with the explanations in the writings of Aquarian Age publishers.

About the Meaning of Human Existence

Although Creation is the highest form of perfection man knows or believes to know, Creation must nevertheless continue to perfect and develop within itself. To reach this goal, Creation requires the assistance of all human beings, no matter how absurd this may sound. That is why the energy of the Creation spirit constantly creates new small spirit "concentrations" which give life to every human body in the form of an immortal spirit form (erroneously called immortal soul) and makes it capable of life, because no man would be able to exist without it. *(See ~ Clarification of the Concept: What is the Meaning of Creation and What Does God Mean? ~ in this chapter)*

The purpose of human existence is, without exception, anchored in spiritual evolution according to the example of Creation. Every spirit form housed within a human body must first work its way through innumerable incarnations from a completely unknowing, new spirit up to spiritual perfection in order to return to its source some day and become one with Creation. Creation then further perfects itself and becomes ever more powerful. Therefore, we human beings are not spared the weary and numerous difficulties we encounter while treading the path of spiritual evolution. On one hand, truths and knowledge already existent are possibly slumbering in our subconscious and must be newly awakened and developed. On the other hand, things not yet existent must first be discovered and then expanded. Despite bonds with all other human life forms, because every human being is an individual at a different evolutionary level, all must climb the rungs of the evolutionary ladder one at a time, without skipping one single rung.

It is self-evident, that the destination of spiritual evolution can never be reached within a single material lifetime; on the contrary, innumerable rebirths are necessary.

What Actually Happens After Death?

When a person dies and departs from physical life, the coarse-substance body decomposes into its constituent parts, whereas the spirit form residing within the body (not, as erroneously claimed, the "immortal soul") changes over to the spiritual realm of the "beyond." All important experiences acquired, gathered and stored throughout the course of a lifetime are evaluated and processed so that a spiritual possession (in the form of lasting knowledge and abilities, truth, wisdom, etc.) can never again be lost. This beyond is not found in some unknown region of the universe, but is around every inhabited heavenly body as a finely-substanced globular, layered shell. For us earth inhabitants, the beyond is located in a layer of finely-substanced matter within our atmosphere, and this layer is divided into seven different realms of evolution. A human spirit form is incorporated into the plane of the beyond according to its evolutionary level.

After a certain time, the processing of the previous lifetime comes to an end and the spirit form leaves the beyond to enter a new body of coarse matter, which then serves as a dwelling place for the new, material life. Following is a quotation from the book Life and Death by Billy Meier: "During innumerable lives, realization, logic, experience, love, knowledge, truth, wisdom, etc. are put together piece by piece like a mosaic. One speck after another is added to those accumulated riches which, in the end, characterize the perfection of the spirit — after unspeakable pains, privations, suffering and needs, joys and love during infinitely numerous lifetimes."

Creation (the energy of the Creation spirit, the almighty Creation power) provides all the necessary conditions for an individual to tread his path through life, but the way to go about doing this is left up to that person, himself. Creation provides the necessary guidelines, which are laid down in the laws and commandments of Creation and are unalterable. Whether or not a person obeys these guidelines and how he organizes the course of a lifetime is, again, his very personal matter.

Creation, therefore, never assumes guardianship or responsibility for the arrangement of anyone's life but allows total freedom of choice in every respect and by no means interferes in whatever the choice may be. It cannot be stressed enough that the individual destiny is neither determined by ethereal powers, guardian angels, spirit leaders, etc., nor by any imaginary "providence." On the contrary, every human being is responsible for his own thoughts, deeds and actions, and thus the old proverb proves to be true that… "Everyone carves his own destiny!" Well unto him who comprehends this and acts accordingly.

Clarification of the Concept:
What is the Meaning of Creation and What Does God Mean?

The term Creation means: Creation spirit, energy of the Creation spirit, universal consciousness — all of which are concepts that mean one and the same thing. Creation is the most tremendous mass of pure spirit energy existing in our universe. Creation is the greatest and most powerful elementary force in the entire universe, inconceivable in its knowledge, wisdom, truth, love, logic, and justice. Creation is the originator of all creations, which means that it created all the worlds and everything pertaining thereto, and is thus both the BEING and NON-BEING of life. In the linguistic usage of spirit teachings, there is no mention of a god, if the almighty power of Creation is meant to be expressed. God means a king of wisdom and is the German translation of the old-Lyrian term, JHWH. It is a name for human beings who possess extraordinary knowledge, ability and wisdom and, as a result of their spirit power, are able to master and accomplish that which national leaders and other rulers, as well as kings, queens and emperors, are unable to do. That is why knowledgeable and able wise men are referred to as "kings of wisdom" — human beings whose spiritual standing is greater than emperors and kings. God was, and today still is, a title for extraterrestrial human beings who possess such qualities. Even Jmmanuel (alias Jesus Christ) said: "God is a human being just like any other human being. Above God stands Creation, which is immeasurably higher, because Creation alone is the immeasurable mystery."

Thus, God is not identical with Creation and has no influence on the spirit life of man (erroneously called the soul life of man).

Why are Extraterrestrials Visiting Us on Earth?

As soon as a human race masters space flight to some extent, its nature is to expand its horizon and explore cosmic space, step by step. And since many races obviously make use of this ability, it is by no means astonishing that our earthly globe is visited by various extraterrestrial intelligences. In response to the question of why they visit our earth, here is an entire series of answers:

- A very small percentage of all visitors were occasionally stranded on our planet, having landed here because of emergencies resulting from technical difficulties.

- Extremely rare are time travelers who have lost their way in time and space due to lack of space-flight technology or erroneous calculations.

- Other extraterrestrials come here out of sheer curiosity; for example, in order to take a short excursion to earth if they happen to be in the immediate vicinity of our blue planet on their space-flight route.

- Reconnaissance patrols also appear now and then from outer space to find out if our planet is already inhabited by man, or whether it would be suitable for settlement and therefore be appropriate as a new homestead for their own race.

- It probably happens now and then, but certainly not frequently, that extraterrestrial visitors come to obtain very specific resources, which are not available on their home planets but are absolutely necessary for the manufacture of a certain product. This, of course, does not mean that they view our earth as a mining colony to be exploited at will and without permission.

- A compelling reason to monitor events in our region of the galaxy came about when we entered the Atomic Age by dropping two atom bombs on Hiroshima and Nagasaki, as well as the atom bomb tests that followed. Because of this, those extraterrestrial security forces who fill a supervisory function throughout outer space were brought to the scene. Since that time, all activities in the realm of military use of nuclear energy have been monitored around the clock in order to intervene in the interest of security throughout universal space, if it becomes absolutely necessary.

- Most extraterrestrial visitors probably appear on the scene for expedition purposes because they want to expand their knowledge. They collect unknown plants, minerals and other things which, when analyzed and found useful, are carried home with them. They conduct all kinds of studies on our planet and then withdraw as quietly and unrecognized as possible after their work is done.

- The study of our life styles and cultural achievements can be quite interesting for them, as it provides valuable information about their own growth through an earlier phase of their development. Observing our destructive behavior allows them to recognize what they should specifically heed in order to prevent similar negative developments in their own people, and how they could better manage their own affairs.

- In the framework of diverse extraterrestrial research activity, earth human beings, especially, stand in the limelight. How could it be any other way? Research provides an opportunity to willingly or unwillingly make contact with earth people in some form or another. As a rule, such contacts are of short duration, rarely lasting months or even years, and are especially short when dealing with personal contacts. They have no desire to demonstrate their power to us because they are extremely happy that they already have this unpleasant phase of development behind them.

In the course of their research work, it occasionally happens that extraterrestrial crews, robots or androids involuntarily take earth people aboard a spacecraft to be analyzed from head to toe with the help of special apparati. For those concerned, this is usually a painless procedure while they are completely unconscious. As a rule, the people who serve as guinea pigs in the literal sense of the word are released immediately after examination. In many cases, the persons in question can only vaguely remember the unusual incident, or not at all, because their respective memories were intentionally deleted. A good hypnotist is capable of retrieving what was deleted from the subconscious, as in the case of the married couple, Barney and Betty Hill, in the USA.[82] On the whole, the persons temporarily abducted, although unharmed, nevertheless become frightened. And as already reported at the beginning, not all extraterrestrials have good-natured intentions. Unfortunately, malicious extraterrestrials also exist who, in their lust for power, hunt for suitable planets to conquer with the intention of taking possession and achieving control of their inhabitants, provided they have the ability to do so. In a few rare cases, such power-hungry creatures also reach earth with their spacecraft. Acts of violence are customary for them, which is why they do not shy away from kidnapping human beings. The worst thing that could happen in this respect is to be kidnapped to a foreign planet in order to serve the wicked ones as slaves or be exhibited at circuses, fairs or amusement parks. Outright kidnappings of earth people attributed to extraterrestrials do occur, but are so seldom that it is hardly worth mentioning. Besides this, potential attacks on earth in order to capture it cannot be completely excluded, as it would be erroneous to conclude "everything good comes from above," as the proverb so nicely states. Nevertheless, there is no need for alarm, at least not as long as we are under the constant surveillance of Billy's extraterrestrial friends.

- Finally, all those are to be mentioned who are concerned about our well-being and therefore help us in various ways. This is especially true of the Pleiadians and their allies, to whom we shall turn now.

Contrary to different opinions, I must stress clearly that the extraterrestrials — wherever they may come from — do not appear here on earth or on other planets according to the order of "God" (whereby is actually meant the almighty spirit of Creation), nor are they angels sent by God. They by no means determine the destiny of an individual or even an entire civilization. Such a thing has never happened and will never happen in the future!

What Goals Do the Pleiadians and Their Allies Pursue on Earth?

The interest of the Pleiadians in the destiny of earth can first be traced to historical events of the distant past. The Pleiadians are descendants of our common ancestors who originated in the Lyra and Vega Systems (from whom the Pleiadians descended) and inhabited our planet a very long time ago. As a result, they influenced the development of the earth population in both negative and positive respects. Unfortunately, they caused a great deal of suffering by grievous wrongdoing. Nonetheless, the inhabitants of earth on their own initiative all too readily accepted and promoted them until they eventually became so malicious that we still suffer the consequences of their various degeneracies to this very day. The blame for the entire misery cannot be cast on the extraterrestrials alone, but in equal measure on the earth people themselves, who not only happily embraced and practiced the false teachings and actions of the extraterrestrials, but developed them in all possible areas into the degraded practices of today. Nevertheless, the Pleiadians have felt partially responsible for the Creation-opposing behavior of their earlier ancestors, as well as the resulting degeneracy (although, as stated, earth people themselves greatly contributed to this).

But we also must not overlook the reverse side of the coin. Without premature contact with the knowledge and capabilities of the extraterrestrials, earth people would still be vegetating along as cavemen in the Stone Age.

Despite the negative influence of the ancient Lyrians and Vegans, earth inhabitants also acquired positive knowledge and capabilities from an evolutionary standpoint, and were catapulted forward by gigantic steps in a relatively short time. Aside from the voluntary commitment to make amends for damage caused by these ancestors, the active involvement of the Pleiadians and their allies has yet another reason. A law of nature says that the stronger and more intelligent human beings should at all times and in all places give the weaker and more needy a helping hand and stand by their side with advice. That is why races with high spiritual development and capable of space flight function as helpers and protectors of human life (cosmic keepers of order) and mentors of spiritual development — but keep in mind— only within a lawful framework based on the laws of Creation.

Several examples of this:

- If the survival of a certain civilization is seriously threatened because its respective sun has exhausted its resources to such an extent that it can no longer be considered a life-giving factor, the inhabitants would be left with no other alternative but to migrate to another planet. If they are unable to save themselves because they lack the necessary space flight technology, help will be rendered by races that are able to conduct a large-scale evacuation from one planet to another.

- Desolate planets that are urgently needed for settlement but are environmentally hostile for human life forms are made as habitable as possible by enormously accelerating the planet's natural development with purposeful measures.

- Every time a civilization has reached a certain phase of development and enters a new level especially suitable for the promotion of evolution, highly developed intelligences offer their services.

- By far the most difficult task is to provide peace and order in universal space within the realm of possibility. If local developments possibly degenerate into a small- or large-scale catastrophe, force must also be applied in order to prevent a greater disaster and re-establish harmony.

As for the situation on earth in particular, we are presently at a very critical and dangerous level, as illustrated in Appendix A. Every kind of help and support should be more than welcome because we are in bitter need of it. No other Age is as well suited to raise spiritual evolution to a higher level than the Age of Aquarius, the pre-period in which we now find ourselves. This is the second important reason why the Pleiadians at this very time are showering their wisdom and helpfulness upon us from their horn of plenty. The way they go about helping us does not always match the desires and ideas of our modern, affluent society. It is often expected of extraterrestrials to set everything right again with radical measures by simply taking over the governmental power of the entire earth which, of course, the Pleiadians certainly would be capable of doing. But they would never be justified in doing this, and such measures would accomplish absolutely nothing in the long run. Rather, we must see to it ourselves that peace, harmony, happiness and well-being reign again one day.

The modus operandi of extraterrestrials is by no means equivalent to that of a surgeon who surgically removes diseased ulcers but is rather like that of a doctor who recognizes the symptoms of a disease and offers the proper therapeutic measures to be taken. But following the doctor's orders and taking the medicine regularly are entirely up to the patient. It is similar with the instructions of the extraterrestrials, especially when dealing with self-created problems. Our extraterrestrial friends may not pull the chestnuts out of the fire for us — no, we have to do it ourselves. They may only provide us with instructions on how to go about doing this. Following these instructions is also never allowed to be forced upon us. Whether or not we heed the warnings and make use of their useful teachings is entirely up to us.

To the disappointment of many UFO fans, the Pleiadians and their allies have never landed in public. But they have nevertheless rendered many valuable services, and they continue doing so to this day. To accomplish very specific tasks, they seek out suitable people whom they influence in various ways to address and carry out greater and smaller goal segments in the framework of a total global concept. Eduard Billy Meier, who functions as a mediator between the extraterrestrials and the earth people, in this regard undoubtedly fulfills the most important function. Billy is the only earth citizen at the present time who is permitted to have personal contact with the Pleiadians. To be able to do his task justice, he was trained and prepared for decades by the extraterrestrials. The Pleiadians have always extended a helping hand if necessary in the promotion of Billy's mission, be it through various protective measures or as mediator for inspirations to come about from the spirit planes of Arahat Athersata or Petale (through mediation of the High Council).

Around 31,000 people receive impulses in a sophisticated form of telepathy in order to advance the evolution of earth humanity. With the exception of five people (four of which have since died), these 31,000 people do not know from where these impulses originate. They presume that the source of these transmitted ideas comes from their own deductive reasoning or subconscious creative mind. *(This information was personally given to Billy on November 17, and December 1, 1989 by the JHWH Ptaah.)*

For example, authors and film producers in particular are selectively inspired to create their utopian novels and science fiction films in order to prepare mankind in a gentle manner for the coming events. More importantly, these inspirations help the insight to grow within us that we are not the only intelligent creatures in the universe. At the same time, earthly science is also stimulated to allow and develop new discoveries and inventions essential for our times and to accelerate research for the future. Scientists and other personalities, therefore, receive thought impulses to promote the natural progression of developments, corresponding to the demands of the time, and direct them into the right channels. The Pleiadians accelerate progress in this way, but only if really necessary and only in exactly-measured doses. Certain experts are inspired to appear in public, but only when their findings can be spread without causing any damage. On the other hand, the extraterrestrial helpers also see to it that no more knowledge is gained than our scientists are capable of handling. Scientists and ruling powers should be prevented whenever possible from rising to the eventual status of gods and exploiting power for their personal advantage (by governing people under a dictatorship or by abusing their technical achievements for power, politics and destruction). Unforeseeable and irreparable consequences could arise therefrom because earth people aren't yet mature enough to handle many things. The Pleiadians are determined to prevent us from making the same mistakes that our early ancestors made, to the detriment of humanity. Of course, this type of intervention and influence can only be carried out to a certain extent, as is established by law. The main objective of the Pleiadians, in my opinion, is to promote our spiritual development, and that is probably why the transmission of the spirit teachings should be of greatest significance. In retrospect, it can also be seen that a virtual wealth of valuable hints, good advice, warnings, messages and teachings of every kind have been transmitted to us through the contactee, Billy, and which continue to be transmitted to this day. I would like to impart some of this important information to you on the following pages. Especially worth mentioning are the extraordinary remedial measures the extraterrestrials have taken for the entire earth population, which will undoubtedly be their crowning achievement and will be discussed at the end of this chapter.

Transmission of Spirit Teachings

The Pleiadians have been instructive elements for the people of earth since time immemorial, and this continues unchanged to this very day.

The correction of spirit teachings that have been twisted and distorted beyond recognition in the course of time is one of the most important tasks to be fulfilled by the Pleiadians. These spirit teachings contain the laws and commandments of Creation. They reveal the truthful teachings about the entire Creation with all of its life forms, etc. Reduced to a basic formula, the teaching of truth has unrestricted validity throughout the entire universe.

During the Aquarian Age, it is more important than ever not to withhold the revelation of truth a single day longer. All progressive thinkers accept the wisdom of the spirit teachings with enthusiasm and gratitude. They know it would be very strenuous to climb the ladder of spiritual evolution without this help and they might even succumb to stagnation.

Incidentally, the Pleiadians hold an exceptional trump card in their hands — they are actually in a position to best convey the truth to us earth people due to their advanced level of evolution. A citation of the Pleiadians in this respect follows:

> "If we therefore convey explanations and interpretations, these correspond to the highest degree of our understanding and knowledge of the highest known truth. But truth is not found through any type of explanations and interpretations given by far lower-developed life forms in a confrontation. What we are conveying is the ultimately known truth up to and with our spirit plane."

A drop of bitterness must nevertheless be swallowed. The Pleiadians do not tell us everything by far that we would like to know. On one hand, there are many things that we earth people are only allowed to learn when we have become spiritual thinkers and when our spiritual knowledge and spiritual wisdom have developed far enough for the next level to become a 'must' for us. On the other hand, the Pleiadians must be silent about various matters because they are required by their laws to withhold knowledge of certain subjects in order to prevent any harm, which we in our ignorance would not even be aware of.

As stated in Appendix A, spreading the spirit teachings can best be accomplished in an era in which we have been living for quite some time. Nevertheless, many problems must first be resolved in order to make headway in spiritual evolution. First, our technical progress is outrunning our spiritual progress by gigantic steps. We presently lack the wisdom and maturity necessary to prevent the negative use of this advanced technology. And compared to the steady overemphasis of material-intellectual matters, our spiritual intellect has been sorely neglected and has fallen behind to an alarming extent. It is crucial to gradually balance this gap and bring about a harmonious balance.

Another problem concerns an evil of no less magnitude regarding the prevailing religious conditions here on earth, which, according to the Pleiadians, is unparalleled throughout the universe. In other words, our very peculiar cult-like religions and their sects are absolutely unique in the entire universe. We cannot begin to imagine the extent of this harm, as the magnitude of global damage resulting from these religious dogmas for centuries and millennia is indeterminable. Therefore, it has become necessary for many of our contemporaries to return to the narrow path of truth, which had been abandoned long ago due to ignorance of the facts resulting from mistakes and false teachings. But in order for the delicate flowers to flourish anew in the garden of truth, the weeds must first be uprooted and the plant parasites effectively eliminated. This work will be arduous and will require a completely new and progressive form of thinking. Many of us, whether we like it or not, must sooner or later depart from the false ideas of our traditional world views in order to finally see and understand the facts as they really are. And for those who wish to correct their false behavior and set their lives on a truthful course, there is only one rightful guiding light and inspiration — the study of the spirit teachings.

WARNINGS!
Unbridled Overpopulation

Originally, each individual strip of land on earth was inhabited by only as many people as that region was able to nourish without using the chemical substances that we add to arable land today in order to increase production. This natural state lasted until about the time of the French Revolution when around 500 million people inhabited the earth. From that point on, the number of earth people increased to an intolerable level within a relatively short period of time. Today (1990), we have already exceeded the number of five billion people and are thus totally overpopulated. Our planet cannot bear this for any length of time. It only provides enough space, food, raw materials— without mankind intervening against the laws of nature — for around 500 million people (529 million to be exact). Under ideal conditions, this would mean not more than an average of one dozen inhabitants per square kilometer of productive acreage. One of the largest problems of our time is the immense overpopulation of earth. The majority of all grievances can ultimately be attributed to this fundamental evil.

- As a result of our disastrous overpopulation, people do not have sufficient living space. They are packed into modern apartment-silos like canned sardines. This inhibits development, promotes aggressive behavior toward fellow-citizens and, on a tong-term basis, creates a breeding ground for dangerous territorial conflicts.

- Since millions of people die yearly from starvation (a large majority of the earth population is permanently on the verge of starvation), it is apparent that the food situation will become even more acute if population growth continues to rise in this speedy manner.

- Also, the problem of unemployment will become more difficult to remedy from year to year. The army of unemployed millions has also increased in the industrial countries on which many a developing country, indirectly, depends. If economic assistance to the Third World in the form of technical know-how and cheap credit should be curbed or even stopped, it would lead to a worldwide economic catastrophe. Many nations would be forced to defend their right to life through the use of sheer force. Making such a decision would by no means be difficult because they would have nothing at all to lose in their life-threatening and completely desperate situation.

- Ever more people need ever more raw materials and energy in the form of fossil fuel (crude oil, natural gas, coal), and electricity, which in turn, literally leads to the total exploitation of the earth. We are relentlessly robbing it of its valuable mineral resources, which can only partially be reproduced, if at all, in the course of millions of years. This immense damage inflicted on our planet year after year is irreparable and, therefore, an enormous evil. A further great danger is also imminent: The lower our supplies of raw materials and energy get (because they are daily decimated), the greater the probability of armed conflicts. Our modern economy can no longer function without these valuable goods and people will forcibly defend them, if need be, or seize them by force.

- Increasing industrialization is, unfortunately, leading to environmental pollution, which increases to ever more serious forms. Our waters, once clean and pure, are gradually transformed into chemical sewers. The poisoning of our atmosphere by no means plays a secondary role. And if this development continues, we shall choke, someday, in "our own muck."

The earth, as an entity, can no longer idly stand by and permit mankind's perilous effects and interventions destroy it as a result of irrational and excessive greed, so the earth will vehemently defend itself. Diverse natural catastrophes will be the consequence in the form of earthquakes, floods, droughts, starvation, climatic shifts and more, all the while increasing in intensity.

In the end, large-scale armed conflicts and a global spreading of incurable diseases and deadly epidemics will in this dreadful manner ensure that the overpopulation is reduced to a somewhat more tolerable level. Therefore, it is of utmost necessity that we take appropriate actions as soon as possible in order to put a stop to this disastrous development.

A good example of teaching is delivered by nature itself, which always takes care that the excess number of any animal population is curbed to a natural number by epidemics or temporary famines, and so forth, so sufficient food will be available for all animals at all times.

Only man in his megalomania dares to disregard and dishonor the venerable laws of nature. Contrary to the faunal life forms, man produces offspring as if on an assembly line, without considering whether the children will have to live from hand to mouth or scrape along in poverty for their entire lives until they perish in misery from sheer hunger. Every reasonable person must realize that extreme but unpopular measures are called for now, meaning that our planetary overpopulation can only be solved through a targeted birth control or by periodic birth stops. Naturally, these measures must be coupled with absolutely essential assistance, taking respective conditions into consideration, which vary from country to country. There is simply no getting around this measure. Every other attempt would simply be a useless, pretentious solution resembling a mere drop in the bucket and would basically prolong the problem, but not solve it. Instead of accepting the bitter truth and acting accordingly, so called "good remedial measures" are often substituted because of a misunderstood humaneness and a completely misunderstood idea of charity. Through such misguided actions, the privation and misery of innumerable human beings are not relieved but, instead, increased. Despite good will, any other "rescue" is absolutely impossible. Each one of us in a responsible position who is not willing to take the effective action in this direction becomes partially responsible for the entire tragedy. Everyone should be aware of this fact.

Destruction of the Vital Ozone Layer

A perilous threat for all of us on earth takes place in our atmosphere, meaning the shifting of the ozone belt. The ozone roof in the stratosphere, which should protect us from the life-threatening ultraviolet rays of the sun, is becoming ever more permeable because of the increasing destruction and the related decrease of the ozone content. To blame for this is air pollution of the first degree, bringing disaster caused by exhaust released from the combustion engines of cars, trucks and airplanes, from factories, nuclear power plants, and households, and from the often mentioned spray cans containing fluorochlorohydrocarbons (FCHC). In contrast to this flagrant disregard of the reduction of ozone content in the stratosphere, exactly the opposite effect is taking place in the lowest layer of the atmosphere where the extremely toxic ozone (O^3) is increasing at an alarming rate.

In view of the immense significance of the stratospheric ozone layer for the existence of all life forms on earth, the Pleiadians gave a warning in this reference during a contact in 1975. Billy sent this warning to competent scientists, governments and chemical factories all over the world in a circular letter. Following, you will find the pertinent information received from Semjase on February 25, 1975:

SEMJASE: For many decades now, we have been monitoring all the spheres of your world, their steadily growing changes and the dangerous consequences caused by fuel gases and other dangerous, harmful substances released by the earth people. For several years now, we have been able to establish that a steadily growing and dangerous change has made itself noticeable in your stratosphere, which portends deadly consequences for all earthly life. To an increasing extent, the ozone belt has been changing, due to the irresponsible influences of human achievement. Various chemicals destructive to ozone rise into the stratosphere as gaseous substances and damage the ozone belt. In addition to fluorochlorohydrocarbons, this is also especially true of bromine gases that smell very evil. In contrast to earth terminology, bromine gases are known in our language as a poisonous gas, also called fluorochlorohydrocarbons, which penetrate the ozone layer and slowly destroy it. This gas has already damaged and destroyed the ozone layer by approximately 6.38 percent. This percentage is already becoming harmful and dangerous for all life forms and is beginning to cause mutative changes. This is a percentage point which has been reached within only 60 years. Especially the bromine gases and FCHCs are slowly destroying the ozone belt, as already mentioned, allowing an increase of ultraviolet rays from the sun to penetrate the atmosphere and cause damage to all life forms. Over various regions, this ozone belt is already dangerously affected and variable in its protection. In three different places, the danger already exists that the ozone belt will break up and will be completely destroyed in several decades if the release of destructive factors is not curbed. If not, holes will be torn in the protective ozone screen and unobstructed ultraviolet sunrays will penetrate your atmosphere, causing a tormenting death for all life forms. Everything within the areas penetrated by rays through the hole would be hopelessly destroyed. Principal offenders are the destructive chemical substances and radiation released by combustion engines and other processes destructive to matter, such as atomic fission and similar evils, which have greatly subjected the entire world and all its life forms to disastrous changes since 1945. Destructive chemical gases are also released by the actions of daily life. Every spray can also release other chemicals besides the FCHC and they also rise into the stratosphere and slowly but systematically destroy it.

Recently, researchers and scientists from various countries have become so much more knowledgeable about the destruction of the ozone belt by various chemicals, especially FCHCs, and want to use them for purposes of war in their irresponsible drive for power. They have already designed the basic idea for building rockets containing the destructive and death-bringing factors of fluorochlorohydrocarbon and bromine substances. Shot high into the stratosphere and exploded, they would tear gigantic holes in the ozone belt, causing all the ultraviolet rays of the sun to penetrate downward. Such a hole would be able to slowly close, but the process would take centuries — if no further destructive substances would continue to penetrate. In addition to this, a vital factor is at hand that the ozone belt is subject to certain movements and travels. A hole would not only destroy a very specific region but would uncontrollably travel to and also destroy other large areas, a fact which is not yet known to your scientists. Furthermore, these facts have been concealed from the public up until now.

Nuclear Threat and the So-called Peaceful Use of Atomic Energy

A nuclear threat resulting from the construction and stationing of atomic weapons of every kind since the end of World War II has been hanging over our heads like the Sword of Damocles. It is a suicidal madness of the highest order of the earth people and contrary to nature and Creation in every respect. However, not only its military use and the atomic bomb tests connected with it, but also the peaceful use of nuclear energy, contain great danger, as the catastrophe in Chernobyl sufficiently proved. It would be like "carrying coals to Newcastle" if I were to list everything on this subject that has been known for a long time. I shall therefore only touch upon several facts which are less known to the general population.

I must first of all point out that besides the known effects of radioactivity, also another type of radiation occurs unknown to us. According to the Pleiadians, not even our best nuclear physicists have the least notion about it. Another negative aspect, also not generally known, is the disturbance of the magnetic field of earth and the resulting polar shift, which are connected with our climatic changes, and which may also be unknown to the general public.

JHWH Ptaah gave the following explanation in this connection in September of 1975:

> **PTAAH:** The earth's magnetic field was actually disturbed by the atomic bomb explosions (as Billy had correctly suspected), which means that the explosions caused a very weak thrust effect on the earth and influenced the caliber of its rotation to a barely detectable degree. The earth was thrown out of its normal rotation and is slowly seeking a new rotation orbit. In addition, its orbital path around the sun was also reduced in very small increments and thrust out of its normal orbit. The earth scientists have committed a malicious crime on their own planet and its entire humanity. The changes forcefully brought about by the explosions have far-reaching significance and can have catastrophic effects. The magnetic poles of the north and south have already shifted considerably within recent years. Consequently, the magnetic North Pole in the north is found today in the area of the Canadian polar sea, while the South Pole has been displaced and is moving in the direction of South America. Around the change of the third millennium (in about 1,000 years), the changes of the magnetic poles of earth will have progressed to such an extent that the South Pole will be located in South America and the North Pole will have moved towards Saudi Arabia. The previously calculated point of the North Pole in the year 3,000 gave a location between Dschidda at the Red Sea and the Islamic Pilgrimage City of Mecca.

Thus, another of Billy's speculations was confirmed by Ptaah:

PTAAH: After the explosion of the atom bombs in Hiroshima and Nagasaki, the atomic radiation spread rapidly and soon enveloped the entire earth. The far greater danger of the specific elementary radiation released through these explosions will yet cause great riddles for the earth scientists. They have not yet mastered these riddles because they do not yet understand their nature and form. In particular, three main conditions for the continuation of life on earth are influenced and damaged by the release of this elementary radiation. The catastrophic process after an atomic bomb explosion on as large a scale as the Hiroshima bomb lasts several centuries and influences all factors supporting life in a negative way. In the pure atmospheric layers around the earth, the ozone balance has been influenced in a catastrophic manner as a result of the released elementary radiation by atomic explosions. This creates an electrical radiating energy that moves in a high frequency range as yet unknown to your science. As a result, this radiating energy mixes with oxygen and creates gigantic quantities of ozone in the lower atmosphere — therefore, in the wrong place. These dangerous changes result in the destruction of all microorganisms, even in the further surroundings, that are of enormous importance for the maintenance of all earthly life. Shortly after an explosion, the ozone values sink rapidly and level off. But the elementary radiation continues to penetrate all matter and is stored there for hundreds of years and during that time it destroys all microorganisms in its vicinity.

The damaging of the ozone belt constitutes another factor in the higher layers of the stratosphere but can be only partially traced back to atomic bomb explosions. *(See ~ Destruction of the Vital Ozone Layer ~ in this Chapter)*

With regard to the peaceful use of nuclear energy, Quetzal explained its use is possible without causing danger to the environment and living creatures; he states as follows:

QUETZAL: The possibility exists for you and it is also used by us (Pleiadians). Earth people are not yet capable of doing this. Nevertheless, they are completely negligent and act irresponsibly in their work with atomic energy. They knowingly create deadly hazards for all life forms. Atomic energy will be useful in every way only if all residual substances and wastes are completely used and processed so that an absolutely radiation-free matter is created. But this is only possible through a transformational process that converts the radioactive mass back into its original non-radioactive state. Matter is thus returned to its initial form. Your scientists are working with radioactive materials before they are able to reverse the process. They are acting criminally in every way and are in violation of the laws of nature.

In response to Billy's question of how the energy problems should be solved (without using nuclear energy), Quetzal gave the following answer:

QUETZAL: Every planet continuously provides its life forms with sufficient and natural energy containing no danger whatsoever. That is, if the planet has normal population numbers and does not succumb to overpopulation. The earth is now overpopulated by around 4 billion people (the total when Quetzal made the statement). The situation is now completely out of control due to greed for power, profit and luxury of earthman. If earthman would be reasonable and introduce a purposeful birth stop (with controls afterwards), then the reduction of the earthly population to a normal level of 529 million would be possible within a short period of time. Thus, the energy problem would also be solved in a natural way, as well as the problem of food provision. The stupidity of earth people along these lines is without limits, because they irresponsibly violate all natural laws. However, they also cannot be addressed about ending this problem. Misguided humanitarian efforts still protect and promote this crime of overpopulation and resulting starvation, etc. The re-establishment of a normal level of earthly humanity will be the correct and only solution to your energy and food problems. Any other solution is illogical and will result in only partial solutions, representing illogical effects due to illogical causes.

In response to Billy's question for a solution to the problem, Quetzal answered:

QUETZAL: … but these solutions are only a matter of time because the problem of an ever-growing overpopulation, and with it the irrationality and greed of earth humans, will continue to grow. It would be completely inappropriate for me to list and explain the possibilities that actually exist in order to thoroughly solve these problems of energy and food. We can name such possibilities only if the earth people themselves strive to achieve a drastic reduction of their planetary population and bring it back to its normal level.

Of urgent necessity are the following measures:

- The immediate halt of all atom bomb tests.

- Prohibition of all atomic weapons whereby all existing material must gradually be destroyed or rendered harmless.

- The closing down of all atomic power plants step-by-step and increasing efforts to put energy sources to use which are not harmful to the environment (solar energy, free energy from space etc.).

As Quetzal further stated, individual problems usually cannot be solved alone, but only in conjunction with others:

QUETZAL: Since every violation of the laws and commandments of Creation triggers real catastrophes, one problem naturally reaches into another. Therefore, a problem can never be viewed separately, but must be seen as the cog of a wheel reaching into the next wheel, because everything existing in the universe is dependent upon a large number of other functions. In general, a revolving wheel exists and continues to develop in a spiral formation depending on upward or downward endeavors; this means that if a person or an entire humanity strives for evolution, the cycle slowly spirals upwards. But if one person or an entire civilization only live for the satisfaction of subjective desires, the cycle will spiral downward, which equates to spiritual stagnation and material degeneration.

Reckless Exploitation of the Earth

Semjase made a very concerned statement in a contact report about the reckless exploitation of the earth by the earth people:

SEMJASE: Mineral ore extraction and the extraction of other minerals on a planet or other stars (heavenly bodies) is only carried out by us (on our home planet of Erra) in an extreme emergency. This process is equivalent to the destruction of a star. A planet or another heavenly body may never be exploited in the way it is done on earth. What the earth people are doing is the same as destroying a planet. The first evil effects of this destruction have been noticeable on earth for decades, whereas the present time itself introduces the pains of planetary destruction. This means that earth people are exploiting their planet and destroying its fundamental life force by robbing it of petroleum, natural gas and the various mineral ores. The earth is suffering from inner displacements, which lead to violent volcanic eruptions and earthquakes, causing the earth to slowly collapse within itself. The same process is also caused by the construction of dams and similar formations, which, due to the enormous weight of accumulated mass of water, gives rise to very dangerous earth movements. Much worse are the underground and aboveground atom bomb experiments, as well as the dreadful underground explosive tests, which are declared to be atom bomb tests, although in truth, they are much more dangerous.

The earth possessed petroleum deposits of 646 billion tons, of which 65 billion tons have already been exploited or destroyed through the ignorance of the earth people. Destruction also resulted from underground atom bomb explosions. In fact, 20 billion tons of petroleum were destroyed. (The numbers refer to the years 1975 and 1976.) A planet like earth produces 140 billion tons of petroleum in the course of one billion years. If the planet has thus enriched its petroleum for 4.6 billion years, it has produced inside itself 646 billion tons of petroleum. But earth people have already exploited one tenth of this in less than a century — an amount it took the earth 500 million years to produce! If the planet wants to regenerate its petroleum content to the original value existent before the exploitation of all mineral ores, gases and petroleum, etc., it will require 811 million years due to the loss of natural resources up to the present time. This process will take almost twice as long as the former production time because mankind has now stripped the earth of many elements needed for this production. The earth's surface, alone, has lost so much fertile soil in less than one century that nature will need many millions of years to make it fertile again.

And the list could go on and on — truly a dreadful chapter of human irrationality and greed!

In closing, I would like to add an excerpt from the conversation between Billy and Ptaah on February 3, 1990. On this occasion, Ptaah predicted, among other things, the catastrophic effect of the raging hurricanes in Europe during February of 1990.

PTAAH: ...Indeed, all of the incidents of natural catastrophes to occur this month as well as afterwards are simply and purely a result of the criminal and reckless destruction of the earth and its atmosphere through the irresponsible actions of the people of this world. Air pollution, radioactive contamination, atom bomb tests and their aftermath of tremendous jolting of the earth, toxication of all life, atomic power plants with all their destructive environmental influences including the deadly radioactive burdening of the atmosphere and all life forms, and gigantic artificial lakes and other similar malicious things, are the causes for events to come, even if the persons responsible and the governments of earth do not want to recognize this fact.

The opposite namely is true, because during and after the coming events, those responsible will talk big and claim that the occurrence of natural catastrophes and devastations of nature (brought about by mankind's destructive urges stemming from irrationality and greed), has absolutely nothing to do with them. That, however, will be only lies and obstinate stupidity as well as lack of understanding and unlimited primitiveness on the part of all those who want to free themselves from guilt. They refuse to acknowledge responsibility in any regard, much less confess their inability to carry such responsibility. In truth, all of these liars have committed crimes against the humanity of earth and against the planet itself, regardless of whether they are among the governing forces or are researchers or whether they are beneficiaries of these destructive actions. Man as such must be added to this list, at least every one who does not cultivate discipline and order and who does not stop the overpopulation but continues to produce countless offspring and thereby burdens and endangers the earth and all earthly life. The weight of all people in excess of 529 million constitutes a tremendous burden for the earth and creates extraordinary pressure at various depths. The earth simply cannot easily tolerate this. Tremendous pressure points produce tectonic changes in areas and cities where masses of human beings accumulate in the hundreds of thousands or even millions. The combined tonnage of all the buildings, vehicles, machines and so forth, which are concentrated at certain points, cause incredible pressures on the surface and inside the earth, resulting in dangerous displacements and breakage points deep inside the earth. (I do not like to speak or even think of all this.) The tremendous weight of humanity at concentrated points, alone, is quite enough to unleash various forms of catastrophes on and for the planet. The secondary cause for catastrophes are generally the earthquakes which, through the primary cause (pressures and displacements and so forth), are unleashed due to the massive weight of human beings themselves! This also holds true for the large amounts of accumulated water contained as artificial lakes and the like, which also cause earthquakes.

But earthman does not consider these facts. On the contrary, the facts are denied, the planet and all its life are continuing to be destroyed. It is high time that the entire madness is stopped and prohibited. Such a stop can still be carried out, and it is really high time to do so. The earth will no longer allow herself to be criminally destroyed. She now starts to defend herself and is striking back, blow for blow. This truly has nothing to do with explanations the know-it-alls and unscrupulous say to their own defense, when they proclaim that special natural occurrences like earthquakes and storms have always swept over the earth from time to time and that the dying forests practically worldwide are not half as bad as claimed by pessimists. In truth, these denials are one more crime committed against earth and all life forms. Actually, the coming events no longer fall within the scope of natural occurrences in repetition but are actually a fighting back by nature and by the planet itself.

A rapid and purposeful change of mankind's ways is of urgent necessity. Man must end all these destructive actions against the planet, against nature and against all life. But even when criminal doings and actions against the planet, life and nature have ended, the planet and nature, as well as life, cannot simply regenerate themselves within a short period of time. The damage alone to nature and the planet will require a regeneration time of 340,000 years, and profound things, such as the regeneration of petroleum, will require many millions of years. Also, the reduction of artificially produced radioactivity (from A-bombs and A-bomb tests, as well as from nuclear power plants and many other radioactive things produced by earth people), will take many thousands and even millions of years.

The quantity and strength of radioactivity, alone, deposited over the polar regions is far more critical and dangerous than that of nuclear power plants. People who fly over the earth's poles in flying machines absorb larger quantities of dangerous radioactivity than those who work in the immediate vicinity of nuclear power plants.

But that, my friend, is enough for today. Please do not ask any more questions.

BILLY: That's also quite enough for me today. Well then, so long and my best regards to everyone.

Warning Against Plans of Conquest

Unfortunately, abuse of technical achievements not only takes place with us on earth but also with other civilizations who also badly abuse their technical achievements to appease their lust for power.

And in this connection, Semjase directed the following warning to the humanity of earth:

SEMJASE: If earthman has achieved the necessary technology to fly to other planets, they must not do so light-heartedly and in the hope that man will always be the winner. Numerous dangers of varied magnitude are lurking in the cosmos itself, and inhabitants of other worlds are not simply helpless when attacked by another race. This could lead to deadly defeats and a total enslavement for earthman, which would be comparable to falling back into primeval times. It could also happen that the planet earth would be totally destroyed. The technical requirements for this have been worked out to maximum perfection by many human and non-human races throughout the cosmos. If earth people wish to carry their barbaric despotic ways and greed for power out into the cosmos, they must take into account their own total annihilation, and no other planetary being would rush to their aid. Other races in the universe do not senselessly fight one another or banish, enslave or exploit others, as is done among the peoples of earth, but they know how to defend themselves and, if necessary, can do this by radical means.

These races continue to be vastly superior in their technical possibilities for quite some time. And wherever this is not the case, they are often under the protection of other more highly developed intelligences whose technology has reached maximum perfection.

This information alone should serve as a serious warning for the future… that we cannot carry our unbridled greed for power and plans of conquest out into the cosmos without being punished

The Necessity of Barbarism Without Degeneracy

The earth is presently in a very critical phase of development. This provides us sufficient cause for concern, especially with respect to the near future of our planet. The negative factors have mainly been pointed out in this chapter. Perhaps I have given the impression that earth people do everything wrong and by no means live correctly. That is not true. earth people, from the very beginning, have been no worse than other human civilizations that must more or less suffer the same "labor pains" and "childhood diseases" and go through about the same stages of development as we. A certain barbarism is part of this course of development and quite necessary for progress in a natural form without degeneration.

With regard to this, Semjase revealed the following:

SEMJASE: ... the earth people go the way required for their evolution. Certainly, they are barbaric and, consequently, are unbridled and often inconsiderate in matters of research. However, barbarism is characteristic of many life forms as it is required by nature and is a way through which life can first be guaranteed. With that, I refer to natural barbarism, which is free of degeneracy. This also applies to far more highly developed races than those of the earth people and does not subside until higher spiritual perfection is achieved and the required realizations have become part of the spirit. There is absolutely no cause for earth people to feel defamed and degraded as evil monstrosities.

They are the descendants of wild ancestors and have to follow their own path of development. Their way leads over much need, misery and toil to realization and knowledge. This requires the hardness of a certain barbarism without which there would be no urge forward, toward something new and better. Barbarism only allows for research and development. The necessary hardness is contained within it to disregard certain conditions that would hinder progress. Barbarism, namely, can nip in the bud the strict religious delusions that hinder progress in every respect. Human beings are capable of carrying on fruitful research only if they set aside religious delusions and seek the truths where they are actually concealed. This does not detract from respect for life or even from the esteem for Creation itself. Quite the contrary, esteem for Creation and for life will first be kindled through research and its discoveries. earth people may recognize that this is really so. For example, no life could be freed from disease if life had previously not been destroyed experimentally in order to analyze the germs of a disease and then find its antidote. To destroy life for the purpose of research requires the hardness of barbarism. All forms of evolution require barbarism because it creates the necessary hardness. Therefore, a person suffering from strong religious delusions is never capable of bringing about a decisive, life-supporting development because they are too one-sided and think and act too humanely, and therefore, degenerate one-sidedly as well. (Of course, animal experiments can be replaced with better methods as soon as such methods are available.)

Indications and Warnings of Cosmic Events
The Destroyer Comet

A gigantic comet called the Destroyer grazed our earth about 75,000 years ago for the first time, causing devastating destruction. Approximately 10,000 years ago when that particularly powerful comet reentered the SOL System, Venus was ripped from its original orbit around Uranus. Thereafter, the comet left the SOL system but invaded it again in the year 16,098 (before our time calculation) and from that time on has returned to us at more or less regular intervals. This cosmic monster has already caused great calamities on earth and will continue to do so if we do not succeed in putting an end to it. Among other things, the Destroyer Comet is also responsible for the catastrophe of the great biblical Flood (6,613 years before our time calculation), to name one concrete example. *(See ~ Chapter 11 for more detailed information. Also see ~ Semjase's Fantastic Moon Story ~ in this chapter)*

In a conversation between Billy and Quetzal, we learned the details about the dimensions of the Destroyer Comet:

BILLY: You have always spoken of a gigantic comet with reference to the Destroyer. Therefore I would find it interesting to know what dimensions this guy actually has.

QUETZAL: Its mass equals 1.72 times that of planet earth and its specific weight varies in comparison to the average weight of the earth. The entire mass of the Destroyer is somewhat denser than the earth. If the earth has a volume of 1,429.9 billion km^3 with a medium density of 5.51 grams/cm^3, then the Destroyer is a giant in comparison with its volume of 1,083.3 billion km^3 and a medium density of 7.18 grams/cm^3, if I may give you the data according to earthly understanding.

BILLY: Interesting — and does the Destroyer also have a rotation of its own, like the earth, for example?

QUETZAL: That is correct, but it rotates more slowly than the earth, which rotates 465 meters per second (1,535 ft. per second) at the equator. The rotation of the Destroyer only amounts to 314.7 meters per second (1,039 ft. per second) on the very same line.

BILLY: Therefore, its spin is approximately three quarters of the velocity of the earth rotation.

QUETZAL: That is correct. The Destroyer's velocity has been increasing for quite some time — in fact, as a result of our efforts. We are endeavoring to send this wandering star off course in order to guide it into regions far away from the SOL System where it can no longer do any harm.

BILLY: Fantastic — then earthman will no longer fear that it will threaten the earth again, if you succeed in your undertaking. (The next great danger would otherwise threaten us in the year 2255, when the Destroyer penetrates our SOL System again.)

QUETZAL: This is correct, and we are quite confident.

BILLY: I have a question to that: Why are you allowed to meddle in the affairs of the Destroyer, if on the other hand, you are not allowed to undertake anything against our other impending danger, such as the anticipated red meteor?

QUETZAL: As an act of vengeance, the Destroyer was partially deflected from its natural course by our early ancestors and, consequently, caused damage in the SOL System which was not of natural cosmic origin. Since we do not know the exact circumstances of that time, we cannot give any closer details or explanations about it.

As the following example illustrates, the Pleiadians have very exact instructions about when they are permitted to help us and when not.

The Red Meteor

QUETZAL: The Red Meteor named in the prophecies is enormous in size and will cause extremely malicious destructions on earth and, in addition to climatic, tectonic and other changes, will also split the earth crust from today's Baltic Sea to the Black Sea. It will swoop from the depths of the cosmos into the SOL system and then on to the earth.

BILLY: Do you mean that we are not dealing with a known comet which always travels through our system in its orbital path?

QUETZAL: This is correct, because this meteor travels in an orbit which will direct it to your SOL system for the first time. In earlier times, it was never in your region of space.

BILLY: And its flight is to end on earth? Aren't you able to undertake any action against it?

QUETZAL: You know very well that we are not permitted to stop this event. The cosmic forces themselves have programmed this event in advance, and it can only be stopped or warded off by the earth people themselves. In their materialistic and misguided disunity and in their delusions of grandeur, they disregard all warnings and prophecies, so this event will inevitably come to pass as a rebuke and retribution, if you wish to see it as such. And because this admonition and retribution must occur, we are not permitted to undertake any actions to ward off this event. earth people should listen to your words and warnings, but that is precisely what they do not do. You are standing in a lost position, like a voice crying in the wilderness, and only a few are willing or shall be willing to listen to your words, to grasp them, think about them and learn to act in the right way. Therefore, those not listening will experience many deaths when the meteor does its deadly work and creates a new continent on the earth through a violent earth gap, from which red-hot lava will gush forth, from the Baltic Sea to the Black Sea.

BILLY: You said that so dramatically and unscientifically. By the way, it would be of interest to me where this earth rift will occur.

QUETZAL: It is our way to also remain human while offering scientific explanations without using a scientific language. Scientific terms prevail primarily only among the earth people who believe they must distinguish themselves with this language. This is a degeneracy of cold-blooded megalomania and, furthermore, it leads to the belittlement of all dangers. This is one of the reasons why we — and all other intelligent and truly thinking life forms — never allow ourselves to fall into using scientific language, but use simple human words, instead, which have to sound somewhat dramatic because the developing drama of the abominable event actually exists. A purely scientific means of expression is always misleading because it is detached and impersonal, thereby belittling and minimizing the dangers.

With reference to the earth rift to be expected, I can tell you that it will divide the land between the Baltic Sea and the Black Sea. Red-hot masses of lava and natural gas and so forth, will also produce a deadly wall of sulfur which will cover the land, drifting westward and will create an additional death zone.

Semjase's Fantastic Story of the Moon

In connection with the birth of the cosmic Destroyer, which has already been discussed, I do not want to deprive you of Semjase's fantastic story of the Moon. Her story should serve as an example, as many other past events that have been conveyed to us by the extraterrestrials are not to be found in any history or other text books.

A Cosmic Catastrophe

The story of the Moon's origin begins with a cosmic catastrophe. It happened about 22 million years ago, when a sun in the Vega Region of the Lyra Constellation was so violently shaken due to unknown explosions that it collapsed, ripping a gigantic hole into the stratum of universal space. During this colossal implosive process, the sun's diameter shrank from 11 million kilometers (7 million miles) to a meager 4.2 kilometers (3 miles), whereby its mass was so densely compressed that a single cm^3 (cubic centimeters) of matter weighed as much as several thousand tons. From that point on, this miniature sun has been hovering as a dark, gaping "hollow" in universal space, devouring everything within a radius of millions of kilometers with an irresistible gravitational force. In the vocabulary of our astronomical science, such formations are called "black holes," the existence of which have already been presumed and postulated for some years now.

The Birth of the Cosmic Destroyer

During the collapse of this star, not only was this sun totally changed, but its entire solar system was completely dissolved, which means that the planets orbiting the mother star were either destroyed or catapulted into universal space as dangerous missiles. One of these catapulted planets finally came into the outer gravitational field of a neighboring solar system and revolved around it for many thousands of years. In fact, it was far outside of the actual orbital paths of the planets but on an unpredictable and therefore dangerous course. Without any life, this frightfully dark wandering planet traveled through the icy cold of the cosmos as an outcast and foreigner in a foreign system.

I shall quote the continuation of the story word for word from a contact report with Semjase:

SEMJASE: In the grip of these far-reaching powerful arms of the sun, it came closer and closer in the course of thousands of years to the actual region of the system's satellites (planets) which it had orbited for such a long time with steadily increasing speed. Imperceptibly, its orbit narrowed more and more and its potential danger continued to grow year after year. With the passing of thousands of years, it suddenly plummeted with unexpected speed into the innermost orbital path of the sun and its planets. Like a greedy monster, it emerged from the blackness of space, proclaiming death-bringing destruction. At first, it was like a shadowy silhouette out of nowhere but then assumed the mysterious and hazy form of a semi-dark round disk. Then, illumined by the reflecting rays of the sun, it approached the orbital path of the outermost planet at an incredible velocity. It was still millions of units away from the actual center of peaceful serenity, which it would soon transform into a raging inferno when its gigantic bulk penetrated the stillness of this harmony. But ages still continued to pass before the giant finally left its orbit and moved dangerously close. Then recognizable as a round ball, the Destroyer reflected the sunlight, while a fine trail of luminous particles was pulled along behind it. Now only several hundred thousand units away from the next worlds, it gave rise to infernal storms on those worlds, destroying large regions which had been cultivated by human beings settled there. Trembling with fright for their hard-earned goods and their lives, which were already hard enough without this, they suddenly found themselves exposed to the violent and merciless forces of the universe. Helplessly condemned to be handed over from life to death, they stared into the sky at the gigantic wandering planet racing ever nearer as a deadly projectile. It was only a question of time before the forces of the cosmos would unfurl their monstrous powers. In the night of the third day after the Destroyer had broken into the orbital paths of the planets — it must have been shortly after midnight — the cosmic wanderer penetrated the elliptical path of the sixth planet. Causing violent cosmic storms, it thrust this planet several units out of its orbital direction and brought it onto a dangerous course towards the sun. Full of horror and fright, the people fled in great numbers into the wide-open flat lands that covered the planet. But the unleashed forces of nature were stronger than their will to live of these human beings. Two-thirds of the humanity residing there were killed by the unleashed inferno of nature. Raging waters ripped away large parts of the continents, while immense areas were buried beneath the red-hot lava of exploding volcanoes and reduced to ashes. The daily rotation time of the planet doubled and the planet orbited the sun in the opposite direction. Because of the cosmic devastation, the survivors were forced to start from the beginning — devoid of all culture — set back into a primitive time of origin. The Destroyer raced further through the system, spreading hell, death and destruction. As a next target, it crossed the orbit of the fifth planet — a world that was on the verge of creating life. This planet was fortunately too far away from the inter- section point to be seriously damaged. Except for mighty storms and smaller quakes on land and water, there were no considerable occurrences worth men- tioning. But the system's fourth planet was to find its destruction in a battle of the worlds. As the smallest of all planets, it stoically traveled its course, crossing and confronting the flight path of the wanderer, as if precalculated. And that is precisely what happened; it came into the irresistible destructive force of the giant. Like wild monsters, the two raced towards one another — a giant and a dwarf planet. But before they collided with one another, violent explosions ripped apart the lifeless, dead dwarf planet. Its fragments were catapulted into the endless expanses of the universe, where they were trapped as shooting stars or meteors by the gravitational forces of other star systems and ultimately burned out in their atmospheres. Other parts of the dwarf planet were pulled into the sun and atomized. Others were pulled into the Destroyer and became part of it.

The Birth of Our Moon

After this long preliminary story, we have finally come to the actual origin of our moon. In the aforementioned explosion of the dwarf planet, something else hap- pened. Half of the dwarf planet, bursting apart, was catapulted into the universe like a giant fist and shot on its wearisome path toward a very distant destination. The heavenly body came a number of times within the range of several suns on its flight path. Through its travels, it underwent a change in form as it was shaken, struck by meteors and shooting stars. After a few centuries, it took on a jagged but rounded form. The surface was deserted and bare and covered with gigantic, deep craters. Due to the forces of various star systems, its velocity gradually slowed down; it changed its course a number of times until it finally was attracted by the sun of our SOL System and, thus, was brought into its present orbital cycle. As a dark, dead planet, it passed through all the planetary paths of the outer rings of our SOL System without causing any damage. Not until reaching the inner rings did it collide with several planetoids, which only tore deep craters into it. This caused it to slightly change its course yet another time with the consequence that it was driven into an orbit parallel with the third planet of our SOL System, which at that time was already producing its first primitive life. This planet was covered with great oceans and thick primeval forests, deadly yet fantastic. From that point on, only thirty-four days passed before the invader caught up with the planet. The forces of the planet were enough to entrap the dwarf invader and caused it to orbit in an elliptical path. And from that time on, it has orbited around the earth — as our Moon.

What the Pleiadians Are Not Allowed To Do

The Pleiadians have, thankfully, made a great deal of valuable information avail- able to us, which represents a great help for us. Nevertheless, their helpfulness also has its limits because of the laws and commandments of Creation, even if some of us, discontented, shake our heads due to a lack of understanding. It is often very difficult for us earth people to understand and accept certain ideas if we think our humanity (as we falsely understand it) is questioned or even maligned. And because of this false understanding, an interference in the course of nature occurs through which the self-regulating balance is dangerously disturbed.

In nature, everything is balanced so that degeneracies (in both a positive and negative sense) are inevitably eliminated. Only among us earth people has this self-regulation been omitted so that, for example, a hopeless overpopulation could occur.

As helpful and necessary as Pleiadian assistance may be, they are not permitted to exceed a certain limit. The Pleiadians correctly obey the natural laws. In accordance with this, they are also not allowed to become involved in our affairs beyond a given extent. Every human being and all of humanity have a prescribed evolution, from beginning to end, from a state of absolute ignorance to the highest perfection. On this path of development, not a single step may normally be left out.

When a more highly developed race comes across a lower one, then it may convey only as much knowledge as the latter can deal with and process in order to advance its evolution and, under certain circumstances, even to accelerate it. An advanced civilization is never permitted to reveal knowledge which the recipient race cannot yet handle. Take children in first grade to whom you would like to teach algebra. Since they are lacking the necessary prerequisites, they would be totally overwhelmed by any attempt to teach them such advanced concepts. It is similar with our extraterrestrial teachers. The Pleiadians have always conveyed to us as much information as they feel they can take responsibility for, and in doing so, have probably often gone to the outermost limits of what is possible. Semjase once made the following statement on the topic of interference: "We do not have the right to influence and accelerate human evolution beyond what is permissible by the laws and commandments of Creation and in accordance with the respective evolutionary level of a life form. Since every life form is justified to think and act according to its own free estimation and according to its own arrangement, we are not permitted to exercise any forcible influences if these are not life-essential. We may, therefore, only be active as teachers."

Are Extraterrestrials Active in Positions of Our Government?

Billy posed the following question in one of the contact conversations:

> **BILLY:** It was recently explained to me that extraterrestrial intelligences are active in various governments of our earth and could even be permanently employed. Is there any truth to this matter; should any credence be given to this information?
>
> **PTAAH:** You can call such things fairy-tales. If this information were the truth, peace would have come to earth long ago and the earthly humanity would have been taught the truth through their governments, . Since we extraterrestrials have no right to forcibly interfere in earthly matters, we must restrict ourselves to the extent that we select earth people in order to have our knowledge conveyed through them. If we had the right to interfere to the extent of being permitted to work in government positions, we would be able to reveal ourselves publicly. We then would have no need to fear that we might be harmed by any governments, military, criminals, etc.

BILLY: It is said that these extraterrestrials secretly and anonymously play a part directly or indirectly in government positions.

PTAAH: That is also not true, which your very own logic can confirm. If that were actually so, then within a matter of days, our ships would no longer be pursued by any authorities, government or military powers. We indeed possess all possibilities of nipping such actions in the bud, and would do so if we were working in any government positions.

Why the Pleiadians Do Not Help Us Financially

At the time when the Semjase Silver Star Center was being constructed in Hinter-schmidrüti in 1975, Billy and the existing group had insurmountable difficulties in overcoming all the pending problems. Although most of the financial misery during the first years has improved substantially as time has passed, we are still far from being free of financial worries. It still takes considerable effort to pay for all the necessary purchases and make ends meet without going into much debt.

The question has often been asked why the Pleiadians do not help us out financially, although it would be very easy for them to do so. Besides, for example, they could certainly influence various gambling games and the like, through which quite substantial profits could be made.

In regard to this, I would like to quote Semjase's explanations about this subject in the year 1975:

SEMJASE: Earth man should consider that, first of all, we have nothing which compares to a means of payment as is customary and commonly practiced on earth. Even if we wanted to, we could not provide you with the financial means that you call money, because we have no such goods at our disposal. We shall never influence gambling games and so forth, because they are of exceedingly malicious value. A third important point to mention is that we do not want to let ourselves be provoked into talking and questions. The earth is your home and not ours. If we are here and want to help the earth people in spiritual and other areas of development, that is a commitment we have made and we shall not allow ourselves to be influenced by the orders of earth people. Our task is a voluntary commitment.

This is our side, and now comes your side — earth people have to make an effort and contribute their own finances. This means that they must also voluntarily make the commitment to shoulder certain things on their own. It is completely wrong for them to think that they can only demand help and goodness without also contributing to this help. earth people must learn that their selfishness and their boundless egoism are completely out of place and have no justification whatsoever. Therefore, if earth people are to be helped, they also have to contribute their part to this help. According to your values, their part consists of procuring the necessary capital and accomplishing all necessary work. If earth people believe they can only take and give nothing in return, they are on an unrealistic course. They will only be capable of overcoming their evil egoism when it has become clear that two opposing factors create a unit. In other words, that giving and taking must be joined together to form a unit. If we convey spiritual goods and knowledge, and so forth, then it is your duty to process these goods and knowledge and also to contribute your fair share of the work in order to attain the whole. Therefore, if earth people think and act illogically according to the motto that taking is more blessed than giving, they will never be free from their evil egoism. And earth people are egoistic, both individually and collectively, which is why exploitation is very widespread in your world.

And on another occasion, Semjase stated the following:

SEMJASE: We unfortunately are unable to provide financial help from our side, but you can count on our advice in every other matter. We shall give you advice on the construction of the Semjase Silver Star Center and all other things. If we were willing to help financially, we would be conjuring up grave danger. Such help of this nature would only mean that the individuals (of the group) would no longer do their utmost to accomplish their purpose and goal. Their fighting spirit would be paralyzed and everything would ultimately be left up to us in the steady hope that we would definitely help out in the case of failure! You, however, live in a world different from ours and have to remain fit for action as individuals. This can only be done if you have to fight out your own earthly concerns on your own. You have to stand on your own two feet financially with regard to achieving your objectives, including building the Center, and you have to fight hard for everything you get. Only in this way, as you [Billy] know from your own work, can the necessary success be achieved, and then every individual involved is connected and is a part of this whole.

I hope that these two explanations are sufficient for all those who wonder why the Pleiadians do not lend us a helping hand in financial matters, not even when our group is up to its neck in difficulties.

Why the Pleiadians Do Not Prevent Wars

The question heard everywhere is: Why do the extraterrestrials or the Pleiadians, in particular, not intervene when earth people bitterly fight and slaughter each other in terrible wars?

Many people simply do not understand why the Pleiadians do not make short work of stopping the wars and creating peace and order, when they have every possible means to do so.

I would now like to relate JHWH Ptaah's comment on this matter during a conversation with Billy:

PTAAH: Interventions are only permitted if recognizable catastrophes of a galactic or intergalactic scope emerge.
BILLY: Does that mean if a world could be completely destroyed or annihilated by its inhabitants, and if the entire system or even the galaxy were endangered by them?
PTAAH: You know the facts very accurately. Every life form must go the way of its own evolution, even if it leads over the path of self-destruction.
BILLY: That sounds somewhat raw and perhaps even barbaric. It's quite clear to me, because it is a law that is also anchored in nature. Whatever degenerates in a negative form will be destroyed because it can no longer endanger good life.
PTAAH: That is correct. You know this law quite accurately. Only by observing these laws can life be guaranteed. It is a malicious and false humaneness if degenerated life is permitted to continue in a form that can become even more degenerate. An elimination represents the only correct obedience of the law of conservation.

Why the Method of Healing Cancer is Not Revealed
An answer by the Pleiadians:

> **PLEIADIANS:** Earth man, individually, must work for the necessary knowledge about these truths because the knowledge will grow from within, and only then will he be able to understand many things and thereby learn the correct forms of action. Were we to reveal this knowledge to them, we would be handing earth people a means which they, in turn, would use for destruction and annihilation, because the knowledge to fight this disease contains many forces and too much power for us to simply reveal and then be responsible for. It is still too early for earth people to possess this knowledge. Only after continued and progressive evolution will they be able to put themselves into the proper place for this knowledge with all of its strength and power and use it moderately and according to the laws and commandments of Creation, and not use it in a negative way.

Special Actions For the Earth Population

As already reported in *Chapter 2 (Cosmic Alliances and Organization for Public Order)*, the extraterrestrials have the right only in very special emergencies to forcibly intervene in the destiny of any civilization. According to a commandment of Creation, the free will of every human life form must be respected and remain untouched even if this freedom is misused for harmful actions. Not until a certain limit is exceeded may intervention take place by making use of what is referred to as "logical force." *(See ~ Chapter 13: Attacks of the Giza Intelligence)*

Lucky Once Again

Not all human life forms are so peacefully minded as the Pleiadians and their allies. Unfortunately, there are also very unpleasant subjects who still live in a dreadful and degenerate barbarism. These inhumane creatures have killed all of their feelings in the course of their evolution. They think and act only in a materialistic way. Unless they manage to remove this negative degeneration, they will die out one day and eliminate themselves. Meanwhile, they pose a tremendous danger, especially for all those who are inferior to them in military power. We should be on guard against them, because they often fight and destroy everything that crosses their path. Such creatures also do not shy away from eliminating entire planets or leading their inhabitants into barbarous servitude as slaves. This may sound like a vision out of a horror film, but it corresponds to reality. Such a malicious punitive action from cosmic space would have happened to us earth people if the Pleiadians and their allies had not intervened at the right time. The population of 16 inhabited planets was in search of new, suitable living space because their system was close to destruction. Their three existing suns had apparently served their time. The vital sunrays were no longer able to fulfill their function to the extent necessary. The inhabitants, therefore, had no other alternative but to look for new habitable planets. These emigrants had taken various planets into consideration for their resettlement and our earth was among them. Whoever thinks that they merely wanted to occupy our already overpopulated earth in order to live here is grossly mistaken. It was planned, instead, that the entire population of earth, with kith and kin, would be slaughtered in the truest sense of the word. The fact that this planned global massacre did not take place we owe to our extraterrestrial friends. With tremendous effort, the Pleiadians and their helpers took care that these emigrants were resettled on other habitable planets.

One can only heave a sigh of relief in amazement and think "lucky once again." This striking example probably shows some of the dangers from cosmic space that have recently been lying in wait for us. Consequently, this matter should by no means be taken lightly. All of us on earth should therefore closely join together in united forces (without the help of extraterrestrials) in order to defend ourselves against such threats.

Warding Off a Cosmic Catastrophe

The use of so-called logical force is also justified if danger arises through the use of certain atomic weapons. Not only the planet on which the atomic war is conducted but the entire solar system, also, could be destroyed by a chain reaction. This, in turn, could cause an even greater cosmic catastrophe.

The greatest danger of unleashing a worldwide atomic war on our earth existed up to the end of 1974. Since the earth is located at a delicate point in our galaxy (as explained in *Chapter 12*... not in one of the spiral arms but on the outermost edge outside of the spiral arm), the destruction of the earth globe could destroy the entire space and time continuum. Under certain circumstances, the aftermath of a chain reaction could trigger the dreadful occurrence of a cosmic catastrophe.

Through unspeakably wearisome, painstaking and complicated measures, this already- provoked disaster was luckily prevented. This tremendously difficult task — according to Asket[84] and the Pleiadians, the most difficult mission ever to take place in the history of this universe — was carried out and successfully mastered by Asket and her assistants of the DAL Universe.

But who could possibly know that? It happened, so to speak, behind the scenes, and earth people had not the slightest notion about it.

In principle, the extraterrestrials are not obligated to help us in every crisis. During local conflicts, wars, natural catastrophes, and so forth, such an unjustified request is absolutely out of the question. This especially goes for the great mess we ultimately got ourselves into. ("You must drink the spoiled soup as you have brewed it.") And all reports that extraterrestrial spacecraft have surrounded the earth and are merely waiting until they have to evacuate us are entirely unfounded. People are absolutely unrealistic. Help in the form of a large-scale evacuation is not to be expected unless, of course, a special case should occur.

Due to the close bond with the destiny of earth, in great probability the Pleiadians would not allow the earth population to be rotted out to the point that not a single person were left. In such an extreme case, they would possibly be allowed to take special actions to prevent the total extinction of mankind on earth.

What Every Man Can Contribute to World Peace

War actions in all imaginable gradations and variations, bloody rebellions, terrorist attacks, kidnappings with terrible torturing, etc. have become such daily occurrences that we almost have become accustomed to them.

Based on the disagreeable fact that human rights in numerous countries are still totally disregarded, it is understandable if the dearest wish of countless victims is nothing more than to live in peace and quiet. And beside a few exceptions, all of us wish a permanent peace might finally come to the entire earth.

All of this is fine and good, but this pious wish will be fulfilled only if every single person makes his own contribution within reasonable bounds. Unfortunately, I can already hear the well-known objections of skeptics ringing in my ears. First of all, skeptics are of the rock-hard conviction that armed conflicts can never be brought under control on earth. They think that there have always been wars on earth and there shall always be wars in all future times. Their second objection, which is heard even more often, is that they cannot imagine that a simple citizen could be capable of contributing to world peace. If we look back on the history of earth, it would be very easy to gain the impression that earth people cannot get along without war. This opinion is not correct; because it is only a question of time before this behavior opposing the law of Creation on earth will forever become a part of the past. In the end, it is dead certain that it is entirely up to us, or to be more precise, up to every single one of us.

Billy explained it very clearly:

BILLY: World peace always begins in small ways. The people of earth can never create peace if they wage war in their own house and in their own personal surroundings. They must first create peace there and within themselves and then with their friends, relatives and acquaintances, and in their daily encounters in their profession and in their spare time. Efforts toward world peace must begin in small circles and then continue in an outward expansion. This requires a unification in small ways without regard to the world situation and/or insidious occurrences.

Unfortunately, more and more statesmen and other leaders are appearing on the scene who attempt to stir up one nation against the other and involve them in bloody feuds by using propaganda and warmongering methods of education.

BILLY: In this connection, man must be his own best friend and must close his ears to the siren songs of the warmongers, because without men who allow themselves to be instigated, there can be no instigation and, therefore, no wars either. Not until man has cleared these hurdles within himself can he start to carry peace out into the world.

Already in 1984, the Pleiadians showed us a splendid way of doing this and every sensible man could do it if he is capable of mustering a certain portion of good will. It has to do with an absolutely unique peace meditation, instructions about which have been conveyed to us by the Pleiadians and which can be obtained from FIGU.

In order to correctly understand the meaning and purpose of our Peace Meditation, it is necessary to go somewhat further back in time.

First of all, I would like to describe a situation that happened several years ago. In the Voice of the Aquarian Age (No. 52, page 8), I wrote the following: "It was in 1984 when Billy received the staggering news in the course of a contact conversation with Quetzal that we would definitely have to bury our hopes of preventing World War III. Prophecies from various sources had indicated this pending catastrophe for a long time and in this respect, the prophecies Billy received from the Petale spirit plane in the autumn of 1981 are being fulfilled. In general, they state: As a result of war actions, natural catastrophes, unknown diseases, starvation, epidemics, etc., no less than two-thirds of the entire earth humanity will be destroyed, and Central Europe, for example, will have almost no chance of surviving at all."

CHAPTER 14 ⚬ What Do the Extraterrestrials Want Here on Earth?

In contrast to his custom of publishing no dates and times or only encoded dates and times of anticipated events, Billy shocked us for once with precise data. According to his own calculations, World War III was to begin on April 25, 1998. But Billy did not consider an unknown time factor in his otherwise absolutely correct calculations. According to Quetzal's research, this date was moved ahead a few years. Therefore, the dismal prognosis looked as if World War III would occur in the year 1984.

As suggested by the Pleiadians, FIGU began the Peace Meditation the same year (1984), with the objective to at least lessen World War III in its brutality and to postpone it for several years.

In this connection, the following statement, among others, has been heard:

> What of it? I have to die one way or another — in the worst case, maybe a little sooner than expected. And when it has happened, at least it is behind me and nothing more can happen to me. (Actually to be pitied are only the survivors, who will have to vegetate along under the most miserable of conditions and struggle to rebuild everything anew out of the rubble.)

I would like to make the following comment to that: Whoever thinks that everything is over after dying as a result of war is mightily mistaken. Exactly the opposite is the case. If a person prematurely loses his life, therefore losing part of his predestined life span, he must make up for the number of lost years according to the law of incarnation by being born one more time than otherwise would be necessary. Such an out-of-turn rebirth can take place shortly after death — in such a case as this, perhaps even before the end of the world war or shortly thereafter. Evidently, there can no longer be talk of having left everything behind by dying.

What the Peace Meditation has effectively brought us, (which has been practiced since 1984), we can proudly answer — is an "astonishing success." According to the statement of JHWH Ptaah, the intensified efforts of some governments and countless individuals towards peace can be entirely traced back to our Peace Meditation.

What has happened in Eastern Europe, alone due to the initiative of Mikhail Gorbachev, would not have been considered possible in recent years by anyone. The fact that World War III has become questionable in the meantime speaks clearly enough for itself.

Of course, credit for this success by no means belongs only to our group and about 3,400 helpers throughout the earth, but also to the extraterrestrials, without whose help our small group would have had no chance of causing such an earth-shaking transformation in such a short time. After all, there are as many as 511 million Pleiadians (that means all inhabitants of the planet Erra, except for the small children), as well as around 3 billion of their allies who regularly support us in our Peace Meditation. And at this time, it is opportune to express our sincere thanks to the 3.5 billion extraterrestrial helpers. Thanks and appreciation should also go to all earth people who have been working in a sensible manner for world peace and who continue to do so.

Unfortunately, I cannot get around pointing out something which, understandably, will not be heard gladly by many well-meaning people who, with noble intentions, make futile attempts at world peace with gigantic demonstrations, incorrect meditations and the like. Although, their efforts are made for a well-intended purpose , they are nonetheless completely ineffective, according to the Pleiadians, because they do not accomplish one iota of what they are actually supposed to achieve.

It perhaps sounds presumptuous, but nothing changes the fact that our Peace Meditation is the only effective means of promoting world-wide peace efforts.

According to Ptaah's explanations, all other peace meditations are useless because the necessary knowledge about the context is lacking, which is needed to achieve effective results. Although it is correct that positive thoughts produce equivalent effects, but as far as they are specifically related to peace among the earth population, this does not hold true. Directly linked to the Peace Meditations is a measure which had been taken by the old Lyrians when they resided earlier here on earth. To promote world peace, they undertook a unique programming of a determined proverb in the memory banks of the earth's atmosphere. This determined proverb, sworn by oath and bound by codex, is a programmed impulse-laden determination sentence from the old-Lyrian language which goes as follows: "Salome gam nan ben Urda — gan njber asala Hesporona." (Peace [in wisdom] be on earth and among all creatures.)[84]

It works in the following way: Whenever this Lyrian sentence is thought or spoken correctly, the thought impulses of the sentence reach inside the mentioned memory bank. These thought frequencies automatically release peace impulses that affect all the people of earth. The impulses received by human beings are correctly understood and made effective in this sense – even if only in subconscious manner.

The method of transmission of thought impulses by our extraterrestrial helpers is tremendously long and also somewhat more complicated, but distance plays no hindering role, no matter how great the distance may be. I emphasize once again: This regulation exclusively pertains to the Lyrian sentence for the promotion of world peace!

In view of the substantially improved political situation of the world, the next question is whether the announced prophecies in relation to the outbreak of World War III are still valid or not. Contrary to predictions of the future, which come to pass one hundred percent, prophecies are basically understood as warnings and by no means must come to pass if man seriously heeds the warning and changes his behavior accordingly.

As far as the catastrophe of World War III is concerned, everything is open-ended at the present time. Excellent progress has undoubtedly been made on the rugged path to world peace, but the danger of World War III is only stopped for the time being and by no means prevented. What we will not be spared with seeming certainty is a world fire, which can and will happen in the form of terrible natural catastrophes (earthquakes, floods, periods of drought, starvation, dying forests, environmental catastrophes, incurable diseases and epidemics, world economic crises, and so forth). Local wars, drug-related criminality and similar, unpleasant events cannot be eliminated from one day to the next, which is quite obvious.

According to Ptaah's statements, more or less serious setbacks are also expected in the freedom efforts of the now-dissolved Eastern Block countries. A great deal of what has already been accomplished will most likely be destroyed. With great probability, everywhere in those regions where the population is not yet mature enough to sustain their newly won freedom, the people will behave so irrationally that their governments will be left with no alternative but to tighten the reigns again and take unpopular actions. Joined with this are the completely unlawful interferences and covert influences by western nations and their secret services. Altogether, these can lead to bloody conflicts, causing a chain reaction, which finally brings on the outbreak of a global war. So the danger of World War III is, unfortunately, by no means prevented.

Should it happen that positive forces gain the upper hand to accelerate and fortify the peace process world-wide, then there is still a justified hope of preventing the great tumult in the form of a world-wide war. Our situation is therefore not entirely hopeless, and with united forces, we should actually be able to accomplish this feat.

However, it will be necessary for the perpetual skeptics and know-it-alls to let themselves be taught by the Pleiadians, who are truly better informed than we. And the Pleiadians guarantee us unmistakably that: "The only correct and effective aid in attaining a permanent world peace is and shall remain the Peace Meditation," as we have done according to the commendable instructions of the Pleiadians with the help of 3.5 billion extraterrestrial friends. Whoever feels addressed and would earnestly like to take part in the promotion of world peace should join our Peace Meditation, better today than tomorrow, because it, alone, guarantees us the very last chance.

Footnotes

82 ▪ The abduction account of Betty and Barney Hill is explained in the book 'The Interrupted Journey"

83 ▪ Asket – Billy had personal and telepathic contacts with Asket for eleven years. The Pleiadians and Asket's people have the same origin, which means they were originally at home in the Lyra and Vega Systems. The old Lyrians and Vegans spread throughout the entire universe in the course of millions of years and even into the neighboring DAL Universe.

84 ▪ The "Salome Meditation" is performed by many people around the world each month. They gather at a specific time and day depending on which dateline they live so that the meditation is experienced concurrently.

CHAPTER 15

Special Updates and Recent Developments

Since the debut of the book, *And Still They Fly!* (German version) in 1991, the UFO phenomena has become remarkably integrated into the public arena. The idea of extraterrestrials visiting our planet is now commonplace and relatively a global notion. These otherworldly icons have permeated many movies produced in Hollywood. And it is not uncommon these days to see a flying saucer with aliens inside in commercials trying to sell us cars or breakfast cereals!

Regardless of how many times the world powers (including the media) have tried to deceive the public about the UFO phenomena, people from around the world and all walks of life continue to see strange things in the sky. They feel the deep truth that we are not alone in the universe.

As for Billy Meier, the Swiss extraterrestrial contactee, a great deal of controversy and intrigue has continued to swirl around him. For this English edition, I have added a new chapter to "fill the reader in," so to speak, about all the new goings-on with Billy and his mission. Some of the following reports will clarify old ones, while others may well surprise you. One might think that after all these years, the life and times of Billy Meier would "go silently into the night," but such has not happened as you will discover.

The Pleiadian/Plejaren Withdrawal From Earth

At the end of January 1995, according to plan, the Pleiadians/Plejaren from planet Erra and their confederates withdrew completely from our earth. This meant that the three secret stations on this planet (in Switzerland, North America, and Asia), previously inhabited continually by approximately one dozen extraterrestrial races since January 28, 1975, were not only vacated but completely eliminated. Nothing remained, therefore, that would indicate the former presence of these stations. During the major contact period between 1975 and 1988, the total number of extraterrestrials stationed at the aforementioned sites amounted to no fewer than 2,862 individuals.

The Pleiadians/Plejaren took their withdrawal as an opportunity to inform us earth people of several facts about which they had remained silent until then, or which they were not permitted to share with the general public. With their departure, they could also lift, among other things, the secret of their true identity, namely, that they do not at all refer to themselves as Pleiadians, as we earth people have generally called them for the past 20 years. Instead, they call themselves "Plejaren" [Play-YAR-en] after their star system, which is known as "Plejares."

This fact was intentionally kept secret from us earth people until the withdrawal of the Plejaren in order to uncover a particular hoax. The above factors take the wind from the sails of all frauds, charlatans and liars who claim they maintain physical or telepathic contact with the Plejaren. "Pleiadians" do not exist, only the Plejaren, as explained.

The Reason for the Withdrawal of the People of Erra and their Confederates

According to Jshwjsh Ptaah, the main reason for the final departure by the Errans and their confederates must continue to remain a secret, at least for the time being. Ptaah, however, presented several other clarifications regarding this subject:

It can now be told that our extraterrestrial friends completely fulfilled their voluntary assignment on our planet. Their departure was timely and took place as planned.

The author's comments: The major objective of the Plejaren was to provide us with instructions, information, and similar material that would advance our spiritual evolution by attempting to direct us earth people back onto the proper path of truth which, unfortunately, we abandoned a long time ago.

Through their contactee, Billy Meier, the Plejaren transmitted the following to earthman: Ancient esoteric wisdom, the true laws and commandments of Creation, and valuable guidelines for an appropriate lifestyle.

Another assignment was to make the earth population aware of the so-called UFO phenomenon in which Billy Meier played the most significant role. Ptaah has stated that the worldwide UFO controversy really gained momentum only through Billy's efforts, which prompted ufologists and various scientists, official agencies, governments, and the military, to seriously begin investigating this topic — although the general public is normally not aware of this. Indeed, this fact is usually vehemently denied by the powers that rule. On February 3, 1995, Ptaah expressed his appreciation to Billy Meier and added that Billy truly had to struggle to earn this "thank you," considering all the hardships thrust upon his shoulders. Such strife included the detrimental effect on Billy's health, the defamations, insults, assassination attempts, hateful tirades, and many other similar matters (e.g., adversities within his own family…)

PTAAH: ... of course it was inevitable that envious and deceptive individuals, along with hoaxers who falsified your photographs and movie footage, would come on the scene in an effort to make you look preposterous and to destroy the work of your Mission. Those people were eager, therefore, to steal your original negatives and movie footage — a relatively easy feat, of course, because of your trusting nature. They copied and recopied your material countless time and falsified your material with the aid of montages and other manipulations, creating the impression that you had used trick photography and photomontages. Included in the scenario were your films and photo negatives, which these unscrupulous characters also retouched and marked with lines, making them appear to be threads, strings, wires or similar material from which items could be suspended. These altered films and photos were later disseminated throughout the world. In fact, forged rolls of film and negatives were given to you without your ever becoming distrustful or suspicious, as you implicitly trusted those who subsequently deceived and discredited you.

Ultimately, the Plejaren withdrawal is linked to future events that had been predicted and with which they are not permitted to interfere in any way. Billy further asked Ptaah.

BILLY: What about your status as the JHWH for this planet. Will your status also terminate with the completion of your assigned objectives?

Until recently, JHWH Ptaah had been in charge of three planets: earth, Erra and Alatides in the Harkonen System.

PTAAH: Well yes, I must turn to other tasks.
BILLY: What a shame. That means earth will now be without an JHWH.
PTAAH: This is not quite accurate, for there still exist descendants of the old gods who will make themselves known. However, I can only share this information with you in confidence, if you are interested.

The author's comments: With these "gods," Ptaah alluded to extraterrestrials who had settled on earth in prehistoric times and who, unlawfully, had themselves revered as creators, while the people on earth presumed that they were gods.

What Consequences Does the Withdrawal Bring?

Although Plejaren assistance will now be evident only in a very limited way, nonetheless, we may benefit in the following areas through their support:

- Their telepathic and personal contacts with Billy Meier will continue until his death, although not at their former pace. (Meier had an average of four personal contacts annually between November 1989 and January 1995.)

- Fortunately, the extraterrestrials' support for the peace meditation has not waned in any way.

- Likewise, with the aid of appropriate instrumentation, impulse contacts will continue, influencing approximately 31,000 earth people. Scientists, physicians, journalists, movie producers and others will continue to receive suitable impulses, disbursed in an acceptable dosage and manner, to advance the evolutionary development of the earth population. In this way, timely and essential developments will be fostered. These advancements will not occur in great clusters, in order to avoid skipping even one step of the evolutionary process. Impulses directed toward science fiction authors or movie producers, respectively, are intended to prepare us earth people for future events.

- Completely withdrawn, with just a few exceptions, were the 7,000 or more unmanned telemeter disks that used to orbit the globe 24-hours-a-day to perform a multitude of reconnaissance assignments. Several of these flying objects still continue, however, to monitor and register important events on this planet. Furthermore, earth continues to be visited daily by two manned Plejaren spacecraft as part of a regular reconnaissance program. The Plejaren remain intensely interested in events transpiring on our planet; above all, they wish to keep abreast of all facets pertaining to the Mission.

After 20 years of secrecy, and as part of their withdrawal, the extraterrestrials officially acknowledged something of which initiated earth people had been aware of for some time, although they were not 100 percent certain. They confirmed the fact that extraterrestrial flying objects had crashed, or made emergency landings, in various countries on earth and that these objects and their dead or nearly dead passengers had been recovered — at all times under the strictest secrecy, to be sure! Ptaah also stated that very conclusive and genuine evidence for the existence of extraterrestrials is held under lock and key — for whatever reason — by governments, military agencies, and secret services who want to prevent the general public from finding out the truth. Sooner or later, however, the secrecy-mongers will be forced to relinquish their secret documents and evidence because the now triggered UFO controversy will endure. These agencies are currently placing an even greater emphasis on hiding the truth through every possible illegal means because certain groups foresee their prospects vanishing. Data provided by the Plejaren reveals that large numbers of flying objects of earthly origin exist in many countries. These objects have a variety of shapes and are not necessarily disk-shaped at all.

An Announcement from Billy:

During my latest contact conversation with Ptaah, some extremely unpleasant facts came to light regarding the two Asket and Nera photographs which, until now, had been indexed in the FIGU photo albums and sold under this "Asket and Nera" caption. Unfortunately, during my conversation with Ptaah, he revealed that the two women depicted on the photos are not Asket and Nera from the DAL Universe, but two American look-alikes, as Ptaah had stated in the 39th Contact of 1975. These photos are malicious forgeries and were switched upon the order of and in collaboration with the "Men in Black." The related, specific explanations can be gleaned from excerpts of the latest contact report

Asket and Nera Photos: An Extremely Unpleasant Matter!

Fig 15-1
Is this a photo of Asket and Nera?

Fig 15-2
Is this a photo of Asket or a guest of a variety show?

that follows below, which will serve to clarify the situation for all friends, members, acquaintances, and interested parties as to the connections and contemptible machinations of the "Men in Black" and their hired helpers. In addition, I would like to mention that the said three photographs with the (FIGU designated) numbers #109, #110, #111 will not be removed from our photo selection. (It is unfortunate that only two pictures are mentioned in the contact report, but #109 was simply not good enough for distribution.) Instead they will receive a new caption stating that the two young women in the photograph are American look-alikes of Asket and Nera who resemble the originals so much that it is practically impossible for anyone to tell them apart — except for the ladies themselves. Here, then, are excerpts from the contact report dated May 14, 1998.

Billy

From *Contact Report #264: Thursday, May 14, 1998, 12:55 a.m.*

PTAAH: Do not hesitate to tell me what you have to say.

BILLY: OK, fine: Once again, something is preoccupying me that I cannot understand. It is linked to conspiracies and defamations which, by and large, don't bother me, but they raise several questions. You are familiar with that schemer and defamer (Kal K.) Korff and this Luc Bürgin. Together, they recently video-taped an interview with my dear ex-wife which they intend to disseminate worldwide in July, apparently with an explanation or exposé regarding the two photos of Asket and Nera that I allegedly photographed from a television set, and which are said not to be Asket and Nera but two American Asket/Nera look-alikes. You mentioned them yourself in *Contact 39* when you stated that two young women live in America who work in the same job, and are almost exact doubles of Asket and Nera.

PTAAH: The two photographs also show the two look-alikes from America.

BILLY: How do you mean that? I personally took the pictures of Asket and Nera.

PTAAH: This is a fact. However, the problem is that you never received the original photographs, which would have been printed from your original negatives.

BILLY: I don't understand?

PTAAH: Are you really unable to remember the incident?

BILLY: What am I supposed to remember?

PTAAH: Quetzal's and my visit on February 3, 1985, when we explained to you a few of the connections as they pertained to the photographs you just mentioned.

BILLY: I have no recollection of this. What happened at that time?

PTAAH: We revealed to you then that you had received forged pictures which depict neither Asket nor Nera.

BILLY: Now I don't understand anything anymore.

PTAAH: Oh, now I see. You really have forgotten everything, and with certainty this is linked to your life-threatening condition at the time, including your partial amnesia. That is why you are unable to remember many of these things.

BILLY: Please don't keep me in suspense now.

PTAAH: At the time we did not wish to deal with these matters on a public level.

BILLY: But I feel that this issue must be addressed if I hold forged Asket/Nera photographs, which I have been selling with such a caption until now. If this is actually the case, they're really going to attack me viciously.

PTAAH: Well, it isn't really your fault. Blame must be directed toward your photographer. He allowed himself to be forced into such fraudulent action by a group of Men in Black, and in doing so, he betrayed you.

BILLY: I am familiar with that riffraff. One of them pursued my daughter, Gilgamesha, once when she was coming home from school. One of them chased her with a knife in his hand. When they couldn't catch her, the cowardly guys escaped in a large, black limousine.

PTAAH: I am familiar with the story. But hear now: It seems that I must again relate all the information to you, and this time in a way that brings it before the public, providing you wish to record this conversation later?

BILLY: For sure.

PTAAH: All right then: From the beginning of the contacts with us, you never allowed yourself to be intimidated by any of the schemes of the Men in Black, regardless of how despicable, dangerous, and indeed, life-threatening they were. As you simply laughed at their assassination attempts and always carried a weapon — with the appropriate gun license, I must add — the Men in Black, instead, resorted to making you look preposterous and highly questionable before the world. Because they were unable to get close enough to you, they aggressively forced people who worked with you, such as photographer S., to discredit you on a future, long-term basis. They coerced S. into forging the photographs you had taken with our permission. In other words, they made him completely forge or adulterate your pictures. Several times during your early contact period with us, your own films, which photographer S. developed and made prints for you, were substituted with totally different, adulterated films. Therefore, from the very beginning you received many counterfeit negatives and photographs or forged pictures. This is also what occurred with the film on which you photographed the images of Asket and Nera, and which you allegedly did receive back only after several months. But in reality what you received was, in fact, a product of the Men in Black who had discovered and photographed the doubles of Asket and Nera in America. These pictures were then processed and given to you by S. You, of course, believed they were the originals, but they were forgeries and deceptively similar to your own authentic photographs. For this reason you did not realize you had been defrauded, and neither did we. In fact, we were unaware of this deceit until the autumn of 1984 when we brought your photos to Asket, because she also wanted to have them. Of course, she noticed the deception immediately, and because of this, we began investigating the matter and discovered that the Men in Black were behind the entire scheme and they were those who had forced the photographer into their services. Due to their order, S. produced the forged photographs and handed them to you as if they were originals — whereupon you always assumed they were the actual photographs you had taken yourself. This was the case also with the pictures of Asket and Nera. With regard to these particular photos, we discovered that S. immediately submitted the film, you had handed to him for processing, to the

Men in Black, as people in your ufological circles call these black men. Within a few days they found and repeatedly photographed the Asket/Nera look-alikes in America, and this is how the two pictures with which you are familiar came into being and which were passed on to you. The Giza Intelligences somehow play a role in this matter also as they have done on other occasions, of which as you are well aware, although we were unable to clarify their exact association in this plot. Clearly, however, they negatively influenced a vast number of earth people by their telepathic impulses in an effort to harm, defame and even assassinate you, which they attempted several times — fortunately without success. Everything was done to make you and your mission appear preposterous; specifically, by accusing you of producing photographic forgeries. The Men in Black wield their impact even today, and so do the decade-old influences of the negative telepathic impulse machinations against you and your mission, which they intend to destroy. The impulses by these Giza Intelligences presumably affect all those people who are working against you and the mission with their schemes, defamations, and other negative machinations, although these individuals never realize they are being influenced by these impulses.

BILLY: What am I now going to do with the photos? Under these circumstances I can no longer use or sell them. Now I really feel like a crook after claiming they were photos of Asket and Nera.

PTAAH: You are not guilty in this matter. But you could simply continue selling them with a new caption explaining that the two ladies are American look-alikes of Asket and Nera.

BILLY: This scheme involving the Asket and Nera photos dates back to 1975 or so, a very long time ago. And yet, the consequences are only appearing now? That's what I call a long-term calculation. This is astounding. The situation actually deserves my respect. But why didn't we record this as part of a contact report? Then we could have openly clarified this matter much sooner.

PTAAH: Unfortunately, it could no longer be handled on your end. After your last contact with Quetzal on October 31, 1984, and after you had finished your OM book, your health was in such an appalling state that for several years you were closer to death than to life. For this reason you were incapable of jotting down the contact conversations. By November 17, 1989, your health and strength had finally improved to the point where you were able to record our conversations again in writing.

BILLY: How is it possible that I forgot all of this…

PTAAH: You know yourself how many things and facts you had to relearn and how many other things you were unable to relearn at all. Furthermore, your memory had been organically damaged, and this is the reason why it cannot be as active as it was previously. Just remember, the power and capabilities your consciousness possessed allowed you to accomplish those many astonishing feats.

BILLY: It is unfortunate, but that's the way it is, I know… But now I just remembered another question regarding the Men in Black and their machinations with the look-alike photos and the photographer: How could the Men in Black find the two American women so easily and quickly, and then photograph them in the right manner?

PTAAH: These Men in Black, as they are called because of the black clothing they constantly seem to wear, have always had access to unfathomable resources — or what normal people or citizens, rather, would consider them to be. It was a simple task for them to locate the two young artists. Once these extremely unscrupulous men set their mind to something, nothing remains hidden from them. The photos of these look-alikes, of whom I actually spoke during the 39th contact on December 3, 1975, were not taken in the presence of the two young women. Instead, their images were copied from movie footage to which the Men in Black had gained access. I believe this genre of film is called a revue. In any case, individual photographs were copied from it and, together with photographer S., they selected those that most closely resembled your own photos of Asket and Nera. This is how they were able to deceive you. The purpose of the entire matter was to create pictures of specific situations deceivingly similar to those pictures you had taken of Asket and Nera. The objective was for you to normally, and unsuspectingly, disseminate and sell these counterfeit, or rather forged, photographs of the two look-alikes to interested parties, believing them to be original pictures of Asket and Nera. This scenario was intended to make you look deceitful some day because they calculated that sooner or later one of your adversaries would examine these photographs and get to the bottom of the matter. The result would be that the forged Asket/Nera pictures in the so-called revue film would be recognized as the photos you were holding of those look-alikes. This was meant to provide the evidence for exposing you as a purported deceiver and make you and your story look preposterous and, subsequently, destroy your mission. All of this was thoroughly pre-programmed in 1975 by the Men in Black. They calculated that the appropriate photo sequences would be found in the near future — which seems to have happened now — and the photos would be fully exploited by your enemies soon afterwards. There is no doubt in our minds that the enemies against you and your mission are purely earthly beings under the influence of the long-term and still-active Giza impulses.

BILLY: Korff and Bürgin also?

PTAAH: Without any doubt.

BILLY: Now that you have brought up so much about the Men in Black, I have another question: Quetzal told me once that these men are also responsible for an assassination attempt on my life. Which attempt was that?

PTAAH: There was not only one attempt. Truthfully, eleven of the fourteen assassination attempts can be traced back to the Men in Black.

BILLY: So, you are saying that on February 3, 1985, you and Quetzal explained all of this to me about the so-called Asket/Nera photos, which truthfully depict the American doubles you had mentioned in the 39th contact? Well, unfortunately, I simply can't recall any of this, I have really forgotten it altogether. Now I want to ask you why you have not reminded me of these facts until now? If I had consciously absorbed this information, I would have removed the pictures from circulation and published the appropriate details in our quarterly publication, the Wassermannzeit.

PTAAH: For all these years we were not consciously aware that you had forgotten our explanations regarding these matters, otherwise we naturally would have pointed them out to you at the appropriate time.

Another Announcement from Billy...
Several New Assassination Attempts Against Billy Meier:
June 8th & 10th 1998

Two noteworthy dates once again, since on these two days someone attempted twice to change me from the living to the dead—probably in response to what I said in *Bulletin #16* and on the Internet regarding the seedy schemes of the "Men in Black" and the Asket-Nera photo forgeries. Kal K. Korff and Luc Bürgin both took negative positions against me again, as they believe they have to aggrandize and promote themselves as the alleged "debunkers of the Billy Meier hoax." To this end, they are not even hesitating to also exploit my confused, dear ex-wife Kalliope for their defamations. And I want it to be known that, because their openly defamatory remarks provoked my clarifications in *Bulletin #16* and on the Internet, they must bear some blame for the new assassination attempts that have been directed against me and my life. And all of this has taken place after several years of quietness in which no assaults were made on me.

Here then are the circumstances regarding the assaults: On June 8, 1998, at 4:40 p.m., I was walking on the premises of the Semjase Silver Star Center from the shed toward the charcoal pile and the Hinterschmidrüti storage area. I had just passed on my right the road sign banning vehicle traffic, and was even with a nearby red maple tree, when a shot suddenly rang out from the left. With the bang of the shot I felt the air move as the bullet whizzed past my forehead—at least this is how I interpreted the gentle breeze. — About 30 minutes later, when a few Center residents and I inspected the actual site of the shooting more closely, and after we had examined the immediate surroundings and beyond, we discovered the entry point of the bullet in the trunk of the red maple tree. The bullet was a 22 caliber. When I stood beside the tree my forehead was at the precise level of the bullet hole.

Unfortunately, we were unable to track down the individual who had fired the shot at me, because the assailant disappeared undetected while I rushed into the house to get my weapon so I would not be unprotected in the event of another attack. — The shot was heard also by Conny Wächter and Aroona, her daughter, who both stood about 30 meters (90 ft.) from me at the time. From her office, Eva Bieri also heard the shot ring out, as did Davide Turla, a Passive Group member, who was approximately 50 meters (150 ft.) away on the Schmidrüti Forest storage area. — I was in Conny Wächter's direct field of vision and she could, therefore, clearly see me. And yet, even she was unable to spot the assailant; but that was not surprising after all, because the three of us later ascertained that the person had been hiding in the dense foliage of the hillside bushes where the assailant could not be seen, although the individual was just 8 meters (24 ft.) away from me. It almost seems to me like a miracle that the bullet missed me at this short range, because it passed my forehead by a mere millimeter or two.

After this unsuccessful attempt, I thought the matter would be over for a while as was always the case before — but far from it. Only 28 hours later in the early morning hours of June 10, at 3:05 a.m., I was once more assaulted. This time the assailant used a cheap throwing-knife and apparently did not have much of a clue about handling such a weapon — to my own good fortune.

Silvano Lehmann, on guard duty that night, was standing below the parking lot near the garage across the open area as I approached him. Twice I heard some strange sounds along the wooded hillside. Although there was a moon in the sky that weakly illumined the parking lot and both Silvano and me, we could see nothing in the direction from where the unusual sounds had originated, as everything was enveloped in the deep shadows beneath the trees. As we listened for one, two or three minutes for any additional telltale sounds in the night, I stood on slightly higher ground than Silvano because I was on the sloped edge of the parking lot facing him. Suddenly I felt a powerful blow against my left kidney and heard a metallic clanging when something dropped on the ground to my left. With my flashlight I scanned the ground in hopes of locating what had hit me and then fallen down. Silvano and I could immediately see that it was a throwing-knife, obviously hurled at me by an inexperienced individual, because it struck me handle first, fortunately, in the kidney area (the knife had probably rotated on its axis as it jettisoned toward me). The pain from the impact was considerable, and it only abated slowly after lingering for several days. Had the knife missed me and continued on its track through the air, it certainly would have rotated again and struck Silvano squarely in the face, since he was standing slightly below me on the lower path, a mere one meter (3 ft.) away from me.

Although we immediately illuminated the dark hillside with our flashlights and quickly searched the trail there, we found nothing except the knife's sheath, which had inadvertently been dropped at the site. The knife-throwing assailant was obviously quicker in disappearing from the premises than we were in reaching his hideout, even though we had sprinted 10 meters (33 ft.) before we reached the trail. Ten meters also happens to be the distance across which the throwing knife had been hurled at me.

I can only state that I find it despicable and sad that somebody would attempt to eliminate the truth in this way. It matters not whether the "Men in Black" are behind these assassination attempts, as they usually would exploit an unstable human being of the earth to do their dirty work, or an assailant who was simply a confused 'Billy Meier' enemy. I strongly doubt the latter and tend to think that it was the scheming "Men in Black." After all, they perpetrated most of the assaults against my life. They did so in a manner whereby they influenced unstable people and forced them into following their commands. They themselves have no desire to execute their own dirty deeds, especially not with their own, highly developed weapons, the secret technology of which would be revealed. This is the last thing they would want because such information must remain a secret.

One way or another, in my opinion, the assailants are wretched fools who will pay an incredibly steep price in the future for taking chances, as they do, in this manner.

Billy

Prophecies and Predictions

(An informative clarification taken from a lecture by Guido Moosbrugger at the Burbank Hilton, Burbank, California: July 20, 1996.)

Prophecies are many times completely misjudged, particularly by people who are very religious. And they are of the erroneous assumption that prophecies are determinations or commandments by supernatural forces, or even by "god" forces. This, of course, is not the case under any circumstances because a prophecy is nothing more than an announcement or a pre-announcement of events to be expected in the future.

A prophecy is not intended to put any feelings of fear or panic into human beings. Rather, prophecies announce future negative events and are intended to serve as warnings. This offers human beings an opportunity to take the required countermeasures in order to greatly reduce or prevent the prophecies from taking place by their own hard work and efforts so that they are possibly averted.

And due to the fact that they are always warnings, as I have just mentioned, it would only be logical to assume that these are negative events that are being announced. It would be totally paradoxical to announce positive events and to want to influence them in a negative manner. Therefore, this explains why prophecies, without exception, contain negative announcements, because only the negative in an excessive form needs a change back to the normal positive state in order to balance everything again. Through the necessary positive influences of thoughts and actions, therefore, negative events can be prevented before they occur, thereby fulfilling the purpose of any prophecies.

True prophecies must never be presented in a text with detailed data regarding the time they are supposed to transpire. Certain hints and certain dates must be kept secret or can only be implied, so to speak, between the lines. There are several reasons behind this:

- Extremely detailed data could lead to fear and panic.

- Absolutely necessary evolutionary steps must not be skipped to evade unpleasant, harmful experiences. For instance, the evolutionary process would be incomplete if one did so.

- One very important and very serious reason why prophecies must not be made available in a completely clear form is that through precise and advance knowledge of certain facts, monumental destruction and catastrophes could be generated and they would be triggered by the excessive feelings of fear, hatred, envy and other such things of all the people who have become aware of the negative events that lie ahead.

- Another very serious reason is the fact that the majority of the earth population at this point is not capable of understanding, consciously assimilating and dealing with the full extent of a prophecy.

Many people believe they would be prepared to deal with such detailed prophecies, but it has been shown that most people would not be capable of handling the entailed knowledge. Therefore, coding must be used as a safety measure to avoid that the still unwise human being is not harmed in his or her consciousness by this premature information. Relatively few people are capable of mastering encodings of a text and to truthfully understand and handle them.

Of course, it is never the prophecies, or even the prophets themselves, who are producing these announced catastrophes, wars and evils of all type among humanity. The human beings themselves determine their own fate through denial, lack of knowledge and lack of obedience to or observation of the laws and commandments of Creation, subsequently triggering these negative events. So if prophets announce unpleasant, horrible things, this signifies that the human beings in general are in a low developmental stage and a new standpoint must be discovered in order to prevent the fulfillment of the prophecy.

Prophecies, as are now given on earth, can only be "diffused" if every single person is immersing him- or herself in the laws and commandments of Creation. If those prophecies are not heeded, as is the case now and has always been on earth, no changes for the positive will take place. If man's thinking, actions and activities are not improved, then a given prophecy becomes a "prediction," which is a fact that cannot be avoided and will fulfill itself with all its consequences. And this will continue to occur until the human beings on earth are willing to climb off of their high horse and find it appropriate, in their arrogance and rebellion, to take the offered prophecies seriously and act accordingly. Any announcements related to cosmic events of any type do not fall into this category of prophecies because universal forces are entirely separate from human beings who have no power over such cosmic forces.

In contrast to a prophecy, a "prediction" of any form is a fact that is already considered "historic" and will take place with 100 percent certainty. This clearly shows that all predictions will occur with 100 percent accuracy and there is not the slightest chance to alter them, not even one iota.

From a section appended to the dialog of Contact #251, by Billy Meier:

Explanation of Prophecies and Predictions:

"… Consequently, contacts with extraterrestrials can only occur on an official level if everything proceeds correctly and man on earth is mature enough to accept the contacts. This will still require more time, during which many things will transpire in regard to discovery of proof that human beings on earth did not originate on this planet, and also that they do not exist alone in the universe or in this galaxy, the Milky Way. Coonsidering events which are yet to transpire before the first official contact with extraterrestrials takes place, a certain chronology of the prospective historic events must be established. To this end, prudence dictates that exact dates are not mentioned, or it might result in conditions that could negatively alter future events. Furthermore, the consciousness of many people could suffer disorders because they might attempt to change things once they learn of coming events — events that cannot be altered in any manner, shape or form, because they are predictions, not revisable prophecies. I will not mention any dates, therefore, although I am familiar with them. For this reason, I will simply list in chronological order the most important upcoming events, or rather incidents and occurrences, etc., that will take place beginning with 1995. This year will show that nature's ca-tastrophes will continue to wreak endless havoc. Events related to the destruction will increase or decrease in number; in other words, occasionally there will be more of them and sometimes less, but overall the incidents will increase. Regarding the overpopulation, unfortunately, no changes for the better will take place; indeed, the overpopulation will increase."

The following are additional excerpts from Contact 251:

An American Strike?
On a broader scale, expect a strike involving the USA and its president, which will stun the entire world.

Fundamentalism, AIDS, Mad Cow Disease, Scrapie Epidemics
In addition, lengthy deliberations will increasingly take place regarding Islamic fundamentalism, which will mesmerize the entire globe. Uprisings, revolutions, wars and other diverse forms of unrest will escalate tremendously, with Islamic fundamentalism playing a very sad part in the scenario. The health of human be-ings on earth is in extreme danger, not only due to the rapid spread of AIDS, but from the rising ill effects of scrapie among humans, whereby the Creutzfeldt-Jakob Syndrome is not the only repercussion. The scrapie epidemic will increase among animals as well. And if this is not enough, another horrible epidemic and disease will break out among human beings. Even though efforts are made to the contrary, the renewed threat of chemical warfare, a long-standing practice, will be on the rise once again.

Nuclear And Biological Weaponry
Likewise, the same holds true for nuclear and biological weapons. The danger of accidents in nuclear reactors will increase throughout the world. Regarding this subject, France in particular must be extraordinarily careful in every way, as one prophecy warns of a strong probability of an accident near Lyon, which can be prevented as long as the responsible individuals undertake the right steps — a prophecy can be changed. Initial efforts are made by a new movement to promote total non-violence; while a woman gains a high and influential position among world powers through the formation of another group. Mass tourism will increase by leaps and bounds, and slowly but surely it will invade and destroy the remain-ing Shangri-Las on earth.

Flights to Mars
First steps will be taken for a flight to Mars, but will not be blessed with good for-tune. However, the next flight, very soon thereafter, will have better luck, although it will encounter certain difficulties due to unexpected technical problems. All of this will transpire shortly after the worldwide misery of unemployment and its related ills are corrected and surmounted.

Signals of WWIII Looming

A new stockpiling of weapons will follow at a time when the worldwide production of weapons is accelerated once again. This will signal the first threat of a looming third world war, as foretold by a prophecy, unless earthman strives to avert this danger through reason and appropriate thoughts and actions. Should man fail to act against the fulfillment of this prophecy, a new and extremely destructive weapon will be built that will produce disastrous effects in the next world war. One important factor in this scenario is the criminal neglect to monitor the earth from space. New weapons will again create quite a stir, and so will the death of 4 heads of state who will die within 7 days of each other. These are the last danger signs, which foretell that within merely 2 years of these events, the long-feared world war will indeed break out unless the human beings of earth finally gain mastery over their reasoning to stop all these ills. Should this not be done, mankind will fail in its attempt to protest and boycott the new deadly weapons, because by this time the armories of many nations will be full to their capacity. Passing laws to prohibit the use of these weapons will be ineffective at this late stage. World War III cannot be averted if man fails to finally become reasonable! The war will begin with conventional weapons and escalate to nuclear, chemical and biological warfare. The world war will begin in November of a specific year, after 5 years of intensive efforts are spent reaching this goal which is preceded by 4 years of unspecified preparations. Should war actually break out, it will last for 3 years and 11 months and will therefore end in October of the fourth year. By this time, the northern hemisphere of the earth will be largely destroyed by nuclear fires and radioactivity, which will annihilate the entire animal and plant world unless man sees to it that the prophecy proves itself to be just a prophecy without fulfilling itself. Should this not be the case, the world will face some additional 11 bitter years of poverty, misery, starvation and many other ills. The nuclear radiation will cause the crippling and mutation of children born at that time, and multitudes who survive the war will be contaminated and burned by radiation. Chemical warfare will cause horrifying and atrocious skin diseases, and biological warfare will produce festering sores and many other ills, not to mention horrible human freaks, etc.

More About WWIII

Should the prophecy of another world war fulfill itself, and should the earth population not immediately begin rethinking and redirecting its entire effort into beneficial routes, the consequences of this World War III will be cataclysmic. Likewise, this holds true for an enormous vengeance-campaign directed against the initiator of the war, which will be initiated and directed by a bloodthirsty man, who is — how could it be otherwise? — another "Representative of God," a pope. Once again, these events are based on the condition that the prophecy fulfills itself through the fault of the human beings of the earth.

New Weapons, More War and Environmental Crises

With the melting of the polar caps there also looms for earth in the not-too-distant future another severe economic crisis that will spread throughout the globe. And another global war, World War IV, will once again threaten this planet and its entire earth population because of their lack of reason. However, several reasonable individuals are able to neutralize the threat, which is again encouraged by the invention of new weapons with great striking power that will be the materialization of those weapons existing now only in science fiction novels. These are death ray throwers, ray canons, ray rifles and ray guns, besides others. In the midst of these developments, three scientists will generate an incredibly inexpensive energy source, although this will not be the only new form of energy, as another will be found that is based on sound vibrations. And again, new and deadly weapons will be developed from this. Scientists tend to utilize everything they can get their hands on, and for this reason it is inevitable that man will stop the Greenhouse Effect and utilize its effects in reverse, thereby preventing a further melting of the polar caps. These actions, in turn, will lower the highly elevated water levels of all oceans.

DNA Manipulations

Prior to these unfolding events, however — always with the assumption that the prophecy fulfills itself through man's own fault — scientists will discover the manipulated gene of ancient times in the DNA chain responsible for the rapid aging in human beings. These events may yet unfold this year, as preparations in this area had already begun in 1994. Whether scientists make their discovery public and utilize their findings to their fullest extent is questionable, however. From the way things look now, public disclosures regarding these discoveries will not be made until a much later date, and probably will still remain this way for a very long time before the public will be fully informed about the discovery. Therefore, a long period of time will pass before the genetic manipulations are reversed by retromanipulation of the pertinent gene. For the time being, scientists will be unaware that the gene they have stumbled upon is the key factor, and that it is this particular gene which was previously manipulated once before, many millions of years ago.

Increased Space Travel

During this period, earthman will increasingly dedicate himself to space travel, which he had neglected for many years. Venus will be particularly interesting for earth human beings during this period, and for this reason man will contemplate sending a manned space capsule to the volcanic planet. Simultaneously, man will avail himself of a new energy source by exploiting the interior energies of the earth. He will develop two new dangerous weapons. The high-pitched, humanly inaudible sounds of the first weapon will be able to destroy any material and will have the capability of absolutely destroying all life forms — an ultrasound weapon in other words. The second weapon will have as its basis high frequency energies, which will also be capable of destroying and killing everything.

New Genetic Discoveries

Discoveries and inventions in the field of gene technology or gene manipulation, respectively, will continue, as events must unfold — contrary to the desires of the opponents of genetic manipulation who even now persist in ranting and raving against it. The time is no longer that remote when, through genetic manipulations, plants and animals will be successfully crossbred, and totally new life forms will be created. Hence, the stupid, antagonistic complainers will scream in vain; they should be grateful instead that science has advanced to a point where genetic manipulations become feasible. Only through genetic manipulations will the future rectification of genetically-manipulated degeneration of earthman be guaranteed, so that they may be able to fit again into the normal progression of negative and positive. The secrets of Creation will, of course, not unravel through this process and will remain a mystery to man for the time being, even though he will actively search for them while on space stations outside of earth. This does not signify, however, that science will be inactive; on the contrary. Scientists will unveil the secret of gravity. In doing so, they will begin mastering certain facets of space and mass. But just before this transpires, earthman will develop the capability of allowing human organs to "re-grow" for organ transplants. These organs will always be adapted to the particular body in need of the organ. As a result, the danger of organ rejection is eliminated. During this period, renewed advances into outer space will occur whereby a large space project, critical to mankind, will take shape, and Albert Einstein's theory of relativity will undergo several additional modifications. One religion will initiate large-scale war activities at that time, resulting in the development and utilization of another new, dangerous weapon that will be capable of changing the climate, a so-called climatic weapon.

Prophecies Beginning in 1995

However, as bad as they may seem, these periods are not as unstable as that of 1995, a year when new discoveries on Mars are possible; and a year when the seeds of a new ideology are sewn that sets it apart from traditional religions. 1995 will also be a year when an unknown, powerful male individual begins to come into prominence, who keeps the world spellbound and gather followers around him, in much the same rat-catching manner as the Pied Piper of Hamelin. For this reason, in one prophecy, he is called the rat-catcher. These events coincide with many innovations and discoveries in technology and science; because 1995 and the ensuing years bring incredible breakthroughs that will change our civilization. One contributing factor to these breakthroughs in the near future will be, finally, the exposure and rectification of an error in the Pi-number calculation.

Climate Control Devices

Prior to the previously mentioned climatic weapon, the entire earth will be subjected to very problematic climatic changes when overall temperatures fall, that is, they drop dramatically. The result will be that land masses and oceans will freeze because of man's insanity. Consequently, a new invention will be developed that, powered by the most economical of energies, artificially heats the earth atmosphere. This is the moment when Japan and China will discover that the prevailing physics are not the last word in knowledge, but that there exists yet a higher level of physics, which extends into fine-matter spheres. Following this realization, science will be discredited for some time. Nonetheless, space exploration will continue and a new world will be discovered in this process; a new earth that will be suitable for supporting human life. The actual period when space travel and its many related discoveries commence is already in the very near future.

Space Travel Succeeds

In general, expeditions into space will be successful, e.g., earthman will discover, or rather locate, ancient human traces and artifacts left behind on Mars. This will present sufficient reason for man to build, furbish and fly new spaceships with even greater ranges into the vastness of space to make ever greater, more interesting and especially more significant discoveries. Initially, these spaceships will travel over relatively long periods of time until propulsion systems are developed that make super-speed space travel feasible without time shifts. Spaceships reaching velocities above the speed of light, indeed speeds several million times the speed of light, will one day become the rule. But until this occurs, several hundreds of years, even millennia, will pass. Still, these aforementioned predictions shall occur in the near and somewhat more distant future and mankind will not be kept waiting too much longer; even elderly people alive today will experience the beginning of these predictions.

The Discovery of Ancient Extraterrestrial Artifacts and Stations On Mars

The discovery, reactivating and renewed operation of ancient extraterrestrial artifacts and stations on Mars in the not-too-distant future and much later in other places, will be accomplished by our more distant descendants. These events are also associated with grave danger, however, as dangerous diseases and epidemics will be brought back to earth due to space travel, along with the exceedingly vicious "wolf," as one prediction calls this horror, which could be a horrifying animal or a deadly epidemic. The definition of the "wolf" is not clear yet and its explanation is still pending. According to the prediction, this deadly factor will be introduced or carried to earth either by ordinary space travelers or by lawbreaking space travelers. Furthermore, in the distant days ahead, the discovery of a new and very significant substance is foretold— one that will benefit man greatly — as long as he is able to utilize it to his own benefit. This entire scenario transpires at a time when a new order exists on earth that satisfies, in an inexpensive manner, all needs of man. New, overall-like suits for human beings will be invented and produced that will enable man to fly through the air freely without the aid of any other devices.

The DNA Fight Against Aging

Barely three decades prior to this event, however, a third DNA information code will be discovered in the human body, and the first concrete steps will be undertaken to eliminate diseases in the elderly, heart diseases and aging. After approximately 25 years, these efforts will prove successful.

The Cleanup of the Ecosphere

Simultaneously, once the appropriate steps are taken, the feasibility of a classless society, as well as technological-biological prerequisites, will emerge that deal with the worldwide cleanup of the polluted rivers, lakes and oceans. This praiseworthy progress will be negated, however, by an extremely negative invention in form of a biological weapon; it will wreak tremendous havoc and induce instant aging in human beings and animals (in seconds).

The "Nocturnal Dawning[85]"

Shortly thereafter the period of "nocturnal dawning" comes into existence, as stated in another prediction. This "nocturnal dawning" will be a new technological achievement whereby the dark side of planet earth is illumined by an artificial sun that was affixed to a space station; this device will not create full daylight, but a bright, dawn-like condition.

The artificial sun in the sky will virtually ring in a new age on a grand scale., the Age of Space Conquest. From here on, space travel definitely will become commercial and turn into a significant, powerful institution by which man, through science, will pursue the secrets of Creation and with it the origin of life and all existence.

Space Travel Institutions Increasingly Ignores Earth Governments

Of course, these events will make science very respectable again, especially as they relate to the institution of space travel, which will capture the attention of scientists. Ultimately, this will not turn out well and will happen as it must: This space travel institution will increasingly ignore the earth governments and science, deal with them unfairly, and will generate conflicts again that provide the greatest prospects for a new war. All of this will come into play barely 15 years after the aging gene is isolated and neutralized, when the human biologic aging process is largely surmounted, and the related previous deplorable genetic manipulation finally reversed again.

Human Beings Converted into Machines

A looming new war will break out and last for approximately 40 years. During this period or about 6 years prior, human beings will be converted into machines, that is into robots for the first time by connecting their nervous system to microscopic electronic-biological apparati and machinery that will serve to guide them. This will cause great problems about 85 years later, when the now powerful scientists begin to play 'God,' as they had done in earliest times, and they will create new hybrids between human beings and animals through genetic manipulations. These new 'semi-humans' will declare their solidarity with the robotic humans. But before this occurs, another 80 years will pass after the creation of the robotic humans, as I mentioned previously. With the creation of the robotic humans, intelligent biologic-electronic-machinelike robots will be constructed. A gigantic space station will be built on which a vast number of human beings will live while the station travels in its own orbit around the Sun.

Mars Revolt, Underwater Buildings and the Sun is Dying

Because of man's inherent attitude, caused by his degeneration, wars and revolts will occur on Mars. These events will transpire when human beings, after conferring with extraterrestrials, construct residential buildings beneath the oceans that will dangerously interfere with the ecological equilibrium of the oceans, landmasses and the air. Once again the time will come when another new, dangerous, fatal weapon is invented that will disintegrate the bones of life forms. Simultaneously, the artificial sun created about fifty years prior will drift from its orbit and, over a mere seventy-two hour period, will plunge to earth. The earth's own rotation and orbit around the Sun will change then and result in the reduction of the length of years, days and nights. Unfortunately, this will also be the time when the first space conflict — a space war — takes place between the earth inhabitants and those human beings who will have migrated to Mars by then. The gigantic space station in orbit behind the Sun will be damaged. At this time a new earth chronology will be considered because the changed length of the days and seasons on earth cannot be used as in the old system.

New Religion will Attempt to Abolish the Christian Sunday, Islamic Friday and Jewish Sabbath

Earth humanity, already under the spell of religions and religious sects at this time, will remain spellbound for several more centuries. Following the installation of the new earth chronology, the founder of a new religion will come to the forefront and revoke the Christian Sunday, Islamic Friday and Jewish Sabbath in order to establish a new holiday schedule. As an experiment, money will be briefly abolished, but underground trading with valuable goods such as precious metals, diamonds and other commodities will continue. Some time later, the insane earth inhabitants will criminally alter the earth's atmosphere into a dreadful form.

Human-animal Hybrids

And another war on earth will occur, as the earth people will have failed in their attempt to become more peace-loving and intelligent. The future will hold nothing positive pertaining to scientists because they will have begun to perform their first genetic manipulations on human beings and animals by this time, and will be creating entities, so-called 'semi-humans', whom they will produce by crossbreeding human beings with pigs and then train them as fighting machines. These entities will be sent to war and also perform a variety of tasks in space. However, this situation will not go well for very long. The entities will oppose their creators, as is also the case with the robotic humans who will have had arms and legs amputated so their nervous systems can be attached to minute electronic-biological devices, whereby these semi-humans will become living navigational devices for spaceships and every type of weaponry, machinery and earth vehicles, to name but a few.

A Man Will Appear and Present the Universal Teachings

… to the entire earth population. He will be remarkably successful, although existing religions and religious sects will follow up with global countermeasures — as has been the case since ancient times. The teachings of the spirit will be included in these teachings, and some forty years later the teachings of reincarnation will have been spread worldwide and accepted by the existing religions. However, prior to this event some unpleasant encounters with extraterrestrials will take place that may result in a satisfactory union depending on which direction man takes — taking the wrong direction will result in disagreeable, possibly even dangerous prospects.

Mankind Learns to Control Volcanoes

Through technological intervention, man will slowly learn to prevent natural catastrophes. Volcanoes, in particular, will be calmed and their activity controlled, as will be the influences of weather conditions. Triggered by the invention or, rather, discovery of a new and very valuable energy source and its rights to ownership, renewed war activities on earth will ensue.

Longevity Increased

Problems will also occur within the human population because their relative immortality, that is, the increase in human longevity, will amount to life spans of from 350 to 450 years. This increase in longevity will also cause increasingly greater problems of overpopulation and all other subsequent obstacles, which will include migrations that will result in new types of interbred peoples. Among them will be a group who call themselves Eurasians. They will demand the Eurasian region for their homeland at a time when the 'semi-humans,' those human-animal, genetically-manipulated creatures and the robotic humans will be creating incredible problems. These difficulties will lead to the serious decline of every space travel program and nearly bring space travel to a complete standstill. The problem will come about because the robotic humans and semi-humans refuse to continue working for normal human beings, and because of their unwillingness to continue a life of subservience and exploitation as living steering devices for spaceships, vehicles, equipment, war machines and such other apparati. These events will transpire at a time when a climatic reversal begins on earth because the Sun is noticeably weakening in activity, triggered by the reduced nuclear fusion within it.

Space Travel has Repercussions

Earth man's urge to explore knows no limits and, consequently, he will penetrate ever deeper into space; unfortunately, this tendency will also produce repercussions. Inevitably, unexpected disasters will occur, for the prediction states that in the not too distant future, earthman will face some extremely terrifying phenomena during his space expeditions that will present great and trying obstacles. One event, supposedly twenty years later, will take place as the frightening and definite conclusion is reached that the Sun is truly a dying star. And an additional thirty-five years later, human beings of earth will face a new horror when one of their exploration spaceships brings a deadly epidemic back to earth that will leave medical scientists completely helpless. By this time, man will known about the essence of Creation for thirty-five years; likewise, the truth will be understood that the negative and positive represent a unit within themselves, although they also form a perfect unit when joined. The previously mentioned space-exploration craft will lift off shortly after this realization, whereupon it will encounter great horrors. Equipped with a completely new propulsion system, the expedition spacecraft is expected to penetrate space to the extent that it will reach the original home planets of the first genetically manipulated peoples. Such an undertaking will still be completely irresponsible on the part of earthman of that period. On one hand, they will have remained trapped in their genetically manipulated degeneration and, on the other, in their megalomania they will vastly underestimate the dangers of space and alien worlds. They will become aware of their failings only midway along their way toward the original home planets of the genetically manipulated people, when the expedition will be confronted by terrifying extraterrestrial life. Ultimately, this space expedition becomes feasible only when the technological apparati, machinery, all electronic instruments and many other items of that period are no longer operated and piloted by human beings. Instead, the technological devices will become equipped with independent, biological intelligence that will make all piloting and operations almost infallible. The robotic humans still performing those functions at that time will rebel against this change of events. Simultaneously, earthly space travel will reach the pinnacle of its development as research forges on, and soon further deductions and solutions will unlock additional secrets of matter.

Robots Rule
Concurrent with this development will begin the rule by the robotic people under the leadership of someone from their own ranks who will be the enemy of all other human life forms and cause a great upheaval, although he will die very soon after these events.

Scientists Ignite a SOL Planet Within our Solar System
During this same period, once again, the megalomaniac scientists will perform an incredible spectacle by producing a gigantic second sun. Although this group of scientists will be small in number, nonetheless, through a dangerous experiment they will ignite one of the SOL planets, which will burn for seven days and glisten in the SOL System as a second sun before it burns out and fades. Jupiter and Saturn could be equally suitable candidates for this experiment as they are uncompleted miniature suns, making the selection of other planets for this future insanity unnecessary.

Brain Research Excels
Great progress in brain research will occur in the same period, including the implantation of micro modules into human and animal scalps. The micro modules will assume and execute all the navigational functions of the brain. At this time, far from earth, an artificial world in another alien solar system will be populated

by an immense migration wave, due to the continued, irrational increases of the earth overpopulation. The robotic people, simultaneously, will become a danger to regular human beings through their own propagation and the siring of many descendants. Due to genetic alterations, these descendants will be born without arms and legs, with their nerve endings already exposed. This will permit easy access to the nerve endings of their extremities, which can then be attached without surgery to various devices and machinery, etc. The robotic people will become a true menace to normal human beings as they will possess unforeseen consciousness-related powers. Over time, they will further develop these powers by way of an above-normal application of their consciousness whereby the brain, through unique, painstakingly constructed energy generators, will be endowed with special energies from the outside. All of this will allow the forces of their consciousness to perform at record levels.

Sun's Nuclear Fusion Decreases

The time will come when further powerful changes take place within the SOL System as the Sun's nuclear fusion decreases. Indeed, the entire gravity field will not only become unmanageable and changed, but large-scale climatic changes will become the daily norm. These occurrences will inspire scientists to record performances because they will want to find methods to counteract the Sun's negative consequences. In fact, these consequences will manifest themselves far sooner than anticipated and will contradict millennia-old erroneous scientific assumptions. Only then will people correctly realize that the Sun is a dying celestial body and that, subsequently, the end of the SOL System is predetermined. Nonetheless, the Sun will continue to exist another billion years, but by then it will be a dead star that will, ultimately, be swallowed up and destroyed by a Black Hole. Therefore, scientists will begin performing at feverish rates. In the process, they will discover that the base for pi was miscalculated. By eliminating the error in pi and correcting future computations based on pi, scientists and their amazing, highly developed technology will have the capability to make unimaginable energies accessible to the people of earth. This will be accomplished through the diversion and utilization of energies from Black Holes within the Milky Way system. Scientists at this time, though, will still be unable to travel to the center of our galaxy to tap the existing Black Hole in that region. Still, it will be unnecessary to go to the center of our galaxy, at least at that particular time, as nearby objects will produce sufficient energy to serve earth's needs. This new energy source, in fact, the type of energy, itself, will enable earthman to develop new forms of space travel. In the wake and expansion of these developments, a travel and transportation factor becomes a reality which, prior to 1995 and long into the future, had been called a fantasy: Time travel.

Time Travel

This discovery/invention, in turn, will enable man to travel into the past and the future, and as well into the vastness of the Universe, something that was hitherto impossible. In the aftermath of these events new human life forms will be discovered, and without a doubt, the human beings of earth will learn previously unfathomable information from these extraterrestrials, as these ETs will possess remarkably greater intelligence than those of earth.

Creation of Artificial, Biological Intelligence

Developments in every field will progress rapidly and result in the creation of artificial, biological intelligences that will be utilized for the guidance and handling of all apparati, devices, electronics, machinery, including flying craft and vehicles. At this time there will be no concern about these biological intelligences becoming independent to later endanger the earth people, as will be the case with the robotic people, who will no longer be of any use and will be exterminated at once.

Space Crash

The time will then come when all space stations and satellites orbiting the earth, Mars and Venus will crash. This will be the result of the Sun's ever decreasing activity having changed to such an extent that monumental gravitational changes of all planets will occur, even to the Sun itself. Scientists will be working at record levels to find solutions for the changes, but they will be unsuccessful. Yet, they will have success in as much as they will discover an incredibly important factor in the Creation formula. Thereafter, another danger from space will threaten the earth world, this time from the depths of the center of the Universe. The danger of this threat will become evident only much later, however. Prior to this event, however, earthman will place artificial suns into orbit around the earth, far beyond the customary distance.

Artificial Sun

Earth man will not have much luck with these satellites either, as one of the artificial suns will begin to glow due to severe damage and scorch large regions on earth. In turn, the aftermath of these events will dangerously affect earth's atmosphere and produce an oxygen deficiency that causes worldwide riots. From this catastrophe another will evolve, because the scorched land and lack of oxygen cannot remain without consequences.. The catastrophe will affect the economy and the entire food processing industry and will result in a famine the likes of which the world has never seen nor experienced over the past thousands of years. This will signify the beginning of the end for conventional space travel, as barely one decade later time travel will become routine through the advancement of technology. Millions of light years will be bridged, that is, traversed, without any time loss, and human beings will no longer experience limitations in their conquest of distances.

More Genetic Manipulations

This also is the time when geriatric research, through genetic reverse-manipulation, will relieve the human population from the premature aging curse; a curse that was brought about long ago in the genes of the initial fighting peoples by the gene manipulators, the "creator-overlords." This reverse manipulation will afford man an even longer life span than that achieved by genetic scientists of earth through prior manipulations whereby human lives increased to an average life expectancy of four hundred years. These new achievements will produce an extremely long human life expectancy of thousands of years. In the ensuing few years, the time will come when intelligent ocean dwellers will begin to contact human beings and communicate with them, and a new race of earth inhabitants will thereby be founded. Then the time will come when aggressions with Martian inhabitants will begin and result in the actual launching of attacks on the colonies. These events will be followed by fifteen years of relative calm, finally bringing good fortune to the earth human inhabitants in their quest to find their actual origin. An earthly space expedition will penetrate into the regions of Sirius and discover there, or rather locate, proof of the Ur-Ur-Ur-ancestry of the human beings on earth, who previously were procreated through genetic manipulations in ancient times by the Sirius "creator-overlords." This discovery will reveal that over many millennia, the earth ancestors fled across long twisting paths, found the SOL System and began settling there. Thus, mankind on earth will eventually find its direction back to its origin — which, of course, will not suddenly resolve mankind's problems by any means.

Mankind of earth is Re-Acquainted With Their Creator-Overlords

Of course, linked to this discovery will also be contact with the very distant ancestors of the previous "creator-overlords," as well as other intelligences from Sirius and will, by then, no longer lead to the pursuit and slaughter of the genetically-manipulated descendants, earthman. The contacts will lead to a collaboration instead, resulting in the definite reversal of the previous genetic manipulation. This action, in turn, will result in the birth of new descendants who will be normal and no longer be degenerate. The circle finally closes and man will become a true human being, in balance with the negative and positive.

The reversal of this previous degeneration-gene manipulation, along with the continually climbing overpopulation … precipitated even more so by the extraordinary human longevity, will result in plans for the eradication of those human beings in whom the genetic reverse manipulation had not yet been performed, on earth as well as on all other worlds colonized by earthman and space stations inhabited by them. [1]This eradication will transpire in the same manner previously proclaimed and demanded by responsible individuals very long ago: A worldwide birth stop over a seven-year cycle. Within this framework, only parents whose degeneration was previously eradicated through genetic reverse-manipulation will be permitted to procreate. Therefore, only those individuals will be legally entitled to produce any offspring. Illegal pregnancies will be assessed as the most abhorrent crime, punishable by death to the guilty parties. This concept will only come about as an inescapable law five years before the period when complete authority over planet earth is placed into the hands of the administrative sphere within the Sirius alliance, and enforced there from.

Continued Space Research, Sun Becomes Weaker

Nonetheless, in these distant days ahead, earth scientists will be ambitious; they will fulfill new objectives, make new discoveries, and capture the last remaining secrets of chemistry. Despite the incredible knowledge that extraterrestrial intelligences will have passed on to the earth scientists, by far not every mystery about everything will have been penetrated or unraveled. Therefore, research will continue into all facets including that of astronomy, and scientists will subsequently penetrate to the center of the Milky Way to investigate its secrets and those of the Black Hole.

The Sun's activity will increasingly cause more concern, as it becomes notably weaker and unable to provide sufficient energy to supply earth and Mars with light and warmth. In these distant, future times, artificial suns will routinely orbit the earth at a considerable distance to brighten and heat its surface. This situation will not remain benign, either, as one can deduce from an event that will occur seventy years after capital punishment for illicit procreation becomes law, when two of these artificial suns will destructively collide with one another, inflicting severe damage.

These, then, are the overall predictions for a succession of future centuries. The sequence of these occurrences has become somewhat intermixed, and only the most significant future events are mentioned.

Footnotes

85 ▪ This may be the "preview" of similar such undertakings in the future: In January of 1999, the Russian government attempted to "make night into day" by aiming an 80-foot space mirror onto the earth's surface. They may have succeeded if the unfurling device had not gotten entangled in an antenna system.

HENOCH
PROPHECIES

PRESENTED BY QUETZAL DURING
CONTACT 215
FEBRUARY 28, 1987 – 2:09 A.M.

Dear reader,

I'm very glad that the second edition of my book *And Still They Fly!* has
been published. I would like to take this opportunity to present my sincere
appreciation to the following people who have helped me in the translation and
correction of this book: Christian Frehner, Marc Juliano, Marianne Schmeling,
Mary Jane Shippen, Jason Steele and Mike Whelan.

In this second edition we have done something new. We have added
Henoch's prophecies. They were transmitted, on February 28, 1987, to Billy by
the Plejaren contact person Quetzal. Quetzal has transformed the old language
into a current one, German, which is understandable at the present time.

Henoch belongs to a lineage of old prophets who have worked on Earth
since ancient times. Henoch was born on February 3, 9304 BC and died on
January 1, 8942 BC. He had an extraterrestrial father, by the name of Kretan,
who originated from the Pleiades/Plejaren.

Unfortunately, the *Book of Henoch* was removed from the *Bible* and
therefore, his beneficent but falsified words can only be read in the *Apocrypha*.

May the following text encourage you to ponder. Take notice, however,
that this is only a prophecy which doesn't have to be inevitably fulfilled if the
human beings of Earth bring about a positive change in their thinking, feelings
and actions.

Guido Moosbrugger

THE HENOCH PROPHECIES

QUETZAL: Before I give you a clear account of the prophecies of Henoch, I would like to point out that prophecies are always changeable and can be changed for the better if man makes positive changes in his thoughts, feelings and actions leading to that which is better and positively progressive. Prophecies always rest upon specific causes; these again result in certain effects, whereby these effects can be changed at any time if only the preceding causes are changed in their form. Therefore, it is possible that negative or evil prophecies do not have to be fulfilled if the preceding causes will be purposely changed in a manner, that positive and good develops instead of negative and evil.

However, this does not apply to predictions, as these rest upon events that cannot be changed, are inevitable and surely and definitely will occur in the future. Predictions rest upon a preview and thus on a direct viewing of the future, and have neither to do with a prophecy nor with a calculation of probability. So when I make a portion of Henoch's prophecies for the third millennium known to you, it does not mean that they actually have to be fulfilled, because the prerequisite of fulfilment in each case would be that the already existing causes continue to exist as also continue to be created in the future, so that a fulfilment of the prophecies can come to pass.

Thus, provided that human beings of earth will become reasonable, the possibility exists that by a reasonable change in the way of thinking as well as a reasonable development in feeling and an equally reasonable way of acting, everything changes for the better and positive, whereby prophecies do not have to be fulfilled. However, if this transformation does not occur, a very evil, wicked and negative time lies ahead for the earth and its entire population in the coming new millennium.

BILLY: Since the Second World War, thoughts, feelings and actions of the human being of earth have changed very much towards the positive and good but all that achieved is not enough in my opinion, as the great transformation towards the better has not been achieved yet, neither by the mighty of this world nor all of mankind of earth itself. In the years gone by, you have made many predictions and calculations of probability as well as mentioning prophetic facts concerning the economic, military and political situation on earth, whereby I was requested to spread this information, which indeed I have done. Governments and newspapers, radio stations as well as TV-stations and many private persons worldwide were informed by me. But the entire effort did not achieve anything because up to now mankind has carried on in the old manner and no attention was paid whatsoever to prophecies, predictions and calculations of probability. And the same will most likely be the case in the future, when I receive permission from you in the coming time to spread the prophecies of Henoch for the third millennium. But nevertheless, I feel that Henoch's message for the future must be made known and distributed, because somehow it may bear fruit yet.

QUETZAL: You apparently never give up hope. Your optimism is honourable and deserves to be heard by human beings, but the way things have developed throughout this century, there is not too much hope that human beings of earth will come to their senses and heed your words. This will be the case only then, when the prophecies prove to be true or even worse, have already come to pass. Probably only then the time will come when the defamations against you will end in regard to your contacts with us, although they will long continue to be vehemently disputed by your enemies as well as by pathological know-it-alls and critics who dismiss them as swindle, lies and fraud. The full truth about our contacts with you will be proven in the distant future, and then mankind will accept our help we offer through you, even when they erroneously assume, we come from the seven-star-system known to human beings of earth as the Pleiades.

BILLY: Semjase and Ptaah already explained this to me. But tell us now what the new millennium will bring to human beings of earth and the planet earth according to the prophecies of Henoch.

QUETZAL: I will do that in a moment, but I would like to explain before beginning that, I am not authorized to give exact indication of years in an official manner.

BILLY: I understand, but it is certainly good that way. However, I would be grateful to you if you could present the prophecies in a somewhat understandable, modern form of language in order for human beings to understand them better. The ancient language and writing style of Henoch would be almost impossible to understand for most of today's human beings. This also means that a language is desired which explains in an open and clear manner the meaning of the prophecies, and that they are not rendered in riddles and mysteries. Because if I were to publish everything, then open, explanatory and non-coded prophecies would be of value as I think, understandable prophecies can only be beneficial; and the interest of people dwindles when a code is used because they cannot understand anything. My experience has proven to me that human beings are more accessible, can be much more readily addressed, pay closer attention and are more interested in something, if the matter is explained to them in a clear and distinct manner. Indeed it is correct that by encoding the prophecies etc., some anxiety will diminish, however, only to become increasingly greater, the less is understood, because imaginations of all kind begin to stir and agitate, creating hellish fears and images.

QUETZAL: Your words are correct. Therefore, I will present the prophecies of Henoch in an easily understandable manner. So listen ...

If the human being of earth continues to live in the same way as he has done up to now, forming his thoughts and feelings in the same manner, indulging in the same actions as he has hitherto, then the words of the prophecies of Henoch could not be any clearer. The point in time, at which these prophecies will begin to be fulfilled, will be when a pope will no longer reside in Rome.

All of Europe will then fall victim to a terrible punishment by evil powers. The Christian religion will collapse and the churches and monasteries will end up in ruins and ashes. Monstrous forces will be created by science and will be released by the military forces and armies as well as by terrorists, which causes great destruction. Millions and even billions of people will be killed by acts of terrorism, by wars and civil wars, and finally in some parts of the world, every third human being, and in other places every fourth human being, will lose his or her life. The nations of the east will rise against the nations of the west, the west against the east. Many deaths will be inflicted upon the people by fighter and bomber aircraft, and bombs and rockets will destroy and annihilate smaller and larger villages and cities. The people will be completely powerless against all this and will live through 888 days of hell on earth, suffering hunger and plagues, which will claim even more human lives than the war itself. The time will be so severe as never before experienced on earth, because ultimately nothing can be bought or sold any longer. All provisions will be rationed, and if a human being steals even a small piece of bread, he/she will have to pay for it with his/her life. Many waters will mix with human blood and turn red, as once in the past the Nile in Egypt turned red with blood. And it will be that the fanatics of Islam will rise up against the countries of Europe and all will shake and quiver.

Everything in the west will be destroyed; England will be conquered and thrown down to the lowest level of misery. And the fanatics and warriors of Islam will retain their power for a long time. However, not only Europe will be affected but ultimately all the countries and peoples of the earth, as the great horror expands to a war that will encompass the entire world. After the turn of the millennium, the papacy will exist only a short period. Pope John Paul II is the third-from-last in this position. After him, only one additional pontificate will follow. Then a Pontifex Maximus follows who will be known as Petrus Romanus. Under his religious rule, the end of the Catholic Church will come and a total collapse becoming inevitable. That will be the beginning of the worst catastrophe that will ever have befallen human beings and the earth. Many Catholic clerics, priests, bishops, cardinals and many others will be killed and their blood will flow in streams. But also the reformed version of Christianity will become just as infinitely small, as does Catholicism.

Due to the fault of scientists, enormous power will be seized by the power-hungry and their military, their warriors and terrorists, and power will be seized as well through laser weapons of many types, but also via atomic, chemical and biological weapons. Also concerning genetic technology, enormous misuse will occur, because this will be unrestrainedly exploited for purposes of war, not lastly due to the cloning of human beings for warring purposes, as this was practised in ancient times with the descendants of Henoch in the regions of Sirius. However, this will not be all of the horrors, as beside the genetic technology and the chemical weapons, far worse and more dangerous and more deadly weapons of mass destruction will be produced and will be used. The irresponsible politicians will unscrupulously exercise their power, assisted by scientists and obedient military forces serving them, who together hold a deadly sceptre and will create clone-like beings, which will be bred in a total lack of conscience and will be scientifically manipulated to become killer machines. Division by division and devoid of any feelings, they will destroy, murder and annihilate everything.

The USA will set out against the eastern countries ahead of all other financial states and simultaneously, she will have to defend herself against the eastern intruders. In all, America will play the most decisive role, when in the guise to strive for peace, and to fight against terrorism she will invade many countries of the earth, bomb and destroy everything, and bring thousandfold death to the populations. The military politics of the USA will likewise know no limits, as neither will their economical and other political institutions, which will be focused on building and operating a world police force, as it is the case already for a long time. But that will not be enough, and in the guise of a so-called peaceful globalisation, American politics will aspire to gain absolute control of the world concerning supremacy in economy. And this will point towards the possibility that a Third World War could develop from it, if human beings as a whole will not finally reflect upon reason and become reasonable and undertake the necessary steps against the insane machinations of their governments and military powers as well as their secret services and call a halt to the power of the irresponsible who have forsaken their responsibility in all areas.

If this does not happen, many small and great nations will lose their independence and their cultural identity and will be beaten down, because the USA will gain predominance over them with evil force and bring them down under her rule. At first, many countries will howl with the wolves of the US, partially due to fear of American aggressions and sanctions, as this will be the case with many irresponsible in Switzerland and Germany but also of other countries; in part others will join in because they will be forced somehow to do so, or will be misled by irresponsible promoters of American propaganda.

Finally, many Asian, African and European states will rise up against the American hegemony, once they recognize that the United States of America is only taking advantage of them for purposes of war, conquest and exploitation. In this way, many countries will become puppet-states of America before reason and realization will emerge in the responsible ones of governments and in many of the population, resulting in a turning away from the USA. However, the great war will hardly be avoidable, because the human beings of earth will probably not accept the directions towards the better, therewith towards true love, true freedom and true peace, and striving instead only towards wealth, pleasures and riches and for all manner of material values and vices and unrestricted power. Thus, huge and deadly formations of tanks will roll across the countries while fighter planes and rockets sweep through the air and bring death, ruin, destruction and annihilation to countries and people.

And the terrible time will come, when the armed forces will get out of control, and this will be the cause of wild and terrible devastation and unimaginable massacres of the people who helplessly will have to watch the violent actions. The majority of human beings will take no heed of your and our warnings, although something could still be saved and the very worst averted if your and our words of love, peace, freedom and wisdom would be followed. Yet, unfortunately that will be questionable.

If the Third World War will actually happen as calculations and observations appear to indicate to be probable now and also during the approaching few decades, then as now, the civilian population will above all have to bear the brunt of the enormous suffering in tremendous numbers in this entire catastrophe, and last but not least, due to the fault of the irresponsible scientists who by cloning will create human machines for military purposes, devoid of conscience and feelings as well as create immensely deadly and all-annihilating computer-like weapons. At the same time the danger could become reality that the human combat machines, the military clones will gain their independence and under their own management will bring death, devastation, destruction and annihilation to the human beings of earth and to the planet. The entire planet will become an arena of unparalleled suffering, which will never have existed before on earth up to that time. The cruel happenings will last about 888 days and cause civilization to collapse. Yet, the terrible scenario will continue, and epidemics and various diseases as well as enormous famine will be spread among the people while the economy of the world will totally collapse, and there will be no possibility to produce any goods. It will be self-evident that all foods and medications etc., will be rationed and whoever steals any of these goods will be punished by death.

The insanity of war will not only extend across the land, but the disaster will equally be spread to the oceans, into the atmosphere even into outer space. But there will also be settlements under the ocean that will be developed in the course of future and these will be attacked and destroyed, claiming the lives of many thousands of people. However, a certain maelstrom of destruction will also originate from the undersea facilities; because in the cities at the bottom of the ocean, groups of submarine pirates will be formed which will burst upward from the depths of the ocean and will become involved in destructive actions of combat with naval fleets on the surface. And at this time, the possibility could become reality that extraterrestrial forces intervene against the western industrialized countries, because these will be responsible for the extreme and enormous disaster of the coming evil times. These extraterrestrial forces will give up their anonymity and their state of secrecy and will assist those who are being terrorized by the irresponsibly acting western countries, should this possibility become reality. In addition, apocalyptic natural catastrophes will occur which will cause all of Europe to shake and tremble, but Europe will continue to exist even after having suffered enormous destruction.

Far in the west, it will be different; the United States of America will be a country of total destruction. The cause for this will be manifold. With her global conflicts which are continuously instigated by her and which will continue far into the future, America is creating enormous hatred against her, worldwide in many countries. As a result, America will experience enormous catastrophes, which will reach proportions barely imaginable to human beings of earth. The destruction of the WTC i.e. the World Trade Centre by terrorists will only be the beginning. Yet all the apocalyptic events will not only be brought about due to the use of unbelievably deadly and destructive weapons, such as chemical, laser and others and by cloned murder-machines, but in addition to this, the earth and nature, maltreated to the deepest depths by the irresponsible human beings of earth, will rise up and cause destruction and bring death onto the earth. Enormous firestorms and gigantic hurricanes will sweep across the USA and bring devastation, destruction and annihilation, as this from time immemorial never before will have happened. Not only America, but also all other western industrialized countries which will still live at the beginning of the new millennium in the delusion they could dominate and rule over underdeveloped countries, i.e. Third World countries, will not only soon lose their influence over these, but must defend themselves against them.

According to the prophecies of Henoch, the truth about industrialized countries is, that they only seem to appear to be true civilizations, but in fact they are not, because more and more toward the end of the twentieth century and the beginning of the third millennium, they will disregard all true love, true freedom and wisdom as well as true peace along with all values of humaneness and all values of men's and women's true being. But not even all the terrible happenings will hinder the USA to continue in proceeding with her actions against all countries. Even when the North American continent will be stricken by the most terrible catastrophe which ever will have been recorded, evil military powers will wreak havoc with computerized and nuclear, biological and chemical weapons, whereby it will also happen that computerized weapons become independent and cannot be controlled any longer by human beings. Overall, this is the most important part of Henoch's prophecies.

BILLY: But there is still more to it, at least, that is what you told me. May I please ask you to continue?

QUETZAL: You are untiring; so I will point out a few more important facts of the prophecies: As of now, new epidemics have spread among the people of earth, however, as Henoch prophesied, quite a number of further epidemics will follow. Not only AIDS will occur worldwide in the nineteen-nineties, but also epidemics such as the so-called mad cow disease, i.e. BSE, out of which different strains of the Creutzfeld Jacob-Syndrome will develop, lasting well into the new millennium.

Also an epidemic known as Ebola will cause many deaths, as well as other unknown epidemics and diseases, which will sporadically arise in epidemic proportions and will be new to the human being, causing great concern. However, most of the evil will be brought about by politics. France and Spain become involved with each other in armed conflicts, and that even before World War Three will have broken out. Yet France will not only engage in armed conflicts with Spain, for within her great unrests will arise, leading to upheavals and civil war, as it is the case in Russia and Sweden. Especially in France and Sweden, machinations as well as dictatorial regulations of the European Union will cause much unrest and many uprisings, but also crimes committed by gangs and organized criminal elements in these countries will cause unavoidable civil wars. In addition, significant tensions will arise between the native citizens and immigrants from foreign countries, who as a rule also observe religious beliefs different from those of the native populace. And in the end, this will lead to severe conflicts. Hatred against strangers, foreigners and people of different religious beliefs will be the order of the day, as well as the rise of neo-nazism, terrorism and right-wing-extremism. Conditions similar to civil war will be in England, Wales and North Ireland and claim many human lives.

The Soviet Union will be dissolved during this decade or, at the latest, by the beginning of the next. The man decisive for this action will be Mikhail Gorbachev. But this will not lead to rest, because the new Russia will continue its long-standing conflict with China over Inner Mongolia, with the result that Russia will lose a portion of this territory to China. And China becomes dangerous, especially to India, as also at this time China maintains uneasy relations with her. China will attack India, and if biological weapons will be used, around 30 million human beings will be killed in the area of and around New Delhi alone. However, this will not be the end yet; because the effect of biological bombs and missiles etc., used, cannot be controlled at that time and terrible epidemics unknown up to that point in time will arise, and will spread quickly to many areas.

Also Pakistan will allow herself to be misled to instigate a war against India, which will be especially dangerous in view of the fact that both countries are developing atomic weapons. Yet Russia will not rest and will attack Scandinavia and in doing so, embroil all of Europe; and months before that, a terrible tornado will have swept across northern Europe, causing great devastation and destruction. It must still be stated, that the Russian attack will occur during the summer, in fact, starting from Archangelsk. Denmark will not be dragged into the war, due to the insignificance of this country. Yet, Russia will not be satisfied with this action of war, as her will for expansion will be ravenous. And consequently, Russia will launch a military attack against Iran and Turkey and will conquer these two countries in bloody fighting, causing enormous destruction. In the Russian expansionist mentality will also be included the drive to gain control of the Middle Eastern oil deposits, as well as to gain control of the south eastern region of Europe. Therefore, she will also invade the Balkan and conquer these countries there in enormous battles, causing ruthless and devastating destruction with many deaths.

This will be the time, when tremendous natural catastrophes will hit Italy and its people, causing severe hardship. But this will also be the time, when Vesuvius could become active again and could spread tremendous havoc. At the same time a war will shake Italy and claim many human lives as well as cause great destruction. Destruction of war will also descend on the northern countries as strong military forces will invade them from the east and will pillage and murder, and as well as use bombs and missiles, like hail coming down, and hitherto unknown deadly weapons of laser- and computer- controlled types which will destroy and annihilate everything, whereby the first target will be Hungary, after that will follow Austria and northern Italy.

Switzerland will also be severely affected, but will not be the actual target; this will be France and Spain. However, the main objective of the aggressors will be to bring all of Europe under their military control and for that purpose, France will be selected to be the headquarters. France, a country, that not only will be invaded by the aggressors from the outside, but will also be conquered from within as a result of collaborative forces and other forces. This can be envisioned as being the many foreigners of a different religion living in France at that time, and specifically Islam, which will be this force working from within.

Once France has fallen, a war to conquer Spain and England will take place, subsequently, an alliance with the forces of the aggressors will be formed, which will invade Scandinavia. For all these French-based military operations, the weapons of mass destruction stored in the arsenals of France will be used and cause evil devastation, destruction and annihilation. The aggressors from the East will force the French army to join their military forces, and lead a war of conquest against the northern countries of Europe, invading and conquering Sweden and Norway, subsequently these northern countries will be annexed to Russia.

Military forces will also attack Finland, whereby many will be killed and an enormous destruction will be caused, followed by a total dissolution of the country and a long time of occupation by Russian forces. This will also be the point in time, when the German citizenry will fight a civil war and simultaneously will be attacked by a large army from the east. Yet, the country and her population will be able to shake off the yoke of the aggressors, at first, however, it will be caught by the power of the invading military forces. After some time, peoples will rise up against the aggressors and invaders, resulting in a struggle for independence all over Europe. At the same time, when a civil war rages in Germany, an enormously bloody revolution will break out in England, which will claim more lives than will be claimed by the civil war in Germany. And because England and Ireland have been at war for a long time already, due to the IRA and the police- and military forces of England, the result will be (because this feud will continue up to that time) that this revolution will spread out to all of Ireland, especially affecting North Ireland. Many lives will be lost during a civil war in Wales, where differences between various parties will arise before the Third World War. Welsh and English forces will clash especially near Cymru and claim many lives and cause great destruction.

But death, destruction and annihilation will not only rage in Europe but also in America, where much suffering will have to be endured, and many deaths as well as destruction and annihilation will be. America and Russia will have the most terrible weapons of mass destruction at their disposal — a fact that is already the case to a certain extent today — and will clash with violent force against each other at that time, whereby Canada will also be dragged into this conflict. The source of this conflict will substantiate the Russian attack on the American State of Alaska and against Canada. This conflict will result in mass killings of human beings as well as devastating destruction, annihilation and epidemics etc., which mankind of earth will ever have seen and experienced up to that time. Not only nuclear, biological and chemical-weapons will be used en masse, but also enormously deadly systems of computer-controlled weapons that are only in the beginning stages of development today, or will be invented and constructed during the third millennium.

As already mentioned, enormous natural catastrophes and rolling walls of fire and violent hurricanes will rage across all America, while in addition, all the terrible effects of war will bring thousandfold deaths, destruction and annihilation. America's largest cities will be absolutely destroyed and firestorms will cause great disaster and misery. Severe earthquakes and volcanic eruptions will also belong to that time, and these will cause much suffering and misery and deaths besides enormous destruction and devastation, as all of nature and the planet itself will rise up against the insanity of human beings on earth. However, tornados, earthquakes and volcanic eruptions will not only rage in America, but also in Europe and in the rest of the world. These activities have already begun at the present time, also during the past decades, with the exception that they will become increasingly more devastating in the future. And man of earth is guilty for the most part, today, as also in the future it is man who destroys the entire environment: All of nature, the atmosphere, water and all the resources of the planet. And through this a shifting of weight inside the earth takes place, caused for example by the creation of gigantic lakes by damming and by creating hollow caverns due to the exploitation of petroleum and gas etc. And thereby unnatural inner earth movements are created, which also lead to unnatural tectonic effects and cause earthquakes and volcanic eruptions, which also in turn cause enormous climatic changes, resulting in horrendous tornados of devastating proportions which, in the end, will set their destructive energies free on the entire world. All of this will also lead to increasingly horrible floods and unusually massive snowfalls, which will advance to the southern countries and finally even to the equatorial regions, because through the insanity of human beings, the earth has begun unnoticeably to spin as a consequence of atomic explosions inside and on the surface of the earth. And this will be the reason that the planet will slowly but surely enter an extraordinary spinning orbit around the sun, while the first phase is already occurring, which causes a change in climate, leading to a new ice age.

Yet the misery on earth will continue, as two terrible civil wars will break out in America, whereby one will follow the other. Afterwards, the United States of America will break apart and deadly hostility will prevail among her, which then leads to the division into five different territories and it cannot be prevented that sectarian fanatics will play a dictatorial role. Anarchy will be the worldwide condition that will prevail and torment human beings over a long period of time, as human beings will also be tormented by the many epidemics and diseases, many of them new and unknown to human beings and for this reason incurable. Due to this fact, the bodies of many human beings will slowly and miserably decay, while unbearable pain will also occur, as well as blindness and terrible respiratory problems that lead to suffocation. The consciousness of many human beings will become impaired and succumb to feeblemindedness and insanity. And all these gruesome occurrences will be traceable to biological and chemical weapons, which are the cause of not fast, but gruesome and slow deaths; as this will also occur due to the use of ray and frequency weapons which are already being developed today.

Finally, the words of Henoch may specifically be mentioned, which includes, that mankind of earth in pursuit of technology for mass destruction and in greed for power, hatred, vengeance and riches will ignore all values of Creation, and will trample upon all values of love, wisdom, freedom and peace, as ancestors of the Henoch-lineage had done before, to plunge itself and the world into screaming misery, death, destruction and annihilation and into the most severe catastrophes, mankind of earth will ever have experienced.

BILLY: But these are still not all of Henoch's prophecies.

Quetzal: That is correct. Yet, the given explanations should suffice.

BILLY: Ah, one moment please my friend. While you presented the prophecies of Henoch, a question passed through my mind, why Switzerland should actually also pay up, i.e., will be overrun by foreign powers of war. Is there a specific reason for this?

As a neutral country, our country should be respected as such and be spared any actions of war.

QUETZAL: If Switzerland would really remain neutral, she would be spared any actions of war. Due to much irresponsibility among the people and the government, the land of peace, as it was called in early prophecies, will lose its real neutrality, despite different explanations and promises of the irresponsible. Indeed, the fact will be that these irresponsible in office will establish contacts to join the UN and NATO as well as the European Union, which in consequence will destroy the actual neutrality of Switzerland, in fact, contrary to all assertions of the responsible in government and the misled population, as I already explained to you. Through the UN and NATO, Switzerland and her citizens will be drawn into actions of war. Indeed, the nature of the UN should be purely peaceful; yet this will not remain so, for it will be unavoidable that the forces of UN will also take up arms in the new millennium. This may possibly only be for defensive purposes, but this still means actions of war, so death will also reap a rich harvest in the lines of the UN-forces.

However, that will not be all, because in the minds of various responsible officials in top positions of Europe, the idea has emerged to create a European Union; and the people belonging to it will experience a great loss of freedom as also the various central governments which will shamefully sell off their entrusted countries to this European Union, which will exhibit very strong dictatorial tendencies. Brussels in Belgium will be the central seat of the government of this European Union, and those responsible there, will cash in on enormous profits that will have to be paid for by the countries and their populations who belong to the Union. They will call these compensations/profits their just pay, for which all countries and peoples belonging to the European Union will have to perform hard labour. For this reason, the responsible ones of the European Union can live high and squander at the expense of the citizens and then laugh about the stupidity of their supporters. The governments of the countries concerned, as well as the European Union in Brussels will gradually go so far, that they will want to hold any refusers, objectors and critics responsible, and want to punish them. And the deplorable dealings of the European Union will finally be the decisive reason that the warring powers from the east will invade Europe and destroy everything and subjugate everyone, if the entire population of Europe and their governments do not act reasonably against everything, so that the threatening prophecies do not fulfil themselves.

BILLY: When shall this connection with the planned European Union become effective? I mean in reference to Switzerland?

QUETZAL: The beginnings for this will already be set by the responsible ones of Switzerland during the coming 1990's, yet the actual connections will only come about in the next millennium. The lack of reason within the government as well as of the majority of the Swiss population will unfortunately be greater than common sense. This will open up all paths for the megalomania of the governing body; and if the citizens of the country do not become reasonable and work against these machinations that lead to slavery and war, the catastrophe can befall Switzerland in the end. The people in the European countries and in Switzerland still have time to prevent all of this and turn it towards the better, although it is questionable that common sense and reason will win and prevent the threat of evil, because this is still possible in the next years, but very soon, it will be too late.

BILLY: Let us hope for common sense and reason, but I think all hope is in vain.

QUETZAL: The way things look, you will probably be right, unfortunately.

The New Era of
the Aquarian Age

Astronomical and Astrological Observations

New Age, a new era, the *Golden Age,* the *Age of Aquarius* — these are actual slogans that accompany us each step of the way in our daily lives, if we walk through life with open eyes and ears and do not bury our heads in the sand and refuse to see all the new developments continuously unfolding around us. Nevertheless, whether we have noticed it or not, we are about in the middle of the transition into this new era called *Aquarius.*

Before taking a closer look at the significance of the Aquarian Age, it would be appropriate that several astronomical facts should first be explained in general terms. As we all know, it would be an illusion to believe that our earth is a resting planet around which all other heavenly bodies revolve. Far more accurate is the exact opposite. The earth goes through a number of different motions, which take place simultaneously. Contrary to the saying of the Greek scientist Archimedes, "give me a fixed point, and I shall turn the world out of its hinges," there is actually not a single heavenly body at rest in our entire universe, and this fact has been confirmed time and again through cosmological research.

Today, as everyone knows, our world rotates around its own axis once every 24 hours, which gives rise to the change of night and day. At the same time, the earth also revolves in an elliptical path around the sun in the course of one year. Yet according to mere observation, it looks as if the sun were wandering around the earth. However, to man this orbital motion of the sun is merely an illusion. Another important factor involved is its precession, which I will discuss at a later point. This brief explanation of the earth's motions will have to suffice for the time being.

To define the position of the stars and their motions, let us imagine the entire celestial sphere as an enormous globular shell around the earth with a celestial equator, which may be envisioned as an extension of the earth's equator and located in the same plane. Both celestial poles (North Pole and South Pole) are marked

323

at the top and bottom of the globular shell and represent the end points (celestial axis) of the extended earth axis.[86]

The earth equator is inclined about 23.5 degrees with respect to the earth orbital plane. In other words, the earth axis inclines 66 degrees and 33 minutes of arc to the orbital plane of the earth. The earth orbital plane, when projected onto the inner wall of the globular shell, is called the ecliptic. The ecliptic is the annual orbit, which the sun appears to take from our viewpoint on earth against the backdrop of fixed stars in the heavens. In reality, this is merely an effect or reflection of the earth's orbit around the sun.[87] The zodiac belt, which was introduced in ancient times, is located along this ecliptic. It is divided into twelve zodiac constellations, seven of which are named after animals. The constellations of the zodiac belt are Aquarius, Capricorn, Sagittarius, Scorpio, Libra, Virgo, Leo, Cancer, Gemini, Taurus, Aries and Pisces.

From an astronomical viewpoint, the Age of Aquarius started when the vernal equinox[88] entered the zodiac constellation of Aquarius. As a result of the slow wobbling motion of the earth axis, the vernal equinox shifts from year to year by 50.116 seconds of arc and thus slides one constellation further away every 2,155 years, and finally passes through the entire zodiac belt of the ecliptic in exactly every 25,860 years. *(See – Explanation of the Concept: Precession)*

Of course, I have now put my foot into my mouth, as my statistical information does not fully correspond to today's astronomical data. In this case, I can perhaps reassure those who may question this fact that my information did not simply appear out of nowhere, but was conveyed to the Swiss contactee, Eduard Albert Meier, by the female Plejaren spacecraft pilot, Semjase.[89] It is quite obvious that extremely complicated calculations were involved in compiling this data.

I compiled a list clearly indicating the important points and periods of time on page A-10 in the section entitled Age of Aquarius in Numbers. The end or expiration point of the Age of Pisces, which also begins the first half of the transition into the Age of Aquarius, was precisely calculated as February 3, 1844 at 11:20 A.M,, Central European Time. At the same point in time on February 3, 1937, the second half of the transition period started. Its full effect will not be reached until 2029. This means that the Age of Aquarius will not actually come into full force until then. Like all other eras, the Age of Aquarius will last for a total of 2,155 years and will come to an end in the year 3999. After that, the Age of Capricorn will begin, followed by the Age of Sagittarius. The entire cycle of precession will not be completed until 25,860 years later, after which time a new cycle will begin all over again.

I shall undoubtedly stir up another hornet's nest when I start to discuss the cosmic influence of heavenly bodies, as this topic deals with astrology, which is not seriously considered (or is even fully disregarded) by most astronomers and other natural scientists. The reason for this is that astrology has not yet succeeded in gaining due recognition as a natural science in our present-day society.

In my opinion, the true meaning of the Age of Aquarius can only be explained in astrological terms, regardless of whether critics agree or not. Of course, it is entirely up to the reader to decide whether to skip over this section or read the chapter to the end. My only desire is to describe this complicated theme as clearly as possible with the confident expectation that I succeed in this endeavor. Before treading on delicate ground, I would first like to reassure you that astrology is considered to be a discipline of the natural sciences by the extraterrestrial Plejaren,[90] like astronomy, astrophysics, physics, chemistry, etc.

Our present knowledge of astrology is so inadequate that we will have to learn a great deal before we are able to even approach the level of the Plejaren. Nonetheless, there are a number of outstanding astrologers on earth today who have some understanding of the subject and take their profession seriously, such as internationally renowned professor Dr. Hans Holzer. These relatively few experts are faced with a multitude of so-called astrologers who are often comprised of swindlers, frauds and plain braggarts and who profit immensely from the gullibility of many people. These criminals ruin the reputation of the upright astrologers whose efforts in this field are sincere. It is quite obvious that not all can be lumped together — the wheat must be carefully separated from the chaff. The critic's position that "astrology is good-for-nothing, anyway," can by no means be regarded as a conclusive argument. Correctly formulated, it should at least read, "improperly used and erroneously calculated astrology is of no value." A clear line must be drawn between facts that actually exist, and pure speculations that have absolutely no value. For example, if someone sincerely believes that the destiny of an individual or an entire nation is dependent on the stars, then that person is severely mistaken and is definitely headed in the wrong direction. On the other hand, it is absolutely correct that the stars have a certain influence on earth and its inhabitants, but never to the extent of determining a person's destiny. The decisive factor is the way in which a person reacts to these cosmic vibrations. This is entirely left up to individual free will, as everyone is capable of making decisions that affects their own destiny. These decisions are exclusively made by one's own power of determination toward his own goals. From an astrological viewpoint, the following types of radiating energy must be taken into consideration:

- By far, the most powerful cosmic influence originates from the tremendous energy of the central sun at the center of the galaxy, from which an abundance of intense radiation flows and is supplied to the stars. The recipients thereof transform the energy — in a manner of speaking — according to their individual needs and respective evolutionary levels. This holds true for both the star systems and the living creatures that inhabit them. Depending on the relative position of the constellation (stars and planets), it allows a greater or lesser degree of the radiating energy of the central sun to reach us and thus determines the intensity of this energy. The vibrations radiating from the individual stars, however, are exceedingly small in comparison to the radiating energy of the central sun of the galaxy.

- The next level of energy is radiated from the various zodiac constellations. The Age of Pisces is characterized by the lowest vibratory frequencies, whereas the Age of Aquarius is characterized by the very highest.

- Not to be forgotten are the vibrations of the individual planets (or planet tones) which are of special importance for astrological evaluations. I repeat, the individual alone determines his or her reaction to cosmic influences in the form of certain vibrations.

I would now like to briefly explain the somewhat sensitive aspect of astrology — the subject of horoscopes. There are both pros and cons on this subject. Of absolutely no value are the mass-produced horoscopes on the market, which are nothing more than a general summarization of weekly prognoses. Such nonsense can indeed be forgotten. On the other hand, it does not mean that horoscopes should be rejected entirely. If a horoscope is to have rhyme and reason, or make a meaningful statement, tremendous knowledge and skills are required in its calculation. Unfortunately, our present knowledge is so inadequate that even an excellent astrologer is unable to give an absolutely reliable forecast of any future event. Using a concrete example, I would like to mention the one aspect of this subject that deals with time of birth and its meaning. When calculating a birth horoscope, it is of utmost importance to know the exact moment of birth, meaning if possible to know the exact second during which the skullcap of the infant emerged from the mother's womb and was exposed the light of the world for the first time. If we do not carefully heed certain circumstances, which seem to have little meaning but are actually of great importance, the rate of success will be considerably lower.

Another important reason why all forms of astrology today can be considered meaningless speculations is the fact that the location of astronomical zodiac constellations of the ecliptic does not correspond to the astrological zodiac signs (of the same names) as they appear in our yearly calendar. As a result of the precession, the vernal equinox shifts according to the sequence of the astrological zodiac signs. For example, instead of shifting from Aquarius to Pisces, it shifts from the Pisces constellation to Aquarius, and so on.

Furthermore, the sections of the twelve astrological zodiac signs are all the same size, whereas the special longitudinal extensions are not the same for all astronomical constellations. It should also be noted that the symbolic meaning of an astrological zodiac sign always remains the same. Its effect will vary somewhat depending on the astronomical constellation in which it happens to fall. The constellation serves as a background, comparable to a backdrop in a theater. I would like to clarify this case with the following example. Let us assume that you once saw a play many years ago, which greatly impressed you. At a much later time, you have an opportunity to see the same play again and you decide to do so. Because of your joyful anticipation of the coming event, it does not occur to you at first that the external framework has already changed. You take your seat and await what is to come. The time finally arrives — the curtain is drawn and the play begins.

But what a difference! Contrary to what you remember, the backdrops are totally different, the actors, costumes, etc. are new. Since the staging has changed, you now have the impression that a completely new play is being performed, although its expression, or character, has not changed. The effect that these changed circumstances have on your life, and the way you plan to use them, is entirely up to you. I would like to emphasize again that the character expressed by each astrological zodiac sign always remains the same within a cycle of 25,860 years, only the respective backdrops change or, in other words, the locations within the various zodiac constellations change.

Many readers may consider all this to be pure nonsense, but whatever your opinion may be, nature allows no one to tell her how she should act … luckily enough, I would say. Nature has ordered life in such a way that all matter is subject to a continuous change between becoming and passing away in periodically recurring cycles. These cycles not only give rise to all types of change but also serve as the evolutionary basis for further development of all life forms.

The Meaning of the Age of Aquarius

First of all, the beginning of the New Age means that our solar system has become immersed in the celestial region of the Aquarius Constellation and, consequently, in an area flooded with the radiant energy from the central sun of the galaxy. Due to the respective positions of other constellations in relation to the constellation of Aquarius, the radiant energy of this central sun affects us with far greater intensity than in any other past or future era. This is also why one refers to this era as the Golden Age, a most appropriate designation.

The Age of Aquarius actually went into effect on February 3, 1844, after we had entered the periphery of the central sun's golden rays. Consequently, we are now in a critical phase of the transition period. On one hand, we are still feeling the impact of the vibrations from the preceding Age of Pisces, which is coming to an end, and on the other hand, the rays of the present Age of Aquarius have started to reach us and are gaining in intensity. What has taken place over the past 185 years can be compared, on a somewhat smaller scale, to the change of seasons from winter to spring which also takes place gradually and not overnight. The expired Age of Pisces was primarily characterized by murder, assault, raw brutality, religious fanaticism, insane beliefs, magic, mysticism, the rise of many different cults and other negative aspects of the worst kind.

Pisces is at home in water, whereas Aquarius is at home in the air. It is as if a flying fish had sprung out of the water and transformed into a bird in flight. This metamorphosis will last a total of 185 years. Struck with blindness, mankind is slowly emerging from the depths of a dark cavern and is increasingly absorbing the light of new knowledge. This transition period can best be characterized by the word upheaval. Former ways of life that had become habitual are now outmoded and in need of change and must be torn down, whatever the price may be and without heeding the losses involved. At the same time, however, the foundation for the construction of a new house is being laid. As a result of the unfavorable consequences of the Age of Pisces, the various changes are unable to take their course without complications that include terrible wars and revolution, terror, fanaticism, power-hungry politicians, hatred, discontent, as well as deception and fraud. The terrible mortgage of the past is now due and payable.

Furthermore, troubled minds have been imagining the very worst for quite some time and have been talking about the total destruction of the world, or something similar. The illusion that all of mankind is doomed to destruction and that life will disappear from the face of the earth will definitely not come to pass. Nevertheless, as everyone knows, the situation is highly critical in many respects. In view of this, I would like to quote a small excerpt from a series of articles titled *Facts Worth Knowing.*[92] Such topics include over-population, military activities and the weapons industry, where we find the entire world contaminated by all sorts of toxic substances and radioactivity. The booklet also examines criminality, power politics, drug addiction, misleading religions, world-wide mismanagement at all levels, financial exploitation, misuse of chemicals and toxins, terrorism, racism, slave trade, prostitution, anarchy, invocation of the dead, spirits and demons; wars and revolt. These things will be accompanied by natural catastrophes in the form of earthquakes, hurricanes, floods, continued destruction of forests, climatic changes, the hole in the ozone layer, nuclear danger, the AIDS epidemic, sexual degeneration and other similar things. These are all signs of the transition period that we are now experiencing.

Undreamed of progress has also undoubtedly been made in all realms of life, especially in the fields of science and technology. In recent decades, an unprecedented number of inventions and discoveries have been made. Unfortunately, spiritual development has by no means been able to keep pace. Consequently, an unbridgeable gap has developed between the enormous scientific and technological progress and the development of ethics and social sciences. At the present stage of our development, we are simply not mature enough to handle the progress made in the natural sciences and technology. This will remain the case for as long as we continue to misuse all new inventions for negative and military purposes and as long as all the fundamental laws of nature are sacrificed for material profits. This discrepancy must be rectified because it hovers over the heads of mankind like the sword of Damocles.[93]

The Age of Aquarius is also frequently referred to as the last days. This is true only to the extent that traditional and outdated aspects of life will disappear, a prediction that will indeed come to pass. This is by no means the final end but, rather, a new beginning that will not reach its full impact until the year 2029.

The high frequency and spiritually-energetic vibration of the central sun are now flooding our earth and giving rise to an epoch of spiritual breakthroughs that will largely evolve into positive manifestations. The radiant energy during the Age of Aquarius will activate the evolution of the planet and its inhabitants over an extended period of time to such an extent that no one will be able to escape its influence.

The new era will bring about fundamental and needed changes, improvements and a new order for everything of former value. The cosmic influences are increasing to such an extent that revolutionary changes, discoveries and inventions occur almost daily. In this illustrious age, tremendous growth will also take place in spiritual realms. According to Semjase, the intellect will no longer be the only decisive factor in life but will be taken over by spiritual knowledge and skills. Everything that restricts and enslaves the spirit will be destroyed after it has exceeded its negative climax.

This new beginning not only has grave consequences for mankind as a whole, but also for each individual. The way a person reacts to these impulses will vary considerably. Some will consider these changes as threats and will desperately hang onto their traditional ways and indulge in their material needs and pleasures more than ever before. Others will be haunted with an inner restlessness and seek refuge in all sorts of religious cults that will spring up like mushrooms and take their followers under their perilous wings. Teenagers, in particular, will fall prey to unscrupulous and negative fishers of men. These healers and false prophets will spread throughout the multitudes and successfully find new victims whom they will shamelessly exploit and misguide. The New Age is demanding its tribute and, therefore, malicious liars and cheats will find very fertile ground for their shady activities. Another category of victims will find their presumable salvation in drugs and will sooner or later turn to crime or end up in the gutter if they do not find a solution. These painful and enduring by-passes may often be discomforting and perilous, but are unfortunately necessary in order for many people to find their way back on course after wandering along dangerous detours.

Lastly, there are a number of people who have undergone greater positive transformations than others and are thus able to receive and process cosmic vibrations to a much greater extent. Luckily, these people do not keep their newly formed consciousness to themselves but radiate it unknowingly into their environment. This in turn triggers effects that promote further evolution.

The Golden Age is the beginning of the real and true life, in the sense of creative-universal order. The human race on earth will approach an unparalleled spiritual peak, but according to Semjase, it will require many centuries before the human spirit is able to reach such a stage of development on this planet. No other age has ever been in a better position to uplift all realms of life to their highest possible levels of development. We are going to experience the most powerful evolutionary period ever to take place on earth. With the gradual progression of the Golden Age, the inhabitants of our planet will advance one step at a time in their overall evolution from kindergarten to high school, in a manner of speaking, and all the unruly school children unwilling to learn will be ruthlessly left behind if they do not rid themselves of degenerative habits. All evil forces must undergo a radical change if they want to survive.

To help alleviate the hard labor pains of the transition period, which will last until February 3, 2029, extraterrestrial intelligences have sporadically appeared with their spacecraft (so-called UFOs) as a means of demonstrating their existence. In singular cases, which have been taking place less and less, they have established contact with specially selected people on earth. These people had to undergo extremely rigorous training and tests before they were ready to receive all kinds of important messages and teachings. Diverse thought impulses from the extraterrestrials are apparently necessary because we must first plow the field of ignorance by the sweat of our brow before we are able or even permitted to reap the fruits of the New Age.

The extraterrestrial brothers and sisters from the Plejaren and their Lyrian allies are primarily responsible for setting the milestones that mark the right path to take into the future, a future which will be strewn with many obstacles. Due to their extensive and varied forms of help, they have contributed more than only commendable services.

As mediators and interpreters between the extraterrestrials and inhabitants of earth, special people have been selected through the ages to fulfill this function and have appeared time and again on the world stage in the form of prophets. To clear up any misunderstandings from the very start, it must be said that prophets — even those who are genuine — by no means hold an elevated position attributed to them today out of ignorance. They are, of course, human beings, and I explicitly stress the words, "HUMAN BEINGS." Because of their extraordinary abilities and superior knowledge, they are able to correct erroneous information passed down through the ages and to proclaim the true laws and commandments of Creation in unadulterated form. Unfortunately, their blunt and very harsh-sounding language of truth has often been misunderstood and criticized by many. This severe tone was deliberately selected because it alone is suitable for this day and age. To be quite honest, you certainly would not whisper to your travel companion sleeping in the next tent to dress quickly because a nearby dam had just broken and a life-threatening flood must be expected immediately. But as we already know, the prophets on earth have always been depicted as liars and cheats, confronted with animosity, persecuted and condemned to death because they dared to reveal the pure truth to the people.

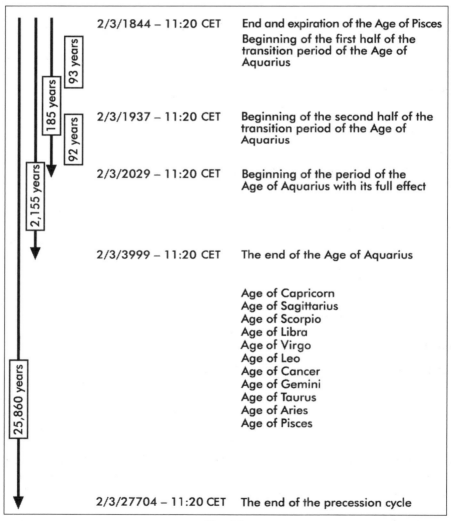

Fig. A-1
The Age of Aquarius in Numbers

Expressed in Semjase's words:

SEMJASE: Many prophets are born in February, both earthly as well as those cosmic-born in Aquarius who will be radical reformers, revolutionaries and teachers of the New Age. The very greatest of these are the ones born into the world at the beginning of the second half of the transition period. Very decisive factors are the hour and minute of birth, because the closer the birth is to the transition point of 11:20 A.M. according to the earth-time calculation, the more pronounced the Aquarian characteristics will be. These prophets are very few in number and are scattered throughout the world.

It is no wonder that the Plejaren have chosen an inhabitant of earth with this date of birth in the present age to serve as a spokesman for them so that the ideas conveyed to him may be further relayed to mankind on earth. This contactee is Eduard Albert Meier from Switzerland who is known worldwide by the name of *UFO Billy* and who is one of the most important *preparers of the way* for the New Age of Aquarius. As already mentioned, many weeds must first be uprooted to enable the flowers of the Golden Age to flourish and one-day bloom in their full glory. Despite all the progress made in some areas of this world, there are still too many doors and gates locked in chains. These doors, if opened, can lead to a better world with lasting peace, good neighborly relations between all the peoples of earth, love and friendship and the willingness to help others.

Although the New Age will bring tremendous progress, it will also demand a radical revision of our former ways of life that have been far too materialistic. We have been impregnated with unreal religious beliefs that continue to be shaped by many corrupt factors such as the greed to possess, the drive for power, egotism and self-righteousness. The time has come to "move heaven and earth" as soon as possible in order to escape the dead-end that mankind has reached. This can only be accomplished by a change in consciousness brought about by the acceptance of universal truth and the fulfillment of the laws and commandments of Creation.

As a result of cosmic influences, new changes of immense proportion are ahead of us, the likes of which the world has never known. These changes are worth using and supporting and everyone can make a contribution so that the Age of Aquarius will shine with golden radiance into the future, which is our hope for all those who are of good will.

Explanation of the Concept: Precession

Under the influence of the gravitational force of the sun and planets as well as the moon, which tends to straighten the inclined axis of the earth, because the axis of the earth slowly gyrates in the direction opposite to the earth rotation. The imaginary extension of the earth axis (celestial axis) rotates around the North Pole of the ecliptic once in every 25,860 years and describes a double cone in space. An additional inclination triggered by the gravitational pull and torque of the Moon leads to a motion so that the extended axis of the earth, or celestial north pole, actually describes a wavy precessional orbit against the backdrop of the heavens. The latter process is known as nutation.[94]

As a result of precession, the vernal equinox shifts from year to year by 50.116 seconds of arc and slides into the next constellation along the ecliptic every 2,155 years. Finally, it passes through the entire zodiac belt of the ecliptic in exactly 25,860 years.

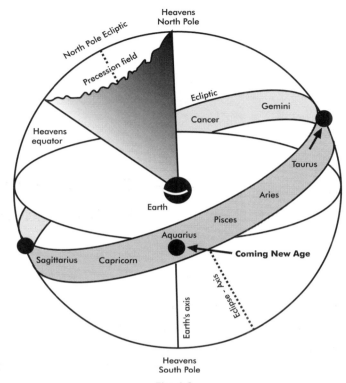

Fig. A-2
The Zodiac and Precession

Footnotes

86 ▪ The earth's axis is an imaginary line that runs from the North Pole through the center of the earth to the South Pole.

87 ▪ The earth's orbital plane is the plane in which the earth revolves around the sun in a year's time.

88 ▪ The vernal equinox is one of the two points of intersection between the ecliptic and the celestial equator – the point the sun crosses on March 21st as it moves from the southern sphere of the heavens into the northern sphere in what appears to be its annual orbit from our viewpoint on earth. The celestial equator divides the celestial globe into a northern and southern celestial sphere. It can be considered an extension of the earth's equator and is located in the same plane.

89 ▪ Semjase is a Plejaren spaceship pilot and one of the most important contact persons with Eduard Meier. *(See – Chapter 2)*

90 ▪ The Plejaren are inhabitants of a region of space near the seven stars in the Taurus Constellation known as the Pleiades. *(See – Chapter 2)*

91 ▪ A FIGU publication referencing the February 1989 issue *(See page 7)*

92 ▪ Damocles: a flatterer who, having extolled the happiness of Dionysius, tyrant of Syracuse, was seated at a banquet with a sword suspended over his head by a single hair to show him the perilous nature of that happiness.

93 ▪ A small, periodic oscillation of the earth's axis which slightly varies or nods the Earth's precessional motion.

Physical and Spiritual Brain Quotients

Clarification of the Concept: Brain Quotient

Every person possesses a material consciousness and a spiritual consciousness and also a material and spiritual brain quotient. This can be expressed in percentages.

While compiling the percentage values for the year 1844, when about 1.4 billion people inhabited the earth, a mistake must have slipped in somehow because the calculation was simply not understandable. It was due to this circumstance that Billy called Bernadette and me into his office in the hope that we could perhaps undo the Gordian knot. But we could not imagine any more than Billy how a percentage value under 10 percent was to occur with this distinct presentation — and that is exactly where the snag was. In order to get out of this fix, Billy decided to tap the cosmic memory bank. At first, he laid his head across the small pad of his arm stump while his right hand held the ballpoint pen ready to write. He concentrated, called up the desired percentage values and noted these down on a piece of DIN-A 4 paper (German standard paper size), one after the other, with his eyes closed. Afterward, as we added the percentage values, we came up with exactly 100 percent. We had obviously overlooked the 1.8 percent. The following percent values were now listed on his scratch paper: 60 – 24.8 - 9.007 - 5.1 – 0.008 - 0.003 - 0.002 and then the missing 1.8.

These percentage values express the levels of the physical brain quotient found among earth inhabitants in the year 1844:

Hence, Billy had once again given us visible proof of his many and varied abilities.

BRAIN QUOTIENTS RESPECTIVE TO PERCENTAGE OF POPULATION		
1.8% =	25,200,000 Earth people under	10%
60% =	840,000,000 Earth people from	10–11%
24.08% =	337,120,000 Earth people from	11–14%
9.007% =	126,098,000 Earth people from	14.5–16%
5.1% =	71,400,000 Earth people from	16–18%
0.008% =	112,000 Earth people from	18–20%
0.003% =	42,000 Earth people from	20–24%
0.002% =	28,000 Earth people over	24%

Fig. B-1
These are the respective physical brain quotients.

Physical Brain Quotient

The physical brain quotient (material consciousness quotient, personality quotient) consists of two integrated factors: the brain value in use and the intelligence value.

The brain value in use shows what percentage of the brain capacity a person is capable of using. The unused remainder completely goes to waste. A material brain quotient of 14 percent means that a mere 14 percent is used for the brainwork in the material realm.

As a matter of rule, the material intelligence value corresponds numerically with the brain value in use. Differences between the two percentage values only occur with disorders of the material consciousness.

In the course of progressive development, a human being learns how to make better use of his material brain quotient, the entire volume representing 100 percent. Theoretically, this value increases by 1 percent within a period of 1,000 years. (100 percent should be obtained in 86,000 years.) Unfortunately, in general practice the outcome is quite different. Attaining 100 percent in 86,000 years is only valid if the evolution were to take a normal course without retrogression, an achievement which practically never occurs. In reality, the continued material development does not permanently increase, but continuously alternates between advancement and retrogression, up and down, similar to the curve of a stock value. Therefore, we have to consider billions of years of development before the highest value of 100 percent is finally reached.

The Spiritual Brain Quotient

The spiritual brain quotient (spiritual consciousness quotient) is a criterion for the spiritual potency of a person or their spiritual evolutionary level. In principle, the percentage point of the spiritual brain quotient can correlate with that of the material brain, which is roughly true in only a few exceptional cases among the earth people at the present time. The lower the spiritual evolutionary level, the more the percentage point decreases. As we can see from the following list, the greatest difference is no less than 7 percent (List from the year 1978).

Towards the top, the percentage point is very clearly limited. It may not exceed a maximum of 1 percent above the value of the material brain quotient. This is a security measure that prevents an over-dimensionizing from occurring within a human life form. The purely spiritual evolution should not become too predominant. The material development would otherwise be short-changed, causing people to be almost incapable of survival by fully neglecting the necessity of preserving the life of their own body.

PHYSICAL & SPIRITUAL BRAIN QUOTIENTS
RESPECTIVE TO PERCENTAGE OF POPULATION
For Earth population in the year 1978,
outlining the following results accordingly:

1	Human Being	with 25.7%	Physical brain quotient
		and 25.8%	Spiritual brain quotient
2	Human Beings	with 25.01%	Physical brain quotient
		and 24.06%	Spiritual brain quotient
14	Human Beings	with 20-24%	Physical brain quotient
		and 17.6%	Spiritual brain quotient
1,246	Human Beings	with 18-20%	Physical brain quotient
		and 16.04%	Spiritual brain quotient
456,021	Human Beings	with 16-18%	Physical brain quotient
		and 15.06%	Spiritual brain quotient
30%	of remaining interest of mankind	14.5-16%	Physical brain quotient
		and 13.8%	Spiritual brain quotient
62%	of remaining interest of mankind	11-14.5%	Physical brain quotient
		and 10.9%	Spiritual brain quotient
4%	of remaining interest of mankind	10-11%	Physical brain quotient
		and 9.6%	Spiritual brain quotient
4%	Humans less than	10%	Physical brain quotient
		and 3-6%	Spiritual brain quotient

Source: Taken from "Things Worth Knowing" #4

Fig. B-2
These are the respective physical and spiritual brain quotients.

"Rule of Internal" by Titius and Bode

In the second half of the 18th Century, before anyone had any notion about the planets Uranus, Neptune and so forth, a German mathematician by the name of Titius calculated the distances of the planets to the sun, while the astronomer, Bode, introduced this finding to astronomical science.

The mathematical formula that forms the basis of the *Rule of Interval*:

- The planetary names are written one below the other in their proper sequential order: Mercury, Venus, Earth, Mars, Jupiter, Saturn, Uranus, Neptune and Pluto (Transpluto and Uni[94]).

- The numerical order, 0, 1, 2, 4 and so forth are written next to each planet.

- Each line is then calculated by multiplying by 3, adding 4, and dividing by 10.

"Rule of Interval" for the Planets of Our SOL-System

The mean interval from the earth to the Sun — the Astronomical Unit, AU, which is about 150 million kilometers (149.6 x 10⁶ kilometers) serves as a number for comparison.

> **10 (see abstract).** The results of this are approximately the mean intervals of the planets to the Sun, expressed in astronomical units (AU). An AU marks the mean interval from the earth to the Sun, which is about 150 million kilometers (149.6 x 10⁶ kilometers), and is used as a standard of comparison. Mars, for example, with 1.6 AU, is on the average 1.6 times as far away from the sun as the earth, and Jupiter with 5.2 AU, is 5.2 times as far away, and so forth.

Sun						Actually measured interval		
Mercury	0 x 3 =	0 plus 4 =	4:10 =	0.4 AU	0.39 AU =	57.9 x 10⁶km
Venus	1 x 3 =	3 plus 4 =	7:10 =	0.7 AU	0.72 AU =	108.2 x 10⁶km
Earth	2 x 3 =	6 plus 4 =	10:10 =	1.0 AU	1.00 AU =	149.6 x 10⁶km
Mars	4 x 3 =	12 plus 4 =	16:10 =	1.6 AU	1.52 AU =	227.9 x 10⁶km
Asteroid Belt	8 x 3 =	24				
Jupiter	16 x 3 =	48 plus 4 =	52:10 =	5.2 AU	5.20 AU =	778.3 x 10⁶km
Saturn	32 x 3 =	96 plus 4 =	100:10 =	10.0 AU	9.54 AU =	1427.0 x 10⁶km
Uranus	64 x 3 =	192 plus 4 =	196:10 =	19.6 AU	19.20 AU =	2869.6 x 10⁶km
Neptune					30.1 AU =	4504.0 x 10⁶km
Pluto	128 x 3 =	384 plus 4 =	388:10 =	38.8 AU	39.4 AU =	5899.9 x 10⁶km

Fig. C-1

Footnotes

94 ▪ Transpluto and Uni (See FIGU *Bulletin #9, Vol. #1*) Reader's questions on the Web site of FIGU-Switzerland — *www.figu.org*.

GLOSSARY

ALENA [ah-LEH-nah] – A contact person to Billy who, on one occasion, helped another extraterrestrial named Menara demonstrate an ancient laser pistol. In Photo #50, Alena can be partially seen holding the laser pistol inside Billy's office.

ARAHAT ATHERSATA – A pure spiritual We-form whose name means "The precious one who contemplates the times."

ASHTAR SHERAN – Is the pseudonym for the extraterrestrial leader Aruseak. He was the cousin of the last boss of the Giza Intelligences Kamagol II, who was striving for world domination. Ashtar Sheran was active on earth in a negative and criminal way, on behalf of Kamagol II and his followers, up to the year 1937.

Sometime in 1983, Ashtar Sheran and his followers were killed during a failed attack against the Timars (Asket's planetary nation from our neighboring DAL Universe.) Following the natural laws of Creation, those who died in the DAL Universe will have to incarnate there. Since Ashtar Sheran's physical body is dead, and his spirit form exists in the DAL Universe, no telepathic or otherwise communication can take place with him or those who exist in the DERN-universe.

ASKET – Asket's home planet exists in a twin universe to our own called "DAL." Her race, the Timars (pronounced "timmarz"), emigrated to the DAL Universe about 50,000 years ago from our own universe, which is called "DERN." They accomplished this by creating a gateway through a highly advanced technology. Asket's people share the same ancient ancestry/heritage with the Plejaren and the earth human races. The Timars exchange their very advanced technical knowledge for the immense spiritual wisdom of the Plejaren. Therefore, the Plejaren, who were once 3,000 years ahead of earthly technology, have recently achieved incredible technical advances and are presently 8,000 years ahead of us.

Although Asket is not a Plejaren, the young-looking, blonde-haired Asket greatly assisted Billy in the preparation for his mission. She contacted Billy for the first time on February 3, 1953 and lasted for eleven year and ended in 1964, returning to her home in the DAL Universe. Asket's subtle influence guided Billy for 12 years through many lands of earth to learn and experience various cultures, belief systems and earthly knowledge in general. Asket also took Billy on time travel trips into the past to allow him to see firsthand the true nature of many historical events. The main concern of her people was to assist the Plejaren in monitoring earthly affairs since they know that we are on a very dangerous course in our evolution. She explained to Billy that we are nearing a time when we cannot only destroy ourselves, but are threatening the balance of cosmic space as well.

BAAVI INTELLIGENCES [BAH-vee] – They have an association with the Plejaren and are called on occasion to perform special tasks for them. They live in the same solar system (Tayget) and dimension as do the Plejaren.

BEAMSHIP – The word "beamship" is an old term for a type of light-based drive. Though such drive systems are not currently used by the Plejaren, the word is used when discussing their spacecraft. During the time of peak interaction with the Plejaren, Billy could identify at least seven variations of "beamships."

COSMIC ALLIANCES – A League of Nations – consisting of 127 billion people that extends far into the cosmos and to which many planetary systems belong. The Plejaren are affiliated with a cosmic alliance to the High Council in the Andromeda Galaxy.

CREATIONAL LAWS AND COMMANDMENTS – For instance, one of the most significant laws states that the errors humans commit should not be condemned, because only by committing errors can humans evolve. Hence, humans can learn from the mistakes they make. After committing mistakes, they will eventually recognize this fact, reflect on them, and remedy their errors. And, as a rule, they will become more knowledgeable and will refrain from making the same mistakes again, at least not in the identical ways; and thus they make progress. This also signifies that humans must thoroughly reflect on all matters so as to recognize where they are prone to making mistakes and to gather new knowledge, which will lead them to success and advancement. Success and advancement will be achieved by pensive thought, and this is another important Creational-natural law without which any evolution is impossible.

A law, therefore, is an established and irrevocable rule which, when implemented and followed, prevents the life form from experiencing harm of any kind. A directive, by contrast, is a mere recommendation which guides the person in a specific direction where some initiative should be taken or disregarded and, as a consequence, something good or bad, respectively something positive or negative, will occur. The following recommendations represent such Creational-natural directives:

'You shall not kill in depravity.'
'You shall not violate your covenant with CREATION.'
'You shall not steal or expropriate from others.'
'You shall not blaspheme the Truth,' and so forth.

DAL UNIVERSE – A twin universe that gently nudges against our own DERN Universe. Asket comes from the DAL Universe. The DAL Universe is where Semjase presently resides while recovering from her head injury and subsequent cerebral collapse, which occurred at the Semjase Silver Star Center in 1984.

DERN UNIVERSE – This is the name of our universe, which contains all known matter that our scientists currently see and a great deal more. As do most universes, the DERN Universe has seven layers or belts and is billions of light-years in size. *Source: FIGU Bulletin #5, Vol. #1 June 1996 (English Version)*

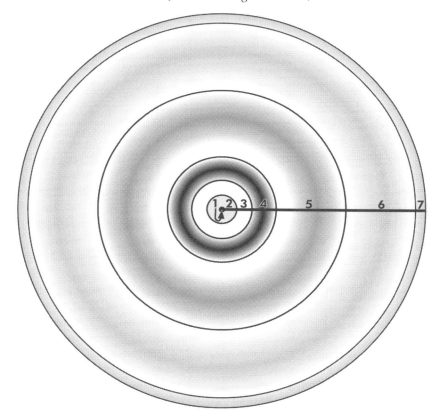

Fig. Glossary -1
A graphic cross-section of our DERN Universe. (Not to scale)

1. **CENTRAL CORE:**
   radius is 3.5 light-years

2. **UR-CORE:**
   1 x 10¹⁴ light-years

3. **UR-SPACE:**
   1 x 10¹⁴ light-years

4. **SOLID-STATE MATTER UNIVERSE BELT:**
   2.5×10^{15} light-years. This belt includes all galaxies, planets, stars, etc.

5. **TRANSFORMATION BELT:**
   1×10^{55} light-years

6. **CREATION BELT:**
   1.4×10^{64} light-years

7. **DISPLACEMENT BELT:**
   1.4×10^{7} light-years

DECALOGUE – A book transmitted to Billy via the Petale Level. It contains the original 12 Commandents which serve as spiritual guidelines for mankind. These directives were given to humans in ancient times but were later manpulated by negative forces which became the tenets of the biblical "Ten Commandments."

DRUANS – They are a highly developed and extremely peaceful human race and are capable of bringing innovations to our own technology. The planet Druan, is located in the NOL System, which belongs to a galaxy whose expanse is about 1.7 times as large as ours, and this galaxy is about 310 billion light years from this SOL System."

GIZA INTELLIGENCES – A group of extraterrestrials whose base of operations was located near the Giza Plateau in Egypt. In 1956, Asket and Billy visited the installation. After rendering themselves invisible to detection, they trekked deep beneath the pyramid complex to find the rogue base. There they found a derelict spacecraft (372 ft. high and 981 ft. in diameter) in an immense hall that was far beneath the earth and a mile from the Giza Pyramid, hence their present moniker — "Giza Intelligences."

The Giza Intelligences were the owners of the craft. There were "extraterrestrial renegades from the Henoch-line who came to earthmany thousands of years previously from the space-time alteration of the Lyra-Vega area."

For hundreds of centuries, the Giza Intelligences were replete with evil intrigue. In more modern times, they were the puppet masters to Hitler and many of his henchmen. Before and during World War II, they helped Hitler throughout his career as the maniacal leader of Germany. Though they were officially removed from the planet with the blessings of the High Council, their negative influences still remain to this day.

HIGH COUNCIL – Residing in the Andromeda Galaxy, the High Council is the name of the central authority of the Plejaren and their allies within the Cosmic Federation. Members of the High Council are so spiritually advanced that they have reached a stage whereby they exist in a half-physical and half-spiritual human state of being.

JHWH [ish-wish] – "King of wisdom." They possess the highest degree of knowledge and wisdom that humans can possibly acquire as long as they have a material body. A king of wisdom has the duty of standing by his people and providing his help and advice. He also presides over inhabited planets but cannot assume the role of a despotic ruler, a predicament that occurred to some extent on earth in earlier times.

Semjase's father, Ptaah, currently presides over three planets, Erra, Terra (our earth) and Alatides. Because of the level of spiritual and material attainment, many of those JHWHs who visited earth in the ancient times were considered gods to the resident humans of earth. Even today, if we earthlings were exposed to a Plejaren directly, we would become so overwhelmed by their level of pure feelings and logic that we could experience unreasonable euphoria or tremendous mental confusion. (This is one of the reasons why the Plejaren do not land on the "White House lawn.")

JSCHRJSCH [ish-rish] –"Queen of wisdom." Semjase was considered (before her accident) to be a demi-jschrjsch.

KOSAN – An intercosmic lanquage the Cosmic Alliances use to communicate with one another.

LYRA-VEGA STAR SYSTEM – The original birthplace of the Plejaren's ancestors.

MENARA [men-NAR-ah] – is a dark-skinned woman from the Lyra System. She belongs to one of the races befriended by the Plejaren who were stationed on earth for eleven years (1975-86). She often acted as contact person in place of Semjase and Quetzal.

PETALE LEVEL – The highest stage of pure spirit forms or pure spiritual energy beings before becoming one with the Creation.

PLANET ERRA [EHR-ah] – The present home planet of the Plejaren. The planet is about the same size as earth and has a similar rotation.

They maintain a balanced population of approximately 500 million people. Much of their work force is either completely automated or run by androids. Even still, all Errans, adults and adolescents alike, perform two hours of manual work each day in order to reach a balance between their spirit and consciousness.

PLEIJA [PLAY-yah] – is Semjase's precocious sister. According to Billy, Pleija is a vibrant, adventurous creature with long, black hair. While visiting with Billy, Pleija took a spin on his moped as Semjase watched on nervously.

PRECESSION – The slow, gradual westward motion of the equinoxes due to the precessional movement of the Earth's axis. The precession of the equinoxes occurs at a rate of 50.116 seconds of arc per year, making a complete circle around the North Pole of the ecliptic once every 25,860 years. *(See ~ Appendix A)*

PTAAH [p-TAH] – Until recently, he was the overseer of earth and several other planetary races. He is the father of Semjase, Pleija and Jucata[95] and is 795 years old.[96] (In earth years, Ptaah would be a healthy 79½ year-old man.) Note: The Ptaah of planet Erra is not to be confused with the Ptah of ancient Egypt or Ptaah, the son of the barbarian JHWH, Arus I who menaced ancient earth.

QUETZAL [KWET-sahl] – is 464 years of age,[97] 1.9 meters (6'4") tall, has blue-gray eyes and light brown hair. He is married to four wives and is the father of six children. During the 11-year contact period (1975-1986), Quetzal was commander of all Plejaren stations in our SOL system. According to Billy, Quetzal possesses enormous abilities, especially in the field of technology. He is also quite a distinguished inventor who has invented and constructed several very useful devices, such as increasing the speed of Billy's typewriter so Billy could type 1,200 characters maximum per minute (20/sec) using spiritual power.

SEMJASE (sem-YAH-seh) – is 354 years old.[98] She is about 1.7 meters (5.5 ft.) tall, slender, young, pretty, fair-skinned, with sparkling blue eyes and light-blond hair. Her extended, somewhat elongated earlobes, provide her with a special feature. This is the only anatomical difference that distinguishes her from our women on earth. Due to her exceptional knowledge, which far exceeds even the average person on her home planet, Erra, Semjase carries the rank of a demi-Jschrjsch (ish-rish), which means a demi-queen of wisdom or a demi-goddess as this type of person was referred to in earlier times on earth in Greek mythology. Having occupied herself with various matters relating to our planet years before she made contact with Billy on January 28, 1975, Semjase is by far the most knowledgeable extraterrestrial regarding our situation here on earth. During the period from February 1965 through June 1973, she remained in the DAL Universe with Asket's people. Upon her return from the DAL Universe to Erra, she came to earth in July 1973 and, in a hidden station, continued to carry out the tasks she previously performed here.

Semjase was once married but lost her husband with whom she had been married for only seven years. Her spouse participated in a foreign galaxy research expedition. Of the two dispatched research ships only one returned home safely after eleven years; the other ship, with her husband on board, unfortunately suffered control damage and crashed into a sun. Semjase bore no children in her marriage.

Unfortunately, on December 15, 1977, Semjase had a life-threatening accident at the Semjase Silver Star Center in Hinterschmidrüti (Switzerland), and was immediately whisked to Erra, her Plejaren home planet, for medical treatment and rehabilitation. In May 1978, she returned to earth and resumed her contacts with Billy until March 26, 1981. From March 1981 until the end of January 1984 she had no contact with Billy since other duties prevented her from visiting him. February 3, 1984, was the date of her final contact with Billy. Due to her accident on December 15, 1977, Semjase suffered a cerebral collapse at the beginning of November 1984 and she was taken directly to the DAL Universe where she is now recuperating with the help of Asket and her friends, the Sonaers. Semjase's father, Ptaah, explains that the complete regeneration of her brain and all PSI powers, abilities and her memory loss during her collapse will likely take about seventy earth years. During this convalescent period, she will spend most of her time in the DAL Universe. No possible communication linkage exists between the DAL and DERN-universes — the only possible communication is achieved when beings actually traverse the distance and bring the communiqué with them. There is no possible mode for a person to establish telepathic, let alone personal, contact with Semjase while she is in the DAL Universe.

SFATH (s-FAHTH) – was an old, venerable man and the first Plejaren to contact Billy when he was five years old. He was Semjase's grandfather. Although his age was not mentioned, Billy estimated that he looked about 90-95 years old. (At the time of his visit, Sfath was almost 1,000 years old.) In 1942, Sfath took young Billy in his pear-shaped, silver craft high over the earth. Placing a helmet-like apparatus over Billy's head, Sfath instilled vast amounts of knowledge and perceptions into Billy's brain. This knowledge would later help Billy fulfill the tasks necessary for his mission, which he still performs to this day. After educating Billy for

*Sketch by Christian Krukowski

several years through mostly telepathic instruction, Sfath handed over the next phase of Billy's education to Asket. Soon after, Sfath passed away.

SOLAR [soh-LARH] – is an extraterrestrial man belonging to the races stationed on earth. He worked many years as an ally of the Plejaren.

SPIRITUAL TELEPORATION – A very fast method of transportng a body from one place to another through dematerialization and rematerialization — with the help of spiritual forces of consciousness (without technical aid). In fact, it is set off quite consciously. A person able to teleport spiritually must be on an enormously high rung of spiritual evolution. Immense spiritual forces are necessary for this. Quite often, a number of spiritual forms join together to create a spiritual assemblage. By combining their efforts they are able to transport effectively.

TALJDA [tah-LEE-dah] – is a yellow-skinned woman from planet Nissan in the Lyra-Vega System, which is one of the planets her people settled several million years ago. Her ancestors came from the planet Kudra, the ancient home planet of a segment of today's Asian earth races. Previously, Taljda had been Billy's contact person a few times.

TELEMETER DISKS – Unmanned, remote controlled flying disks for surveillance and exploration. They range from 0.4 in. to 17 ft. in size. Several FIGU members have seen glimpses of these machines. On at least one occasion, a small telemeter disk showed up on a photo that was innocently taken by one of the FIGU members as it zipped around the exterior of the main house.

TELEPATHIC CONTACT – consists of two forms:

1.   Primary telepathy is functional within planet boundaries.

2.   Spiritual telepathy is functional within universe boundaries and is instantaneous. Billy had to learn over 50 million spiritual symbols, some comprising up to 800 squiggly lines. Most of Billy's official contacts began with a telepathic message telling him when and where the contact would take place.

Footnotes

95 ▪ Jucata is no longer alive. No information is available regarding the circumstances of his death.

96 ▪ On June 14th, 1976, Semjase told Billy that Ptaah, her father, was 770 years old.

97 ▪ Due to the lack of a reference pont (birthdate in earthly terms) Quetzal's current age cannot be verified.

98 ▪ Semjase's current age cannot be verified.

RESOURCE LITERATURE

ANALYSIS OF MAJOR RET. COLMAN S. VONKEVICZKY – MMSE, Director of ICUFON USA

ARAHAT ATHERSATA – Aquarian Age Publishing House (Wassermannzeit Verlag) FIGU (German language only)

ASTRONOMY – by Peter Lancaster Brown, Orell Füssli Publisher, Zurich 1974 (German language issue)

EXTRATERRESTRIALS AND THE EARTHMAN'S LONGING FOR PEACE – by Maarten Dillinger, R.G. Fischer Publisher, Alt Fechenheim 73, D-6000 Frankfurt 61, 1984 (German language only)

ILLUSTRATED ATLAS OF THE UNIVERSE – by A. Rükl and Walter Kraus, 1988 Artia, Praha, Publisher, Werner Dausien, Hanau/Main (German language only)

THE UNIVERSE – by Iain Nicolson and Patric Moore, Mosaik Publisher GmbH, Munich (German language only)

INTRODUCTION TO ASTRONOMY – by Karl Thoene, Publisher Hallwag, Bern (German language only)

PHOTO INDEX – Aquarian Age Publishing House (Wassermannzeit Verlag) FIGU (German language only)

LETTERS OF CORRESPONDENCE OF THE SPIRIT TEACHINGS AND STUDIES – Aquarian Age Publishing House (Wassermannzeit Verlag) FIGU (German language only)

GENESIS – Aquarian Age Publishing House (Wassermannzeit Verlag) FIGU (German language only)

AND STILL THEY FLY! – *Second Edition*

HOBBY BROCHURE – 9/90, page 61 (German language only)

COURSE OF ASTROLOGY VOLUME 1 – by Dr. H. Freiherr von Klöckler M.D., Publisher, Herman Bauer K.G., D-7800 Freiburg i.Brg. (German language only)

LIGHT YEARS – by Gary Kinder, Publisher, The Atlantic Monthly Press, New York 1987

MARATHON IN THE UNIVERSE – by Reiner Klingholz, Georg Westermann Publisher, GmbH, Braunschweig 1989, 2nd edition 1990 (German language only)

MEYER'S MANUAL OF THE UNIVERSE – by Karl Schaifers and Gerhard Traving, Bibliographic Institute Mannheim, Vienna-Zurich, 6th edition (German language only)

TRI-MONTHLY JOURNAL, "VOICE OF THE AQUARIAN AGE" – Aquarian Age Publishing House (Wassermannzeit Verlag) FIGU, CH-8495 Schmidrüti ZH/ Switzerland (German language only)

OM – Aquarian Age Publishing House (Wassermannzeit Verlag) FIGU (German language only)

OPEN LETTER – by Gary Kinder, MUFON UFO Journal #28, April 1987

PROPHECIES – Aquarian Age Publishing House (Wassermannzeit Verlag) FIGU (German language only)

SEMJASE REPORTS – Billy's contact reports, spirit teachings, explanations and experiences with extraterrestrial, Plejaren life forms — Aquarian Age Publishing House (Wassermannzeit Verlag) FIGU (German language only)

SUN, MOON AND PLANETS – by Erhard Keppler, Piper Publisher, Munich, 2nd edition 1990 (German language only)

THE MEIER INCIDENT, "THE MOST INFAMOUS HOAX IN UFOLOGY" – by Kal K. Korff with the editorial assistance of William L. Moore, USA

UFO CONTACT FROM THE PLEIADES – by Lt. Col. Wendelle C. Stevens, Ret., USA 1982

UFO DOCUMENTED COLLECTION, HUGIN SOCIETY FOR POLITICAL AND PHILOSOPHICAL STUDIES – registered organization, D-5802 Wetter 4, P.O. Box 13 (German language only)

TERRIFIC WORLDS – Planets, Moons and Comets – by Rudolf Kippenhahn, licensed edition for the Book Club Ex Libris Zurich 1988 - German Publishing House Stuttgart (German language only)

FORTY ENCOUNTERS WITH EXTRATERRESTRIALS IN BRAZIL – by Dr. Walter K. Bühler, Rio, Ventla Publisher, D-6200 Wiesbaden 13 (German language only)

JOURNAL OF FACTS WORTH KNOWING "VOICE OF THE AQUARIAN AGE" – Aquarian Age Publishing House (Wassermannzeit Verlag) FIGU (German language only)

AN INTERVIEW WITH A UFO CONTACTEE – A comprehensive booklet and excellent reference on the Billy Meier case containing over 40 detailed answers to by Billy Meier questions, conducted in 1995 by FIGU lecturer and author Guido Moosbrugger. Complete with side-by-side German and English, as well as new photographs taken of the interview held at the Semjase Silver Star Center, this booklet explains many topics surrounding the mission, life and spirit teachings of Billy Meier and the Pleiadian/Plejaren extraterrestrials. *$7.00 (68 pages)*

AN IMPORTANT WORD CONCERNING THE OCCULT FORCES AND MEDITATION – An in-depth look at the dangers of occult forces on their various levels including the process of forming self-created entities and forces in the psychic realm. The principles of a successful meditation are discussed, presenting an analysis of the adverse forces that the meditating student will inevitably encounter. *$5.00 (22 pages)*

A SURREPTITIOUS ENVIRONMENTAL CATASTROPHE ~ The Desert Will Win – An important environmental booklet describing the destruction of nature and the extensive desertification now occurring on earth. Overpopulation is also discussed as being the number one cause of these environmental problems affecting us all. *$1.00 (10 pages)*

ATTACKING QUESTIONS FROM JAPAN – Straightforward questions from Japan concerning the meaning of freedom, the function and bylaws of FIGU, error and atonement, clarification of true contactees, the history of the Chinese and Japanese races, excerpts from recent contacts and other topics. *$5.00 (30 pages)*

BILLY MEIER ~ His Contacts With Extraterrestrials – A basic introduction to Billy Meier and his contacts with extraterrestrials. This booklet details some of the overwhelming evidence provided by Billy and his extraterrestrial friends such as the photographs, metal samples, 8mm films, witnesses, and the initial investigation. This is a perfect booklet for someone who is just discovering this unique and well-documented UFO case. *$5.00 (19 pages)*

THE CHALLENGE OF OVERPOPULATION – Written by Fuctuoso Suzara, this pamphlet addresses the overpopulation problem in the Philippines. Fuctuoso covers population control methods, contraception and various programs that need to be implemented. *$1.00 (6 pages)*

CONTACT 235 – Verbatim dialog of a contact on Feb. 3, 1990 between Billy and Ptaah including discussions on crop circles, the true concept of polygamy, other earthly contactees as well as contact liars, earthquakes and human contributions to natural disasters. *$5.00 (36 pages)*

CONTACT 241-243 – A three-contact booklet containing verbatim dialog between Ptaah and Billy. They discuss details on smoking, various earthquakes, the Greenpeace organization, the formation of our galaxy, the renewed possibility of contact with another extraterrestrial race around the turn of the century, and many more subjects. *$10.00 (39 pages)*

CONTACT 249 – Ptaah and Billy talk about other extraterrestrial races visiting the earth. They also discussed Billy's book "An Introduction to Meditation," the overpopulation, BSE and the number of deaths due to religion. *$5.00 (34 pages)*

DESIDERATA – A thought-provoking poem and helpful reminder of the important things in life and proper ways of thinking, written by "Billy" Eduard Albert Meier. *Free w/ purchase (6 pages)*

49 QUESTIONS – Have you ever pondered about life? Why do we live? What about extraterrestrials? Why are they really here? What about earth? Why are we here and who or what created us? What is love? Why is the world turning upside-down? Word War III? Meditation? Inside this extensive text, you will discover the answers to these questions and many more. *$5.00 (44 pages)*

HUMAN BEINGS AND HUMANNESS – Insightful words on the unique characteristics of human beings and what it truly means to be a human being. Also, twenty-three essential pieces of advice for mankind and one's daily walk on the path of evolution. *Free w/ purchase (7 pages)*

LIFE IN THE SPIRITUAL AND PHYSICAL – An intensive examination of man's struggle to find true spiritual values, as well as the real meaning of life in the material realm. Laws and harmony creation, inner values, egotism of mankind and a definition of true happiness are just a few of the topics covered in this enlightening book. *$1.00 (30 pages)*

OUR MANIFESTO – A very informative booklet that defines the goals and efforts of the group founded by Billy Meier called FIGU. FIGU is a German acronym that stands for "Free Community of Interests for the Frontier and Spiritual Sciences and Ufological Studies." *$1.00 (18 pages)*

OVERPOPULATION BOMB – Billy Meier outlines man's indisputable, calculable exploitation of planet earth and the criminal depletion of its resources through overpopulation and global mismanagement. Discrimination towards women and the servile role they endure even to this day in many nations is explained and correlated to the increasing overpopulation problem. *$1.00 (26 pages)*

THE PEACE MEDITATION – In our opinion, one of the most important pieces of information pertaining to the Billy Meier mission. Learn everything you've wanted to know about the bi-monthly meditation for peace practiced by thousands around the world. Numerous negative prophecies have been dissolved through this meditation according to the Pleiadians/Plejaren. All your questions will be answered in this highly informative booklet. *$1.00 (10 pages)*

TORTURE AND THE DEATH PENALTY – Two important topics contrary to nature's laws are candidly explained. The reasons why torture and the death penalty are illogical and ineffective are covered as well as the necessary application of truth and logic concerning these issues. *$1.00 (26 pages)*

TALMUD OF JMMANUEL – Who was Jmmanuel, the man known to us as Jesus? What was his connection to extraterrestrials and was he really resurrected? These questions and many more are ultimately answered in this clear German/English translation from the original 2,000 year-old Aramaic scrolls discovered in a burial cave. *$18.00 (272 pages)*

THOSE WHO LIE ABOUT CONTACTS – Information on liars, cheats and frauds in the UFO community and false claims of contact with Ashtar and Hatonn among others. Quotations from the books "OM" and "An Open Word" present a profile of the man called Mohammed explaining much about his actual task on earth. *$5.00 (41 pages)*

SEE ORDER FORM ON THE BACK OF THIS PAGE.
MAKE A COPY AND MAIL CHECK OR MONEY ORDER TO:
FIGU SOCIETY USA, P.O. BOX 730, MOUNDS, OK 74047

FIGU SOCIETY USA ORDER FORM

		QTY.	Subtotal
And Still They Fly! $26.95	x [_____]	= _____
An Important Word Concerning the Occult Forces and Meditation $5.00	x [_____]	= _____
An Interview With A UFO Contactee $7.00	x [_____]	= _____
A Surreptitious Environmental Catastrophe ~ The Desert Will Win . . . $1.00	x [_____]	= _____
Attacking Questions from Japan $5.00	x [_____]	= _____
Billy Meier ~ His Contacts With Extraterrestrials $5.00	x [_____]	= _____
The Challenge of Overpopulation $1.00	x [_____]	= _____
Contact 235 . . . . $5.00	x [_____]	= _____
Contact 241-243 . . . . $10.00	x [_____]	= _____
Contact 249 . . . . $5.00	x [_____]	= _____
49 Questions $5.00	x [_____]	= _____
Life in the Spiritual and Physical $1.00	x [_____]	= _____
Our Manifesto $1.00	x [_____]	= _____
Overpopulation Bomb $1.00	x [_____]	= _____
The Peace Meditation $1.00	x [_____]	= _____
Talmud of Jmmanuel $18.00	x [_____]	= _____
Those Who Lie About Contacts $5.00	x [_____]	= _____
Torture and the Death Penalty $1.00	x [_____]	= _____
Desiderata . . . . Free with purchase	$4.00 S&H	= _____
Human Beings and Humanness . . . . Free with purchase	TAX	= _____
	TOTAL	= _____

Make check out to "FIGU Society"
FIGU Society USA, P.O. Box 730, Mounds, OK 74047
ALLOW 2-4 WEEKS FOR DELIVERY

A LITTLE BIT OF KNOWLEDGE, SENSE AND WISDOM – The long way to understanding and to the realization of the consequences of the creational principle of cause and effect in our life and development; and what is necessary in order to achieve our goal of evolution.

AN OPEN WORD – The criminal and contemptuous machinations of religions, Christianity in particular, the church and its sects; the million-fold bloody madness of all those, and its degenerate, exploiting, criminal, assassinating works and actions that falsify the truth — laid open in the *Open Word* and written in a free and uncensored language.

ARAHAT ATHERSATA – Message to the earthly humanity from a high spirit form; explaining facts of human behavior in religion, politics and the sciences, etc.

ATLANTA – Volume 3 of an adventurous crime novel trilogy by Billy: Atlanta is a well-educated, smart, self-responsible and strong woman to whom an unfortunate stroke of fate plays an evil trick. She would be broken down by it if the shining hero Gelion would not break free and conquer the darkness of hell through which she must walk.

BOOKS OF NAMES – A total of 6,360 interplanetary names (male and female) in their original form and their meaning. Received and recorded by Billy (in three volumes).

BOOK OF WITNESSES – Witnesses' reports of their experiences with "Billy" Eduard Albert Meier, his abilities and contacts with human beings from the Plejaren and their federation; with many black-and-white pictures.

DIRECTIVES – These are guidelines and behavioral regulations for the processing, attainment and conservation of psychic, physical and consciousness purity and health. They are drawn up within the framework of the laws and commandments to follow the hygienic care of the body, psyche, spirit and consciousness which are anchored in the teachings of the spirit.

DECALOGUE – The "Ten Commandments" in their original form, including two other commandments withheld from humanity until now.

EXISTING LIFE IN THE UNIVERSE – Billy Meier's contacts with the Plejaren; extraterrestrial life; the SOL system, comets and meteors; universal life…

FROM THE DEPTHS OF THE UNIVERSE – Billy tells the story of his contacts, from the beginning until today. Content: How all began; My first contact; Asket's explanations; Attacks; Documentation; Unbelief; What the extraterrestrials told me about the human beings on earth; What the extraterrestrials told me about their home world; Travels through space and time; The extraterrestrials' message for us human beings; The future development of earth… etc.

GENESIS – The teachings of the origin of Creation as well as the development of the universe, heavenly bodies, flora and fauna and the human life forms according to the laws of Creation with the evolutionary guidelines for man resulting here from.

GO TO HELL, GELION / BY THE POWER OF LAW – Volume 2 of an adventurous crime novel trilogy by Billy: Two novels of the adventures of Gelion which he had to come through before he encountered Atlanta.

INTRODUCTION INTO MEDITATION – Is an introduction to truthful meditation, its use and its effectiveness in the human life.

THE LAW OF LOVE – Is about love as the foundation of all existence, the lawfulness of love, its definition and its meaning in human life.

LIFE AND DEATH – About the continuing existence of the life-giving spirit of man in the realm beyond after the death of the physical body and about the life of man as such and man as such, with everything of importance in the realm within him and the realm outside of him.

MAN ON EARTH, I WISH YOU… – In his legacy, Billy gives us an extraordinary gift into our hands that makes our life rich and worthwhile to live, if we manage the good handed over to us with care and prudence, if we are using it sensibly and responsibly, and if we let it grow in our life.

OM – The most important Laws and Commandments of Creation, rules of order and guidelines; aim and task of man in his material and spiritual life, laid out and explained by JHWH Ptaah and his prophet, Billy.

THE PHANTOM / WHITE-SLAVE TRADER – Volume 1 of an adventurous crime novel trilogy by Billy: Two novels of the adventures of Gelion which he had to come through before he encountered Atlanta.

PHOTO BOOK – A coffee-table book with many photos.

PHOTO INDEX – Description of all previous photos with information on the location, time and date of the pictures and the photographer. (No pictures)

THE POWER OF THOUGHTS – The roots and fruits of all human phenomena are one's own consciousness and its thoughts, through the power of which everything is transformed into reality…

PROPHECIES – Prophetic explanations and predictions of the coming events on earth since 1976 on.

THE PSYCHE – Help in the life of man.

PLEIADIAN/PLEJAREN CONTACT REPORTS – Billy's contact reports, spirit teachings, explanations and experiences with extraterrestrial Plejaren life forms (from volume 1 on).

THE ROSE COLORED CRYSTAL – This book contains eleven fairy-tales for children and adults with an instructive content.

TALMUD JMMANUEL – Original translation of a two thousand-year-old script found in Jerusalem in 1963, which describes the life and work of Jmmanuel (alias Jesus Christ). Recorded at that time by order of Jmmanuel through one of his disciples.

THE WAY TO LIVE – In 500 verses, paragraphs and explanations, the human being in his life and striving is made accessible to the reader. It is explained to him how he can and should shape his life if he is willing to align himself with the creational truth; and it is explained how he can recognize the way of living and thinking of other human beings and their character.,

MUCH ADDITIONAL INFORMATION, BOOKLETS, AUDIO-VISUAL MEDIA, A POSTER, PHOTOS, T-SHIRTS, STICKERS ETC. CAN BE ORDERED FROM:

FIGU, SEMJASE SILVER STAR CENTER, CH-8495 SCHMIDRUETI/ZH, SWITZERLAND *WWW.FIGU.ORG* OR THROUGH FIGU'S INTERNET SHOP: *HTTP://SHOP.FIGU.ORG*

Steelmark LLC

8086 South Yale, Suite 173
Tulsa, OK 74136
Tel: 918-827-6453
Fax: 918-827-5561

Visit **STEELMARK ONLINE** for the latest news and information, online forums, chat room, UFO photo gallery and free downloads. Steelmark Online: *www.steelmarkonline.com*

AND STILL THEY FLY – And Still They Fly has its own website where you can get updated information and even download some physical proof for yourself. At the site, you can download the Pleiadian/Plejaren spacecraft sounds, which are discussed in the book, and play it back on your computer or portable mp3 player. Visit us at: *www.andstilltheyfly.com*

THROUGH SPACE AND TIME – A photo journal of "Billy" Eduard A. Meier

This is a new Steelmark publication. This coffee table sized photo journal contains the best of Billy's photographs. More information can be found online at: *www.throughspaceandtime.com*

PLEIADIAN DEPARTURE – An upcoming release which encompasses the 251st contact from the Billy Meier case. More information can be found online at: *www.pleiadiandeparture.com*

FIGU GROUPS

SWITZERLAND
FIGU – Headquarters
Semjase Silver Star Center
CH-8495 Schmidrüti / ZH
Switzerland
Tel: +52 385 1310
Fax: +52 385 4289
Website: *www.figu.org*
E-mail: *info@figu.org*

USA
FIGU Society USA
P.O. Box 730
Mounds, OK 74047
E-mail: *swhitney@billymeier.com*

FIGU – Los Angeles Study Group
P.O. Box 2520
North Hills, CA 91393-2520
E-mail: *mjuliano@billymeier.com*

GERMANY
FIGU Süddeutsche Studiengruppe
Postfach 85
D-88140 Wasserburg/Bodensee
Deutschland
de@figu.org
http://de.figu.org

JAPAN
FIGU - Japan
3-11-2-305 Minamino,
Hachioji-shi, Tokyo
192-0916 Japan
Fax: +81 426 37 1524
jp@figu.org
http://jp.figu.org

NETHERLANDS
FIGU Studiegroup Goes NL
Secretariaat
Trompstraat 8
4461 GK Goes
Holland/Nederland

CANADA
FIGU - Canadian Study Group
P.O. Box 703 Station P
Toronto, Ontario
Canada M5S 2Y4
ca@figu.org

Did you enjoy reading this book?

The following pages contain several new books from Steelmark on the Billy Meier contacts. The following books are either available now or will soon be available. More information on the publication status of these books is available at their respective websites, or at the Steelmark Online website at *www.steelmarkonline.com*

Steelmark

Unlocking the truth of the ages.

The Talmud of Jmmanuel
ISBN 0-9711523-3-0

Who was Jmmanuel, the man who became known as Jesus?
What was his connection to extraterrestrials? And was he really
resurrected? The answer to these questions and many more
are ultimately answered in this clearly rendered, side-by-side
German/English translation from the original, 2000-year-old
Aramaic scrolls discovered in a burial cave by "Billy"
Eduard A. Meier in Jerusalem in 1963.

Celestial Teachings
Emergence of the True Testament of Jmmanuel
by James Deardorff
ISBN 0-9711523-4-9

In this well-reasoned book, meteorologist James Deardorff makes a compelling argument for the authenticity of , an ancient scroll that suggests that the origin of the Christian New Testament may well be extraterrestrial. Dr. Deardorff's arguments are always sound and often dramatic; such as the observation that stars don't point-UFO beams do. Deardorff shows how the original teachings were altered over time and finally transformed into the Gospel of Matthew. This stunning book is not for the timid or even for the conventionally religious. It is for the seeker who is not afraid to contemplate new and daring ideas.

Through Space and Time
A photo journal of "Billy" Eduard A. Meier

ISBN 0-9711523-5-7

A high-quality, hardcover compilation of Billy Meier's world-renowned UFO photographs – many of them never before seen in public – alongside a comprehensive, autobiographical account of his extraterrestrial contacts and many other experiences. Never before has a photo journal been produced on the Billy Meier contacts with such stunning resolution and clarity while also providing vivid, fact-filled accounts by Meier and other eyewitnesses to the events. Surely, a book to inspire awe and wonder for years to come...

(Final editing is presently underway on Through Space and Time and it will be available shortly after you have finished reading *And Still They Fly!*) *www.throughspaceandtime.com*

Decalogue
ISBN 0-9711523-6-5

Decalogue was transmitted to Billy Meier between October 14th and November 17th, 1975 by a highly evolved WE-spirit form that identified itself as PETALE. *Decalogue* is the Ten Commandments in their original form, which also includes two additional commandments that have been withheld from humanity… until now.

Currently undergoing translation into English, *Decalogue* will be available from Steelmark at some time in the near future. Please visit our website for an updated status on *Decalogue* at *www.steelmarkonline.com*

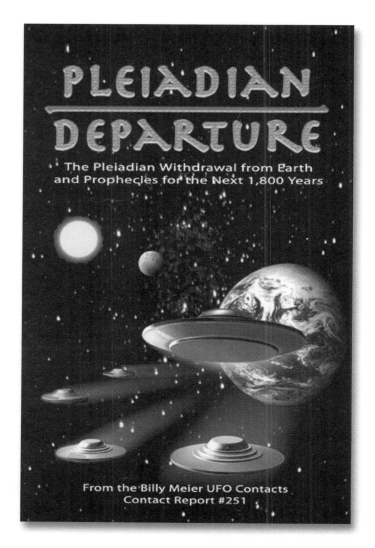

Pleiadian Departure
ISBN 0-9711523-7-3

Pleiadian Departure is a new publication that will soon be released by Steelmark. Encompassing the entirety of Billy Meier's 251st contact on February 3, 1995, this book provides detailed information on the unexpected, yet necessary, withdrawal of the Pleiadians from earth. In addition, *Pleiadian Departure* is filled with an historic account of earth mankind as well as compelling prophecies of things to come.
www.pleiadiandeparture.com

Stay Informed
by Steelmark

Steelmark regularly sends out new information and updates on the Billy Meier Contacts. To be added to our contact list, fill in the information below and mail this pre-addressed card back to Steelmark.

Name: _____

Address: _____

_____

City: _____ State: _____ Zip: _____

E-mail: _____

ASTF 3-04

more Information

Stay Informed
by Steelmark

Steelmark regularly sends out new information and updates on the Billy Meier Contacts. To be added to our contact list, fill in the information below and mail this pre-addressed card back to Steelmark.

Name: _____

Address: _____

_____

City: _____ State: _____ Zip: _____

E-mail: _____

ASTF 3-04

more Information

Postage
Required.
Post Office
will not deliver
without proper
postage.

Steelmark LLC
8086 South Yale
Suite 173
Tulsa, OK 74136

Postage
Required.
Post Office
will not deliver
without proper
postage.

Steelmark LLC
8086 South Yale
Suite 173
Tulsa, OK 74136